Bob Dylan,
Bruce Springsteen,
and American Song

Bob Dylan, Bruce Springsteen, and American Song

LARRY DAVID SMITH

PRAEGER

Westport, Connecticut
London

Library of Congress Cataloging-in-Publication Data

Smith, Larry David.
    Bob Dylan, Bruce Springsteen, and American song / Larry David Smith.
       p. cm.
    Includes bibliographical references (p.) and index.
    ISBN 0-275-97393-X (alk. paper)
    1. Dylan, Bob, 1941—Criticism and interpretation. 2. Springsteen, Bruce—Criticism and interpretation. 3. Popular music—United States—Analysis, appreciation. I. Title.
    ML400 .S657 2002
    782.42164'0973—dc21   2002067935

British Library Cataloguing in Publication Data is available.

Library of Congress Catalog Card Number: 2002067935
ISBN: 0-275-97393-X

First published in 2002

Praeger Publishers, 88 Post Road West, Westport, CT 06881
An imprint of Greenwood Publishing Group, Inc.
www.praeger.com

Printed in the United States of America

The paper used in this book complies with the Permanent Paper Standard issued by the National Information Standards Organization (Z39.48-1984).

10 9 8 7 6 5 4 3 2 1

copyright acknowledgments

to
NICOLA JOSS *and* PETE TOWNSHEND

contents

preface

On March 7, 1997 I met with Pete Townshend to correct lyrics and confirm facts for my forthcoming book, *Pete Townshend: The Minstrel's Dilemma*. Townshend's participation was long in the making and the direct result of Nicola Joss's commitment to my work. For over seven years, I'd written, faxed, telephoned, and generally hounded Ms. Joss (Townshend's personal assistant) in pursuit of my ambition to create a scholarly account of Townshend's career. As a narrative critic, I was fascinated by the focus and breadth of Townshend's writings; however, I required his permission to present my findings since, in the absence of concrete examples of his approach, the work would drift into analytical descriptions and interpretative paraphrasing. Of course, Townshend was reluctant. Why should any artist yield their copyrights or their time for projects that offer little-to-no compensation in either artistic or commercial terms? Always kind—and consummately professional—Townshend abstained from direct participation in the project. Eventually, he agreed to read chapters as they emerged (with no promise of anything). I spent five years researching, writing, and massaging the project without any guarantees. I mailed the manuscript to Townshend in late April 1995.

Townshend wrote me on his fiftieth birthday—May 19, 1995—with a colorful, and thoughtful, response. He granted permission to use his writings under the condition that I correct the errors in transcription that plagued many of the examples. Though he agreed to allow me to use his work, he maintained his distance: demanding that I do my job, and announcing that he would stick to his. I pushed for access. He kept me at bay and taught me the wisdom of his position. When his schedule permitted, we met (he graciously provided workspace and hospitality), corrected mistakes, and discussed situations. Never did he attempt to influence an interpretation or a conclusion; he allowed me to do my job, just as he'd urged for years. During our session, he looked up from the manuscript, flicked his glasses off, spun them around—yes, in a wind-milling fashion—and declared, "There is no academy on how I go about my craft!" That is, there are no books on the complicated negotiations that render commercial art. There are serious (and not-so-serious) biographies, sensationalized histories, and partisan interpretations of songwriters and their products, but there is no systematic study that considers the writer's biography, creative imperative, artistic influences, stylistic tendencies, and corresponding artistic/commercial negotiations.

Well, Pete, there is now.

This volume, *Bob Dylan, Bruce Springsteen, and American Song*, builds directly upon *The Minstrel's Dilemma*. In it, I explore Bob Dylan's and Bruce Springsteen's songwriting careers as well as their individual contributions to the musical tradition that is American Song. This volume is dedicated to Nicola Joss and Pete Townshend, since the idea comes from Mr. Townshend's observation, and the opportunity to pursue the idea comes from Ms. Joss's undying support. Mr. Townshend's and Ms. Joss's generosity cannot be overstated. They did more than make one book possible; they facilitated a *program's* emergence.

Before we begin, please allow me to thank Kevin L. Brown for his hard work, support, and guidance. I could not have completed this project without Kevin's help (the Fact Family should be proud!). Thanks also to Glenda Hall, Mike Hemphill, Michael Holmes, Larry and Jane Gibson, Tom and Nancy Oxley, and Glenn Smith for their varied contributions to this project's development. And, of course, thanks to Eric Levy and Greenwood Publishing for their continued support.

Special thanks go out to Lynne Okin and Jeff Rosen of Special Rider Music for their kind permission to quote Bob Dylan's lyrics as well as to Jon Landau, Jamie Feingold, and the folks at Jon Landau Management for their kind permission to quote Bruce Springsteen's lyrics. These people were more than professional, their generosity—like Joss's and Townshend's before them—makes this work possible. They allowed me to "do my job" to the best of my ability.

As I noted in *The Minstrel's Dilemma's* preface, my earliest musical memory is of my mother playing the boogie-woogie on the church piano after Sunday morning service (of course, after she was certain that the preacher was safely outside!). It is, perhaps, my most treasured recollection. The music's rhythm, the church setting, and her rebellion by playing the devil's music in the Lord's house; but most of all, I remember that sparkle in her eyes as the music came over us both. It was a uniquely American experience involving uniquely American sights and sounds. It is to that memory that I offer the following account of two American artists that, I feel, embody that spirit of rhythmic rebellion.

introduction

The December 12, 1965 issue of the *New York Times* features an intriguing article by Thomas Meehan in which he discusses the state of American literature by
posing the literary question of that day: Who is public writer number one?
Meehan opens: "For the past three and a half years, since the death of William
Faulkner . . . American literary critics have been nervously scanning the horizon
in search of a novelist or poet who can be definitely called the nation's Public
Writer No. 1, in the way that Faulkner and, before him, Hemingway, answered to
this title." To settle the matter, an informal survey of English students at three
Ivy League universities was commissioned. Meehan reports "a number of jaws
dropped noticeably" when the results were announced and twenty-four-year-old
Bob Dylan was declared the winner. For survey respondents, Dylan (described as
a "combination of Harpo Marx, Carol Burnett and the young Beethoven"), unlike
other contemporary writers, voiced their concerns, as a Brown University senior
observed: "We don't give a damn about Moses Herzog's angst or Norman Mailer's
private fantasies. . . . We're concerned with things like the threat of nuclear war,
the civil-rights movement and the spreading blight of dishonesty, conformism
and hypocrisy in the United States . . . and Bob Dylan is the only American writer
dealing with these subjects in a way that makes any sense to us." The English
major maintained that Dylan's song "A Hard Rain's a-Gonna Fall" provokes more
student interest "both in a literary and a social sense, than an entire volume of
Pulitzer Prize verse by someone like Robert Lowell."

This may be the first time in *world* history that a songwriter achieved the
celebrity status accorded "public writer number one." Consider music history:
ancient song defied authorship; medieval song resigned authorship; Renaissance
song laughed at authorship; industrial song used authorship; and 1960s society, it appears, celebrated authorship. Notice Meehan's parade of celebrity
images and how these characterizations are deployed within a serious assessment of supposedly thoughtful students at elite institutions for an article for
one of the most prestigious publications in American journalism. George M.
Cohan, Vincent Youmans, Lorenz Hart, and Cole Porter (among others) achieved
considerable fame during their songwriting careers, but none of them stood a
chance of upstaging Mark Twain, John Steinbeck, Scott Fitzgerald, or Ernest
Hemingway as the nation's preeminent wordsmith.

An interesting development appeared with the singer-songwriter's emergence in the 1900s, when the musical world embraced the celebrity author/per-
former. This condition invited both the partisan (e.g., academics, journalists)
and the mischievous (e.g., journalists, academics) to examine a song in terms of
its author and that individual's stance on the featured subject. Unlike songs by
Broadway's Oscar Hammerstein, Motown's Holland/Dozier/Holland, or Nashville's
Fred Rose, these songs were associated with a face, a personality, and a public
image. One is hard pressed to imagine Stephen Foster's persona hovering over
the performance of one of his ridiculous "coon songs" the way Bob Dylan's persona permeates the performance of one of his songs. A new form of celebrity
was introduced by the singer who publicly represented his or her own words, and
attribution emerged as the dominant concept for formal and informal criticism.
Dylan described his relationship with his work for *Newsweek* in 1997:

> But I'm not the songs. . . . It's like somebody expecting Shakespeare to be Ham-
> let, or Goethe to be Faust. If you're not prepared for fame, there's really no way
> you can imagine what a crippling thing it can be. . . . Some days I get up and it
> just makes me sick that I'm doing what I'm doing. Because basically—I mean,
> you're one cut above a pimp. That's what everybody who's a performer is. I have
> this voice in my head saying, "*Just be done with it.*"

Later, *Newsweek* inquired about Dylan's status as the "poet for his generation,"
to which he replied: "I don't think of myself in the highfalutin area . . . I'm in the
burlesque area." How interesting that an interview in which Dylan complains
about his celebrity status is manipulated to feed that image.

Burlesque performer or poet for his generation, Bob Dylan represented a
musical innovation that reverberated around the world. The celebrity-singer-
songwriter integrated the Hollywood image of the professional singer and his or
her particular style with the literary image of the author and his or her individual message. This marriage of style and content opened new creative and commercial doors for artists; however, once through those doors, the union occasionally suffered over-attention (or inattention), jealousy, stagnation, or
voyeurism (among many possible complications). Yet, innovative singer-songwrit-
ers such as Jimmie Rodgers, Woody Guthrie, Hank Williams, and Chuck Berry
successfully negotiated their way through the maze of interests that comprise
the music industry and each achieved distinction in his own way. The cult of personality that developed in association with the American mass media in the
mid-twentieth century would represent both blessings and curses for the recip-
ients of public adoration. The means through which celebrities managed this
attention would prove to be as important as the talent that provided the initial
recognition.

In *Pete Townshend: The Minstrel's Dilemma* I approach this phenomenon from
a narrative perspective. There I explore two questions: What was Townshend's stylistic response to his artistic situation, and how did his version of "the minstrel's
dilemma" impact his art? The latter dealt with Townshend's professional status
and the fact that no single entity controls commercial art; therefore, artists

must actively engage a diverse industry full of competing agendas. Each work is the product of negotiations between artists and production personnel (e.g., engineers, producers), artists and business personnel (e.g., managers, promoters, artist, and repertoire staff), artists and their musical colleagues (e.g., fellow band members, studio musicians), artists and their audiences (e.g., fans, media), within the artist (e.g., internal conflicts over artistic direction, and so on), and more. The "minstrel's" choice between doing what satisfies that individual's creative impulse and doing what satisfies the commercial interests associated with the art may involve considerable deliberation. That careers are prolonged or shortened in direct relation to the resolution of these issues demonstrates the centrality of this historic conflict.

My other concern involved Townshend's stylistic response to his creative/commercial situation. For this I applied my critical technique—narrative synthesis—to evaluate Townshend's writings as stories. After investigating the characters, values, and plots evidenced in individual songs, albums, short stories, poems, films, music videos, and theatrical projects, I determined that the lifework articulates a single story across its respective phases. This story line (titled "The Seeker") explores the individual's search for identity in specific settings (from intrapersonal, to interpersonal, to group, to societal contexts). Not *all* Townshend songs follow this story line; nevertheless, when the lifework is considered in its totality, "The Seeker" theme is dominant. Despite the pressures associated with a dynamic commercial environment full of independent agendas, Townshend somehow managed to "tell his story." Townshend's dedication to this narrative imperative was so intense that he revived projects in order to complete their stories. The *Tommy, LifeHouse,* and *Quadrophenia* projects were reborn on stage, their endings revised, and their stories sharpened in a fashion that provided closure for their author.

The Townshend project demonstrates the power of *auteur* theory in studies of songwriting. The convergence of biography, creative impulse, artistic philosophy, and stylistic tendency that renders the auteur and his or her *oeuvre* (or lifework) reveals the force of personality and creative drive that enables the successful implementation of a given vision. Here I use the auteur/narrative strategy to explore two artists' contributions to the evolving songwriting tradition that is American Song. In order to appreciate Bob Dylan's and Bruce Springsteen's individual contributions to American Song, we must first define that musical form. For assistance, I turn to Alec Wilder's study of American music and his use of James T. Maher's account of its origins. Maher asks us to imagine a performance "at the edge of Echo Canyon in Grand Canyon National Park" that includes the following:

> The Fisk College Jubilee choir . . . Scott Joplin, Ben Harney, and Eubie Blake playing ragtime piano . . . a country fiddler . . . a Negro cotton hand chanting field "hollers" . . . a back country blues singer . . . a good southern Negro ragtime orchestra . . . a small Negro ragtime dance band from a New Orleans Saturday night function . . . a handful of immigrants each intoning some old-country favorite remembered with love and comfort . . . W. C. Handy leading his

travelling band-orchestra-dance-band . . . a group of Carolina mountain people
singing remembered British North Country modal ballads . . . a cowboy singing a
round-up tune . . . [and much more]. . . . Imagine this great melange of sounds
pouring down into the canyon, mixing below, then returning in a single echo and
you may get some idea of what happened as American popular music achieved
a native idiom between 1890 and World War I.

Like the country itself, Maher suggests, American Song is an evolving blend of
influences. The "echoes" emanating from Maher's Grand Canyon assume distinct
forms at different times; nonetheless, they all fall within the parameters of
established musical categories. For a few moments, let us explore these traditional classifications and their manifestations in that fascinating "melange of
sounds" that is American Song.

Music historians Donald Clarke and Richard Crawford offer fine analyses of
popular music's evolution and America's musical maturation, respectively. Both
writers present thorough definitions of the three master categories that organize all music: the classical, popular, and traditional forms. Crawford writes:

I propose a categorical distinction between "composers' music," for works
whose notation embodies the authority of the composer, and "performers'
music," for works whose notation is intended as an outline to be shaped by
performers as they see fit. The first category, ruled by the written directives
of composers, is the classical sphere, a realm where works aspire to transcendence: to outliving the time and place of their creation. The second, ruled
by performers who shape composers' scores to fit the occasion, is the popular
sphere, a realm where works aspire to accessibility: to acceptance by the target audience. With written compositions split into two categories, music that
circulates orally may then be considered a third: the traditional (or folk) sphere,
often linked with particular customs and ways of life. Tending to preserve each
culture's linguistic and musical practices, the traditional sphere is ruled by a
belief in continuity.

Clarke concurs as he traces the evolution of "church music" and its contributions to music's "technical development" through the Renaissance, the rise of
secular opera, and into the eighteenth century's symphonies, string quartets,
and concertos. Clarke explains: "When these forms emerged during the glorious
flowering of Viennese music, they were based on sonata form, the rules govern-
ing their composition corresponding to what was regarded as the logical order-
liness of philosophy and the arts in classical Greece: hence 'classical' music."
Complementing the classical form is its popular counterpart, which Clarke
defines "as a song written for a single voice or a small vocal group, accompanied
by a single chord-playing instrument or a small ensemble, usually first performed
in some sort of public entertainment and afterwards published in the form of
sheet music (or mechanically reproduced in the twentieth century); it is written
for profit, for amateur listeners and performers." Finally, Clarke maintains that
in "all times and places there was also folksong, invented and performed by the
less privileged classes: lullabies, love songs, work songs, story songs and so on."

The authors present three distinct musical orientations that pursue artistic agendas unique to that particular form: transcendence, accessibility, and cultural continuity.

Crawford traces the varied works of music historians and their claims regarding the impact of classical and popular music on the emerging American art form. Citing the research of John Tasker Howard (in 1931) and Gilbert Chase (in 1955), Crawford notes a shift in emphasis with regard to the prime mover behind American Song's development: "While Howard had proclaimed composers to be the primary agents of American music history, Chase took his stand with American genres—spirituals, blackface minstrelsy, folk songs and fiddle music, shape-note hymnody, Native American songs, ragtime, blues, and jazz—that relied on the way they were performed. As much as compositional types, these genres were performance traditions that took over and recast any music their practitioners played or sang." For Chase, a "composer-centered" view of American musical history "would miss the heart of the subject."

Again, Clarke supports such conclusions. He contends that the mid-1800s witnessed a division in American music into the "absurd terms from nineteenth-century anthropology" known as "highbrow and lowbrow" art. Clarke makes several compelling points. He observes that America's "contradictory attitudes" about Europe produced disdain for foreigners who "were despised for patronizing America" and admiration for their formal music, which, ironically, was considered to be "superior." Publishers, therefore, designated informal song to be the "trash" of the "common people" and concentrated on Europe's formal music as the stuff of high art. Such admiration did not extend to paying royalties. While performing rights societies were emerging in Europe (and collecting royalties), American publishers continued to take Europe's music without paying; hence, American composers of formal music were left in the lurch, their services overshadowed by stolen European music for which publishers requested higher rates due to its perceived superiority. The result was a retardation of American formal composition and a proliferation of the domestic "trash" that was America's informal music.

Crawford suggests that H. Wiley Hitchcock's 1969 work places notions of highbrow and lowbrow music to rest. Hitchcock introduced "two complementary streams" of American Song, the classical and the vernacular traditions (which Hitchcock defined as "music not approached self-consciously but simply grown into as one grows into one's vernacular tongue"), which Crawford describes in this fashion: "Formulated as attitudes toward rather than properties of music, they allow a classification of works that does not proclaim the superiority of one class over another—though admittedly, such classifying is itself a cultivated act." Hitchcock's "streams" provide a useful starting point for our understanding of a musical environment that quickly evolved from traditional songs into songwriting traditions.

These musical domains developed in fashions consistent with their musical agendas. The technical requirements necessary for transcendence, the consuming trends that are conducive to accessibility, and the informality of cultural vernaculars require creative conditions that facilitate precision, popularity, and authenticity, respectively. Classical conservatories, musical entrepreneurs, and cultural societies pursue formally what civic associations, local businesses, and family gatherings do informally; that is, they provide contexts for the playing, studying, selling, and promoting of their respective musical wares. As a result, the classical, popular, and vernacular approaches integrate and segregate according to the creative whims of the musical minds of the times. These musical boundaries are, in no way, rigid. For example, Black vernacular music from plantation life was influenced by European vaudeville's staging to create the "coon" tradition that gradually evolved into American vaudeville. Classical compositions were borrowed or emulated by Hollywood producers to generate popular soundtracks for films. Vaudeville routines were refined, refitted, and reintroduced by Jerry Lieber and Mike Stoller (and their 1950s musical "playlets") as well as by Berry Gordy (and his 1960s Motown acts). And in the most famous synthesis of all, Southern Black church music (and its Afro-rhythmic influences) merged with Southern hillbilly traditions (and its Anglo-melodic heritage) to produce that sensational hybrid, rock and roll. On the other hand, university conservatories labor to preserve and extend classical music's integrity and ultimate transcendence, Nashville and Broadway songwriters stick to prescribed formulas to ensure their music's accessibility for target audiences (thereby guaranteeing sales), and folk festivals promote traditional methods of instrumentation and singing in order to encourage cultural continuity. In every case, the musician's creative agenda either preserved an original form or co-opted various strands of influence in service of that individual's artistic mission.

The research on these various trends is extensive and far too vast to list here. Studies of classical forms and popular expressions offer compelling insights into the technical qualities of America's formal music and the commercial aspects of her popular sounds. America's classical music remains tied to its European heritage in fundamental ways, while the popular sphere has witnessed a number of striking innovations. American vaudeville (with its "coon show" antecedents), Tin Pan Alley's enterprising marketing, Broadway's domestic adaptations of European operetta, the Big Band era's pioneering orchestrations, the ascendance of jazz, Nashville's and Hollywood's co-optation of Tin Pan Alley commercial formulas, the New York songwriting factories (e.g., the Brill Building) that revised and extended Tin Pan Alley methods, and, of course, the musical cross-breeding between the popular and vernacular spheres that created Memphis soul, Motown theatrics, folk-rock, rock music, hip-hop, rap, and more represent but a few of the musical innovations from that vast "melange of sounds" known as American Song.

The vernaculars and their popular offspring have stimulated the pens of critics interested in the histories of these musical forms. Peter Guralnick's research into the origins of soul music (*Sweet Soul Music*), country music (*Lost Highway*), and the blues (*Feel Like Going Home*) complements Francis Davis's exploration into the history of the blues (and its companion PBS video), Charlie Gillett's research into rock and roll's emergence (with his *excellent* treatment of industrial variables), Bill Malone's study of country music, David Jasen and Gene

Jones's historical treatment of Black songwriting, and the outstanding 2001 video/book package, *American Roots Music*, to shed much light on the history and development of these diverse musical traditions (this is, assuredly, but a partial listing of the many strong efforts to sharpen our knowledge of this subject matter). Moreover, video productions such as Time-Life's *The History of Rock 'n' Roll*, PBS' *Rock 'n' Roll*, and Ken Burns's extensive treatment of American jazz (again, there are many more such offerings) offer direct testimony from the participants of this musical evolution. Finally, writers such as Bill Flanagan, Bruce Pollock, Jimmy Webb, and Paul Zollo offer compelling insights into the practice of songwriting through extensive interviews with practitioners (Flanagan, Pollock, and Zollo, respectively) or personal accounts of the creative process (Webb). That there is more to this avenue of research indicates the rich qualities of the American musical heritage.

Within these musical orientations, the interplay of words and music varies. Classical forms—principally opera—downplay the "lyrics" in favor of musical orchestration and theatricality. Occasionally, this results in performances in which singers deploy a language different from that of the audience. Popular songs rely on trite expressions and heavy repetition presented through simple melodies in order to promote accessibility. Oftentimes, these seemingly innocuous expressions are rich in metaphor and are deceptively colorful. But it is the vernaculars and their reliance upon their respective "native tongues" that pose the most intriguing mixes of words, music, and performance. The steady syncopation and heavy repetition of the blues, the airy indifference and moralistic storytelling of folk, the earthy instrumentation and jumbled language of zydeco, and the restrained rhythms and spiritually infused vocables of Native American song display their own blends of music and lyrics that directly serve the cultural roles pursued by that approach. When left to their own devices, these musical expressions capture the unique cultural heritages associated with that artistic tradition; when allowed to intermingle, they expose music's potential to transcend context through individual initiative.

Such musical diversity would seem to prohibit any thematic interpretation of American Song's lyrical content; nevertheless, writers of varying orientations ply their trades in search of some central organizing principle. For instance, Alec Wilder contends: "There is a fugitive essence and personality that distinguishes a song as American. . . . For a song to possess an American character it requires a subtler distinction than the presence of marked syncopation. Sometimes it is the lyric, which causes the listener to take for granted its native source. Sometimes it is the shape of the song, its unacademic looseness, and sometimes simply that it doesn't sound like an importation." Wilder's "subtle distinctions" are evasive and, as he readily admits (unlike most of his colleagues in music criticism), he established "arbitrary qualitative rules which often may seem academic to the point of snobbishness." Be that as it may, he has a point regarding American Song's "fugitive essence and personality." Jim Cullen contributes to this line of thinking when he describes the "republican character" of American art and how that orientation has filtered down through the works of Stephen Foster,

Walt Whitman, Mark Twain, Woody Guthrie, John Steinbeck, Bob Dylan, and Bruce Springsteen (among others). For Cullen, "If the *politics* of republicanism is *representative democracy, then the art of republicanism is representational democracy.*" Cullen considers Whitman to be the progenitor of an artistic worldview predicated on a "working-class romanticism that endows ordinary objects with grandeur." Cullen writes:

> In the most literal of terms, Walt Whitman was a representative democrat, depicting ordinary people in ordinary language while finding the music, drama, and beauty . . . of their lives. And his identification with them was total. . . . Whitman was a master at distilling the popular culture of his time and demonstrating its expressive possibilities in a society struggling to realize both freedom and equality in life and art.

From there, Cullen articulates the essence of his position: "Simplicity, mobility, hope: this is the art of republicanism." *Simplicity, mobility, hope,* with a dash of rebellion (i.e., Wilder's "fugitive essence and personality"), these are the thematic raw materials of American Song that mix and match according to musical genre, commercial orientation, and artistic application.

To be sure, there is no standard manifestation of these themes. A rap or rock song may evoke images of social mobility through rebellion. A country song may promote acceptance as an avenue of hope. A blues number or a folk tune may use simplicity to convey a basic emotion or principle, repeatedly. A Native American offering may apply prayer as a vehicle for hopeful transcendence. Though Cullen's argument is not exhaustive, it is thorough; hence, it offers a meaningful starting point for an exploration of two American songwriters and their individual contributions to American Song's development.

One important influence in American Song's thematic maturation involves the work of Woody Guthrie. Woodrow Wilson "Woody" Guthrie was born in Okemah, Oklahoma in 1912 and, in the words of country music historian Bill Malone, "occupies an unusual position in American country and folk music" to an extent that makes him "difficult to categorize." According to Malone, Guthrie "began as a hillbilly singer with strong traditional roots and advanced to the position of America's most revered urban folksinger and writer." All indications are that Guthrie was a restless man (perhaps as the result of the Huntington's Chorea that plagued his family and, eventually, took his life), with a hobo lifestyle that directly fed his musical repertoire. His travels across the Southwest, into California (where he established a reputation as a radio personality, singing hillbilly tunes), and back across the country exposed him to the varied plights of Americana—an experience that infused his hillbilly music with a "flowering of radicalism." Malone elaborates: "Guthrie felt a strong emotional kinship with the homeless and often-persecuted migratory workers, especially his fellow Okies, and he began to compose songs which expressed his sympathies as well as his anger at the system which caused their misfortunes." His discontent grew to the point where the "post-1940 Guthrie would always be known as a protest singer."

Guthrie was a prolific writer (writing over 2,000 songs and poems). After a stint with the Almanac Singers (featuring Pete Seeger and Lee Hays among others) and their "propagandist approach" to folk (in Charlie Gillett's terms), Guthrie settled into his role as the dean of American protest. Songs such as "This Land Is Your Land," "Tom Joad," "Union Maid," and "This Train Is Bound for Glory" are cutting-edge protest songs that were, occasionally, widely misunderstood. Gillett reports that Guthrie's lack of an exclusive contract restricted his exposure as a recording artist; nevertheless, his words echoed from the voices of others who delivered his message to "millions." Jim Cullen argues: "As much as any artist in American history, Guthrie bridged the cultural and political strands of republicanism, fusing populist themes with vernacular language." In *American Roots Music*, Alan Jabbour describes the Dustbowl Poet in this fashion:

> He was a folksinger in the classic sense of having a large repertory of traditional songs learned from his family and community. But he also became a prototype of a "folksinger" in the emerging popular sense. A compulsive writer with a keen eye and a sharp wit, he began composing songs on contemporary issues, drawing on classic folk tunes and genres for his settings.

Guthrie, Jabbour relates, "popularized the 'talking blues' genre of story song/ social commentary" and, upon his death in 1967, was a "legendary model for singer/songwriters of the next generation." He concludes: "America has inherited from Woody Guthrie the image of folksinger as troubadour of the people, composing songs in a roots style that helps grass-roots people reflect on their lives and lots."

Woody Guthrie was a poet. He used the musical forms around him to frame his perspectives on what he saw happening before him. In the process, he built a celebrity image that fueled his ability to commentate on his times. His vernacular blend of folk, blues, and country generated messages from a celebrity wordsmith. His vigor, forthrightness, and confrontational attitude was, indeed, a *prototype* for those that followed. He fits squarely in Cullen's republican tradition of American art and its emphasis on simplicity, mobility, hope—again, with a strong dash of Wilder's fugitive personality, or rebellion. Bob Dylan built his image around Guthrie; Bruce Springsteen shaped his lifework on Guthrie's rhetoric. Woody Guthrie established his own tradition within American Song's vernacular category. It is to this genre that Dylan and Springsteen offer their respective contributions, as their offerings both build upon and depart from the Dustbowl Poet's innovations. In our age of electric guitars and power chord-driven attitudes, Guthrie's little (or not-so-little) sign on his acoustic guitar, "This Machine Kills Fascists," would look just wonderful on a Fender Stratocaster. Woody Guthrie may well be the father of rock music and its rebellious messages that challenge the status quo through individual initiative and personal resolve.

This project explores Dylan's and Springsteen's musical careers through three related questions: What does auteur theory and narrative synthesis tell us about their songwriting? What were their individual contributions to American

Song? How do they build upon the Guthrie tradition of American songwriting? To respond to these inquiries, our critical journey unfolds in three parts. First, we consider the stories told by these two American auteurs—Bob Dylan (in part one) and Bruce Springsteen (in part two). There we examine their respective biographies, creative impulses and artistic philosophies, their oeuvres, and conclude with a consideration of strategically selected exemplars that capture their particular songwriting styles. After which we compare the writers' responses to their individual songwriting situations in terms of their language use, narrative styles, production methods, and performance orientations. Unlike the *Pete Townshend* project's detailed presentation of the auteur's oeuvre and its critical objective of generating a historical account of those writings, this project compares two published bodies of writings. Both songwriters have issued books presenting their lyrics (unlike Townshend), and the number of biographies, studies, and personal accounts of the two songwriters' histories provide a detailed public record of those activities. Consequently, I use those existing materials to build my case regarding Dylan's and Springsteen's evocations of American Song and their individual contributions to that tradition's development.

In his critique of Richard Crawford's book for the *Los Angeles Times*, Ken Emerson takes issue with Crawford's decision to privilege musical performance over other considerations. For Emerson, "one could just as easily argue that the history of our music revolves around its reception and consumption" as well as other variables. Similarly, noted music critic and Dylan expert Paul Williams warns against the use of "developmental" approaches to art criticism, and we would be wise to consider his reservations:

> Talking about an artist's work chronologically can be deceiving—it makes us, writer and reader both, tend to treat each individual work as though it is part of a process of development, part of some heroic saga of personal and artistic growth (or decline). . . . There's truth and much of interest in all this, but it can distract us from the fact that each work, each performance, also exists outside of time, and in fact derives its primary power from its content rather than its context.

Williams then counters his own argument and advances a chronological treatment of Bob Dylan's development as a performing artist. Why the instant contradiction? The answer flows as quickly as the question: The nature of the inquiry demanded a broader view. Just as with Emerson's critique, the key is in the level of analysis. Is the critic concerned with an individual act, a pattern of progress (or decline), or a particular facet of a broader process? Therein lies the fundamental decision point. Since Dylan's performances—like his songwriting—evolved (and that is the key concept here) as his career advanced, Williams expanded his point of emphasis in order to build his case.

Although Williams advocates appreciating an individual song/album on its own merits, the various aspects of the writing, the incongruities between words "performed" and words "written," and the limited observations associated with micro-

analysis may move the critic toward broader views. To capture the evolving qualities of Dylan's and Springsteen's writings, the respective works are treated as
unfolding narratives. Obviously, the musical, performance, and interpretative
dimensions of the art are essential components as well, but I concentrate on the
lyrics and their narrative attributes. In other words, this study endeavors to
focus, and in turn, avoid the potential oversimplifications associated with multi-
level analyses. For example, how can a critic hope to capture such diverse dynamics as sound quality (both within the music or in its engineering, live or recorded),
performance (oh my!), audience response (indeed, which audience?), industry
response/influence, peer response/influence, and interpretation in one stroke?
That each of these levels of analysis contains multiple variables further compli-
cates an already impossible task. While our final chapter considers music production and performance factors, such explorations service observations regarding the oeuvres' narrative qualities. Therefore—like Paul Williams and Richard
Crawford—we stake our claim and mine it. Focus is crucial to sensitivity.

     That the *New York Times* would characterize Bob Dylan as the nation's pre-
eminent wordsmith says a great deal about 1960s American society. That the
Brown University senior would single out Dylan's "A Hard Rain's a-Gonna Fall" as
a statement of his or her generation's concerns over "dishonesty, conformism
and hypocrisy" says even more. "A Hard Rain" employs traditional American folk
music instrumentation to generate the sound—literally the *feel*—of a powerful
piece of protest music. An examination of the song's lyrics suggests anything
but a traditional piece of American folk protest. "A Hard Rain" deploys Dylan's
pioneering form of narrative impressionism that paved the way for serious songwriting innovations. Dylan's idiosyncratic images reveal an impressionistic writing style that transformed songwriting from a Brill Building/Tin Pan Alley craft
into spontaneous, free-flowing art. This transformation facilitated a new phase
in American Song's development, and the following pages trace Bob Dylan's and
Bruce Springsteen's contributions to that constantly evolving "melange of
sounds."

part one
Bob Dylan

Virtually any attempt to assess Bob Dylan's impact on music history is bound for understatement. What standard can be applied to measure his influence on an art form he so completely transformed it would never return to its previous state? Other innovative artists certainly preceded him, yet few have had the mass effect of the individual who synthesized idiosyncratic poetry, celebrity histrionics, and American Song's musical heritage into an unprecedented cultural force. Moreover, the personality trait that enabled this historic confluence—Dylan's rebellion—never, ever dissipated. If anything, it intensified over time. It strengthened his resolve, saved his life from the abyss of celebrity, and delivered his art from the doldrums of public expectation. That strange intersection where rebellion and courage meet—that fertile yet unpredictable ground—spawned an artist who single-handedly redefined his profession—many times, at his own expense. For outsiders, fame is affordable and attractive. For those who have touched that dangerous flame, it often exacts a price that cannot be paid—not in this life, anyway.

   The April 12, 2001 issue of Rolling
Stone features an article by Mark Jacobson
that presents one price of fame: the obsessive
fan. Jacobson's colorful piece considers the science
of Dylanology: "In all of American pop culture, there's no
obsession that comes close in intensity or complexity to the
strange and tender madness that is Dylanology." Jacobson interviews a madman who sifted through Dylan's garbage in pursuit of god-
knows-what, describes an unbalanced fan who managed to secure Dylan's
used cigarette butts in order to obtain the DNA necessary to clone the artist,
and submits his repentance for a review of the auteur's 1978 film, Renaldo and
Clara (in which Jacobson wished Dylan were dead!). In the thick of the madness,
Jacobson cites the activities of music critic Paul Williams—a man who has dedicated much of his professional life to the systematic study of the individual who
transformed the musical world. When asked about his motivations for his work,
Williams replied: "If Shakespeare was in your midst, putting on shows at the
Globe Theatre, wouldn't you feel the need to be there, to write down what hap-
pened in them?"

   The Bob Dylan–William Shakespeare connection is a steady staple among
the millions of words dedicated to the exploration and exploitation of the songwriter's long and diverse career. The cult of personality that gave birth to
"Dylanology" has had its way with the English bard as well, as Gary Taylor confirms in his fine treatise on the science he deems "Shakesperotics." Taylor
writes: "The study of Shakespeare has been in turmoil since at least the mid-
1970s. Scholars are redefining what he wrote, how he wrote it, what it meant in
his own time, and what it means to ours. Lines are being redrawn, even now; old
stories are being told with new twists; our collective image of Shakespeare as a
person and a poet is disintegrating and reforming." From there, Taylor contemplates the partisan—and occasionally mischievous—evaluations that define—
and continually redefine—what history makes of the writer who reshaped
Western theater.

   But what if Shakespeare had endured such critical scrutiny in his own time?
What if he had every word of every work analyzed by legions of critics vigorously
pursuing independent (and occasionally contradictory) agendas the very day his
work became public? Furthermore, what if these critics were an essential element
of the media system that financed the commercial art industry? What would
Shakespeare do? How would he cope with Shakesperotics? The results could well
resemble the life and times of Bob Dylan. Dylan not only experienced the most
intense critical pressures of any wordsmith in his day, he educated that audience and helped create the profession that praised him, cursed him, and—as
Jacobson laments—even wished him dead. Subsequently, Jacobson contends
that Dylan may be the most discussed artist in history.

   An overview of Dylanology necessarily begins with the biographers. These men
have worked long and hard to present as comprehensive an account of their subject's life as possible. I must conclude that the men and women interviewed for

these projects are fully qualified to
write textbooks on interviewing techniques.
The biographers have also combed through studio records, public documents, financial statements,
and—most importantly—one another's work in their
dogged pursuit of their subject matter. I dare not critique
their efforts, but merely encourage a vigorous reading of their
labors so that one may draw one's own conclusions. Chronologically, we
have Anthony Scaduto's (1971) *Bob Dylan: An Intimate Biography*, Robert
Shelton's (1986) *No Direction Home: The Life and Music of Bob Dylan*, Bob
Spitz's (1989) *Dylan: A Biography*, Howard Sounes's (2001) *Down the Highway:
The Life of Bob Dylan*, and Clinton Heylin's (2001) *Bob Dylan: Behind the Shades
Revisited*. Heylin's work also includes the indispensable 1995 chronology of Dylan
recording sessions from 1960 to 1994 and a 1996 account of his daily activi-
ties from 1941 to 1995 (the quintessential example of Dylanology).

Complementing the biographers are academic critics and their attempts to
render systematic interpretations of Dylan's work. Although theoretical mischief
occasionally raises its partisan head, these writers more often than not state
their case and pursue it. The academy's interest in popular art rivals any contemporary topic and Bob Dylan's career has inspired many a scholarly work.
Several examples include: Betsy Bowden's (1982) *Performed Literature: Words
and Music of Bob Dylan*, Aidan Day's (1988) *Jokerman: Reading the Lyrics of Bob
Dylan*, William McKeen's (1993) *Bob Dylan: A Bio-Bibliography*, and Wissolik and
McGrath's (1994) *Bob Dylan's Words: A Critical Dictionary and Commentary*.
Academic periodicals also offer considerable material for Dylanologists from
critics/theorists from a host of disciplines plying their trades to various
aspects of Dylan's lifework. (Such efforts are far too numerous to list here;
please consult McKeen for a thorough account of the academy's output up to
that point in time.)

Journalists contribute to Dylanology in a variety of fashions. Journalistic periodicals not only serve the commercial, informative, critical, and promotional needs
of a complicated international industry, they produce writers who bring their craft
to book-length accounts as well. Those who endorse size as an evaluative crite-
rion, must appreciate Michael Gray's impressive 877-page analysis, *Song and
Dance Man III: The Art of Bob Dylan*. Joining the fun are Paul Williams (1991's *Bob
Dylan, Performing Artist: The Early Years 1960–1973*; 1992's *Bob Dylan, Per-
forming Artist: The Middle Years 1974–1986*; and 1996's *Bob Dylan: Watching the
River Flow*), Greil Marcus (1997's *Invisible Republic: Bob Dylan's Basement Tapes*),
Tim Riley (1999's *Hard Rain: A Dylan Commentary*), and edited volumes by Carl
Benson (1998's *The Bob Dylan Companion*), Thomson and Gutman (2000's *The
Dylan Companion*), and Craig McGregor (1972's *Bob Dylan: A Retrospective*).

Dylanology is a vast, all-consuming passion—much like its colleague,
Shakesperotics. Thinkers of all stripes endeavor to expand our understanding of
these two artists. Taylor closes his review of Shakesperotics with this revealing
analogy:

> A singularity . . . is the center of a
> black hole; it is a mathematical point in
> space having no length, breadth or depth, a
> point at the center of a once vast, now collaps-
> ing star where matter is crushed by its own irresis-
> tible gravity into literally zero volume. Even light cannot
> escape from a black hole; time itself stops. If Shakespeare has
> a singularity, it is because he has become a black hole. Light, in-
> sight, intelligence, matter—all pour ceaselessly into him, as critics are
> drawn into the densening vortex of his reputation; they add their own weight
> to his increasing mass. . . . But Shakespeare himself no longer transmits light;
> his stellar energies have been trapped within the gravity well of his own reputa-
> tion. We find in Shakespeare only what we bring to him or what others have left
> behind; he gives us back our own values.

Taylor continues by describing Shakespeare's greatness—a "star" among others in the "galaxy." But, he argues, the writer was also just another human ("like us but not us") who faced the limits imposed by "space and time" like any other mortal: "The culture that turns him into a god produces a schizophrenic criticism, mixing abasement and appropriation." Taylor acknowledges Shakespeare's "power" and its potential to "corrupt" and "disfigure" the critical process just as the "politician easily corrupts his entourage" before closing with this wisdom: "But criticism, at it best, struggles to be free; like the press at its best, its function is to doubt what we have been told; it is skeptical; it is suspicious of power. Sycophancy is no more admirable in literature than in politics."

Perhaps this is the point where Dylanology and Shakesperotics intersect: a sycophantic, schizophrenic criticism driven by unique combinations of celebrity mysticism and individual agendas. A place where Dylan and Shakespeare undergo transformations into singularities burdened by the impositions of critics reifying their values and supporting their respective worldviews. How does criticism free itself from these constraints? To what may the critic turn to avoid the increasing mass that engulfs the criticism and the subject's work? As I suggested in our introduction, the pivotal concept associated with this—or any other argument—is its level of analysis.

One starting point, as Clinton Heylin and Paul Williams independently recognize, is in acknowledging the difference between the "artist" and the "man." The biographers cover the man and, occasionally, the artist. The two converge in the lifework. As a result, the oeuvre reveals the auteur. To be sure, the auteur contains the man. It is a dynamic that massages much mystery. Although Mr. Dylan can hide the man, the auteur responds to the impulse, and the impulse negotiates the public evidence that is the work. Consequently, I focus on the art as my level of analysis. By stepping outside the shadows of celebrity "sycophancy" or metaphysical "corruption" and allowing the work to speak for itself, we may capture a glimpse of the "star" and appreciate the light emanating from that celestial body. While it is impossible to extract the art from its context, it *is* possible to allow the art to speak from that context, as "free" as possible of the various impositions that may color the analytical process. It is from that perspective that I offer this contribution to Dylanology.

chapter one

the artist

The Arts and Entertainment Network's *Biography* series opens its program, "Bob Dylan: The American Troubadour," with an important observation: "Bob Dylan was never born. He was never a toddler, never went to summer camp, and appears in no high school yearbook." Nevertheless, music historian David Ewen initiates his discussion of "Bob Dylan" with this "biography":

> Dylan attended the public schools in Hibbing and was graduated from Hibbing High School, no mean achievement for a boy who was more often away from Hibbing than in it. Between his tenth and eighteenth years he ran away from home seven times, traveling by any means of locomotion available—by foot, box-cars, by hitching rides—and covering a wide area from the Dakotas to California. He was learning at first hand the meaning of personal suffering and want, as well as inequality and injustice. He was running away from the domination of his parents and the constrictions of a small town, but actually he was being helplessly driven by a nervous restlessness, an inability to stay put anywhere for any length of time—a trait to which he was addicted all his life. But these years of *Wanderjahre* were not without their blessings. As has already been described, it enabled him, when he was ten, to get his first guitar. (Later on he learned to make music also on an autoharp, harmonica, and piano.) A year later it made it possible for him to meet Big Joe Williams, and recognize the importance of the blues. And when he was thirteen, it brought him a job with a traveling carnival, an experience during which he met all sorts of people—from roustabouts and day laborers to gamblers and prostitutes—and to sing songs for them to his own guitar accompaniments.

Ewen's historical analyses of musical styles and personalities make significant contributions to our understanding of the art form and its practitioners, and yet, his presentation of Dylan's life is fictional. The man who became Bob Dylan attended public school in Hibbing, Minnesota and recognized "personal suffering" for a variety of reasons, but Ewen's description of his traveling adventures, his home life, and his musical influences is false. Still, Ewen's erroneous account communicates the pervasiveness of the Dylan Myth—a story propagated by an ingenious, ambitious young personality in pursuit of professional success.

The author of this mythology, Robert Allen Zimmerman, was born in Duluth, Minnesota on May 24, 1941 to Abraham and Beatty Zimmerman. After a bout with polio and the subsequent loss of his job with Standard Oil, Abraham moved the family to the mining town of Hibbing (Beatty's hometown) and joined his brothers' retail business (an electric wiring/appliance company). There the Zimmermans raised two children (David was born in early 1946) in the middle-class climate of postwar America—an America where segregation by race, religion, or economics was rampant. The family's Jewish heritage and their business dealings with the destitute and disadvantaged introduced Zimmerman to prejudice, misfortune, and their consequences (young Bob had to repossess appliances, for example). Otherwise, all accounts indicate that Zimmerman endured a normal upbringing in a small town void of economic extremes. As he related to Cameron Crowe, Hibbing "was not a rich or poor town, everybody had pretty much the same thing and the very wealthy people didn't live there, they were the ones that owned the mines and they lived thousands of miles away." This socioeconomic uniformity may have nurtured a rebellious spirit that was reinforced by the area's physical environment. In 1978, Dylan described the Iron Range of Minnesota to Ron Rosenbaum:

> Well, in the winter, everything was still, nothing moved. Eight months of that. You can put it together. You can have some amazing hallucinogenic experiences doing nothing but looking out your window. There is also the summer, when it gets hot and sticky and the air is very metallic. There is a lot of Indian spirit. The earth there is unusual, filled with ore. So there is something happening that is hard to define. There is a magnetic attraction there. Maybe thousands and thousands of years ago, some planet bumped into the land there. There is a great spiritual quality throughout the Midwest. Very subtle, very strong, and that is where I grew up.

Whether Zimmerman's artistic inclinations were inspired by the Iron Range's environmental magic or Hibbing's sociological blandness, the youngster displayed a propensity for performance at an early age. Reports reveal he enjoyed recording and hearing his voice, commanding attention at family gatherings (a strong rendition of "Accentuate the Positive" was a staple), and entertaining the public (weddings, birthdays). Interestingly, it was not uncommon for the child to demand his audience's full attention as a condition of performance—a trait that foreshadowed an often cantankerous artist–audience relationship.

Young Zimmerman's creative portfolio included poetry (writing poems for his parents' birthdays when he was around ten), music (starting with the piano, the saxophone, and turning to the guitar at around age fourteen), and painting. As he explained to Robert Shelton, he did not hunt, fish, or play sports; instead, "I just played the guitar and sang my songs. . . . All I did was write and sing, paint little pictures on paper, dissolve myself into situations where I was invisible."

Complementing those interests was his exposure to two cornerstones of 1950s American teen life: cinema and radio. Zimmerman was a frequent patron of the local movie house and an avid consumer of late-night radio. Film stars James Dean and Marlon Brando appealed to his introverted rebellion and played a central role in his personality's formation. Moreover, his late-night forays into the musical world by way of high-powered Southern radio stations influenced his understanding of blues, country, and their offspring, rock and roll. The mail-order record business allowed Zimmerman to purchase the music he heard on the radio, thus he was able to accumulate—and assimilate—a vast array. It is not surprising, then, that Bob Zimmerman emerged from this blend of creative influences with a keen awareness of and appreciation for artistic image. Bob Spitz explains the impact of Dean's film, *Rebel Without a Cause*, within this developmental process: "If ever the term 'born-again' applied to Bob Dylan it was then, following this celluloid revelation. He had gotten a glimpse of the future up on the screen in the form of James Dean, teenage rebel, and it appealed to his sensibility. He was inspired by the whole package—the defiant posturing, the attitude, the mumbling, and especially The Look. The look established a state of mind that allowed you to slip into the role with relative ease."

Zimmerman's enactment of "The Look" sharpened with the acquisition of a motorcycle, the requisite leather jacket, and biker attitude. Shelton writes of brotherly art where David photographed Bob riding his motorcycle or posing about with props. The teenager was consumed by the Dean/Brando image, and that perspective informed all facets of his life. Zimmerman's identification with Elvis Presley, Little Richard, and Hank Williams (a veritable 1950s Rebellion Hall of Fame) fueled his image-laden musical ambitions. He may have entered this world with artistic proclivities, but Zimmerman developed those abilities through a rebellious image that he projected *through* those activities—that is, his creative motivations did not service his muse as much as they channeled his rebellion.

Zimmerman's musical maturation featured a host of happenings ranging from his participation in singing groups (e.g., The Jokers), in rock and roll bands (e.g., the Shadow Blasters, The Golden Chords, Elston Gunn and The Rock Boppers), his attendance at concerts (e.g., the Winter Dance Party in January 1959 just nights before the show's participants—Buddy Holly, Richie Valens, and the Big Bopper—were killed), his encounters with area radio personalities ("Jim Dandy" from nearby Virginia, Minnesota), and, in the summer of 1959, a brief tryout as Bobby Vee's piano player (sources differ regarding Vee). Of these musical experiences, two stand out: his bands' performances during his high school's "Jacket Jamboree" and at the "St. Louis County Fair" in the late 1950s. Both events featured hostile audiences with rude responses (booing, laughing) to the sound and fury of Zimmerman's rocking, Little Richard–inspired act that apparently disturbed everyone but Bobby Zimmerman. At this early point in his life Zimmerman displayed a quiet resolve to express himself that could not be shaken by external factors. It was as if the teenager performed for himself—an inner, unshakable audience fully cognizant of and devoted to his personal mission.

The biographers chronicle Zimmerman's life with teenage friends and creative cohorts during his adolescence. They were, without question, thorough in their interviews (e.g., John Bucklen, Larry Fabbro, Echo Helstrom, Leroy Hoikkala) and their findings are informative. Howard Sounes reveals that Zimmerman's first song was written about actress Brigitte Bardot; Clinton Heylin indicates that his first tune was a revision of Jimmie Rodgers's "A Drunkard's Child" (titled "The Drunkard's Son"); and Bob Spitz claims the first composition to be "Big Black Train." Although the details occasionally differ, the research suggests that Zimmerman was an imaginative young man with a penchant for storytelling. His ability to recast the popular songs of the day (Hoikkala remembers his lyrical revisions of current songs; often asserting his authorship over the results), his capacity to weave tall tales (Helstrom recalls a particular concoction about a large, threatening snake wrapped around a tree, even though Minnesota and such snakes are an unlikely combination), and his propensity for word games offer concrete evidence of a wordsmith in the making.

Of particular interest is the Bucklen–Zimmerman word game, "Glissendorf." Sounes and Heylin describe the "mind game" (Sounes) or "word game" (Heylin) the two teens played at the expense of their audience. Heylin provides an example of a "Glissendorf" exchange between the boys: "I see it's raining. / It isn't raining. / You say it isn't? Okay, if you wanna be difficult, it isn't. So let's move on. What's the next first thing to come to your mind? / The what? / The what? Just what I thought. I won! You won! / I don't understand. / That's exactly right. You don't understand. You don't understand." The game's purpose was to confuse the observer or, as Sounes concludes, "it left the other person wondering if they had missed something." The biographers report that there were occasions when a "Glissendorf" victim became angry or hurt by the game—a response that concerned Bucklen and delighted Zimmerman. In any event, the youthful experiences involved in creative revisions of existing songs, imaginative (occasionally, off-the-wall) storytelling, and word games designed to confuse/exclude their "victims" represent the creative foundation of a personality that would one day apply those traits in other contexts.

In the fall of 1959, Zimmerman enrolled at the University of Minnesota, moved to Minneapolis, and entered the bohemian world of the university's art district, Dinkytown. Dylan described this pivotal period to Cameron Crowe: "I came out of the wilderness and just naturally fell in with the beat scene, the Bohemian, BeBop crowd. . . . I had already decided that society . . . was pretty phony and I didn't want to be part of that . . . also, there was a lot of unrest in the country. You could feel it, a lot of frustration, sort of like a calm before a hurricane, things were shaking up." He recalled that Dinkytown's inhabitants were "poets and painters, drifters, scholarly types, experts at one thing or another who had dropped out of the regular nine-to-five life." The writings of Kerouac, Ginsberg, Corso, and Ferlinghetti affected Zimmerman more "than any of the stuff I'd been raised on" such that "everyday was like Sunday, it's like it was waiting for me, it had just as big an impact on me as Elvis Presley."

The Dinkytown musical environment stressed folk music, and Zimmerman shifted gears quickly. Since his musical background was diverse, he proved to be a quick study (Heylin notes that a Dinkytown girlfriend's father's record collection facilitated the shift in genres). The fire of the rock and roll spirit remained ever-present—Zimmerman merely applied that intensity to the musical task at hand. When a Dinkytown friend provided a copy of Woody Guthrie's memoir *Bound for Glory*, Zimmerman's ambitions discovered an anchor in Guthrie's hard-traveling, hard-living, man-with-a-message persona. With his name change, the ingredients were in place for the first incarnation of the "Bob Dylan" characters. Zimmerman would combine a bohemian biker-poet attitude, American Song's blues/country traditions, and the Guthrie image to produce an unprecedented musical hybrid. David Hajdu explains Guthrie's significance: "In Guthrie, Bob found more than a genre of music, a body of work, or a performance style: he found an *image*—the hard travelin' loner with a guitar and a way with words, the outsider the insiders envied, easy with women, and surely doomed. An amalgam of Bob's previous heroes, the Guthrie he found in *Bound for Glory* was Hank Williams, James Dean, and Buddy Holly—a literate folksinger with a rock and roll attitude." Spitz concurs: "If Bobby had an idea of 'Dylan' before, then *Bound for Glory* provided him with a blueprint from which he could build his identity."

There is controversy over the motives for Bob Zimmerman's new persona. Writers (and others) debate whether he wanted to shed his past, romanticize his present, or solidify his musical future. Several biographers suggest that Abraham Zimmerman's relationship with his son had deteriorated so much that young Zimmerman rebelled against the family name. Others argue for a rejection of his religion or his community. While I don't necessarily dismiss these conclusions, I suspect that this imaginative young man was focused on image-building of one sort or another, and, as his "creation" gained a voice in Dinkytown, he continued to embellish that persona in a fashion that enhanced its marketability.

After hitchhiking his way across the country for several months, "Bob Dylan" arrived in New York in December 1960 or January 1961 (depending upon the source). Dylan entered New York's folk scene with an impressive 1961: he moved to Greenwich Village and MacDougal Street in February, he visited Woody Guthrie in early February (in a New Jersey hospital) and developed a relationship with the dying legend, he was billed on a show with John Lee Hooker in April, he played harmonica for a Harry Belafonte recording session in June (his first professional session), he performed throughout the folk community and received a favorable review from *New York Times* music critic Robert Shelton on September 29, he played harmonica during Carolyn Hester's recording session for Columbia Record's legendary producer John Hammond on the next day and signed a contract with Hammond/Columbia that afternoon, he delivered his first major performance at Carnegie Chapter Hall on November 4, and on November 20 and 22 he recorded his first album for Columbia (*Bob Dylan*, released in March 1962). Scaduto cites Miki Isaacson's recollections of the performance style that charmed New York folk circles:

> He used to do all these kooky things, and they never seemed like a routine. He could even make a comic act out of tuning his guitar, get up on stage and fiddle

with the guitar strings and pretend he wasn't able to get it right and cursing under his breath, and we would all be in the aisle with the joy of it. And I'll never forget the thing he did with his harmonica. His eyes were so bad that we didn't know if it was a joke or real, but he'd begin taking harmonicas out of his pockets and laying them down on the table, pulling out one and saying, very sotto voce, "Now where is that E flat harmonica?" then pulling out another one, and not being able to find it. And saying, "Who's got that damned harmonica?" And it broke us all up. It was so Chaplin-like.

Dave Van Ronk agrees in the *Biography* video when he describes Dylan's initial stage act as "excruciatingly funny" with its "Chaplinesque mannerisms" and between-song monologues.

Bob Dylan's 1961 was a dynamic—even explosive—period in which he created and refined an image that was part Guthrie, part Chaplin, a little James Dean, and somewhere in the mix, a portion of Little Richard. The result was a countrified, self-effacing folk singer with an intense drive to express himself. In less than a year he managed to enter the New York folk family, master their musical style, and place himself in a position to surpass his mentors. *Bob Dylan* featured two examples of the means through which the aspiring artist would transcend his newly acquired peers: his songwriting. The album's two original songs, "Talkin' New York" and "Song To Woody," demonstrate Dylan's understanding of folk traditions through their humor, topicality, and musicality. The rest of 1962 provided additional proof of the songwriter's skills, as Dylan penned "Blowin' in the Wind," "The Death of Emmett Till," "Masters of War," "When the Ship Comes In," and "A Hard Rain's a-Gonna Fall" (among many others). Had Zimmerman merely created a character to mimic the words and mannerisms of others, the act probably would have died out. But when he delivered these strong compositions in support of that image, Dylan introduced a new, refreshing act that could make the crossover from folk's narrow constituency into broader, more commercially viable audiences.

The next two years (1962–63) solidified the Guthrie/Dylan image as his public performances, recordings, and social activism received considerable attention. Although *Bob Dylan* had minimal sales (resulting in his Columbia moniker, "Hammond's Folly"), the youngster's career continued its rapid growth: January 1963 witnessed Dylan in London recording with folk singers Richard Fariña and Ric von Schmidt, Hammond's Folly's second album *The Freewheelin' Bob Dylan* was released in May, he appeared at a voter registration rally in Mississippi in July, he excelled at the Newport Folk Festival in late July, he marched on Washington, D.C. in August, and he recorded his third album in October. Bob Dylan was everywhere: writing liner notes for other artists, writing songs for other singers, writing columns for magazines, writing poems, and writing song after song after song. This period's anthems and camp-fire satires revised and extended the folk songwriting tradition through Dylan's deft articulation of various events via his unique adaptation of Guthrie's style. Supporting that style was, once again, the ever-growing Dylan Myth. Dylan explained to *Rolling Stone* that his "biography" was born when a concert producer requested a statement for promotional purposes:

You know, I'm a songwriter, I'm not a biography writer, and I need a little help with these things. So if I'm sitting in a room with some people, and I say "Come on now, I need some help, gimme a biography," so there might be three or four people there and out of those three or four people maybe they'll come up with something, come up with a biography. So we put it down, it reads well, and the producer of the concert is satisfied. In fact, he even gets a kick out of it. . . . But in actuality, this thing wasn't written for hundreds of thousands of people . . . it was just a little game for whoever was going in there and getting a ticket. . . . That's just show business. So you do that and pretty soon you've got a million people who get it on the side. . . . They start thinkin' that it's written all for them. And it's not *written for them. . . . You got all these other people taking it too seriously. Do you know what I mean? So a lot of things have been blown out of proportion.*

As the David Ewen example suggests, the biography got blown more than a little bit out of proportion (*Time*, among others, took the bait). Dylan recreated his past in other venues as well. Robert Shelton's biography cites an imaginative construction of Dylan's life during the post-performance interview for his initial *New York Times* article, a radio interview with Cynthia Gooding on March 11, 1962 is rich in biographical fabrications, and Howard Sounes notes Dave Van Ronk's recollection of Dylan's insistence that he was part Native American (specifically, a Sioux) and how he demonstrated Indian sign language for an amused (and disbelieving) audience. Such storytelling was merely an extension of Bob Zimmerman's penchant for tall tales; however, these inventions were standard practice in show business as well. In every respect, Hammond's Folly was hard at work creating a different type of celebrity. Facilitating it all was the writer's propensity to interject his persona into his songs, which elevated *the author's role* in the expression. His appearances in Mississippi, Newport (joining a celebrity chorus of "We Shall Overcome"), and Washington, D.C. made "Bob Dylan" more than a songwriter; he became a spokesperson for his generation's fight against the status quo. Much like the historic confluence of factors that rendered "Elvis Presley" (the name being more than the person), "Bob Dylan" was the product of an equally historic synthesis of artist, media, and social conditions.

Everything changed in November 1963 when *Newsweek* published a detailed account of Bob Zimmerman's life on Minnesota's Iron Range. The article discussed his parents, their faith, their economic situation, and their relationship with their son in detail, and in so doing, dispelled the myth about orphans, road trips, and strange encounters with the infamous. The trend advanced the next month when Dylan appeared before the Emergency Civil Liberties Committee to accept its Tom Paine Award for social activism. There he delivered a speech that infuriated his audience and raised additional questions regarding the legitimacy of the "Bob Dylan" character. The star of the 1963 Newport Folk Festival, the darling of the Northeastern liberal elite, the voice of his generation now faced a formidable public-relations problem in that his audience not only doubted his identity, it raised questions about the authenticity of his songs and the sincerity of his motives.

Dylan's third album *The Times They Are a-Changin'* (released in January 1964) offered a coherent package of songs and poems that directly addressed the situation. The poems—titled "11 Outlined Epitaphs"—contain a series of "state of the artist" statements regarding his personal history, his views on Guthrie, and his perspective on the press, his art, and his public image (among other things). Balancing that is the album's powerful assortment of topical songs (e.g., "Ballad of Hollis Brown," "North Country Blues," "Only a Pawn In Their Game"). Few recording artists have ever generated such insightful, heartfelt, and *intense* depictions of the luckless and locked out. Whether or not Bob Dylan was a fake, he was a formidable songwriter.

The next thirty months were a whirlwind for Dylan. Under the direction of aggressive manager Albert Grossman, Dylan now participated in tours that were filmed, recorded, and promoted in a systematic, professional manner (e.g., the spring 1965 tour of England was filmed by D. A. Pennebacker and released as the movie *Dont Look Back* in 1967). The budding auteur's songwriting turned away from topicality and toward self-expression by way of a series of albums that transformed the practice of songwriting from craft to art. *Another Side of Bob Dylan* (released August 1964), *Bringing It All Back Home* (March 1965), *Highway 61 Revisited* (August 1965), and *Blonde on Blonde* (May 1966) changed popular-music writing through their cryptic metaphors, outrageous characterizations, and obfuscated messages. The Woody Guthrie, countrified troubadour spokesperson recreated himself into a James Dean, biker-poet.

Actually, the New Dylan was more representative of Bob Zimmerman than the Dinkytown/Greenwich Village version. The James Dean Dylan backed off the Oklahoma accent and country witticisms, traded his thumb for a motorcycle, dismissed his feigned extroversion in favor of his natural introversion, and generally turned his back on *all* causes save his own. This rebel was, in fact, without a cause, and that freedom inspired Dylan's muse—an artistic instinct that existed long before Dinkytown and its folk platitudes. The transition was completed on July 25, 1965 when Bob Dylan "plugged in" at the Newport Folk Festival. His appearance that Sunday evening (the headline night of the festival) featured an electric band (with Dylan on electric guitar) that roared through several songs before shifting gears to solo Dylan's brief acoustic act. Once more, we witness a curious blend of fact and fiction as the Newport audience's response was misconstrued and widely circulated. Ric von Schmidt's comments to Anthony Scaduto indicate that the sound mix was inappropriate for the electric band therefore, members of the audience began yelling that they could not hear the vocals. The response escalated as it traveled through the audience toward the rear and all of the commotion confused everyone. The yelling turned to "chanting" (in von Schmidt's words) and the normally self-assured Dylan appeared shaken. (The specifics of all this are source-dependent.)

Press reports of the Newport "booing" and the folk community's indignation over Dylan's use of electricity spread around the world and, of course, the outbursts recurred at many subsequent shows. The battle was on. The cute, self-effacing boy that charmed New York turned into a combative, self-assured man willing to stand his ground against whatever. When Dylan toured with his new electric band, The Hawks, he withstood his audience's hostility in the same fashion as Bobby Zimmerman endured at the Jacket Jamboree and St. Louis County Fair. After a peaceful show at the Hollywood Bowl, Dylan told Hawks' drummer Levon Helm: "I wish they *had* booed. . . . It's good publicity. Sells tickets. Let 'em boo all they want." The James Dean Dylan may have been confused initially, but those feelings faded quickly, the rebellion solidified, and the songwriting prospered. When the folk community issued "open letters" condemning Dylan's shift in presentational style, the songwriter fired back in song, "Positively Fourth Street," and its confrontational response. The New Dylan had a New Cause.

The first half of 1966 was chaotic. Newlywed Dylan (he married Sara Lowndes in November 1965) traveled to Nashville to record *Blonde on Blonde* from January through March, conducted an extended world tour with The Hawks from May into June (featuring infamous concerts in England with unprecedented crowd responses), and accumulated footage for his second film, *Eat the Document*. Shelton's biography captures the intensity of this period and its impact on Dylan. The situation was difficult for others as well. Levon Helm eventually quit touring with Dylan, as he comments in his autobiography: "I couldn't have taken what Bob endured. We seemed to be the only ones who believed in what we were doing. But the guy absolutely refused to cave in. It was amazing, but Bob insisted on keeping this thing together." Even after England, the pressures for new songs, for further touring, for the second film (it was under contract to ABC), and for delivery of his novel (*Tarantula*, contracted with Macmillan) were exacting their toll on the artist. The combination of touring life, substance abuse, audience hostility, journalistic hazing, and Grossman's commercialism placed Dylan in a dangerous—physically dangerous—position. Something had to break.

And it did on July 29, 1966. Unfortunately, the break occurred in Dylan's neck as the result of a motorcycle accident near his home in Woodstock, New York. The injuries sustained when his motorcycle's wheel locked required prolonged rest, and Dylan obliged by withdrawing from touring for seven years. The mishap also relieved his responsibilities to ABC (for the film), to Macmillan (for the book), and to his audience (for Dylan, anyway). Paul Williams offers these insights into the legendary accident:

> In fact, his actual injuries had been minor. He suffered a cracked vertebra in his neck, was dazed, went to the hospital, had to wear a brace for a while. The story that he had been almost killed and completely incapacitated by the accident was put out by his manager as justification for delaying the promised book and television movie, and for canceling the 64 concert commitments. . . . For his part, of course, Dylan used the accident as an excuse and opportunity to tell his manager no—no, he wasn't going back out on the road for a while, no he wasn't going to say when he would turn in the book, complete the TV film, make his next album. But the accident was certainly more than an excuse. It was a turning point.

Williams claims that Dylan rejected celebrity life, changed lifestyles (quitting cigarettes, drugs, philandering), started reading the Bible, and assumed the traditional family-man role. *Crawdaddy's* founder concludes: "The accident was a moment of awakening, an opportunity for a life-changing, probably life-saving, reassessment, leading to a dramatic shift in personal values."

The next seven years featured a new incarnation of the Bob Dylan character that stressed traditional American music and personal privacy. Gone was the James Dean character who had the good stage sense to die in a motorcycle accident. Still, the New Dylan allowed the previous versions to play out with the release of his first "greatest hits" compilation in April 1967 and the film *Dont Look Back* in May while he recovered in Woodstock with his family and band. The recordings from Dylan's daily sessions with The Hawks (guitarist Robbie Robertson, organist Garth Hudson, pianist/drummer Richard Manual, bassist Rick Danko, and drummer Levon Helm) demonstrate the influence the musicians asserted over one another as the backing band evolved into a creative partnership. The results reveal a relaxed, engaging Dylan free of celebrity stances, with a renewed commitment to American Song (*The Basement Tapes*, the two-album set from these sessions, was released in 1975). The albums from this period—*John Wesley Harding* (released in December 1967), *Nashville Skyline* (April 1969), *Self Portrait* (June 1970), *New Morning* (October 1970), *Dylan* (November 1973), and *Planet Waves* (January 1974)—are unimaginative by the standards set by the previous era. Nevertheless, they reveal an artist in transition, and how that individual relied on his musical instincts to rebound from the creative wasteland of celebrity.

Dylan's hiatus into family life involved limited public appearances: the Woody Guthrie Memorial Concert in January 1968, television's *The Johnny Cash Show* in June 1969, the Isle of Wight festival in August 1969, and the concert for Bangladesh in August 1971. On other fronts, he moved back to New York in September 1970, published *Tarantula* in May 1971, released his second edition of "greatest hits" in November 1971, filmed *Pat Garrett & Billy the Kid* in Mexico in late 1972–73 and recorded a soundtrack album (released July 1973), and published the first edition of his lyrics and drawings (*Writings & Drawings*) in December 1973. Although Dylan rejected the high-profile celebrity life, his commercial engines ran efficiently on a regular schedule.

Dylan's focus on domestic life facilitated his successful transition from one sort of artist/celebrity to another. The earnest apprentice turned into the brash success who evolved into the mature professional. The experienced veteran returned to performing in 1974 and his remarks to Ben Fong-Torres capture his state of mind:

A family brings the world together. You can see it's all one. It paints a better picture than being with a chick and traveling all over the world. Or hanging out all night. But . . . I still get that spark. I'm still out there. In no way am I not. I don't live on a pedestal. Fame threw me for a loop at first . . . I learned how to swim with it and turn it around—so you can just throw it in the closet and pick it up when you need it.

Dylan picked up his fame, joined a new record label (Asylum), and returned to public performance via a state-of-the-art national tour ("Tour '74"—promoted by Bill Graham), a studio album (*Planet Waves*), and a double-album live recording of the "Tour '74" show (*Before the Flood*, released June 1974 on Asylum). Rejoining The Hawks (renamed The Band) for a Graham tour placed Dylan on familiar footing for his return to stage. Levon Helm describes the tour's opening night in Chicago:

> We understood that people were excited by Bob's comeback from a long public absence, but we were astounded anyway when we walked onstage in the darkened hall in Chicago and saw the entire audience stand and hold up their flaring lighters in a roar of tribute to Bob. Imagine nineteen thousand candles in the dark, people calling and whooping. It was a moment, I'll tell you. I could see the normally taciturn Dylan was moved. He walked over to the drums and looked at me, about to say something, but instead he turned back to the microphone and launched into an old song of his called "Hero Blues," which caught everyone off guard, including us.

Throughout the tour Dylan dealt with the celebrity, "icon of the sixties" issue. This response to *Newsweek* was typical:

> Idols are old hat. They aren't people, they're objects. But I'm no object. . . . When we think of idols we think of those carved pieces of wood and stone people can relate to—that's what an idol is. They do the same thing to someone like Marlon Brando—they attach themselves to certain people because of a need. But I'm just doing exactly what a lot of other people would be doing if they could. I'm not standing at an altar, I'm working in the marketplace.

(Fascinating comments from the *creator* of the image that generated the idolatry.)

The marketplace offered considerable yield, but Dylan remained uninspired. His public comments from the era suggest an artistic reckoning. The liner notes for the *Biograph* retrospective communicate Dylan's response to that tour. He told Crowe that he was merely playing the role of "Bob Dylan" and The Band was simply playing "The Band": "It was all sort of mindless. . . . It was just more of a 'legendary' kind of thing . . . it was just a big show, a big circus except there weren't any elephants." Then he complained that the "bigger and louder something was, the more energy it was supposed to have" when, in actuality, it was "big industry moving in on the music." Dylan concluded that the situation was "like the armaments manufacturers selling weapons to both sides in a war, inventing bigger and better things to take your head off while behind your back, there's a few people laughing and getting rich off your vanity." The disappointment was clearly frustrating.

Dylan rejoined Columbia Records and returned to his old studio in September 1974 to record an album of new songs. As the project neared completion, he suddenly revised those plans, re-recorded much of the album that December in Minneapolis, and somehow managed to issue *Blood on the Tracks* in January 1975. The strength of the new songs commanded significant attention through-

out the musical world and signaled the creative return of the seasoned songwriter. Columbia released the *Basement Tapes* in June and that fall Dylan
embarked on his most ambitious musical tour, The Rolling Thunder Revue. *Newsweek* characterized the tour as a "circus like caravan of 70 musicians, filmmakers, old-line Village beats and mainline crazies" on buses traveling throughout
"New England for gigs in places like Durham, N.H., and Lowell, Mass." *Newsweek's*
Michael Orth describes the tour's opening ceremony:

> One dawn last week, Bob Dylan slid behind the wheel of his new mobile home and
> drove to a rocky point behind a Gatsby-like mansion in Newport, R.I. Soon he
> was joined by folksinger Ramblin' Jack Elliott, poet Allen Ginsberg, Ronee Blakley
> . . . Roger McGuinn . . . an assortment of lesser-knowns and hangers-on, and
> Rolling Thunder, a celebrated Cherokee medicine man. The group formed a circle
> around a small fire, and Rolling Thunder, who had earlier phoned the Coast
> Guard for the exact time of sunrise, raised an eagle feather, pointed it heaven-
> ward, then waved it at the gathering. "Music comes from the earth to fill our
> souls," Rolling Thunder intoned. One by one, each of the celebrants sprinkled
> some tobacco into the smoldering fire, and when it was Dylan's turn, he
> stepped forward and whispered: "We are of one soul." At the ceremony's end, he
> had a tear in his eye.

Long-time Dylan friend/advisor Ginsberg addressed the tour's therapeutic value
for its central character: "This is the great moment of Dylan taking off his mask.
. . . He's accepted the myth created around him and is transferring it into artistic energy. He's alchemizing it into gold." Sounes describes the four-hour show's
strategic qualities (Dylan's "contributions were carefully timed for maximum dramatic effect") and Heylin cites participants Jacques Levy's and Mick Ronson's
recollections regarding the show's spontaneous music (Ronson reported that
Dylan constantly revised songs) and theatrical orientation (a "traveling vaudeville
show," according to Levy). The production occasionally entered towns unan-
nounced, and in so doing, represented the antithesis of the carefully staged, thoroughly promoted "Tour '74."

The pioneering tour opened in Plymouth, Massachusetts on October 30, 1975;
Dylan's fifteenth studio album, *Desire*, was issued in January 1976; the Rolling
Thunder's second leg opened in April (with a different cast); the May 23rd performance at Colorado State University was filmed and aired on NBC in September;
the concert album, *Hard Rain*, was also released in September; and Dylan appeared
with The Band for its final concert/film, *The Last Waltz*, in November. Throughout
the prodigious Rolling Thunder experience, film crews combed the stage, the dressing rooms, the buses, and wherever else the traveling troupe might roam. The raw
materials of this footage commanded much of Dylan's attention in 1977, and later
that year, his preparations for a new, revised world tour also occupied the artist.
The new tour dismissed Rolling Thunder's multiple-act packaged approach in favor
a gospel-influenced, musically innovative presentation of the Dylan canon. Many of
the revisions shocked audiences; nevertheless, the Jacket Jamboree survivor
steadfastly guided his new company around the world throughout 1978.

In January 1978 Dylan's celluloid masterpiece opened in theaters. *Renaldo and Clara* was a four-hour tour of Dylan's imagination that received widespread critical condemnation. A *Los Angeles Times* review addresses the film's function: "The object here, it seems fairly clear, is to reveal Dylan's world, internal and external." Charles Champlin concludes that *Renaldo and Clara* "is a very long experience for all but the hopelessly enraptured" although it is "also a very personal, fresh, original and provocative work." Music critic Robert Hilburn also covered the movie for the *Los Angeles Times*: "At once mocking and reinforcing his own almost mythical pop status, Dylan has crammed enough provocative symbolism into this nearly four-hour production to keep Dylan-cologists aflutter for years. . . . It's a bold, if flawed work that has the independence and some of the vision of Dylan's music." Gregg Kilday's review—also for the *Times*—probes deeper into the film's symbolism. He argues that Dylan has "calculatingly filtered his personality through a series of archetypal poses" (ranging from "the wandering urban troubadour" of the *Freewheelin'* period to the "haunted poet-imagist" of the *Blonde on Blonde* era to the "playful country boy" of *Nashville Skyline* phase to the "wizened medicine man" from the *Desire* stage) that were "fashioned" from an "ever-changing succession of masks" that "provide the key" to *Renaldo and Clara*. Dylan elaborated for Kilday:

> It deals with those images, but it goes beyond those images. The image is broken apart and you see what's behind the images. You see the truth behind the idle truth, a kind of resurrection of the common man as opposed to gratification of the image or the ego. . . . The idea of the mask was to reveal the inner self—all these words I'm throwing at you have been used so many times before, but I mean just that—the mask is more a replica of the inner self than the face. We knew we had to do the movie with masks in order for it to be successful.

Just as "11 Outlined Epitaphs" captured the "state of the artist" for those times, *Renaldo and Clara* features another blend of fact and fiction as Dylan toyed with his public image, his relationships with his soon-to-be-divorced wife and singer Joan Baez, as well as a host of other topics. For Dylan, film simply provided the means to his creative ends, as he told the *Washington Post*: "I don't know nothing about making movies . . . I don't consider myself a filmmaker in the fashionable sense of the word or in the scholastic sense of the word. I don't think of myself as a filmmaker. If DeVinci [sic] were alive or Van Gogh, or if Rembrandt were alive, they'd be making films too."

Although he edited the movie down to a more acceptable two hours, the negativity of the reviews apparently inspired Dylan to leave the film business with his brother while he toured with his new band and their new arrangements. In February and March of 1978 Dylan toured Japan and Australia; in April the company returned and recorded the *Street-Legal* album (released in June 1978), and afterward, toured England, Europe, and the United States. That November, Columbia issued the *Live at Budokan* double album in Japan where it was recorded earlier that year (released later in the United States). Many things were happening to Bob Dylan at this point in his life. The complications of divorce and settlements (especially regarding his five children, four of whom Dylan fathered) joined a growing dissatisfaction with his professional life to create a serious predicament. That several critics described his new show as a Las Vegas act, and consequently compared the aging Dylan with the aging Elvis Presley did not help the situation. To cope with his new problems, the auteur turned to an old skill and changed his mask; this time, he deployed yet another widely recognized persona and unveiled "The Answer" to his personal and professional dilemmas.

When Bob Dylan announced that he had committed his life to Christ, he not only introduced a New Dylan for his audience, he also presented a new forum for an old trade. Dylan—the master of the topical song—now shifted subjects as his next three albums—*Slow Train Coming* (released in August 1979), *Saved* (June 1980), and *Shot of Love* (August 1981)—used gospel's musical traditions to convey messages of warning and celebration. Yet religion had always found a place in Dylan's music, as this 1974 statement to Ben Fong-Torres indicates:

> Religion to me is a fleeting thing. Can't nail it down. It's in me and out of me. It does give me, on the surface, some images, but I don't know to what degree. Like da Vinci going in to paint the *Last Supper*. Until he finishes it, no one knows what the *Last Supper* is. He goes out and finds twelve guys, puts them around this table, and there's your *Last Supper*. Or Moses. He found a guy and painted him, and forever, that guy will be Moses. But why Moses or the *Last Supper*? Why not a flower? Or a tree?

Paul Williams agrees that this highly publicized personal/artistic innovation may not have involved any change. Williams maintains that Dylan applied the same skills he used to personalize traditional folk tunes to articulate his moral messages except, this time, he tried to keep his celebrity status out of the process. Dylan told Williams:

> I wrote those songs—I didn't plan to write them, but I wrote them anyway. I didn't like writing them . . . I just didn't want to write those songs at that period of time. But I found myself writing these songs, and after I had a certain amount of them, I thought I didn't want to sing them, so I had a girl sing them for me at the time, Carolyn Dennis. . . . I wanted the songs out, but I didn't want to do it because I knew it wouldn't be perceived in that way. It would just mean more pressure. I just didn't want that at the time.

The moral trilogy extended the musical orientation initiated in *New Morning*'s, and later *Street-Legal*'s, gospel sound. That trend carried over to the tours that supported the new records. After an October 20, 1979 appearance on *Saturday Night Live*, Dylan's gospel tour opened in San Francisco and continued throughout most of 1980 and 1981. These extensive tours of North America, England, and Europe focused exclusively on the new songs as Bob Dylan, once again, stood before hostile audiences hoping to hear "Blowin' in the Wind" and the rest of his historic repertoire. With time, he compromised and included songs from earlier periods; nevertheless, the intensity of his initial commitment was sustained and he seemed to take any criticism in stride. In 1984 he explained that situation to

Robert Hilburn: "The reaction . . . was disheartening at times. . . . But it doesn't wound you because you get used to the ups and downs. You get to where the praise doesn't mean anything because it's often for the wrong reason, and it's the same with the criticism. Besides, I don't think I'll be perceived properly till 100 years after I'm gone. I really believe that. I don't think anybody has really even caught on to 'Blonde on Blonde' yet."

Hilburn's reviews from November 1979 shed considerable light on this facet of the auteur's career. After attending the first night of the gospel tour, Hilburn defended Dylan's decision to focus on his new music: "While this approach sacrifices some 'entertainment value,' it would be too restricting to limit a man of Dylan's artistry to a conventional pop role. The most important American rock figure since Elvis Presley, Dylan should be given full artistic range. The test shouldn't be the age of the material but the quality of it. On that level, Dylan has not let down his audience on this tour." Two days later Hilburn extended his Elvis analogy after witnessing the Los Angeles debut of the tour:

> Dylan may surely revive some of his old tunes in future shows, but his tour's emphasis on new material is something both he and his audience needed. Before this tour, Dylan seemed headed for the same artistic impasse that ultimately trapped Elvis Presley. The audience adoration of his past made movement difficult for Dylan, but by refusing to be bullied any longer by the '60s crowd, he has again asserted his own vitality. That's what makes this tour "born again" in more ways than one.

Dylan's moral period ebbed in 1982 and the musical world heard little from him that year. In April 1983 he returned to the studio with a powerful assortment of songs that evolved into *Infidels* (released November 1983) with several compelling outtakes (e.g., "Foot of Pride" and "Blind Willie McTell") appearing years later on the compilation *Bootleg Series* boxed set. These songs represent the final turning point in the author's career. From this point on, Dylan assumed the posture of the professional musician: Writing songs with varying levels of intensity (and success), maintaining an active stage presence, avoiding the pressures of celebrity, and generally settling into the seasoned veteran's role. Dylan summarized his stance for *Rolling Stone* in 1985: "I've made all the difference I'm going to. . . . My place is secure, whatever it is. I'm not worried about having to do the next thing or keeping in step with the times. I've sold millions of records. I've done all the big shows. I've had all the acclaim at one time or another. I'm not driven anymore to prove that I'm the top dog." He reiterated his position in 1986 to the same publication:

> If I'm here at eighty . . . I'll be doing the same thing I'm doing now. This is all I want to do—it's all I can do. . . . I think I've always aimed my songs at people who I imagined—maybe falsely so—had the same experiences that I've had, who have kind of been through what I'd been through. But I guess a lot of people just haven't. . . . See, I've always been just about being an individual, with an individual point of view. If I've been about anything, it's probably that, and to let some people know that it's possible to do the impossible. And that's really all. . . . If

I've ever had anything to tell anybody, it's that you can do the impossible.
Anything is possible. And that's it. No more.

Rolling Stone reprinted that remark in its coverage of Dylan's fiftieth birthday and used it as a form of capstone comment; that all-important "final look back." How interesting that a statement suggestive of a creative goodbye would actually preface an extended period of steady productivity. The "cause" may be absent (personal or public), but the muse remains active, albeit in a different artistic direction.

Since 1983's *Infidels*, Dylan has issued nine studio albums of varying styles and orientations. *Empire Burlesque* (May 1985) features a return to the gospel sounds of the late 1970s with a touch of producer Arthur Baker's dance-mix influences. *Knocked Out Loaded* (July 1986) and *Down in the Groove* (May 1988) involve curious blends of covers, co-authored, and original material. *Oh Mercy* (September 1989) signals a rebirth of Dylan's songwriting and the positive impact of producer Daniel Lanois. *Under the Red Sky* (September 1990) raises questions regarding the writer's artistic intentions (although it includes an all-star cast of musicians). *Good as I Been to You* (November 1992) and *World Gone Wrong* (October 1993) represent a return to Woodstock and the *Basement Tapes* through Dylan's covers of traditional material that influenced his musical maturation. *Time Out of Mind* (September 1997) represents Dylan's first Grammy Award–winning album (his first Grammy was awarded in 1980 for Best Male Vocal) as well as Lanois's continued influence. And 2001's *Love and Theft* presents the "musician" Dylan described in 1986 through a rollicking review of American Song's varied sounds (*Love* was nominated for three Grammys: Album of the Year, Best Contemporary Folk Album, and Best Male Vocal [for "Honest with Me"]). Throughout it all, the Dylan commercial machine issued two boxed-set compilations (*Biograph*, November 1985; *Bootleg Series*, March 1991), four live albums (*Real Live*, December 1984; *Dylan and The Dead*, February 1989; *MTV Unplugged*, April 1995; *Live 1966*, October 1998; with multiple foreign releases), and two more greatest-hits compilations (*Greatest Hits Volume 3*, November 1994; *The Essential Bob Dylan*, October 2000; and still more foreign releases). The late 1980s also witnessed Dylan's participation in his first all-star band, The Traveling Wilburys, and its two recordings (*Vol. 1*, November 1988, and *Vol. 3*, October 1990). Finally, the auteur has appeared on a variety of tribute albums celebrating the music of Charlie Patton, Jimmie Rodgers, Hank Williams, and Sun Records as well as soundtracks for the film *Wonder Boys* (Dylan won an Oscar for "Things Have Changed") and the television series *The Sopranos*.

During that time frame, Dylan performed at major charity events ("Live Aid" in 1985, "Farm Aid" in 1985), appeared in the film *Hearts of Fire*, conducted a series of "never ending" tours, received a variety of awards from around the world (inducted into the Songwriters Hall of Fame, 1982; the "Founder's Award" from ASCAP, 1986; inducted into the Rock and Roll Hall of Fame, 1988; "Commandeur de Arts et des Letters" from the French Ministry of Culture, 1990; the Kennedy Center Medal, 1998; Grammy Awards, 1991, 1998; "Polar Music Prize" from the

Royal Swedish Academy of Music, 2000; Golden Globe, 2001; Academy Award, 2001; and he has been nominated for the Nobel Prize in Literature in 1997, 1998, 1999, and 2000), performed with a host of artists (e.g., tours with Tom Petty, the Grateful Dead, Paul Simon), endured a night of public celebration at New York's Madison Square Garden (October 1992), performed before the Pope at the Vatican (September 1997) and—somehow, someway—Bob Dylan has achieved the impossible: He has escaped the glare of celebrity spotlights while remaining professionally active. The Dylan image machine has gone dark and the artist now assumes a stealth-like presence that enables him *to be* and *not to be*, simultaneously. Ultimately, Dylan has achieved his life-long ambition, as he related it to Paul Zollo: "What interested me was being a musician. The singer was important and so was the song. But being a musician was always first and foremost in the back of my mind."

The Bob Dylan Story is a fascinating tale of success and failure, presence and absence, commitment and detachment, and a variety of other polarities. It is a tale of extremes. As the *Biography* video argues: "But even as his music has so often held a cracked mirror to the hopes, despairs, and confusions of a changing society, Dylan himself has always resisted definition. From folk trouba-dour to rock and roll trailblazer, from reclusive superstar to weathered icon, Bob Dylan's life has been an American song of unending self-discovery." The 90-minute profile concludes: "Yet Dylan has always remained an enigma, an intensely human paradox. Constantly reinventing himself, but always authentic. Cynical but hopeful. A poet and a rock star. Confessional, but always just out of reach." The *New York Times'* Jon Pareles concurs: "During a recording career that now spans 35 years, Dylan has been a cornucopia of inconsistency. Visionary and crank, innovator and conservator, irritant and stimulant, skeptic and prosely-tizer, rebel and sellout, pathfinder and lost patrol: Dylan has been all of those things, and many more. He may well be the most restless figure in rock history, constitutionally incapable of doing the same thing twice."

The Dylan phenomenon is also a major sidebar to a greater happening in that his history parallels the rise and development of contemporary mass media. The confluence of factors that played significant roles in Dylan's career matured along with the artist—music journalism, musical image making and personal publicity, the singer-songwriter composite, music production, and more devel-oped with Dylan. With so many aspects of popular culture changing around him—and thereby adding to the moment's confusion through the uncertainty of institutional immaturity—how did Dylan manage to survive? What could have sustained him throughout the ebb and flow of a forty-year career? That is our next subject.

chapter two

the impulse

Biography is an essential element of authorship; however, the artistic impulse that inspires and sustains the artist is the prime mover of the creative process. The inspiration and commitment necessary to transform the abstractions of human existence into the concrete representations of art require skills—talents—of uncommon ability. The specific details of an artist's life may provide the raw materials for the creative act, but the artistic impulse determines the content and style of the subsequent expression. The impulse that motivates the artist embodies that individual's artistic philosophy, creative influences, inventive strategies, and stylistic choices. It is the epicenter of authorship.

Our examination of Bob Dylan's creative impulse begins with his comments regarding artistic function. On this topic, his views are quite consistent. For example, in March 1978 he told *Playboy*: "I want to be moved, because that's what art is supposed to do. . . . Art is supposed to take you out of your chair. It's supposed to move you from one space to another." He echoed that view in July when *Melody Maker* cited Dylan's dictum, "The purpose of art is to inspire." Later that year, he philosophized to *Rolling Stone*: "Art is the perpetual motion of illusion. The highest purpose of art is to inspire. What else can you do? What else can you do for anyone but inspire them?" Dylan sharpened his position with these 1983 remarks to the *Chicago Tribune*: "The purpose of music is to elevate the spirit and inspire. Not to help push some product down your throat." A year later he described music's therapeutic value for the *Los Angeles Times*:

> It puts you in tune with your own existence. . . . Sometimes you really don't know how you feel, but really good music can define how you feel. It can make you feel not so much alone. That's what it has always done for me—people like Hank Williams, Bill Monroe, Muddy Waters, Robert Johnson. . . . I'm afraid roots music is going to be obsolete the way we're going. I hope people go back to it. But most people [who make records] don't care about feeling. They just want success.

And in 1993 Dylan told the *Boston Herald*: "Art to me doesn't mirror society. The very essence of art is subversive to society, and whatever society is putting out, art's got to do something else."

Dylan's comments on art are straightforward. Art is to challenge the status quo through emotional appeals. Not surprisingly, he denounces art's commercial dimension and emphasizes its inspirational or spiritual attributes. Notice how he anchors his view in personal experience as he stresses the significance of "roots music" and its emotional impact on him. He elaborated on his musical influences for Robert Hilburn:

> My music comes from two places: white hillbilly music—Roscoe Holcomb, stuff like that—and black blues—people like Son House, Charley Patton, Robert Johnson. These are the two elements I've always related to best, even now. Then, all of a sudden in the '60s, I heard Woody Guthrie, which just blew my mind—what he did with a lyric. So, I stopped everything and learned his songs. That's what kept me going. I wanted to see how far I could take those elements, how well I could blend them together. Sometimes my music has gone a little to one side, then it drifts back to the other, but I'm always headed in the same direction.

Six years later Dylan continued his discussion with Hilburn:

> At a certain point, though, I realized I had found something musically that no one else had found. I just stumbled onto it because I had been doing the regular stuff for a long, long time. . . . When I started, I combined other people's styles unconsciously. . . . I crossed Sonny Terry with the Stanley Brothers with Roscoe Holcomb with Big Bill Broonzy with Woody Guthrie . . . all the stuff that was dear to me. Everybody else tried to do an exact replica of what they heard. I was doing it my own way because I wasn't as good technically as, say, Erik Darling or Tom Paley. So I had to take the songs and make them mine in a different way. It was the early folk music done in a rock way, which was the first kind of music I played. On the first album, I did "Highway 51" like an Everly Brothers tune because that was the only way I could relate to that stuff.

Dylan reiterated his views to the *Chicago Tribune* in a conversation about Bruce Springsteen and his musical heritage. He observed that "Bruce knows where he comes from" and how Springsteen "has taken what everybody else has done and made his own thing out of it." Still, he expressed concern that artists who use Springsteen as a role model will overlook *his* influences: "If you copy somebody—and there's nothing wrong with that—the top rule should be to go back and copy the guy that was there first. It's like all the people who copied me over the years, too many of them just got me, they didn't get what I got." The artist is not only to inspire audiences through emotional appeals that help them define their feelings and question their situations, he or she must also understand the creative influences that enabled the achievement of that artistic end. Throughout this process, Dylan's audience remains constant, as he related to John Cohen and Happy Traum: "The most you can do is satisfy yourself. If you satisfy yourself then you don't have to worry about remembering anything. If you don't satisfy yourself, and you don't know why you're doing what you do, you begin to lose contact. If you're doing it for *them* instead of you, you're likely not in contact with them. You can't pretend you're in contact with something you're not." In 2001 he told *Rolling Stone*: "I have to impress myself first, and unless I'm speaking in a certain language to my own self, I don't feel anything less than that will do for the public, really." Bob Dylan's art pursues emotional inspiration through self-satisfaction: He probes his feelings, satisfies a personal ambition (that embraces his musical roots), and shares the results. His primary audience has not changed across his forty-year career. It may be the key to his longevity.

Dinkytown and Greenwich Village added one final ingredient to the artistic formula that renders Dylan's work. Bob Zimmerman wrote poems as a child and displayed an interest in poetry in high school (hence, according to Hibbing sources, the "Dylan" moniker—supposedly after poet Dylan Thomas), but Dinkytown's and New York's bohemian environments stimulated the young wordsmith's predilection for the art form. With time, Dylan expanded his list of influences to include poets and novelists, as these comments to *Melody Maker* indicate:

> Yes, Rimbaud has been a big influence on me. When I'm on the road and want to read something that makes sense to me, I go to a bookstore and read his words. Melville is somebody I can identify with because of how he looked at life. I also like Joseph Conrad a lot, and I've loved what I've read of James Joyce. Allen Ginsberg is always a great inspiration.

As Dylan's muse synthesized American Song's Black and White musical heritages with his rock and roll proclivities, he gradually added poetry to the mix. Or did he? There are moments when Dylan backs away from that stance. Cohen and Traum's interview probed Dylan's relationship to and use of poetry, and he hesitated, noting: "I understand what's there, it's just that the connection sometimes does not connect." He explained: "My thoughts weren't about reading, no . . . they were just about that feeling that was in the air. I tried to somehow get a hold of that, and write that down, and using my musical training to sort of guide it by, and in the end, have something I could do for a living." Throughout Dylan's career he absorbed every available influence and quickly applied that knowledge to his work (movie dialog, popular expressions, existing song lyrics). If critics wished him to be a poet, why not? It fed his image. When these elements were combined with his commitment to that image, he transcended the respective influences. The *image*—topical troubadour, Newport Mod, paternal patriot, poetic preacher, or professional musician—drives the application of a cultivated musical instinct—his *training*—that seeks to inspire audiences to challenge themselves through emotional expressions that satisfy his personal agenda. Such an approach does not ignore logic or rationality—or even his audience; it merely accents the emotive and probes those personal feelings. (Dylan's "Outlined Epitaph #4" speaks directly to his preference for the emotive over the logical, political, or institutional "truths" associated with societal structures. When Dylan accepts Christ as his *personal* savior, we witness an interesting tension between an individual's *spiritual* orientation and the institutional rhetoric associated with *religion*.)

How Dylan goes about his trade is revealing. He often appears reluctant to discuss his creative strategies; nevertheless, when he opens up, he is instructive. Furthermore, his writing techniques evolved throughout his career: The style that yielded his early work is not the same strategy that rendered subsequent entries. Perhaps we should begin with definitions. Dylan told Shelton that "songs are just pictures of what I'm seeing—glimpses of things—life, maybe," and he told Hentoff that his "songs are pictures and the band makes the sound of the pictures." In 2001 he explained to *Rolling Stone* that a "song is just a mood that an artist is attempting to convey." And in 1978 he offered this detailed description of these inspirational "pictures" and "sounds" to *Playboy*:

> The closest I ever got to the sound I hear in my mind was on individual bands in the *Blonde on Blonde* album. It's that thin, that wild mercury sound. It's metallic and bright gold, with whatever that conjures up. That's my particular sound. I haven't been able to succeed in getting it all the time. . . . It's the sound of the street with the sunrays, the sun shining down at a particular time, on a particular type of building. A particular type of people walking on a particular type of street. It's an outdoor sound that drifts even into open windows that you can hear. The sound of bells and distant railroad trains and arguments in apartments and the clinking of silverware and knives and forks and beating with leather straps. It's all—it's all there. . . . All pretty natural sounds. It's water, you know, water trickling down a brook. . . . Words don't interfere with it. They—they—punctuate it. You know, they give it purpose. And all the ideas for my songs, all the influences, all come out of that. All the influences, all the feelings, all the ideas come from that. I'm not doing it to see how good I can sound, or how perfect the melody can be, or how intricate the details can be woven or how perfectly written something can be. I don't care about those things.

Dylan's conversation with Bill Flanagan builds on these views: "Well, songs are just thoughts. . . . To hear a song is to hear someone's thought. . . . I'm a messenger. I get it. It comes to me so I give it back in my particular style." When asked about the process through which these "messages" are articulated, Dylan claimed "not a whole lot of real thought goes into this stuff" in that it is "more or less remembering things and taking it down." He continued: "A lot of people ask, 'What comes first, the words or melody?' I thought about that. It's very rare that they don't come together. Sometimes the words come first, sometimes the melody comes first, but that's the exception. Most of the time the words and melody come at the same time, usually with the first line." Dylan's remarks to Jann Wenner are helpful:

> Well, I try to get it when it comes. I play the guitar wherever I find one. But I try to write the song when it comes. I try to get it all . . . 'cause if you don't get it all, you're not gonna get it. So the best kinds of songs you can write are in motel rooms and cars . . . places which are all temporary. . . . You go into your kitchen and try to write a song, and you can't write a song—I know people who

do this—I know some songwriters who go to work every day, at 8:30 and come home at 5:00. And usually bring something back . . . I mean, that's legal too. It just depends on . . . how you do it. Me, I don't have those kind of things known to me yet, so I just get 'em when they come. And when they don't come, I don't try for it.

For Dylan's early work, songwriting was a spontaneous happening ("not a whole lot of real thought . . .") that captured a particular moment (or "thought") through that Little Richard–inspired "wild mercury" sound, as he told Flanagan: "The saddest thing about songwriting is when you get something really good and you put it down for a while, and you take for granted that you'll be able to get back to it with whatever inspired you to do it in the first place—well, whatever inspired you to do it in the first place is never there anymore."

The spontaneous qualities of Dylan's writings through *Blonde on Blonde* may be their most prominent attribute. A film, a newspaper article, or some other stimulus generated a "thought" and, as he disclosed to Shelton, "I just sit down and the next thing I know, it's there." There Dylan acknowledged "the song comes fast, or it won't come at all" and that a simple occurrence inspired lengthy writing sessions (lasting "twenty-four or thirty hours, fourteen hours at a time"). On another occasion, he related to Paul Zollo: "The best songs to me—my best songs—are songs which were written very quickly. Yeah, very, very quickly. Just about as much time as it takes to write it down is about as long as it takes to write it." Although the process was spontaneous, he explained to Rosenbaum that he does edit: "I reject a lot of inspiring lines . . . I reject a lot. I kind of know myself well enough to know that the line might be good and it is the first line that gives you inspiration and then it's just like riding a bull. That is the rest of it. Either you just stick with it or you don't. And if you believe that what you are doing is important, then you will stick with it no matter what." When Rosenbaum inquired if the melody flows as naturally as the first line, he replied, "Sometimes, and sometimes I have to find it." Dylan's 1964 comments to *Melody Maker* shed additional light on that creative process:

You ask if I have any difficulty producing songs. You know, they come up and stay in my mind sometimes—sometimes a long time. I just write them out when the right time comes. The words come first. Then I fit a tune or just strum the chords. Really I'm not a tune writer. The songs for me are very confining, or something. I'm not writing that many songs. I've written a lot of things with no structure, written them only because I like to sing them. "Hard rain's a-gonna fall" . . . I wrote the words of it on a piece of paper. But there was no tune that really fit to it, so I just sort of play chords without a tune. But all this comes under the heading of a definition, and I don't care really to define what I do. Other people seem to have a hard time doing that.

When *Rolling Stone's* David Fricke asked why he seemed reluctant to define his writing, Dylan countered: "I'm not reluctant to talk about my songwriting, but no one has ever really asked me the right things. . . . It's like a guy digging a ditch. It's hard to talk about how the dirt feels on the shovel." Maybe so, yet few ditch diggers describe the magical qualities of their labors. For example, when Kurt Loder inquired about the lyrics from several of his early songs, Dylan replied:

> As I look back on it now, I am surprised that I came up with so many of them. At the time it seemed like a natural thing to do. Now I can look back and see that I must have written those songs "in the spirit," you know? Like "Desolation Row"—I was just thinkin' about that the other night. There's no logical way that you can arrive at lyrics like that. I don't know how it was done. [Loder: "It just came to you?"] It just came out *through* me.

Here we get to the crux of the matter: The 1960s Dylan was a messenger—a purveyor of existing "messages" or "thoughts" that traveled *through* him via his creative method. Virtually all of the interviews cited above support this position, as the auteur consistently stated that he did not invent songs; to the contrary, he was a medium for the songs—the songs found him. He reinforced that observation to Bill Flanagan: "A lot of times you'll just hear things and you'll know that these are the things that you want to put in your song. Whether you say them or not. . . . They just sound good, and somebody thinks them. . . . I didn't originate those kinds of thoughts. I've felt them, but I didn't originate them. They're out there, so I just use them." Dylan did not sit down with a notepad, a thesaurus, and a rhyming dictionary in order to chart out his message. He endeavored to place himself in a situation so that he may "receive" a thought, process that "message," and present it through his "particular style." His remarks to Paul Zollo indicate the importance of environment to his receptive process: "Now for me, the environment to write the song is extremely important. The environment has to bring something out in me that wants to be brought out. It's a contemplative, reflective thing."

Although Dylan purportedly despises definitions, his comments to *Melody Maker* leave little doubt about his perceived role: "I'm just the postman. I deliver the songs." The "postman" analogy is helpful. Dylan did not "originate" the letter; the "message" was not from him. He was merely the conduit, the channel, the medium. He told *Newsweek*: "I used to think . . . that myself and my songs were the same thing. But I don't believe that any more. There's myself and there's my song, which I hope is everybody's song." Not only did Dylan desire to share a song's "ownership" (what the postman delivers is the receiver's property), but he shied away from any detailed comprehension of the letter's contents. To that end, he told *Time*: "My songs are not for me to understand. I don't make that a part of it. While I'm doing them I have an understanding of them, but that's all." Herein lies an interesting contradiction. If Dylan is unaware of a work's contents, how can he achieve his artistic goal of personal satisfaction? His comments to Cohen and Traum answer that question:

> It's like this painter who lives around here—he paints the area in a radius of twenty miles, he paints bright strong pictures. He might take a barn from twenty miles away, and hook it up with a brook right next door, then with a car ten miles away, and with the sky on some certain day, and the light on the

trees from another certain day. A person passing by will be painted alongside
someone ten miles away. And in the end he'll have this composite picture of
something which you can't say exists in his mind. It's not that he started off
willfully painting this picture from all his experience. . . . That's more or less
what I do.

That is, Dylan may have a feel for the various elements—or thoughts—that go
into a given expression, and that feel may be personally satisfying; however, the
"composite" that emerges from these different images is audience-dependent. Tim
Riley uses "Maggie's Farm" as an example of how Dylan's "grab-bag imagery" facilitates "flexible interpretations." Riley contends that the song is a "list of complaints, from everyday chores and employer hassles to bureaucratic oppression"
that "stand up to the recontexualization a lot of listeners impose on them." At
that point, the mail is not the postman's. Dylan's personal satisfaction comes
with a successful delivery—a pleasing manifestation of his musical "training."

All of which leads to the conclusion that Dylan's pre-accident songwriting was
more art than craft. Anthony Scaduto quotes former companion Suze Rotolo:
"Dylan was perceptive. He felt. He didn't read or clip the papers and refer to it
later, as you would write a story, or as other songwriters might do it. With Dylan
it was not that conscious journalistic approach. It was more poetical. It was all
intuitive, on an emotional level. . . . It was more than just writing, it was like something flowing out of him." Scaduto also cites a Dylan comment to songwriter Pete
Seeger: "I don't sit around and write songs with the newspapers. . . . It's usually
right there in my head before I start." Scaduto's interview with Mikki Isaacson
provides a noteworthy example of the 1960s Dylan-at-work. She recalled a summer trip and how Dylan wrote songs while riding in the back seat: "He had a spi-
ral notebook, a small steno book, and he must have had four different songs going
at once. He would write a line in one and flip a couple of pages back and write a
line in another one. A word here and a line there, just writing away."

Image is central here. The impulse that drove the work involved a narrative
imperative to move the audience through the story's emotional portrayals that
were, in turn, fueled by the writer's projected image. Dylan's celebrity image personalized—and framed—these inspirational messages. Dylan's image of *himself*
is fascinating. His view that he was a "messenger" who merely received messages—that he was the "postman" who delivered somebody else's mail—and
articulated that content through the *style de jour* provided the basis of the
writer's stylistic decision-making. Since the song already existed, and Dylan was
the medium, he wrote and recorded in a spontaneous fashion. Lyrics were rarely
edited, melodies were freely borrowed, and recording involved free-flowing performance. The spontaneity—a literal casting of one's creative fate to the wind—
was the centerpiece of the inventive process. The narrative imperative (with its
commitment to American Song) provided the artistic anchor. Each edit, each
additional take, each compromise detracted from the intuitive qualities and
inspirational power of the original message. Dylan aspired to keep it simple: raise
the antenna, be sensitive, receive, and deliver with passion ("Little Richard" to
the end). In 1978 he described this orientation to Jonathan Cott: "You must be

vulnerable to be sensitive to reality. And to me being vulnerable is just another way of saying that one has nothing more to lose. I don't have anything but darkness to lose. I'm way beyond that." With nothing to lose, the artist has everything to gain.

The irony of it all is that the "postman" became an international celebrity. The thought, the inspiration, assumed a secondary status as the "medium" became the "message." This was no accident. Dylan dressed the postman up, provided him with clever lines and mannerisms, and interjected him into somebody else's mail. The message or thought may have originated outside the postman, but "Bob Dylan" brought that parcel to everyone's house and everybody ignored everything else. (The overstatement is minimal.) The paradox is staggering: The carefully contrived Hollywood image overshadowed the spontaneously generated work of art.

A major change occurred in 1974 as the art evolved into craft. Dylan's interview with *Rolling Stone* and, once more, Jonathan Cott, describes this creative evolution in detail:

> Right through the time of *Blonde on Blonde* I was doing it unconsciously. Then one day I was half-stepping, and the lights went out. And since that point, I more or less had amnesia. Now, you can take that statement as literally or metaphysically as you need to, but that's what happened to me. It took me a long time to get to do consciously what I used to be able to do unconsciously. It happens to everybody. Think about the periods when people don't do anything, or they lose it and have to regain it, or lose it and gain something else. So it's taken me all this time, and the records I made along the way were like openers—trying to figure out whether it was this way or that way, just what *is* it, what's the simplest way I can tell the story and make this feeling real. So now I'm connected back, and I don't know how long I'll be there because I don't know how long I'm going to live. But what comes now is for real and from a place that's . . . I don't know, I don't care who else cares about it.

Dylan explained that the *John Wesley Harding* and *Nashville Skyline* projects were, in a sense, writing lessons, as the former involved a precise use of language while the latter featured expressions placed "between the lines." The two cover albums that followed (*Self Portrait* and *Dylan*) indicate that Dylan's "connection" with his muse was strained: "I was trying to grasp something that would lead me on to where I thought I should be, and it didn't go nowhere—it just went down, down, down. I couldn't be anybody but myself, and at that point I didn't know it or want to know it." He admitted that he "was convinced" that he "wasn't going to do anything else" until he met a New York art teacher who taught him "how to see." Dylan discussed with Cott Norman Raeben's impact on his creativity:

> He put my mind and my hand and my eye together in a way that allowed me to do consciously what I unconsciously felt. And I didn't know how to pull it off. I wasn't sure it could be done in songs because I'd never written a song like that. But when I started doing it, the first album I made was *Blood on the Tracks*. Everybody agrees that that was pretty different, and what's different about it

is that there's a code in the lyrics and also there's no sense of time. There's no respect for it: you've got yesterday, today and tomorrow all in the same room, and there's very little that you can't imagine not happening . . . doing it unconsciously was doing it like a primitive, and it took everything out of me. Everything was gone, I was drained. I found out later that it was much wiser to do it consciously, and it could let things be much stronger, too. Actually, you might even live longer, but I'm not sure about that.

The 73-year-old Raeben entered the auteur's life through a friend of Sara Dylan's who shared his definitions of philosophical abstractions such as love, truth, and beauty with the Dylans. According to Paul Williams, Dylan was captivated by the precise definitions Raeben issued for these god terms (how ironic!) and started attending his classes. A period of stylistic crystallization ensued in which the songwriter mastered his craft and, for the first time, invited others to participate in the process. The *Desire* project followed and featured Jacques Levy as Dylan's co-author. Although Dylan related to Cott that "I don't remember who wrote what" during the collaborations, the fact that *anyone* participated in this previously intimate act was newsworthy.

The Rolling Thunder Revue occupied Dylan after *Desire*'s release and his pen rested until its return to topicality and the oeuvre's moral period. After the spiritual fervor faded, the narrative imperative that supported the work experienced a loss of intensity because Raeben's techniques enabled a craft while they disabled an instinct. Raeben may have taught the artist how to connect his eye, hand, and mind, but that connection had little to do with Dylan's inspiration. A particular topic may move the writer to rediscover his narrative magic, yet the intuitive inclinations that supported the "muse as medium" phenomenon occurred less frequently. A period of narrative flippancy followed that would continue through the early 1990s. Dylan had always toyed with words, lines, and images; now he dallied with entire songs (and, occasionally, albums). Creatively, the songwriter resigned himself to a different standard as the artistic process reversed itself. The intuitive writings that were spontaneously recorded were replaced by deliberate statements that were systematically produced.

Paul Williams offers a compelling case in point regarding Dylan's post-Raeben writing techniques. Williams notes how many of the phrases in 1985's *Empire Burlesque* project came from movies: *Maltese Falcon, Key Largo, The Big Sleep, To Have and Have Not, The Hustler,* and more (including *Star Trek*). Williams claims that the songwriter had "successfully used 'ready-mades'" throughout his career and such practices merely extended the postman's reservoir of source material. Perhaps. Another explanation may be that when he *tries* to write, Dylan experiences difficulty, as these comments to Bill Flanagan indicate: "Anything I try to write about, I can't do it. If I try to write *about* something—'I want to write about horses' or 'I want to write about Central Park' or 'I want to write about the cocaine industry'—I can't get anywhere with that. . . . What's anything about? It's not about anything. It is what it is." *This* from one of music history's great topical songwriters? Is this to suggest that Dylan did not "try" when he wrote about the John Birch Society, Hattie Carroll, Woody Guthrie, or the Bear Mountain picnic?

I think not. What Dylan means is that he does not write in the fashion of a professional—Brill Building or Nashville—songwriter. To sit down and chart a story's development or a project's structure is to "try" in Dylan's artistic vernacular. Subsequently, ventures that require structure in order to sustain any semblance of coherence (e.g., the *Renaldo and Clara* film or the *Tarantula* book) suffer in their delivery and their inspirational impact is diluted. In the 1980s Dylan's recordings became more and more structured, the producer's role expanded, and the auteur's writing grew increasingly calculated. He was, in every respect, trying to write. Though he acknowledged that his creative peak had passed, he regularly entered the recording situation and, at times literally, forced albums out—many times, it appeared, with callous disregard for song selection. For additional insight into the evolution of his inventive strategies, let us briefly consider Dylan's recording style.

Nat Hentoff's 1964 *New Yorker* piece cites producer Tom Wilson's view regarding the songwriter's recording style: "You don't think in terms of orthodox recording techniques when you're dealing with Dylan. You have to learn to be as free on this side of the glass as he is out there." Producer T-Bone Burnett characterized Dylan in the studio to Greg Kot as "unproduceable, truly unmanageable" and described how he would record the artist: "If I were to produce a record with Bob, what I'd do is sneak next to his house and hang a microphone from the bedroom window while he was writing a song, and when I'd gotten enough songs I'd give it to the record company." Burnett's views are reinforced by Paul Williams's argument that Dylan recordings are "performances" as opposed to "compositions." Williams explains that contemporary recording techniques detract from the holistic qualities of the final product in that producers build the song "piece by piece" (i.e., each musician plays or sings his or her part independently and the production personnel assemble the various bits). He continues: "When this occurs . . . I would not describe the resultant piece of music as a performance. . . . It seems to me more closely related to a composition . . . my point is simply that when I include Dylan's studio recordings under the heading of performances, I do so because by and large he has chosen to perform live or as live as possible in the studio environment."

Dylan subscribed to this recording formula for two reasons. First, the postman/medium did not require ensemble recording techniques to capture and disseminate the messages/thoughts he received—the freer the flow, the cleaner the message; and second, the postman despised the approach. Biographers report how Dylan's first recording session (for Harry Belafonte) featured countless takes that required everyone to play their respective parts over and over and over. Afterward, the apprentice declared "Never again!" and his subsequent experiences with Big Joe Williams and John Hammond reinforced his position. As Dylan stated earlier when he described his "wild mercury sound" and its "natural" qualities: "I'm not doing it to see how good I can sound, or how perfect the melody can be, or how intricate the details can be woven or how perfectly written something can be. I don't care about those things." Tim Riley describes Dylan's recording style from this period: "This is like learning how to drive during freeway rush hour—reaction is all, and every moment is charged with a sense of nervy anticipation. The musicians didn't know what the next line was, never mind what sort of sardonic topspin Dylan's delivery would give it. It's gut-charged music-making without a net."

Another aspect of Dylan's spontaneous recording style involved his attitude toward the recording industry and its agenda. During Flanagan's interview Dylan admitted that

> a lot of my records have been made because it's—quote—time to make a record. . . . Sometimes I've never done the songs before—I'll just write 'em and put 'em somewhere. Then when I'm making a record I'll need some songs, and I'll start digging through my pockets and drawers trying to find these songs. . . . Sometimes great things happen, sometimes not-so-great things happen. But regardless of what happens, when I do it in the studio it's the first time I've ever done it.

That Dylan told Flanagan that producers "usually get in the way" and that how producers are "fine for picking you up at the airport and making sure all the bills are paid at your hotel" indicates his attitude about the production process. Perhaps Dylan's third producer, Bob Johnston, said it best in these remarks to Shelton: "Dylan is so intense, he is quite unlike any other artist I've worked with. I don't really 'produce' his albums, but just do my best to make him smile when he leaves the studio."

Dylan's attitude toward the production process was exacerbated by the technologies of the 1980s. In 1985 he expressed his frustrations to David Fricke:

> My difficulty in making a record . . . is that when I record something in a studio, it never sounds anything like it when I get the tapes back. Whatever kind of live sound I'm working for, it always gets lost in the machines. Years ago, I could go in, do it and it would translate onto tape. It gets so cleaned up today that anything wrong you do doesn't get onto the tape. And my stuff is based on wrong things.

Throughout the 1980s Dylan roamed from producer to producer (including producing himself), searching for someone who could capture the sound perfected "years ago." His 1993 comments to Greg Kot elaborate on the problem:

> Modern recording technology never endeared itself to me. . . . My kind of sound is very simple, with a little bit of echo, and that's about all that's required to record it. I'm most disappointed when producers overlook the strength of my music. The way most records sound these days, everything is equalized. My kind of music is based on nonequalized parts, where one sound isn't necessarily supposed to be as loud as another. When producers try to equal everything out, it's to dismal effect on my records.

Once more, any attempt to edit the postman's mail detracts from the original message and hinders the delivery process. Electronic innovations are artistic distractions (digital, ensemble recording is the functional equivalent of e-mail for this postman). For a letter to arrive slightly crumpled with indecipherable handwriting is part of the message's beauty. Word processers or digital soundboards may clean up the final product, but they dilute the emotional impact of the original idea/thought. The more Dylan recordings drifted toward "composition," the more calculated the lyrics became; hence, the postman's relationship to his mail changed and his parcels reflect that stylistic shift.

After close to 35 years of struggle, the process reverted to its original approach with 2001's *Love and Theft*. There the auteur reached the perfect compromise, in that he was able to achieve a state of calculated spontaneity in the studio. With a road-tested band able to anticipate every musical move, the songwriter revisited his old, spontaneous writing technique. He explained the state-of-his-writing to *Rolling Stone*:

> Well, I follow the dictates of my conscience to write a song, and I don't really have a time or place I set aside. I don't really preconceive it. I couldn't tell you when I could come up with something. It just happens at odd times, here and there. It's amazing to me that I'm still able to do it, really. . . . When you're young, you're probably writing stronger and a lot quicker, but in my case, I just try to use the traditional values of logic and reason no matter what age I've ever written any of my songs.

He elaborated on his creative method for the *Los Angeles Times*:

> Some things just come to me in dreams. But I can write a bunch of stuff down after you leave . . . about, say, the way you are dressed. I look at people as ideas. I don't look at them as people. I'm talking about general observation. Whoever I see, I look at them as ideas . . . what this person represents. That's the way I see life. I see life as a utilitarian thing. Then you strip things away until you get to the core of what's important.

The quest for that thin, wild mercury sound—and the words that punctuate it—continues. A 35-year creative search ends exactly where it began.

The most amazing aspect of Bob Dylan's creative impulse is its simplicity. No part of his inventive process is complicated; in fact, the more sophisticated the act, the less meaningful the expression is for the author. This is, in every respect, art—not craft. The instinctive, free-flowing qualities of Dylan's storytelling—whether the narrative appears in song or poetry—are their defining characteristics. He told Paul Zollo: "In my mind it's never really been seriously a profession. . . . It's been more confessional that professional. . . . Then again, everybody's in it for a different reason." Still, the writer's creative context directly influenced the content of these spontaneous "confessions": An aspiring folk singer applies that genre's traditional vernacular, an emerging poet employs that art form's intuitive imagination, a celebration of Americana expands on that art form's history, a poetic preacher synthesizes art and morality, and a professional musician manages the tensions associated with a commercial process that involves art *and* craft. In many respects, it is as if a pure act is constantly threatened by impure influences. Although Paul Williams warns against forsaking a work's content when considering its developmental context, Dylan's career indicates the extent to which that content *is* shaped by *its* context. Whether he is writing the words or music or recording both, Dylan's art is the product of intuitive powers that represent the heart and soul of his talent. To interject his brain is to dilute the process. Bob Dylan is a medium with a special talent for shaping the emotional messages that flow through him. He may convert that thought into a folk song, a poetic abstraction, a country tune, a hymn, or a pop song. In all cases, the auteur *feels* the message/thought, articulates that intuition through the critical lens of American Song, and renders a self-satisfying expression that, hopefully, arouses his audience's emotions. If the process seems magical, well, maybe it is.

chapter three

the oeuvre

We now turn to the manifestation of biography, creative impulse, and stylistic tendency that is the lifework or oeuvre. Here we explore the maturation of the songwriter's art as it engages the commercial world. As we begin, we must remain cognizant of the fact that no expression appears without a creative purpose or a commercial function. Even when Bob Dylan's work drifts into radical eccentricity, it pursues an identifiable objective (personal, professional, or some combination). The work's content is directly related to its context. Moreover, Dylan's stories display a distinctive American flavor. Critics may assert the impact of various influences within his writings, but each attribute—whether derived from folk tunes, beat poetry, roots music, or cinema—filters through the author's American worldview. This creative predisposition operates on a conscious level, as Dylan related to Robert Shelton and Melody Maker in 1978: "Creatively, I couldn't live anywhere but America, because I understand the tone behind the language. . . . All my feelings come out of America. When you leave America, you get peace. America is a very violent place, so when you leave, you get that peace—to create. My language is still American, though, I don't know the language, the rules or the structure of other countries. I was never a kid in any other country." Regardless of its creative intent or form, Dylan's songwriting deploys an intuitive structure that serves as the tool (the "rules") through which he articulates his "feelings" about life's experiences. He elaborated on this thesis for Rolling Stone in 2001:

> Every one of the records I've made has emanated from the entire panorama of what America is to me. America, to me, is a rising tide that lifts all ships, and I've never really sought inspiration from other types of music. My problem in writing songs has always been how to tone down the rhetoric in using the language. I don't really give it a whole lot of soulful thought. A song is a reflection of what I see all around me all the time.

The body of work that streams from those "reflections" divides itself into six branches: 1) a "folk-posturing" period, 2) a "Newport Mod" era, 3) an "Americana" phase, 4) a moment of stylistic crystallization, 5) a "moral" stage, and 6) a final installment, "American Song, Revisited." Each period features its own creative imperative as stories vary in their artistic function and subsequent characteristics. Once more, since my critical strategy focuses on synthesis, individual works receive respect for their unique qualities while being construed as parts of a greater whole. By considering the oeuvre from a developmental perspective, we may view the narrative impulse's negotiations within an ever-changing musical world. Throughout this give-and-take, Dylan's instinctive evocation of American Song provides his creative foundation. Whether he advocates societal change, outlaw justice, personal salvation, or relational reconciliation, Dylan applies a distinctly American voice to articulate that stance. He discussed this concept with Cameron Crowe: "You got to be strong and stay connected to what started it all, the inspiration behind the inspiration, to who you were when people didn't mind stepping on you, it's easy to say but the air gets thin at the top, you get light-headed, your environment changes, new people come into your life." That "American Song" provides that "inspiration behind the inspiration" will become abundantly clear as we move through the oeuvre.

Dylan's rebellious battle to "stay connected" with his "inspiration" is the centerpiece of his art. The *dedication* of the folk period, the *imagination* of the satirical phase, the *perseverance* of the Americana period, the *sincerity* of the moral period, and the *commitment* of his return to American Song represent the manifestations of that drive for self-expression. All the while, these creative ambitions co-existed with equally powerful commercial motivations. The results brought the Hollywood celebrity machine to popular music songwriting. First, the auteur invented the "Bob Dylan" character. That character was created and sold. Then came the words. And what words they are!

the folk-posturing period

This portion of Bob Dylan's career began long before his arrival in New York, his first appearance on stage in Greenwich Village, or his affiliation with John Hammond and Columbia Records. As we have seen, young Bob Zimmerman intuitively understood image making to an extent that his personal development involved the gradual creation and refinement of the persona that became "Bob Dylan." All those hours watching movies, listening to the radio, and posing for his brother's photographs influenced Zimmerman's awareness of the power of image, and as a result, prepared him for the public stage. With his departure from Hibbing and his entry into the bohemian culture of Dinkytown, the emerging Dylan character left rock and roll on the Iron Range and turned to folk music as his professional entry point. Even if young Dylan merely used the folk music scene as a vehicle for his ambitions, this genre of American Song influenced his creativity in fundamental ways. In 1978 he described his folk heritage to *Playboy*:

> The first thing that turned me on to folk singing was Odetta. . . . That was in
> '58 or something like that. Right then and there, I went out and traded my
> electric guitar and amplifier for an acoustical guitar . . . from Odetta, I went to
> Harry Belafonte, the Kingston Trio, little by little uncovering more as I went
> along. Finally, I was doing nothing but Carter Family and Jesse Fuller songs.
> Then later I got to Woody Guthrie, which opened up a whole new world at that
> time. I was still only 19 or 20.

What he "uncovered" he used to feed his professional biography, form his folk persona, and develop his new act. From Dinkytown to New York, Dylan proved to be a formidable student of music, culture, and literature.

Dylan's "folk-posturing" phase extends from Dinkytown and his introduction to Guthrie through the release of his third album in early 1964. The three albums that comprise this period (*Bob Dylan*, *The Freewheelin' Bob Dylan*, and *The Times They Are a-Changin'*) represent but a portion of the budding auteur's writings from the era. Dylan's liner notes for albums (e.g., "11 Outlined Epitaphs" for *The Times* and for Peter, Paul and Mary's *In the Wind*), his "open letters" and commentaries (published in *Hootenanny* and *Broadside* magazines as well as concert programs—e.g., "For Dave Glover"), along with his poems celebrating Guthrie ("Last Thoughts on Woody Guthrie") and his fabricated biography ("My Life in a Stolen Moment") join a considerable list of songs that were omitted from album projects to create a broad, diverse writing period. (Several songs excluded from albums include "Talkin' Bear Mountain Picnic Massacre Blues," "Talkin' John Birch Paranoid Blues," "The Death of Emmett Till," "John Brown," "Walls of Red Wing," "Lay Down Your Weary Tune," "Percy's Song," and "Who Killed Davey Moore?") Actually, no phase of Dylan's career contains the narrative diversity of this initial segment, although everything flowed from a carefully contrived image that anchored his perspective on that day's topic.

With *Bob Dylan*, Dylan initiated a recording career that deploys specific stylistic signatures to articulate stories that serve a host of narrative functions. His ability to absorb the nuances of a particular genre, to co-opt the internal workings of specific musical styles, and to reproduce that understanding by way of strategic expressions represent the heart of Dylan's *talent*. Throughout this study, notice Dylan's loyalty to creative function as he applies his skills to identifiable ends: Securing an audience with some community (professional, personal), representing the ideals of a specific cause, articulating a personal attitude, or praising the virtues of some value orientation. With that in mind, *Bob Dylan's* function is without mystery. Since Dylan aspired to become a professional musician, he used the Guthrie sound to present traditional folk music that appealed to an established audience. Released on March 19, 1962, the 37-minute, 13-song album cost $402 to produce as John Hammond's production style joined Dylan's emerging penchant for minimalist recordings to render two efficient sessions. Everything about *Bob Dylan* suggests a controlled, limited commercial venture.

The album explores three topics: love, the traveling musician's life, and death. *Bob Dylan* contains six songs about death ("In My Time of Dyin'," "Man of

Constant Sorrow," "Fixin' to Die," "Highway 51," "Gospel Plow," "See That My Grave Is Kept Clean"). The remaining songs celebrate love ("Pretty Peggy-O" and "Baby, Let Me Follow You Down"), lament love ("You're No Good" and "House of the Rising Sun"), and describe the musician's life ("Talkin' New York" and the Guthrie tribute, "Song to Woody"). To be sure, these songs tell stories from an American worldview. The first-person death narrations invoke Christian values in predictable ways as characters cope with the present as a path to redemption ("In My Time of Dyin'"), endure the projected pain of leaving loved ones behind ("Fixin' to Die"), contemplate their funeral arrangements ("Highway 51"), and seek respect for their resting places ("See That My Grave Is Kept Clean"). Little metaphorical mischief appears through these straightforward yarns: Dylan tells us who's doing what, why, and to what end in a direct manner, as the singer sticks to the Guthrie script through a regional dialect that would control this phase of his career.

The two original compositions established narrative orientations that reappear throughout his lifework. "Talkin' New York" demonstrates Dylan's sense of humor, his capacity to recast history, and his application of the "folk process" (i.e., the use of established lyrics and music within the context of a "new" song). That Dylan borrowed lines from Guthrie tunes and musical phrases from a variety of sources created little controversy at this point in his career, since such practices embodied the folk music songwriting tradition. As he assembled his story, Dylan engaged in another practice that would one day cause frustration: he interjected his *persona* into the narrative, and in so doing, elevated the author's role in the story (i.e., what is *Dylan* saying here?). Although locals have taken him to task because his New York debut was nowhere near as harsh as the song suggests (the Village scene nurtured young Dylan), he was clearly talking about *his* life, which would inspire critics (formal and informal) to search for such details in most of his subsequent work. The other original song ("Song to Woody") reveals Dylan's ability to sharpen his pencil and produce a story about a specific set of circumstances. These "topical" narratives not only articulate some view on some subject for some audience, they also create a context for attribution. Much like "Talkin' New York," "Song to Woody" speaks to a broader topic from a subjective point of view. Both in their thematic orientation and musical enactment, these two original compositions foretell the future.

Critical responses to *Bob Dylan* display the opposite trait. The music press was in its infancy during this phase of Dylan's career, therefore few writers focused on the music's internal workings and dutifully pursued celebrity matters and marketed images. History, on the other hand, yields insight into this initial work. For example, Paul Williams notes Dylan's "weird and obviously contrived accent" and Patrick Humphries cites Dylan's view that he sounded like a "Woody Guthrie jukebox." Virtually all historical observations stress that this was an artist in pursuit of a job, as Dylan used the narrative tactics of an established musical genre to gain entry into the professional world. The price of that entry would grow as opportunity quickly evolved into oppression. Still, a creative baseline was established with *Bob Dylan* through the songwriter's capacity to use song as instrument ("Song to Woody") and expression ("Talkin' New York") as well as a mischievous propensity to obfuscate the two.

Dylan's second album, *The Freewheelin' Bob Dylan*, is a marked departure from the $402, two-session *Bob Dylan* production. Originally entitled *Bob Dylan's Blues* and fundamentally revised just weeks before its release (making original pressings quite valuable), *Freewheelin'* represents one of the long-standing icons of the American blues tradition—a "crossroads." This surprisingly complicated artistic intersection featured one road and the "folk process" in which Dylan freely borrowed lines and melodic phrases to suit his purposes. A second road involved Dylan's topical songs, his personalized messages, and their hybrid: the personalized topical song. Here the celebrity songwriter placed a personal stamp on the perspective, advanced in a manner that elevated the role of authorship—the work is more than a song, it is a *statement*. And finally, our third road contained a simple, albeit powerfully symbolic entity: electricity.

The Freewheelin' Bob Dylan—released in late May 1963—was the second and last Dylan record produced by John Hammond (officially ending the original "Hammond's Folly"). The 50-minute work contains 13 compositions that emphasize elegiac accounts of romantic and societal issues. Joining that thematic is an expression of personal nostalgia ("Bob Dylan's Dream"), a personal celebration ("Bob Dylan's Blues"), and two personal fantasies ("Talking [or "Talkin'"] World War III Blues" and "I Shall Be Free"). Controlling the album—and establishing a thematic trend that permeates the oeuvre—are the nine songs of complaint that embrace love (the traditional "Girl from the North Country," "Down the Highway," "Don't Think Twice, It's All Right," "Corrina, Corrina" [an adaptation of a Joe Turner tune], and "Honey, Just Allow Me One More Chance" [an adaptation of a Henry Thomas original]) and contemporary society ("Blowin' in the Wind," "Masters of War," "A Hard Rain's a-Gonna Fall," and "Oxford Town").

Three stylistic tendencies control the work: The continued use of personal references, the advent of surreal imagery, and the intensity of the emotions conveyed. To this point in popular music history, few songwriters had interjected their personalities (real or contrived) into their work to the extent Bob Dylan did in *Freewheelin'*. That two songs use his *name* in their titles advanced this personalization-of-song content. Dylan may not have aspired to become the "voice of his generation," but he was surely positioning himself for that role. Furthermore, "Down the Highway" refers to Dylan's girlfriend (Suze Rotolo) in such a direct manner as to call attention to such matters in virtually all of his songs. The writer baited the hook of attribution, audiences took that bait, and Dylan would regret this invitation into his private world.

As if to balance this self-inflicted trend, *Freewheelin'* introduced another storytelling signature: The use of surreal imagery. Whether he was hiding behind these opaque renderings or revealing his propensity for word games, Dylan deployed a free-form writing style quite outside the folk tradition. "A Hard Rain" and "I Shall Be Free" feature an internal logic that prohibits their consideration as narratives. Instead, they involve bitter ("Hard Rain") or playful ("I Shall") value-laden expressions with minimal characterization or plot progression. Still, when construed with the highly personalized commentaries of the other tracks, one instinctively searches for the "message." After all, these songs are presented through a musical genre that stresses authenticity. By co-opting the folk tradition's posture, Dylan invited his audience to search for something that may not exist—even though he directly ridicules folk songwriting and its Tin Pan Alley style in the introduction to "Bob Dylan's Blues." "I Shall," in particular, foreshadows the Newport Mod's chaotic wordplay and its irreverent, no-holds-barred imagery. It is all one big laugh (or cry).

The third narrative trait is another function of the auteur's personality: The expression's intensity. Few songs in the history of popular music display the anger conveyed through "Masters of War." The song is staggering in its invective. The use of Biblical characters not only invokes widely held American values, it leaves little doubt about the nature of these characterizations. By identifying the "Masters of War" with Judas, Dylan advances the highest form of betrayal—a treachery so complete it is unforgivable. Since the Christian story of Jesus Christ is predicated on "forgiveness" and the central character's martyrdom for the principle, to suggest that Jesus would not absolve these characters is to cast considerable damnation. Dylan used clear language and a recognizable story to tell a tragic tale of societal victimization and ultimate revenge. The intensity of the retribution unveils a storytelling signature that would at times dominate Dylan's writing.

The Freewheelin' Bob Dylan is a seminal piece of songwriting. The writer may have feigned political stances to suit his creative ends, but he did so through a narrative style that exemplified his emerging talent. The pivotal descriptor here is intensity: the intensity of the humor ("Talkin' World War III Blues"); the intensity of the sarcasm ("Don't Think Twice, It's All Right"); the intensity of the anger ("Masters of War"); and the intensity of the questions posed and left unresolved ("Blowin' in the Wind"). Bob Dylan's intensity would eventually change songwriting, and this character trait would foster as much personal sorrow as creative joy.

Critical responses to Freewheelin' gain strength through historical perspective. Clinton Heylin's recording-session chronology claims that the album "is essentially a 'best of' from one of the most creative years in Dylan's life," since its blend of blues and topical song join a provocative list of outtakes to render a wide-ranging project. Patrick Humphries argues that the album "sits uneasily between castigating, 'finger-pointing' songs . . . and the frivolous," since the disparity between the intensity of "Masters" and the playfulness of "Talkin' WWIII" "jarred" the listener. Tim Riley also addresses the record's uneven qualities as it "expands folk's naturalism" while it "tinkers with the language of surrealism." As these examples suggest, most commentators emphasize the project's developmental qualities. The folk façade was beginning to crumble—a natural disintegration instigated and sustained by the writer's creative impulse.

This period of growth was spatial in nature, not linear. Returning to my "crossroads" metaphor, we note the variety of influences exerting themselves simultaneously. The application of the "folk process" and Dylan's samplings from different sources echoed Guthrie's songwriting advice and its devotion to ideas—a songwriting approach that emphasized the proverbial ends over the means. The adaptations of storied tales such as "Girl from the North Country," Robert Johnson's "Crossroads Blues" (in "Down the Highway"), and Henry Thomas's "Honey, Just Allow Me" fit squarely within the folk music songwriting tradition. Clinton Heylin and Michael Gray dedicate significant portions of their respective explorations into Dylan's lifework to the original sources of these borrowed materials. Furthermore, John Bauldie's explanations of specific songs' musical heritages for the Bootleg boxed set conveys Dylan's approval of such practices as well (remember, he cares about those "roots"). And yet the author deviated from the folk process through his personalized topical songs that suggest poetry. Riley describes Dylan's "A Hard Rain's a-Gonna Fall" as a "verbal binge that gets him labeled a rock poet." The track "sounds" like a topical, protest song, but actually begs the question via free-association wordplay, not folk platitudes. Here Dylan stands on the verge of a serious songwriting innovation. In that vein, we turn to our final influence: electricity. Dylan returned to the Iron Range and his musical heritage during these sessions with rock and roll versions of "Mixed Up Confusion," "It's Alright, Ma," "Corrina, Corrina," and "Rocks and Gravel." Whatever inspired the omission of these "electric" tracks from Freewheelin' merely delayed an urge that was as much a part of "Bob Dylan" as his concern for image and predilection for word games. In any event, Dylan's experience in this creative crossroads was not unlike any other heavily traveled intersection: It's how you exit that counts.

Dylan emerged from the Freewheelin' adventure as a national celebrity. Just four days after the record's release, Time described him in this manner:

> Beardless chin, shaggy sideburns, porcelain pussy-cat eyes. At 22, he looks 14, and his accent belongs to a jive Nebraskan, or maybe a Brooklyn hillbilly. . . . At its very best, his voice sounds as if it were drifting over the walls of a tuberculosis sanitarium—but that's part of the charm. . . . But he has something unique to say, and he says it in songs of his own invention that are the best songs of their style since Woody Guthrie's.

From there Time advances Dylan's biographical mythology of runaways, circuses, and hall-of-fame musical encounters. (How interesting that a national news magazine would print such uncorroborated celebrity propaganda.) The trend gained momentum that summer when "Dylan went to the Newport Folk Festival of July 26–28, 1963, an underground conversation piece, and left a star." Shelton observes that "Dylan's apprenticeship was over" after Newport 1963, and the village pet was about to become the voice of his generation.

The increased attention rendered a shift in the media's treatment of the newly crowned king of the American protest song, and this change in reporting would affect Dylan's world. The November 4, 1963 edition of Newsweek features the aforementioned report on Bob Zimmerman's youth on the Iron Range and quickly dispelled all of the talk of runaways, broken families, and earthy musical contacts. The change in publicity gained momentum on December 13, 1963 with Dylan's appearance before the Emergency Civil Liberties Committee and his acceptance of the organization's Tom Paine Award for social activism. Whether Dylan's intoxication or his general discomfort inspired his remarks is irrelevant; what is important is the public reaction to his identification with John Kennedy's alleged assassin, Lee Oswald. By saying that he identified with Oswald's motivations, Dylan not only alienated his immediate audience, he provided additional fuel for the fire initiated by the *Newsweek* article. Dylan's intuitive publicity machine now faced its first public-relations challenge.

The auteur seems to have anticipated it all with his third album, *The Times They Are a-Changin'*, released on January 13, 1964. The album's liner notes ("11 Outlined Epitaphs") complements its thematic orientation to issue a coherent "state-of-the-artist" message. Public opinion about "the voice of his generation" began changing toward the end of 1963, but that character had already undergone significant characterological modifications by that time. The Chaplinesque figure who charmed New York with his heartfelt songs of oppression was in a state of flux and *Times* captures that transition. Heylin's session chronology notes the overlap between *Times* and *Freewheelin'* in terms of their "style, tone, and content" and how several strong songs (e.g., "Seven Curses," "Eternal Circle," "Percy's Song," and "Lay Down Your Weary Tune" among others) were cast aside in favor of topical songs of popular interest. The general argument suggests that Dylan was writing for his market, albeit reluctantly. (Once more, Dylan recorded "That's All Right, Mama" and expressed his rock and roll inclinations— to no avail.) The album's transitional qualities may be best exhibited by the last-minute addition of the final track, "Restless Farewell."

Produced by Tom Wilson, *The Times They Are a-Changin'* contains ten original compositions (running 45:37 minutes). Recorded in six sessions (with several one-take tracks), *Times* presents a seasoned folk veteran carefully articulating the hopes and fears of his constituency, often through the use of protracted examples. The five songs of societal complaint ("Ballad of Hollis Brown," "With God on Our Side," "North Country Blues," "Only a Pawn In Their Game," and "The Lonesome Death of Hattie Carroll") convey the victimization of decent folks by cold-hearted oppressors whose day of reckoning is coming. These tragedies portray murder on the farm ("Hollis Brown"), domestic abandonment ("North Country"), sociological manipulation ("Only a Pawn"), historical atrocities ("With God"), and judicial elitism ("Hattie Carroll") through a direct, understandable narrative style. The two songs of societal celebration ("The Times They Are a-Changin'" and "When the Ship Comes In"), Dylan's last-second tale of personal transition ("Restless Farewell"), and the two love complaints ("One Too Many Mornings" and "Boots of Spanish Leather") round out an album with a purpose. "Farewell" is, without question, a personal song. Dylan recalls the money he made and spent, his time with his friends, and his decision to move along; bids adieu to his women and those with whom he's battled; reflects on his writing and describes his disgust with the media and gossip mongers—in all cases, he exits without remorse. It is a thoughtful farewell to the pleasures and pains that accompanied his professional apprenticeship. It portrays a sincerity that is so unusual that it is untrustworthy.

Times' themes are without mystery. Dylan wants his audience to know why Hollis Brown killed his family, why William Zanzinger should be punished, why victims must understand their situations so they may respond accordingly, and how history may be rationalized. Though he may occasionally shift perspectives ("Boots of Spanish Leather" and its male—female narrators and the female narrator in "North Country"), "Bob Dylan" is taking a stance against these perceived injustices. In many respects, these songs comprise a folk singer's sampler of delightfully depressing tunes to be performed around campfires, with the audience holding hands as they identify with the plights of the oppressed before returning to their Ivy League schools and their trust funds. After all, when Dylan performed at Newport, the odds were that William Zanzinger—not Hattie Carroll—was in attendance.

This irony did not escape Dylan. The music of the oppressed was the blues—either in its traditional New Orleans (Afro-rhythmic) or Appalachian (Anglo-rhythmic) forms—not Northeastern folk. The conflict over representing the protest movement (that he may or may not identify with) or self-expression was intensifying; moreover, Dylan's growing animosity toward the news media aggravated the situation in no uncertain terms. *Times* seems to relate an attitude that "Yes, I can write this stuff, if you want it." Correspondingly, the personal observations featured in "11 Outlined Epitaphs" reinforce the sentiments expressed in "Restless Farewell" to suggest that Dylan was, in every way, taking stock of his situation. The "Epitaphs" are quite a contrast to their "biographical" predecessor, "My Life in a Stolen Moment" (a blend of fact and fiction). The liner notes' use of the term "epitaphs" suggests an ending or transition as well. The take on his Minnesota roots (#2), his commentary on organized politics and his preference for the emotive over the logical (#4), his rejection of hero worship (#6), his discussion of the folk process and authorship (#8), his tirade against journalists and their agendas (#9), and his identification with the many wordsmiths who have impressed him in one manner or another (#11) offer personal accounts on topics of concern to the artist, his audience, and his profession. Not all of these statements are negative: Dylan praises poetry (#5), his village friends (#10), and his creative challenge (again #11) just as much as he rails against journalists, insincere activists, and idolatry.

What stands out in all of this is the poignancy of the writer's observations. His acute awareness of his characters' worldviews as they appear on the Iron Range, in depressed farming communities, and in unfair relationships; his understanding of the activists fighting for civil rights, fighting against imperialism, and for their right to be heard; and his cognizance of the celebrity's dilemma directly inform his stories. Many of these accounts are quite sophisticated for an author of Dylan's age. The evidence suggests that the songwriter wanted to be heard, not investigated. He wanted to be appreciated, not worshiped. And he wanted to express himself—not be a mascot for a movement. Dylan had successfully entered the world of professional music and his new challenge involved his career's direction.

The folk-posturing phase of Bob Dylan's lifework is the most diverse, innovative, and ambitious period of his career. The traditional folk songs, the topical songs, the emerging surrealism, the satirical songs, the liner notes, the magazine commentaries, the public speeches—and most significantly—the carefully contrived image all convey an intense dedication unlike any other timeframe. These were not casual happenings. The drive that inspired young Dylan to travel to New York to hawk his wares intensified and diversified during this period. The friendly folk singer who arrived in New York in 1961 had changed by the spring of 1964, as this description in *Life* indicates: "[Dylan is] not exactly the image of the clean-cut boy you'd like your daughter to bring home to dinner. He is sloppy, disheveled, unshaven. He talks angrily and irreverently. But he is the most important writer of folk songs in the last twenty years." The young Woody Guthrie apprentice did not talk "angrily and irreverently" (although he may have appeared "sloppy" and "disheveled") and his "jive Nebraskan accent" displayed a charm, and a naivete, that inspired the New York folk community to assume an active role in his development. Robert Shelton's *New York Times* review provided the fuel for a celebrity skyrocket that raised questions about his loyalty to the artistic movement that nurtured him. Dylan would now have to resolve the conflict between serving others (and applying his talent in an instrumental manner) and serving his muse (and expressing himself). The apprentice faced teachers wanting to collect a fee for their services.

Dylan's comments to Shelton in *No Direction Home* capture the folk-posturing phase of his career:

> I hate to say this . . . but I latched on, when I got to New York City, because I saw a huge audience was there. . . . I knew I wasn't going to stay there. I knew it wasn't my thing. . . . Anytime they tried to think I was like them, I knew I wasn't like them. I just told them whatever happened to be in my mind at the time. I didn't have any respect for any of the organizations. In New York City, they are all organizations. I had respect for the people.

Chief among these "people" was the man who motivated the move to New York: "Woody used his own time, in a way nobody else did. He was just a little bit better . . . just a little smarter. . . . His influence on me was never in inflection or in voice. What drew me to him was that hearing his voice I could tell he was very lonesome, very alone, and very lost out in his time." Not only did Bob Dylan identify with Guthrie's projected image as the lonesome hero, he intuitively understood how Guthrie "used his own time" to pursue a personal agenda. That is, he understood Guthrie's act and he was hell-bent on applying that knowledge.

As he mastered his trade through his adaptation of Guthrie's model, he developed stylistic tendencies—narrative signatures—that were unique to Bob Dylan. His command of the satirical topical song (in its humorous and serious modes), the advent of his impressionism, and the intensity of his storytelling style energized a songwriting tradition soon to be abandoned. You see, this phase of Bob Dylan's career was *educational* in nature. Next we observe how the innovative young talent *applied* his lessons, as we turn to one of the most creative periods of any writer's professional life.

the Newport Mod era

When Bob Dylan walked onto the stage that Sunday evening—July 25, 1965—he faced a Newport Folk Festival that two years before anointed him the king of the American protest song. But he didn't *look* like the king of American protest at all (Howard Sounes says he looked "extraordinarily ostentatious"). Dylan had just returned from London where he was introduced to Carnaby Street fashion and English youth subculture. The fact that British youth culture—especially the "Mod" movement—was so attentive to every aspect of fashion, dialect, and musical affiliation impressed an individual who shared those same concerns for personal image. Consequently, Dylan did what Dylan does: He incorporated that style into his own act. He co-opted Mod fashion and the Mod attitude while he ignored Mod solidarity. (After all, American Song features a powerful streak of personal independence—that "fugitive essence.") His clothing, attitude, and willingness to face his audience with his artistic innovations represented a fascinating synthesis of personal history and Mod philosophy. He was, then, the original Newport Mod. Nik Cohn—a writer who knows more than a little about the Mods—describes the change:

> In place of the Minnesota boy scout, a whole new face emerged, watchful and withdrawn, cold and arrogant and often mean, full of conscious hipnesses. In particular, he became secret—he stonewalled and played games and pulled faces, let nobody intrude and, when he decided to put someone down, he'd stare at them without expression until they crawled, he'd be merciless. Definitely, this machine could kill. . . . At any rate, if his changes made him paranoid, they also improved his writing out of all recognition. No more schoolboy sermons and no more good intentions, his songs now were sharper, fiercer, stronger in every way. His melody lines got less hackneyed, his imagery less obvious, his jokes less cute. Instead, he was harsh and self-mocking and hurt, he laughed with his teeth, he packed real punch.

As Cohn indicates, the Newport Mod phase of Dylan's oeuvre features a fundamentally different artist from the folk-posturing period: The charming apprentice evolved into a combative celebrity unsure of his friends or his enemies. The creative sponge who absorbed all influences internalized that knowledge, confronted his ambitions, and rendered an artist of whom Bob Zimmerman would be proud. That is, when the New York folk community and the national media affronted Bob Dylan, they received Bob Zimmerman's response, as the Iron Ranger's rebellious spirit was summoned as a means of coping with the demands of celebrity. The artistic perseverance perfected at the Jacket Jamboree and St. Louis County Fair provided a valuable resource for a young artist determined to follow his creative agenda. That outlook not only helped Dylan face the pressures of celebrity, it supported the most creative, unrestrained portion of his lifework.

Nowhere was this controlling image more evident than in Dylan's new battleground: The media interview. Dylan transformed an opportunity for publicity into a performance that left any trace of Woody Guthrie behind in some abandoned dustbowl. Sporting dark sunglasses and a Mod attitude, Dylan turned the tables on reporters in a fashion that disarmed aggressive journalists and disabled more polite professionals. On some occasions, he merely turned questions around in confusing or off-hand ways; on other occasions, he used questions as launching points for elaborate flights of fancy. The 1966 *Playboy* interview with Nat Hentoff offers a wonderful example of the latter. The reporter asked what inspired Dylan to play rock and roll:

Carelessness. I lost my one true love. I started drinking. The first thing I know, I'm in a card game. Then I'm in a crap game. I wake up in a pool hall. Then this big Mexican lady drags me off the table, takes me to Philadelphia. She leaves me alone in her house, and it burns down. I wind up in Phoenix. I get a job as a Chinaman. I start working in a dime store, and move in with a thirteen-year-old girl. Then this big Mexican lady from Philadelphia comes in and burns the house down. I go down to Dallas. I get a job as a "before" in a Charles Atlas "before and after" ad. I move in with a delivery boy who can cook fantastic chili and hot dogs. Then this thirteen-year-old girl from Phoenix comes and burns the house down. The delivery boy—he ain't so mild: He gives her the knife, and the next thing I know I'm in Omaha. It's so cold there, by this time I'm robbing my own bicycles and frying my own fish. I stumble onto some luck and get a job as a carburetor out at the hot-rod races every Thursday night. I move in with a high school teacher who also does a little plumbing on the side, who ain't much to look at, but who's built a special kind of refrigerator that can turn newspaper into lettuce. Everything's going good until that delivery boy shows up and tries to knife me. Needless to say, he burned the house down, and I hit the road. The first guy that picked me up asked me if I wanted to be a star. What could I say? . . . [*Playboy:* "And that's how you became a rock-'n'-roll singer?"] No, that's how I got tuberculosis.

Later in the interview Hentoff asked about "message music" and Dylan's role in its development: "Myself, what I'm going to do is rent Town Hall and put about thirty Western Union boys on the bill. I mean, then there'll *really* be some messages. People will be able to come and hear more messages than they've ever heard before in their life." This was the New Bob Dylan: The Newport Mod. The talented individual who penned all of those delightful topical songs and entertained audiences with his colorful stage act now applied that sense of humor to media interviews, press conferences, and all aspects of his public image. Almost twenty years later, Dylan explained to Robert Hilburn the rationale behind this new version of Glissendorf: "If you took it [all the questions] seriously and gave serious answers, you'd just get hurt. You had to respond in a way that wouldn't hurt you. The press was always battering me around—from the beginning. They just print anything. You can't take it seriously." During this phase of his career, Dylan would take few things "seriously." His media interviews, his studio and concert performances, and all of his writing were infused with a self-indulgent attitude—a Mod attitude—that protected him from being "battered around." From this point on, as Robert Shelton and Paul Williams argue, *everything* would be performance—an image-based orientation that controlled Dylan's pen and that material's enactment. The auteur was focused: Bob Zimmerman's armor served Bob Dylan well.

The Newport Mod era presents a celebrity postman with an active imagination. Although he occasionally issued letters of contempt for personal or professional reasons, the bulk of this era's mail involved imaginative flights of fancy that changed popular-music songwriting forever. The four albums from this period—*Another Side of Bob Dylan* (released August 1964), *Bringing It All Back Home* (March 1965), *Highway 61 Revisited* (August 1965), and *Blonde on Blonde* (May 1966)—join liner notes and other "essays" (e.g., *Tarantula*) to create an substantial body of esoteric, flamboyant art. Without question, these works pursued an expressive narrative function, as Dylan related in the *New Yorker* magazine:

> Those records I've already made, I'll stand behind them, but some of that was jumping into the scene to be heard and a lot of it was because I didn't see anybody else doing that kind of thing. Now a lot of people are doing finger-pointing songs. You know—pointing to all the things that are wrong. Me, I don't want to write for people anymore. You know—be a spokesman. Like I once wrote about Emmett Till in the first person, pretending I was him. From now on, I want to write from inside me, and to do that I'm going to have to get back to writing like I used to when I was ten—having everything come out naturally. The way I like to write is for it to come out the way I walk or talk.

Dylan conveyed that view just prior to recording *Another Side of Bob Dylan* in an all-night recording session attended by Nat Hentoff (this time, with the *New Yorker*) and several of the songwriter's friends. In a classic example of spontaneous recording, Dylan (and Tom Wilson) recorded the entire album in one evening (June 9, 1964). Heylin's chronology indicates that there were few outtakes from this concentrated enterprise that stressed an expressive, creative orientation. The songs flowed through Dylan in a natural, unforced manner—no editing, no overdubbing—pure expression.

Another Side is, as the title suggests, a transitional statement. The album's eleven tracks (running over 50 minutes) feature three thematic orientations ranging from a trademark Dylan satire ("Motorpsycho Nitemare"), to seven songs about relationships ("All I Really Want to Do," "Black Crow Incident," "Spanish Harlem Incident," "To Ramona," "I Don't Believe You," "Ballad in Plain D," and "It Ain't Me, Babe"), to three songs that preview future writing trends ("Chimes of Freedom," "I Shall Be Free No. 10," and "My Back Pages"). These last three tracks involve Dylan's emerging impressionism in which the author moves from pure wordplay ("I Shall Be Free No. 10") to a technique I call "narrative impressionism" ("My Back Pages" and "Chimes of Freedom"). These two styles will dominate the Newport Mod period, as the former approach allows Dylan to play with words and sounds in a whimsical, free-form fashion while the latter uses refrains and musical punctuation to create the illusion of narrative structure. In both cases, we discover that one person's metaphor is another person's folly.

Three stylistic attributes control this album: A shift away from the topical song subject-matter, the steady increase in impressionism, and the demise of the humorous satire. The change from societal concerns to relational matters demonstrates the accuracy of Dylan's remarks to Hentoff. What has not changed is the intensely personal qualities of these offerings. Whereas "It Ain't Me, Babe," "All I Really Want to Do," and "Black Crow" speak in general terms that lend themselves to analogy (Is the songwriter addressing his audience?), songs such as "Ballad in Plain D" and "To Ramona" directly address personal situations. All of these relational complaints are presented in plain, clear language. Dylan writes that relationships need not be abusive ("All I Really"), that the circumstances around a relationship can be harmful ("To Ramona"), that it hurts when our lovers ignore us ("I Don't Believe You"), and that Carla Rotolo was the problem with his relationship with Suze Rotolo ("Ballad in Plain D"). He may not have mentioned the sisters by name, but the song's contents are so pointed that they leave little doubt about their subject. That he publicly acknowledged the lyric's personal qualities heightened the song's "finger-pointing" attributes.

The increase in Dylan's impressionism—in its organized and disorganized forms—is a direct extension of the Newport Mod persona. The Iron Ranger was at home in creative formats that allowed his imagination to run wild—especially if it were at someone else's expense. His Hibbing, Dinkytown, and Village cohorts have testified to Dylan's active—often strategic—imagination, and his propensity for tall tales appears in his professional biography, responses to media inquiries, album-liner notes, and other public commentaries. Now his songwriting embraced those storytelling skills through songs that engaged in various forms of free-spirited wordplay (e.g., "I Shall Be Free No. 10" and its crazy vignettes) and more organized impressionism. Building on the style established with "A Hard Rain's a-Gonna Fall," Dylan used brief lyrical refrains and repetitive musical structures to frame the surreal images featured in "Chimes of Freedom" and "My Back Pages." These songs sound like story ballads as they present characters doing different things, but nothing ever happens. There is no plot progression; instead, we consider characters in a thunderstorm contemplating a litany of life's injustices ("Chimes") and a narrator's cloudy pronouncements on human relations ("My Back Pages"). The emphasis is on imaginative description as Dylan's wordplay assumed control.

This album's transitional qualities are also evident in our last stylistic trend, the demise of Dylan's trademark satires. "Motorpsycho Nitemare" is in the tradition of Dylan's "Talkin' New York," "Talkin' Bear Mountain," and "Talkin' John Birch" with its portrayal of crazy characters doing weird things in service of the story's moral, in this case, the stupidity of bigotry. Dylan's adaptation of the "traveling salesman" story is skillful in its depiction of ignorant bigotry and the conditions that foster that attitude. It is unfortunate that Dylan soon abandoned this storytelling technique: He wrote some funny songs, and his sense of humor was an effective storytelling tool.

Another Side of Bob Dylan leaves Woody Guthrie and the protest movement behind in favor of a younger artist (according to "My Back Pages") free of the burdens of being the voice of his generation. The colorful satires, the poignant protests, and the melodramatic epics fade away in favor of expressive, playful, and occasionally melodramatic poetry. Hentoff offers this lofty analysis of Dylan's new approach: "Whether concerned with cosmic spectres or personal conundrums, Dylan's lyrics are pungently idiomatic. He has a superb ear for speech rhythms, a generally astute sense of selective detail, and a natural storyteller's command of narrative pacing. His songs sound as if they were being created out of oral street history rather than carefully written in tranquility." As the artist turned to writing the way he "walks and talks," he deployed the deft skills Hentoff describes; however, nothing was "tranquil" around Bob Dylan. This was not the poet of his time sitting on Walden Pond contemplating his generation's condition, and this would be a hard pill for contemporary critics to swallow. Brown University English majors and the Northeastern media may have desperately wanted a thoughtful, enlightened poet with a vast command of provocative language, but they received Bob Zimmerman instead. As a result, critics like Hentoff consistently search for the poetic (and autobiographical) qualities of expressions that are more spontaneous than systematic, more superficial than substantive.

In March 1965 Dylan entered a six-month period that would be as controversial as any half-year of any artist's career. The release of *Bringing It All Back Home* that March, the spring tour of England and the filming of *Dont Look Back*, the historic Newport festival that July, and the August issue of *Highway 61 Revisited* made for one turbulent six-month period. The two records from this era do more than extend the impressionistic trend initiated in *Another Side*; as Mikal Gilmore observes, they "effectively killed off any remaining notions that folk was the imperative new art form of American youth, and conferred on rock a greater sense of consequence and a deeper expressiveness." Gilmore continues: "Dylan framed perfectly the spirit of an emerging generation that was trying to live by its own rules and integrity, and that was feeling increasingly cut off from the conventions and privileges of the dominant mainstream culture. In the same manner that he had once given voice to a new rising political consciousness, Dylan seemed to be speaking our deepest-felt fears and hopes—to be speaking for us."

Gilmore relates what is certainly the consensus opinion about this phase of Dylan's artistic development. The songwriter may have aspired to write for himself, but his audience would have none of that. How interesting that the songs from this period are taken as anthems—a generation's objection to the status quo—when, in fact, they are so abstract, so idiosyncratic. One may take a line here, a line there, and use them as polemical inspiration, yet when the songs from these two albums are considered on their own, they liberate the artist, not his audience. This is the essence of Dylan's growing artistic quandary. Perhaps he should have rented that music hall, hired those Western Union messengers, and invited the media to the show.

Bringing It All Back Home represents an extension of the writing and recording styles associated with its predecessor. Heylin's chronology notes that the album was fashioned in three sessions (on January 13, 14, and 15, 1965), with several songs recorded in one take. Produced by Tom Wilson, the album was initially intended to feature one side of acoustic songs and another with an electric band. Dylan later changed the sequence and that approach was abandoned, with the "electric" songs interspersed throughout the album. The record contains eleven tracks (running over 47 minutes) that fall into two orientations, with one exception. The exception involves the satire ("Bob Dylan's 115th Dream") that synthesizes Dylan's "tall tale with a moral" tradition with the impressionism that dominates the other songs. Here the writer weaves a dream/story that portrays mean-spirited people in various encounters with the narrator—a dreaming Bob Dylan. The recording opens with Tom Wilson's famous belly laugh (a richly symbolic act) and instantly restarts with Dylan's surreal imagery placed in a convoluted historical context (beginning with the Mayflower's voyage to America and ending with Christopher Columbus's arrival). Throughout the story, the narrator encounters weird people in even stranger scenes that show no respect for anything; nonetheless, the story holds together through its dream logic (by the way, in this story, America is a pretty unfriendly place).

The rest of the album may be divided into two forms of wordplay: one organized, the other disorganized. The organized wordplay involves Dylan's narrative impressionism in which the song's theme and musical structure provide a loose framework for the surreal imagery floating throughout. Dylan explores three topics through this strategy: romantic relationships ("She Belongs to Me" and "Love Minus Zero/No Limit"), societal relations ("Maggie's Farm" and "It's Alright, Ma [I'm Only Bleeding]"), and individual freedom ("Mr. Tambourine Man"). The love songs articulate the various characteristics of the narrator's romantic interests and leave us to contemplate those traits. But nothing ever happens. The lovers are described in terms of their strength, compassion, and independence (with a bit of vulnerability and abusiveness tossed in) through repetitive lines and underdeveloped scenes. The songs suggest a typical blues or pop song infused with surreal imagery.

This strategy holds with "Maggie's Farm" and "It's Alright" as well, in that clever lines and creative characterizations paint pictures of social relations with varying degrees of clarity. While "Maggie" leaves little doubt about its oppression theme and the narrator's determination to escape, "It's Alright" changes topics from line to line. The music provides a driving tension, with the chorus issuing a sarcastic response to the negativity portrayed in each verse. The song is relentless in its value-laden exposition of societal ills. Through it all, the contrast between metaphor and folly may involve a distinction without a difference. This trend also appears in the landmark work "Mr. Tambourine Man." Here the narrator laments that he or she has been abandoned, longs for an escape with Mr. Tambourine Man, and fantasizes of a carefree moment in which he or she shuns that undesirable situation. Mr. Tambourine Man may be the answer to our worries, but we have no idea what kind of answer he represents (God, drugs, music, a Gypsy leader, or a fellow with an extremely large tambourine?). He is just an escape: The grass is greener somewhere else.

Dylan's five songs of wordplay ("Subterranean Homesick Blues," "Outlaw Blues," "On the Road Again," "Gates of Eden," and "It's All Over Now, Baby Blue") range in complexity from the vacuous qualities of "Outlaw Blues" to the mischievous metaphors of "Gates of Eden." These songs may feature a recurring line to anchor the various verses ("Outlaw Blues" is an exception), but they are totally incoherent when construed as narratives. For example, in "It's All Over Now" it appears as though a relationship is ending, yet Dylan shifts scenes and characters with each verse in a way that not only prohibits any plot progression, it confuses everything. A traditional rock and roll tune such as "Outlaw" need not bear the lyrical burden of a Broadway song, but Dylan appears to go out of his way to confound things. Finally, to offer a narrative reading of "Subterranean Homesick Blues" is the functional equivalent of generating a narrative interpretation of ants scurrying about on an anthill (and that analogy is probably unfair to the ants). There is an awful lot of activity present; however, to ascribe any order to those individual acts may involve more than a little bit of projection. Robert Shelton is absolutely right when he says that these songs are "musical Rohrshachs" with the potential to display a vast distance between artistic intention and audience interpretation. Dylan's imagination was having its way (no Western Union boys here) and he invited his audience to join in the fun.

The merriment continued with Dylan's sixth album, *Highway 61 Revisited*, released on August 30, 1965. Three days before the record's release (and just over a month after the electric performance at Newport), the *New York Times* interviewed Dylan about the new "folk-rock" trend and its relationship to his work: "It's all music: no more, no less. . . . I know in my own mind what I'm doing. If anyone has imagination, he'll know what I'm doing. If they can't understand my songs they're missing something. If they can't understand green clocks, wet chairs, purple lamps or hostile statues, they're missing something, too." From there, Shelton captures the state-of-the-writer: "Some of Mr. Dylan's lyrics are obviously 'camp' fantasies, while others are poetically profound. Many are sufficiently elliptical to spur squadrons of interpreters." And no one understood this more than the auteur—the postman who merely opened his mailbag, arranged the letters in his own idiosyncratic way, delivered the mail, and laughed at the results.

Stephen Erlewine reports that *Highway 61* proved "that rock 'n' roll needn't be collegiate and tame in order to be literate, poetic, and complex." That may be true. It may also be true that *Highway 61* proved that rock and roll can be fun. This nine-track (running over 51 minutes) landmark work demonstrates Dylan's muse at play. There are no humorous satires, no painful elegies, no topical protestations on this album. This album uses recognizable musical formats to support random—often surreal—images that may or may not be related. The four songs that follow the narrative impressionism strategy complement the five tracks of unrestrained wordplay to render an unprecedented work of art. The success of the previously released single, "Like a Rolling Stone" (along with the Newport happening) aroused the public's interest in the controversial celebrity songwriter, and Dylan delivered a collection of musical Rohrshachs that were, indeed, "sufficiently elliptical to spur squadrons of interpreters."

The four works of impressionism explore two tried-and-true topics, *relationships* ("Like a Rolling Stone," "It Takes a Lot to Laugh, It Takes a Train to Cry," and

"From a Buick 6") and society ("Highway 61 Revisited"). From the portrayal of "Highway 61" as a harbinger of evil (home to murder, theft, and intrigue), to the celebration over the projected misfortunes of an ex-lover ("Rolling Stone"), to the narrator's longing for his baby ("It Takes a Lot"), to the narrator's celebration of his girlfriend's heroic qualities ("Buick 6"), these songs establish loose story-telling contexts for a succession of images of varying intensity. For example, the absurd characters and surreal scenes in "Rolling Stone" render a cloudy account of hard lessons and romantic revenge. Whereas these descriptions are certainly imaginative (and critically stimulating), nothing ever happens. The narrator just needles away. As Howard Sounes observes: "There is some irony in that fact that one of the most famous songs of . . . an era associated primarily with ideals of peace and harmony—is one of vengeance." Vengeance notwithstanding, the focus is strictly on the descriptions of characters or scenes: one gains the impression that a master storyteller is going out of his way not to tell a story.

The album's centerpiece is its five songs of wordplay: "Tombstone Blues," "Ballad of a Thin Man," "Queen Jane Approximately," "Just Like Tom Thumb's Blues," and "Desolation Row." These songs range from random gibberish ("Queen Jane Approximately") to organized chaos ("Desolation Row"). Any structure evident is musical, not narrative. The chorus in "Tombstone" adds a deceptive foundation for a parade of images built around famous characters (Paul Revere, Belle Starr, Jack the Ripper, John the Baptist, Galileo, Beethoven, and more). The song conveys values—even lessons (e.g., don't be afraid to face your pride, question authority and knowledge)—in the context of an extended word game. Again, nothing ever happens. The circus imagery of "Ballad of a Thin Man" and "Desolation Row" frame a relentless series of descriptions that appear to serve accusatory ("Ballad") and sociological ("Desolation") functions. As Shelton observes about "Desolation Row," this approach may "best be characterized as a 'folk song of the absurd.'" On occasion, the wordplay appears systematic and suggestive of a code or system. Little wonder that extremists combed through Dylan's trash and developed elaborate lexicons for interpreting these rhythmic expressions that are delivered with such passion!

But what if there is no code? What if the postman is delivering letters to himself? Dylan described this change in his writing to Nat Hentoff and Playboy: "But *Like a Rolling Stone* changed it all: I didn't care anymore after that about writing books or poems or whatever. I mean it was something that I myself could dig. It's very tiring having other people tell you how much they dig you if you yourself don't dig you." With *Highway 61* and the events of the spring and summer of 1965, Bob Dylan was clearly focused on "digging" himself. The auteur was serving his muse and that "thin wild mercury sound" in his head, not his audience. But his audience continued to hang on, as Hentoff's observations indicate: "No longer protesting polemically against the bomb, race prejudice and conformity, his songs have become increasingly personal—a surrealistic amalgam of Kafkaesque menace, corrosive satire and opaque sensuality. His lyrics are more crowded than ever with tumbling words and restless images, and they read more like free-verse poems than conventional lines. Adults still have difficulty digging his offbeat language—and its message of alienation—but the young continue to tune in and turn on." The principal characteristic of Dylan's "message of alienation" was the alienation of any message. As "young people continue to tune in and turn on," they were grasping onto Dylan's *image* and doing what they will with his words. If there was a message in all this, it was "don't take this too seriously"—a missive that was, to say the least, roundly ignored.

The musical portion of the Newport Mod phase concludes with the double-album project, *Blonde on Blonde*. *Blonde* represents yet another transitional statement, in that one-half of the album continues the impressionistic wordplay from the previous projects while the other half foreshadows Dylan's songwriting future (a trend that also embraced his songwriting past). Heylin's chronology reports that the album's production process was a marked departure from the spontaneous sessions that characterized Dylan's recording to that point, and therefore represented "the writing on the wall for all subsequent terrors in the studio." Dylan, his new producer (Bob Johnston), and his touring band (The Hawks) entered Columbia's New York studios in October 1965 and initiated a process that would extend through the end of January 1966. With little coming from those sessions, Dylan dismissed The Hawks and traveled to Nashville with Johnston (a producer with considerable experience in Music City), Robbie Robertson (The Hawks' guitarist), and Dylan veteran Al Kooper (from the famed "Rolling Stone" sessions) to complete the recording. There Johnston brought in several seasoned Nashville musicians to work with an artist quite unlike anything the Nashville regulars had ever experienced. Nashville musicians work in tightly supervised, professionally efficient sessions—a stark contrast to the Dylan method that relied on the improvisational skills of the accompanying musicians.

Heylin's chronology also cites a 1965 conversation between Dylan and Allan Ginsberg in which the songwriter described a recording process in which, according to Ginsberg, Dylan entered the studio, visited with the musicians, talked (Heylin describes it as "babble") into the microphone, listened to the replay, jotted down what he liked, and recorded the new material. Now, this is not the stuff of the patented Nashville Sound! In any event, legend has it that the musicians played cards as Dylan "composed" his songs, stopped the game to record a new song, and resumed the game while Dylan prepared the next track. Whether or not this is true, the spontaneous, "in the spirit" recording style that successfully captured the spontaneous, "in the spirit" messages was evolving in Nashville. Not until 2001's *Love and Theft* sessions would Dylan deploy this unique recording style to capture meaningful original material.

Blonde on Blonde reflects this transition in every way. Released on May 16, 1966, the fourteen-track double-album (running over 73 minutes) offers two songs in the free-form, wordplay style ("Visions of Johanna" and "Stuck Inside of Mobile with the Memphis Blues Again"), five songs that employ the narrative impressionism technique ("Rainy Day Women #12 & 35," "Pledging My Time," "I Want You," "Leopard-Skin Pill-Box Hat," and "Sad Eyed Lady of the Lowlands"), and seven stories about relationships ("One of Us Must Know [Sooner or Later]," "Just Like a Woman," "Most Likely You Go Your Way and I'll Go Mine," "Temporary

Like Achilles," "Absolutely Sweet Marie," "4th Time Around," and "Obviously Five Believers"). The relational songs establish a narrative trend that extends through the remainder of the lifework, while the wordplay and impressionism grind to a halt. The cavalier wordsmith's spontaneous utterances—like his spontaneous recording sessions—would now give way to more strategic, less inspirational art. It was as if the critics finally got what they always wanted—a thoughtful poet—and Dylan's art would never be the same again.

The two songs of wordplay are distinct in their respective orientations. "Visions" employs a smooth, simple, coherent instrumental structure as a platform for a series of unrelated statements. There are no developed characters, few value-laden expressions, and certainly, there is no plot structure. A line or two (or three) may appear to pursue a thought, but the song quickly shifts to another image and its idiosyncrasies. This is the state-of-the-art of Dylan's wordplay: playful, imaginative, evasive. "Stuck Inside of Mobile" is just as playful, but it follows an alternative strategy. This swinging instrumental track features a series of nine surreal vignettes anchored by the recurring three lines about Mobile and Memphis. While each verse displays some internal coherence (in its own crazy way), the vignettes are unrelated to one another—therefore no plot progression. Much like his narrative impressionism, Dylan's recurring lines and the musical structure create the illusion of coherence, but there is no common subject shared by the various vignettes.

The five songs that follow the impressionistic strategy are, of course, more structured. The social commentary floating in and out of "Rainy Day Women" communicates Dylan's views on the vicissitudes of celebrity and its potentially oppressive qualities through a Salvation Army band sound full of partying sound effects (people whooping it up). Consequently, the song makes fun of itself in a fashion that invites the interpretation that it is a "drug song." Drug song or not, "Rainy Day Women" is a compelling example of Dylan's impressionistic technique in that the nonsequential nonsense sounds like a story (and in this case, betrays his thoughts on oppression—to that end, Heylin's biography recommends that we consult Proverbs 27:15 to unlock Dylan's oppression message). This trait holds for the four impressionistic songs about relationships as well. From "Pledging My Time" and its slow, blues-oriented sound, to "I Want You" and its light, merry pop tune, to "Leopard-Skin" and its solid rhythm and blues approach, to "Sad Eyed Lady" and its eleven minutes of verbiage, these songs engage in systematic wordplay in which potential gibberish becomes potential metaphor through its context of usage. The music and the recurring lines build a platform for wordplay that may—or may not—be significant. In all cases, once more, nothing ever happens—just a constant litany of surreal descriptions of varying complexity followed by the recurring tag line.

The other half of Blonde follows strategies last heard on Another Side. Although the intensity seems to have abated, these seven songs of relational complaint fluctuate in their directness, ranging from "Obviously Five Believers" and its simple, repetitive blues structure to "One of Us Must Know" and its straightforward portrayal of relational angst. At times, songs such as "Temporary Like Achilles" and "Absolutely Sweet Marie" drift close to Dylan's narrative impressionism; however, I argue that there is at least a hint of plot progression in these tracks, and that separates them from the impressionistic strategy. Throughout, we observe a blend of Dylan's penchant for bizarre imagery and his acute ability to hone in on a specific point and elaborate on that subject. This narrative style—a blend of surrealism, idiosyncrasy, and topicality—will be the dominant writing approach for the next 30 years. *Blonde on Blonde* is important: It captures the past, the present, and the future in one statement. The postman's "particular style" would now *have* to evolve from intuitive, spontaneous writing and recording (i.e., art) to more calculated, organized writing and recording (i.e., craft), and *Blonde* represents a pivotal point in that evolution.

Before leaving this phase of Dylan's work, we must pause for several compelling examples of the Newport Mod's muse at play. Nowhere is Dylan's wordplay more active than in his nonsongwriting endeavors. In his music, the instrumental aspects of the presentation add structure to both the author's and auditor's experiences; as a result, the utter chaos conveyed through Dylan's personal language is controlled and, quite honestly, often more palatable. In the absence of music, Dylan's words work in isolation, their strengths and weaknesses to be judged on their own; they cannot hide behind his voice, pronunciation, or instrumentals. Although he wrote several pieces for album liners and music periodicals during the folk-posturing period, Dylan's nonmusical writings from this era offer unique insights, and we would be wise to consider them.

The liner notes from the *Another Side*, *Bringing It All Back Home*, and *Highway 61* albums offer examples of the writing style that rendered the *Tarantula* project. "Some Other Kinds of Songs . . . Poems by Bob Dylan" (the notes to *Another Side*) extends the format from "11 Outlined Epitaphs," as the auteur presents eleven poems addressing a host of topics. (The album contains but five of the eleven poems, Dylan's *Lyrics 1962–1985* presents the work in its entirety.) In *No Direction Home*, Shelton claims that the effort "further documents Dylan's experimentation with verbal music and his often elusive world view." From scenes of Paris (poem #2) to a commentary on the Jack of Diamonds (#4) to a vignette about a female hitchhiker (#8), these sketchy statements are tough sledding. Although Shelton describes these expressions as verbal music and "fortune-telling cards that reveal his emerging inner self," I prefer to apply his earlier comment regarding Dylan's impressionistic lyrics: that is, these artifacts read like "Literary Rohrshachs" that purposefully confuse the basic principles of communication. This is unadulterated "expression" with little-to-no regard for "communication"—the author is speaking to himself.

The trend holds for the liner notes "Bringing It All Back Home" and "Highway 61 Revisited" as well. The notes for "Bringing" are more detailed, potentially coherent statements that toss about celebrity names in a sportive fashion (e.g., complaining that Allen Ginsberg did not perform at the presidential inauguration). Shelton calls these notes "*Tarantula*-like nervous thought-fragments, name lists, and wild juxtapositions" that convey "a farewell to perfectionism . . . acceptance of chaos, [and] a description of fear." (Uh, ok!) Shades of *Tarantula* continue with the "Highway 61" notes that dismiss the emphasis on celebrity references in favor of crazy-named characters with quirky natures in strange scenes. These expressions complement the album with their word games and surreal tomfoolery. Dylan's "inner self" is running amuck (and apparently having a grand time). Moving from those notes to Dylan's "Alternatives to College" piece is a smooth transition (Heylin reports that this bit was originally written for *Esquire* magazine). If you merely turn the page between the two writings, you hardly realize that one ended and another began. With imagery such as Felix the Cat as a college professor and Jane Mansfield as an astronaut—well, we drift dangerously close to wordplay for wordplay's sake. These are, assuredly, *Literary Rohrshachs*—make of them what you will.

The writings culminate in the ultimate Literary Rohrshach: *Tarantula*—the book of "words" (in Dylan's terms) that Heylin describes as a "series of in-jokes" and Sounes refers to as "a hundred and thirty-seven pages of liner notes." Dylan's 1969 interview with *Rolling Stone* discusses the evolution of the *Tarantula* project in much detail. Dylan told Jann Wenner that the project emerged because of reporters' inquiries regarding other forms of writing: "And I would say, 'Well, I don't write much of anything else.' And they would say . . . 'Do you write books?' And I'd say, 'Sure, I write books.'" After that, Dylan claimed, all the major publishers started sending him book contracts and he merely accepted the largest one and "then owed them a book." He continued: "But there was no book. We just took the biggest contract. Why? I don't know. . . . So I sat down and wrote them a book in the hotel rooms and different places, plus I got a lot of other papers laying around that other people had written, so I threw it all together in a week and sent it to them." Soon afterward, Dylan received his copy to proof-read, rejected it (saying, "My gosh, did I write this? I'm not gonna have this out"), and relayed to the publisher that he had "corrections" to make. He wrote another "book" and sent it in only to repeat the process ("I just looked at the first paragraph—and knew I just couldn't let that stand"). After taking the manuscript on tour in an attempt to meet the publisher's deadline, Dylan's frustration grew: "But still, it wasn't any book; it was just to satisfy the publishers who wanted to print something that we had a contract for. Follow me? So eventually, I had my motorcycle accident and that just got me out of the whole thing." The publisher's notes to *Tarantula*'s original edition concur with Dylan's observations. After copies of galley proofs and advanced review copies filtered out through the press (and others), Macmillan and Dylan decided to publish the original set of writings, as the publisher states: "People change and their feelings change. But *Tarantula* hasn't been changed. Bob wants it published and so it is now time to publish it. This is Bob Dylan's first book. It is the way he wrote it when he was twenty-three—just this way—and now you know."

Tarantula contains 47 entries with crazy titles (e.g., "A Confederate Poke into King Arthur's Oakie") attributed to different authors (e.g., "Popeye Squirm"). Several entries kick about celebrity names in strange, unwieldy contexts; others introduce characters with wild street names that may (or may not) say something about those characterizations. And yet, once again, nothing ever seems to happen. Once the reader gains a feel for what is happening, everything changes. In these impressionistic antinarratives, characters appear and do things, they suddenly disappear as the context instantly changes planets, and then reappear doing something totally unrelated to the previous act. These expressions involve a concerted effort to make plot progression or continuity impossible. Often, one finds oneself looking at words instead of reading, or as Matt Damsker writes for *Rolling Stone*: "Maybe it amounts to a lot more typing than writing, but *Tarantula* captures the teeming tenor of the bard at a moment when he seemed singularly capable of naming the unnameable [sic]."

But what do we expect? The author was unequivocal in his explanation of what he was, in fact, doing. Bob Dylan had nothing to say with *Tarantula*. It was writing for the sake of writing (or more accurately, *publishing* for the sake of *publishing*). He received a contract and placed himself in the unfortunate position of having to deliver a manuscript with no purpose other than fulfilling his contractual obligation. That Macmillan accepted and published a work that its author disavowed says everything. The disbelief must have been intoxicating for Dylan, who was relentlessly churning out words that meant little to him and everything to everybody else.

While this was an inventive, unrestrained period for Dylan's writing, it was also a frustrating phase in his artistic maturation. Dylan's audience was so enraptured by his early songwriting (and that image) that it now analyzed every syllable of every song for additional insights. Dylan articulated his frustrations to Robert Shelton when he complained that the lyrics to "Rolling Stone" were being over-analyzed and misunderstood. In particular, interpretations regarding a line about attending school aggravated the author: "I wasn't making this song about school. . . . My language is different than theirs. I mean REALLY TOTALLY DIFFERENT! The finest school, I mean, might just be out in the swamps." This was Bob Dylan's artistic predicament: As Dylan grew beyond his carefully crafted image and matured into the artistic personality that embraced Bob Zimmerman's youth, he was stone-walled by an audience and an industry that refused to accept his creative progression. The writer who strategically interjected his persona into his art now faced an inability to remove that image from his work. He was in a creative cul-de-sac of his own making.

What starts with poetic promise drifts into idiosyncratic insolence articulated via a personal code that may—or may not—resemble metaphor. Thematically, this irreverent imagery contains a running commentary about the dark side of human nature. There are few sunny days, warm fuzzy feelings, or hopeful fantasies here; instead, we witness interpersonal vengeance, societal exploitation, and diverse forms of weirdness. Dylan examines this subject matter from unconventional angles: Characterization is often limited to name only, strange acts convey confused values, and rarely—if ever—does anything ever happen. Scenes, characters, and activities change so quickly as to prohibit any opportunity for plot progression. Expressions such as "Sue's wearing a kangaroo hat while she smokes a cheap green cigar and reads The Koran at her crossdressing sister's bar mitzvah" dissolve to the next line and its idiosyncrasies.

The music and an occasional recurring line provide a sense of continuity for an expression that is anything but coherent. Dylan's convincing vocals confuse matters further. At least he laughs or snickers occasionally and lightens the tone of this probing superficiality that demands a rejection of narrative logic. These expressions arouse emotions because there is nothing else there. It was all the ultimate inside joke. It was Glissendorf, Revisited.

the Americana period

The motorcycle accident of July 1966 was a welcomed reprieve for Bob Dylan. The physical discomfort associated with the wreck must have been relieved by the unburdening of his commercial load. *Tarantula* and *Eat the Document* were placed on hold. The concert tour was cancelled. Any recording plans were cast aside. The Iron Range's biker/poet—our original Newport Mod—achieved a heroic ending—true to form. Dylan's understanding of image maintenance is impeccable and he would now deploy those skills to recreate himself once more. After introducing American Song to his brand of impressionism, the auteur would now rely on its fundamental elements for his next transformation. As Dylan settled into a traditional American family, his art followed; as always, the *context* feeds the muse.

Few writers have captured Dylan's situation with the clarity Greil Marcus achieves in his 1997 book, *Invisible Republic*. Marcus argues where Dylan "got what he got" and how he returned to those roots to recover from the damage incurred over the previous five years. Among his problems, Dylan's relationship with his fans was particularly strained, and their antics worsened. Their immaturity was unprecedented (the irony of socially conscious folk fans "booing" is mind boggling) and Marcus describes Dylan's ridiculous predicament:

> Dylan's performance now seemed to mean that he had never truly been where he had appeared to be only a year before, reaching for that democratic oasis of the heart—and that if he had never been there, those who had felt themselves there with him had not been there. If his heart was not pure, one had to doubt one's own. It was as if it had all been a trick—a trick he had played on them and that they had played on themselves. . . . That was the source of the rage.

Rage. Unbelievable!

The Newport Mod phase achieved two artistic goals: First, it allowed Bob Zimmerman's imagination to run rampant with the raw materials the Bob Dylan creative sponge absorbed during his Dinkytown/New York apprenticeship; and second, it provided a sane outlet through which he could deal with all those Western Union fans and their rage—a "there's your message, have at it" response to the Messiah-seeking branch of the Dylan constituency. The intensity of the creative urge that supplied all those words—many of them unrelated, and therefore, unnaturally assembled (try it at home, folks)—combined with his manager's commercial zeal to drain Dylan of all his energy. To suggest that the Newport Mod period nearly killed the auteur is a supportable claim.

The personal/professional pause after the motorcycle accident offered yet another opportunity for Dylan's biography to assert itself. Just as Dylan used Zimmerman's expressive focus to combat his detractors, the artist returned to the "inspiration behind the inspiration" that supported his work as a means to recover, replenish, and rebound. That is, he would turn to his narrative imperative—American Song—to reorient his muse. The biographers discuss an incident in Dinkytown in which Dylan "borrowed" some rare records from a friend and music critic, Jon Pankake. One of the liberated records included Harry Smith's *Anthology of American Folk Music*, a collection of 84 classic American songs presented on six albums. Without seeking permissions from the original artists, Smith assembled these recordings of blues, folk, gospel, and instrumental songs and created a handbook to explain the respective song histories. That Dylan was fascinated—and informed—through Smith's project is beyond question. Combined with the knowledge from his late-night radio adventures, the mail-order distribution system that brought that music to Hibbing, Jim Dandy's instruction, and the Village's musical education, Smith's *Anthology* rounded off Dylan's informal but thorough musical training. This knowledge surfaced in Woodstock, New York in 1967.

Not long after the motorcycle accident, several members of The Hawks moved to Woodstock, where Dylan was recuperating and enjoying life with his growing family. The Hawks rented a house painted a shade of pink—thus the group dubbed their abode, "the Big Pink." Soon Dylan developed a daily schedule he adhered to with regularity in which he traveled to the Big Pink after dropping his daughter off for her school bus, typed away as he brewed high-test coffee while the band awakened, and—once everyone was primed for the day—moved into the basement to, literally, play with music. The biographers describe the open windows, the dog on the floor, and the relaxed, free-flowing qualities of these musicology exercises in which the musicians played old, traditional songs, recorded them on minimal (but effective) equipment, and eventually used the practice as the springboard to new material. The results were deemed "The Basement Tapes." After the musicians pressed acetates of some of the new music for Dylan's music publisher to use as demos in order to attract artists to record them, the tapes began leaking out. The bootlegging became so rampant that *Rolling Stone* actually reviewed the illegal records and furthered the legend (again, Columbia released a version of the Basements in 1975).

Marcus offers his take on the Basements and their significance: "As over the years more and more of the basement performances appeared . . . one could begin to hear something more than a number of interesting songs, or a moment in a particular career. Heard as something like a whole . . . the basement tapes can begin to sound like a map. . . . They can begin to sound like an instinctive experiment, or a laboratory: a laboratory where, for a few months, certain bedrock strains of American cultural language were retrieved and reinvented." From there, Marcus describes the Basements as a typical American town, "Smithville." Smithville is "an imagined America with a past and a future" in which the "jail is full," the Fourth of July is the year's greatest holiday, most of the town is "drunk," the Bible is ubiquitous, the citizenry is "restless," and people talk "funny." This is the backdrop for the Basements. This is the backdrop for the remainder of Bob Dylan's career. Heylin's chronology responds to Marcus when he claims that the Basements represent "a bounty of American song unparalleled in modern music (methinks I can smell the knotted pine of Americana, Greil)." The Basements' importance cannot be overstated.

The Basement Tapes appear in a variety of forms—some legal, some not so. Here again, Heylin's account of Dylan's recording career is invaluable in its presentation of the songs recorded throughout 1967. The official Columbia release contains but a portion of the treasure trove of songs generated in the light, depressurized atmosphere of the Red Room (at Dylan's house) and the Big Pink. From the playfulness of "Million Dollar Bash" and "Lo and Behold!" to "Clothes Line Saga" and its backyard conversation between neighbors to "Please, Mrs. Henry" and its sexual innuendo to the love gone wrong of "Tears of Rage" to the religious imagery of "Sign of the Cross," the Basements inspired Heylin to conclude: "The greatest irony of this is that 1967, the year *after* the accident, is by far the most prolific year of [Dylan's] life." Heylin claims that over 30 original Dylan compositions were recorded during the summer of 1967 as the musicians played the old tunes as a starting point for generating new songs, and Dylan used traditional phrases as that "first line" from which songs originate.

The Americana period is a major transitional moment in the lifework. The stylistic tendencies that allowed the postman to deliver songs of celebration, complaint, satire, and impressionistic wordplay have matured and settled into a creative repertoire. Dylan's impressionistic flights of fancy, his satirical humor and morality, his topical incisiveness, and his idiosyncratic commentaries have all been established and refined. The muse, however, was tired. Recall Dylan's comments regarding the state-of-the-muse after *Blonde on Blonde*, and his inability to "receive" any more "thoughts" and spontaneously relate them through his "particular style" (in his own words, he had "amnesia"). All indications suggest that Dylan's creative well ran dry and he turned to American Song to replenish that reservoir. This phase contains six albums (besides the Basements) that I group into three segments: first, *John Wesley Harding* (released in December 1967) and *Nashville Skyline* (April 1969); second, *Self Portrait* (June 1970), *New Morning* (October 1970), and *Dylan* (November 1973); and third, *Planet Waves* (January 1974) and the "Tour '74" reunion. Here we observe Dylan struggling with his creative instincts, trying to rediscover the spontaneous reception of the inspirational signals that supplied his art. By returning to his musical roots, Dylan revived his creativity and extended his career.

The *Harding* and *Skyline* projects were produced by Bob Johnston in Nashville and involved several of the musicians from the *Blonde* sessions. The results present a smooth, professional sound with brief songs (no visits to "Desolation Row" here) that celebrate and condemn love as well as other facets of human relations. Marcus contends that *Harding* constitutes "an altogether austere, suspicious, ironic version of the whole basement project, a black-and-white movie to the basement tapes' sepias and washed-out Technicolor." Maybe so. Released during the psychedelic age of the Beatles' *Sgt. Pepper* album and the Rolling Stones' *Their Satanic Majesties Request* response (among the other heavily produced records of that time), *Harding* departs from that approach—and *Blonde on Blonde's* cutting-edge orientation—toward the traditional world of the Basements and American Song. Jon Landau used the album as an opportunity for a state-of-the-artist message and concluded that *Harding* represents "a fundamentally American artistic statement" that conveys that "Dylan's influences and sources are primarily peculiar to American culture." Landau reports that the record presents "a new Dylan myth—the myth of the moderate man" in which the "adolescent quest for certain truths, static imagery, finality and the underlying hostile world view which allowed him to create his compelling but ultimately unsatisfying visions have been superseded." For Landau, *Harding* is a "profoundly egotistical album" with an "essential lack of insecurity" that reveals Dylan to be "a truly independent artist who doesn't feel responsible to anyone else, whether they be fans or his contemporaries."

Dylan may not have felt "responsible" to his "fans or contemporaries," but he did respond to his record label with a 38-minute, 12-track recording that *Time* describes as "shapely and graceful [with a] simplicity [that is] deceptive." *Harding* features six thematic orientations: two epic portraits ("John Wesley Harding" and "I Dreamed I Saw St. Augustine"), three relational complaints ("As I Went Out One Morning," "Dear Landlord," and "I Pity the Poor Immigrant"), a satire ("The Ballad of Frankie Lee and Judas Priest"), two individual complaints ("Drifter's Escape" and "I Am a Lonesome Hobo"), two celebrations of love ("Down Along the Cove" and "I'll Be Your Baby Tonight"), and two versions of Dylan's impressionism ("All Along the Watchtower" and "The Wicked Messenger"). *Harding's* thematic diversity involves a complicated blend of past and present. The return of Dylan's satirical style via "The Ballad of Frankie Lee" and its enigmatic parable about mistaken paradises recalls the moralistic tales of earlier times. The song uses cloudy metaphors in a systematic fashion that synthesizes the folk-posturing period's narrative structures with the Newport Mod's personal language (Riley calls the song a "mock linear narrative"). The story moves along at a steady pace, its progression is coherent, but several of Dylan's metaphors are difficult to unpack. Nevertheless, the ending leaves little doubt about the moral of the story. Dylan revisits his impressionism as well via "Watchtower" and "Wicked Messenger." Clear, direct language is used to initiate stories that stop after establishing the respective characters. Dylan told John Cohen and Happy Traum that the two songs "have the cycle of events working in a rather reverse order," which, in turn, opens the songs to a variety of interpretations, "anything we can imagine is really there." The story structures are in place (and they appear intriguing), but Dylan leaves us standing at the narrative altar, wondering what could have been.

One trend that drifts across the various themes in *Harding* involves Dylan's use of portraiture. "Harding," "St. Augustine," "Wicked Messenger," "Poor Immigrant," and "Lonesome Hobo" spend considerable time developing their respective characters. Whether the narrative stresses the positive or negative qualities of its subject matter, Dylan describes the heroic, never-foolish outlaw ("Harding"), the virtuous St. Augustine, and the failed lives of dishonest people ("Lonesome Hobo" and "Immigrant") in a straightforward fashion. The Biblical imagery (Heylin cites Bert Cartwright's count of 61 Biblical references throughout the album), the enigmatic metaphors, and the songs' brevity work with the writer's penchant for portraiture to produce yet another hybrid of Dylan's storytelling signatures. Although he had certainly developed characters in the past, such characteriza- tions typically appeared in service of the narrative. In these songs, the narrative serves the characterization. Dylan songs often move too fast to embellish any single character (or scene, for that matter), so the energy spent developing these characters suggests a shift in songwriting strategies.

The songs of relational contention and celebration join the two individual complaints in their narrative simplicity. This is, assuredly, the stuff of traditional American Song and its pop and country manifestations. The snappy pop tune "Down Along the Cove" and the smooth country-and-western track "I'll Be Your Baby Tonight" convey their romantic celebrations in cute, direct, and loving styles. The complaints are a bit more complicated in "As I Went Out" and its por- trayal of a threatening woman in chains and Tom Paine's successful intervention or in "Dear Landlord" and its cryptic characterizations (everyone has a different interpretation of "Landlord"). *John Wesley Harding* features a broad spectrum of narrative strategies and may well be the most diverse—or superficial—lyrical entry in the lifework. Tim Riley concurs: "The record is remote on several levels: The lyrics are opaque-vernacular; the music . . . is skeletal, yet inscrutable; the songs are riddles posing as revelation."

Where *Harding* fits in the oeuvre may be best observed through the album's liner notes. There Dylan presents a cloudy tale of three kings and their efforts to understand a new Bob Dylan record. The kings consult the story's central character, Frank, who responds by ripping off his shirt, waving it around (drop- ping a light bulb and crushing it with his feet), punching out a plate glass win- dow, and pulling a knife. This apparently satisfies the kings, who leave Frank, his wife, and his friend contemplating the visit as repairmen replace the window. The story is weird, but coherent (much like "Frankie Lee"). Unlike the previous editions of liners notes, Dylan presents a clear, slightly surreal, story. It introduces and develops characters, there is plot progression, and the plot conveys the value of knowledge (among other things). This is the *Harding* package: Playful, moralistic, and a long, long way from *Highway 61*. It is as if Dylan is revisiting each story- telling strategy and attempting to unlock the door to that particular approach.

Dylan returned to Music City and extended this narrative trend with 1969's *Nashville Skyline*. Unlike *Harding*, this 27-minute, 10-song album focuses on a sin- gle topic. Predictably, the love songs explore two themes: celebration (the return of "Girl from the North Country" with Johnny Cash, "To Be Alone with You," "Peggy Day," "Lay Lady Lay," "Country Pie," and "Tonight I'll Be Staying Here With You") and complaint ("I Threw It All Away," "One More Night," and "Tell Me That It Isn't True"). The Newport Mod is not only dead, he is long forgotten. This is a warm, friendly work that conveys heartfelt sentiments in brief, coherent snippets. Bob Johnston and the Nashville musicians complement Dylan's vocals to create what *Newsweek* calls "a relaxed get-together of expert musicians who seem to know each other's—and Dylan's—moves as if they were playing at the Grand Ole Opry."

The playful metaphors in "Country Pie" (in which the narrator just *loves* all flavors of pie) and the cloudy love triangle in "Lay Lady Lay" (a song written for the movie *Midnight Cowboy*, but delivered too late) are smooth complements to the direct portrayals of the character who had it all and now has nothing ("I Threw It All Away"), the character who pleads with his lover to denounce the rumors of infidelity ("Tell Me That It Isn't True"), the character who aspires for an evening of bliss ("Peggy Day"), and the determined traveler storming his way to his woman ("Tonight I'll Be Staying"). These two- to-three minute pop songs follow the standard recipes of American Song's country genre in a manner that, once again, demonstrates Dylan's capacity to co-opt a musical style. He told *Newsweek*: "The songs reflect more of the inner me than the songs of the past. They're more to my base than, say, 'John Wesley Harding.' There I felt everyone expected me to be a poet so that's what I tried to be. But the smallest line in this new album means more to me than some of the songs on any of the previous albums I've made." After pondering those earlier songs, Dylan continued:

> Those songs were all written in the New York atmosphere. I'd never have written any of them—or sung them the way I did—if I hadn't been sitting around listening to performers in New York cafes. . . . When I got to New York it was obvious that something was going on—folk music—and I did my best to learn and play it. I was just there at the right time with pen in hand. I suppose there was some ambition in what I did. But I tried to make the songs genuine.

Again, the context dictated the expression's form. The address plays a significant role in the mail's delivery, and the latest missives originated in "Nashville."

As Dylan escaped the scrutiny of the "New York atmosphere," he rediscovered the narrative imperative that supported his art. The detail associated with *Harding*'s portraits, the record's cloudy qualities (several songs are not as direct as their musical formats suggest), and the intensity of the romantic, relational, and individual complaints revise and extend the storytelling strategies evidenced thus far. With *Harding* and *Skyline*, characters are more than names, metaphors are more accessible, and the author's relationship to his work seems more sincere. Of principal interest is the fact that the postman *wrote* these letters. The days of discovering "thoughts" and delivering them in the postman's particular style have evolved into a new, more deliberate writing technique. Dylan tried to be a poet in *John Wesley Harding* and he tried to release his "inner" self with *Nashville Skyline*. These works were anything but spontaneous (few things are spontaneous in Nashville!). They were the wave of his creative future.

The next portion of the Americana period involves a radical shift from the orientation that generated the *Harding* and *Skyline* projects. Celebrity was, once again, invading the auteur's life. The artist-as-Messiah faction of Dylan's fan base disrupted the Woodstock environment and inspired a return to Greenwich Village. This, unfortunately, made a bad thing worse, as fans rummaged through his trash, demonstrated in front of his house, and harassed his family. Compounding the situation were newfound difficulties with his manager, Albert Grossman, and Dylan's discovery of unjust contractual conditions (Dylan rarely read contracts) regarding his music publishing. To respond, our narrative jokester revised an old solution for his new problem. Just as Dylan adamantly refused to play Western Union boy for the American protest movement, he would now push away his True Believers and confound his manager in an act of artistic defiance.

The *Self Portrait, New Morning,* and *Dylan* projects are best considered in relation to one another. All three records emerged from a series of recording sessions in Nashville and New York that involved the "amnesia" that followed *Blonde on Blonde.* With *Harding* and *Skyline* Dylan "tried" to evoke the spirit of the Basements through the patented Nashville Sound. As his professional situation became increasingly complicated, Dylan "tried" another tactic. He shared his motivations for the *Self Portrait* project with *Rolling Stone's* Kurt Loder and explained his response to an audience that was increasingly debilitating:

> Well, fuck it, I wish these people would just *forget* about me. I wanna do something they *can't* possibly like, they *can't* relate to. They'll see it, and they'll listen, and they'll say, "Well, let's go on to the next person. He ain't sayin' it no more. He ain't givin' us what we want," you know? They'll go on to somebody else. But the whole idea backfired. Because the album went out there, and the people said, "*This* ain't what we want," and they got *more* resentful. And then I did this portrait for the cover. I mean, there was no *title* for that album. I knew somebody who had some paints and a square canvas, and I did the cover up in about five minutes. And I said, "Well, I'm gonna call this album *Self Portrait.*" . . . And to me, it was a joke. [Loder asks why a double album?] Well, it wouldn't have held up as a single album—then it *really* would've been bad, you know. I mean, if you're gonna put a lot of crap on it, you might as well *load it up!*

These comments to Cameron Crowe are also instructive:

> *Self Portrait* . . . was a bunch of tracks that we'd done all the time I'd gone to Nashville. We did that stuff to get a (studio) sound. To open up we'd do two or three songs, just to get things right and then we'd go on and do what we were going to do. And then there was a lot of other stuff that was just on the shelf. . . . So I just figured I'd put all this stuff together and put it out, my own bootleg record, so to speak. . . . Also, I wasn't going to be anybody's puppet and I figured this record would put an end to that.

This was Dylan's new artistic attitude. With his manager allegedly abusing his publishing income, his critics overanalyzing every syllable of his work, his fans rummaging through his garbage, his connection with his creative instinct strained, and his contract with his record company under negotiations, Dylan decided to record cover versions of country, traditional, and pop songs, thereby resting the muse and reducing the publishing royalties. Clinton Heylin's recording-session information sheds much light on how the various tracks were divided into their respective albums. Of the three albums, *Dylan* is the least interesting (that's probably not fair to the versions of "Big Yellow Taxi" and "Mr. Bojangles"). The biographers consider it to be Columbia's revenge album, since it was released (November 1973) during Dylan's brief stint with Asylum Records. That Columbia has never issued the project in compact disc is indicative of its standing within the oeuvre.

The 24-track, 74-minute double-album *Self Portrait* (released June 8, 1970) was produced by Bob Johnston and recorded in Nashville and New York, with Johnston overdubbing many parts in Nashville. A thematic interpretation of *Self Portrait* is pointless. The blend of covers ("Early Morning Rain," "Let It Be Me," "Gotta Travel On," "Blue Moon," "The Boxer," and more) and lackluster traditional adaptations ("In Search of Little Sadie," and "Little Sadie"—same song) are so uneven as to almost make listening prohibitive. The horror is evident in the sequence from tracks 6 ("Little Sadie" I) to 7 ("Let It Be Me") to 8 ("Little Sadie" II). Sandwiched around the voice of his generation *crooning* "Let It Be Me" is the identical song—the latter entry adding musical coherence to the previous version that does everything (*everything!*) wrong. This could only be intentional. Lou Reed's *Metal Machine Music* denied his record company of viable "product" during a contractual dispute in the way that *Portrait* insulted everybody with the crassest art. The version of "Rolling Stone" could easily be used as a motivational tape for karaoke performers—It Is guiltless. (I suppose I should beware of overstatements, since this version is from the Isle of Wight show; still, give it a listen and see what you think.) *Time* captures the sentiment through a review that suggests that "these exercises in nostalgia will be no help for the Dylan faithful, who regularly look to him for an indication of pop music's next new direction," and closes by mentioning a song on which Dylan does not sing ("All the Tired Horses") as a case in point: "How's that for a new direction?" And yet, there are moments when *Portrait's* warm, accessible sound is reminiscent of the unofficial *Basements* and the false starts, playfully spontaneous singing, and general tomfoolery that makes the unofficial version so superior to its official counterpart. For instance, "Minstrel Boy" has *got to be a joke.*

That the Dylan commercial machine was aware of *Portrait's* limitations is evident by the speed with which *New Morning* came to the rescue. Released October 21, 1970, this would be the last studio album produced by Bob Johnston (with Dylan, that is). The 12 songs (running almost 36 minutes) on *Morning* focus on loving relationships with three exceptions: one song of personal celebration (the autobiographical "Day of the Locusts") and two nonstories ("Three Angels" and "Father of Night"). The nonstories differ from Dylan's abstract wordplays in that they offer clear, coherent lines that simply describe ("Angels") and praise ("Father") their respective topics. The love songs, of course, focus on good and bad things (e.g., "Time Passes Slowly," "Went to See the Gypsy," and "Sign on the Window"). The record is dominated by the six songs celebrating love: "If Not For You," "Winterlude," "If Dogs Run Free," "New Morning," "One More Weekend," and "The Man in Me." The joys of love are communicated through a variety of musical genres: a waltz ("Winterlude"), a scat jazz routine ("If Dogs"), classic pop songs

("If Not"), rhythm and blues ("One More"), and gospel (the mournful "Sign" and prayerful "The Man"). (The two nonstories feature a hymn-like quality that was interspersed throughout *Morning.*) The shift in musical approaches contributes to the album's pacing and reduces the narrative redundancy that occurs when songs say the same thing repeatedly.

Morning's gospel sounds are an important development because they fore-shadow the future via their backing vocals, moral overtones, and probing content. Thematically, *Morning* raises issues that would continually resurface during the next fifteen years. Its gospel tone and spiritual sentimentality represent the shape of things to come as Dylan transcends earthly affairs for loftier consid-erations. Though the visit was brief, it was meaningful. This sound now incubates for almost ten years: *New Morning* raises questions that Dylan would one day answer with conviction. That aside, *Morning* is—in every respect—a fine pop album and a stark contrast to the contractual filler that surrounded it. Filler or original material, Dylan did not tour in support of any of these recordings and made limited public appearances, playing guest roles on various artists' records, absorbing the praise and profits of his second greatest-hits release, and trying his hand at filmmaking and sound design with the *Pat Garrett* project. The lat-ter project's evocation of American Song's cowboy/western heritage allowed Dylan to explore that genre in a focused way (too bad the film's final cut failed to present Dylan's work as he intended it).

In 1973 the Americana phase closed where it began: Recording with The Band. The *Planet Waves/*"Tour '74" project generated the only studio album not issued by Columbia; nevertheless, the legal and contractual negotiations that engulfed Dylan's life were probably relieved by a gathering of familiar faces. When Dylan signed an album-by-album contract with David Geffen's Asylum Records and agreed to his first tour in eight years (staged by Geffen and Bill Graham), he re-entered public life in a big way. Probably because of his publishing dispute with Grossman Dylan's pen had been still for some time, and the opportunity to record with The Band stimulated his muse. *Planet Waves* was recorded without a pro-ducer (engineer Rob Fraboni worked with mediator Robbie Robertson to fill this role) in five sessions (two of which were basically mixing sessions) in Dylan's new home state, California. The album was released in January 1974 just after Dylan and The Band opened "Tour '74" in Chicago. The tour was as extravagant as any staged to that time, and Dylan heard few "boos" from his adoring audience.

Heylin's session chronology claims that most of the songs for *Waves* were written during the month preceding the November 1973 recording sessions and that there were but two outtakes from these focused activities. The resulting 11 tracks (running just over 42 minutes) convey that which had never before been captured in the studio: The Dylan–Band sound that was perfected during the Basement experience. This in no way resembled the sound heard during the 1966 tours; to the contrary, *Waves* displays The Band's unique approach to American Song with its dynamic interplay between Robertson's guitar, Hudson's organ and accordion, and the Helm/Manual/Danko rhythm section. Complementing these musical treks across Americana (every song feels like a carnival or a funeral) were Dylan's words and their performance.

Planet Waves addresses one topic only, with one exception. Dylan's "Forever Young" (offered in two versions; one fast, one slow) is a prayer for his children's futures. Although the two versions demonstrate the impact of pacing on the listening experience, the lyrics ring true in both instances. "Forever Young" is a strong song. Love dominates the other nine tracks through songs that complain about ("Going, Going, Gone," "Hazel," and "Dirge") and celebrate that haphazard emotional state ("On a Night Like This," "Tough Mama," "Something There Is About You," "You Angel You," "Never Say Goodbye," and "Wedding Song"). The tough love expressed through "Tough Mama" (she's a load, but she's mine), the disappointment in "Hazel," the messages of sincere adoration ("Something There Is" and "You Angel You"), and the story of eternal commitment ("Never Say") explore many facets of loving relationships. Obviously, affairs of the heart were on Dylan's mind.

While these songs of "love gained" and "love lost" blend Dylan's lyrics and The Band's sound in an unprecedented manner, Waves contains three songs that not only stand out on this record, they stand among the best songs of Bob Dylan's career. The aforementioned "Forever Young" joins "Dirge" and "Wedding Song" as powerful exemplars of Dylan's talent. That "Dirge" and "Wedding"—polar opposites, thematically—appear on the same album demonstrates the auteur's capacity to empathize with both sides of his subject matter. The intensity conveyed by these two songs was noticeably absent during Dylan's "amnesia" and inspired much curiosity regarding his writing's return to that emotional level. To the extent that "Dirge" condemns the narrator's lover, "Wedding" praises her. If the biographers are right and "Wedding" exalts Sara Dylan's virtues, what then could have motivated the aggression portrayed in "Dirge"? The invective is overwhelming. The self-loathing, the anger, and the song's descriptive power (e.g., slavery and mystical metaphors) are photo negatives of "Wedding" and its adoring worship. I hesitate to suggest that Dylan is exploring his relationship with his wife (although all evidence suggests he was), but he is clearly examining loving relationships through a depth of emotion that is downright unhealthy. To articulate one or the other sentiment is one thing, but to pair them on the same work (written within a month of each other) is amazing (and ammunition for all that talk about Dylan's "Gemini personality").

To celebrate the new album, Dylan and The Band hit the road with a national tour that did much for the money changers and little for the auteur. "Tour '74" reminded Dylan of all that was wrong with his profession and placed him in another unhappy situation. All those questions about the "sixties" joined an unfulfilling celebrity lifestyle, the continued litigation with Grossman, the demise of his marriage, and the absence of creative motivation put the auteur into an artistic funk that would last for close to five years. A review of "Tour '74" by the New Yorker's Ellen Willis suggests the type of pressure Dylan endured. There Willis describes a letter she received from Greil Marcus concerning the lyrics to Planet Waves that were previewed in Newsweek. Marcus worried that the lyrics appeared "complacent" and ambivalent (was "Dirge" included!?!) and, unfortunately for Willis, she shared those sentiments as well. She wondered if Dylan had "the power to move us—to matter—as he once did" and feared that the record and tour would contain "more domesticity and low-keyed, moderate angst" ("Dirge" ?!?). Willis explains her stance this way: "My theory was that Dylan was consciously working against the grain of his genius in order to communicate honestly about his own strategy for survival." After reviewing the show (she loved it) and the album (she wants to love it, too), she discusses the preponderance of love songs: "This kind of symbolism can be embarrassing. Dylan has always tended to get sticky about women—to classify them as goddesses to be idolized or bitches to be mercilessly trashed. Yet his conviction that he has been saved by love is so poignant and so obviously genuine that it transcends the stereotype. Which is, in a sense, what popular culture is all about."

What a burden. The expectations. The scrutiny. The demands. And most of all, the assumptions. The assumption that Dylan was trying to communicate (much less "honestly"), that his words were personal, and the overall view of popular culture as personal testimony and public therapy. These were the conditions under which popular artists plied their trade. Under such circumstances, who would aspire to be "public writer number one?" How much money would one require in exchange for the public dissections, the hero worship, and the unrelenting pressure to "inspire" people who would be much better off inspiring themselves? After enduring this for as long as Dylan did, several things are unquestionably clear: This was not about the money, not about the fame, and—most assuredly—not about the polemics. Bob Dylan endured all of this because he had no choice. This was all about his life's calling. The question was, ironically, how would he survive it?

the crystallization-of-style period

We now reach that point where Dylan transformed his art into a craft. The auteur fought through the "amnesia" that followed his motorcycle accident via the *Harding, Skyline, Morning,* and *Waves* projects with varying degrees of success. Once his classes with Norman Raeben connected his eye, mind, and hand as a painter, he transferred that technique to his pen and rendered *Blood on the Tracks, Desire,* and *Street-Legal.* The various songwriting strategies from the previous periods crystallized into a creative repertoire that the artist consciously applied to the topics before him. For subject matter, the author—as always—turned to his context and, unfortunately, his deteriorating domestic situation and its aftermath. Clinton Heylin's biography quotes Dylan on Raeben's teachings, and life afterwards: "Needless to say it changed me. I went home after that and my wife never did understand me ever since that day. That's when our marriage started breaking up. She never knew what I was talking about, what I was thinking about, and I couldn't possibly explain it." Instead, he wrote *Blood on the Tracks.*

What can be said about our opening entry, *Blood on the Tracks?* The album contains nothing but relational complaints with one exception, and that song involves back-stabbing (literally). These romantic elegies differ somewhat in their storytelling strategies; however, there are no word games, no moralistic satires, no impressionistic narratives. These songs articulate relational anxieties through coherent stories told in straightforward language. For many, this is Dylan's "masterpiece." For Dylan, this may have been an opportunity to exorcise his demons, and hopefully, reinvigorate his muse.

Tracks (released January 1975) features 10 songs (running almost 52 minutes) and appears in two versions. The original New York recording presents the songs in a more instrumentally sparse, but lyrically intense fashion. In order to temper the lyrics and lighten the record's emotional impact (and, perhaps, autobiographical qualities), Dylan re-recorded most of the album in Minneapolis in a last-minute effort arranged by his brother. With the help of a group of Minnesota-based musicians, Dylan enlivened several songs (musically) and deflated others (lyrically) as his extemporaneous method of record production was replaced by a more deliberate, self-conscious process. The postman now walked a new route.

The nine romantic elegies differ in their intensity. From playful memories and accounts of lessons learned ("Tangled Up in Blue") to heavy-hearted recollections of love lost ("Simple Twist of Fate," "You're a Big Girl Now," "Meet Me in the Morning," "If You See Her, Say Hello," and "Shelter From the Storm") to a straight-on frontal attack ("Idiot Wind"), Dylan blends fact and fiction through unambiguous, succinct accounts of love gone wrong. Several of these songs appear to strike dangerously close to home: The persecuted man who is saved, then abandoned ("Shelter"), the utter desperation of a jilted lover ("You're a Big Girl"), and the flippant gamesmanship of "If You See Her" convey the heartfelt insights that often accompany personal experience. The "love hurts" thematic is so fully developed that one narrator anticipates the pain through "You're Gonna Make Me Lonesome When You Go" (along with the sense of warning emanating from "Shelter"). The abandonment theme may well be the record's dominant characteristic, with the narrators' responses shifting from tale to tale: The confusion in "Simple Twist," the anger in "Idiot," the pain in "You're a Big Girl," the cavalier attitude in "If You See Her," and the suspicion in "Shelter." The narrator from each song—as Tim Riley suggests—sounds "like the same person" and, therefore, intensifies the various accounts. This is, in every respect, romantic angst to the pain threshold.

Nowhere does this trait appear more than in "Idiot Wind." The writer who penned the merciless societal complaint of the 1960s ("Masters of War"), the intense personal attacks that were "Ballad in Plain D" and "Positively Fourth Street," and inspired a generation to confront—and reject—the status quo through songs such as "Only a Pawn in Their Game" and "The Times They Are a-Changin'" now embellished deep-seated personal emotions through the same narrative strategy. That Dylan was moved to edit his anger in the Minnesota revision of "Idiot Wind" demonstrates the lessons learned from previous outbursts. The narrator complains about his treatment in the press, the distorted views people hold of him (and their inability to approach him), and the turmoil of celebrity life before turning to personal statements that appear to address his wife, his children, and their relationship. Once the smoke clears, the song closes with a declaration of freedom and an admission of sorrow as the central character shares the responsibility for the damage inflicted on everyone. The song is as powerful as any within the oeuvre.

Among these lighthearted, carefree accounts of relational devastation we note the evolution of a traditional Dylan song strategy. The folk-posturing period's satirical approach returns with "Lily, Rosemary, and the Jack of Hearts" and its nine-minute saga of relational intrigue (ending with murder by penknife, of course, executed by a wife who stabs her husband in the back). The colorful scenery and characterizations recall the days of "Talkin' Bear Mountain," "Motorpsycho Nitemare," and "Talkin' World War III" as Dylan takes an old format and revises it. This time, these moralistic tall tales branch out into two new directions: Portraits that emphasize societal complaint, and sagas such as "Lily." The song's narrative qualities were enriched by the Minnesota revisions, in that the additional instrumentation enlivens the story's pacing. Dylan introduces a host of characters (Big Jim—owner of the town's lone diamond mine—and his exasperated wife Rosemary, Lily the vivacious showgirl, a drunken judge, and the mysterious Jack of Hearts) through a fast-paced account of a night at the local music hall and the activities at the bank next door (Jack's colleagues robbing the safe). Things happen quickly: The bank is emptied, the murder occurs, the judgment is rendered, and the song leaves us to contemplate it all. The story is masterful with its subtle humor, cryptic characterizations, and cloudy ending. Without question, this is the sole ray of light in an otherwise dark exploration of human emotions and relational conflict.

When Dylan accepted Christ as his savior, he shared *personal* sentiments in the context of a *group* experience. The expression's intensity was tempered somewhat by the spiritual environment and the duty to share an intimate act publicly. There is no Great Commission for affairs of the heart. There is no creed that demands that lovers go out into the world and share the pain with non-lovers. In the absence of such a Great Commission, it requires courage (or carelessness) to disclose the feelings of loss associated with a decision to end one's family. Whether the artistic motive involves revenge, remorse, release, or rebellion, the individual who shares such an intense loss does so at considerable personal peril. The axiom that personal turmoil is fertile ground for artistic expression be damned, no one engages in public therapy for financial profit—the costs always outweigh the rewards. Little wonder Dylan had difficulty understanding why so many praised the product of his pain. The fact that he continued to revise the lyrics for years to come suggests something of his discomfort with *Blood on the Tracks'* contents. Or perhaps Norman Raeben taught Dylan how to start writing and forgot to tell him how to stop. In any event, the clarity, the depth—simply, the emotion evidenced here elevates this work, not only in Dylan's oeuvre, but in popular music history as well. In all of popular music, there is only one *Blood on the Tracks.*

I wonder if Norman Raeben ever had to deal with art critics? The biographers report that he was fond of calling his students "idiots." I wonder what he taught his students about those who make their livings off of the works of others? I wonder what god term Raeben conjured up for that profession? The critics were hungry for *Blood on the Tracks*. Their responses are, in virtually every respect, contradictory: *Newsweek* wonders about Dylan's "plea for pity," the *New Yorker* contemplates the author's vulnerability, *Crawdaddy* notes Dylan's confusion, *Creem* characterizes Dylan's state of mind, and *Rolling Stone* considers the album's status within the literature of the Western world (and, as a result, takes one small step for journalism, one giant leap for Dylanology). Let us take a moment to consider the specifics.

Maureen Orth writes for *Newsweek*: "Dylan's music is excellent. It's acoustic and spare. There are frequent flashes of the old poetry, and his voice wails hauntingly. What's disconcerting is the covert plea for pity present in many of the songs. Dylan seems to think himself a victim—a curious role for one sitting so firmly atop the rock pile." Ellen Willis considers the state-of-the-artist: "For all their failures, Dylan's happy-husband years taught him something precious: vulnerability. He is able, in a way he rarely was before, to express love, hurt, need without hiding behind a protective irony. And that ability has enabled him to inte-grate the 'old' and 'new' Dylans, the sixties and the seventies—an accomplish-ment that poses a challenge to all of us." Jim Cusimano addresses the art and the auteur:

> Although the line between art and life is shaky in Dylan's work, it's still there. The core experience of *Blood on the Tracks* is a man's loss of a beloved woman. Most, though not all, of the lp is an investigation of the emotions generated by that core experience, which he approaches through various points of view, tones of voice and objects of address. . . . It's difficult to know whether he's trying to fondle his feelings or purge them.

Charles Nicholaus also assesses the state-of-the-artist:

> Bob Dylan is pussy-whipped. There are more general ways to state it, of course. You could say, for instance, that he has so idealized his vision of The Woman that he cherishes her potential infidelities and betrayals as much as her poten-tial for salvation. But that is so much rodomontode [*sic*]. Baldly, put in the vernacular so it can't be mistaken for something else, or avoided altogether, he is pussy-whipped.

Rolling Stone's response is extraordinary. The magazine devoted three arti-cles to the record: serious (I mean *serious*) reviews by Jonathan Cott and Jon Landau as well as a series of critical vignettes from the world of music journal-ism (featuring Chet Flippo, Robert Hilburn, Greil Marcus, Dave Marsh, John Rock-well, Paul Williams, and others). Cott's analysis is an exemplar of noncontextual criticism in which he takes a line from a song here, a statement from there, a piece of classical literature from somewhere, and synthesizes it all into a grandiose critique of All Things Dylan. Cott's conclusions are impressive (I *think* he enjoyed the record), but his procedure is maddening. What writer could endure that form of scrutiny and sustain any level of artistic (or personal) integrity? Jon Landau, on the other hand, most assuredly did not enjoy the album and used his displeasure to attack the artist's historical standing and to foreshadow his shift in careers from music critic to music producer. After a detailed comparison of Dylan's, Charlie Chaplin's, and Elvis Presley's careers, Landau attacks Dylan's method of recording ("Dylan's electric albums have often been pointlessly sloppy, sometimes badly recorded and not nearly as good as some of the material warranted"), his "frequently horrible harmonica playing" ("it sounds like a bleating sheep"), and his eventual standing in popular music history (after comparing Dylan's recordings with notable examples, Landau concludes, "I find him wanting"). The man who would soon manage Bruce Springsteen surmised: "*Blood on the Tracks* will only sound like a great album for a while. Like most of Dylan, it is impermanent."

I wonder what Norman Raeben told his idiots about critics?

After *Tracks*, Dylan's art entered a phase in which he invited all sorts of participation in the creative process. Stopping unknowns in the street and asking her to record with him simply because she carried a violin case, auditioning musicians and producers in search of that "sound" from years ago, and inviting established writers to join in the newly discovered craft of songwriting are but a few of the innovations to emerge with Dylan's new participatory approach to art. Whether the craft had room for input or simply that misery loved company, the auteur changed how he created his work. Not surprisingly, the ultimate participatory expression, The Rolling Thunder Revue, opened in the fall of 1975. Dylan was actively seeking creative inspiration from external sources, including—for the first time—a thesaurus and a rhyming dictionary.

The extent to which Raeben's lessons had been assimilated appears in Dylan's next record, *Desire*—the only co-authored album in the lifework. That Dylan learned to do consciously what had heretofore been unconscious is evident in Jacques Levy's participation—an act that contributed to the work's narrative qualities: These songs contain stories with fully developed scenes, coherent plot progression, and, correspondingly, less emotion and minimal abstraction. To the degree that something is gained (narrative coherence), something is lost (emotional intensity). Heylin's biography explains that the Dylan–Levy writing team came about by happenstance (they were in a bar and the idea of writing together emerged) and cites Levy's recollection that it was a "totally cooperative venture." After helping the auteur with "Isis" that very night, Dylan enlisted Levy's assistance on a topical song idea, his first in over a decade. Levy claims that Dylan was having difficulty finding that famous first line, and that he assisted by placing the subject in a "storytelling mode." The results, "Hurricane," solidified the writing team that rendered *Desire*.

Desire (released January 1976) contains 9 tracks (running just over 56 minutes) with seven songs co-authored by the Dylan–Levy team (the two exceptions are "One More Cup of Coffee" and "Sara"). Produced by Don DeVito over a series of six sessions in July and October 1975, *Desire* features two songs of societal complaint (the portraits, "Hurricane" and "Joey"), two sagas ("Romance in Durango" and "Black Diamond Bay"), one love celebration ("Mozambique"), and four relational complaints ("Isis," "One More Cup of Coffee," "Oh, Sister," and

"Sara"). Levy's influence supported an advance in the satire's evolution by way of the two portraits and the two sagas; additionally, Dylan's songwriting travels abroad more than on any previous work through songs that articulate faraway scenes, international intrigue, and—thanks in large part to Scarlet Rivera's violin—foreign sounds. All evidence indicates that Jacques Levy did, indeed, help the auteur place his songs' ideas in a "storytelling mode."

The two portraits are actually photo negatives of each other. In one, a famous Black man is victimized by a racist judicial system hungry for revenge; in the other, a famous White man is victimized by a system outside the law—a culture with its own code of conduct. "Hurricane" says little about boxer Rubin Carter, in favor of scenic embellishments that unveil the ludicrous qualities of the prosecution and the hideous consequences of the racism. "Joey" follows a different strategy, as the story focuses on the central character's heroic traits. Both stories end negatively—Dylan is embarrassed by a judicial system that practices uncontrolled racism and is angered by the law of the streets—hoping that true justice will have its way in both cases. Unlike the subtle humor and playfulness of "Lily," "Hurricane" and "Joey" use the same attention to detail to reintroduce the czar of the topical song and his anger, frustration, and indignation.

The two sagas are similar in their narrative enactment. Both songs emphasize scenic conditions through "Black Diamond Bay" with its tale of mystery, suicide, and natural disaster (as conveyed by a television report); and "Romance in Durango" with its "lovers on the run" scenario. We know little about any of the stories' characters because the narrative concentrates on the scene; simply, *where* things occur is as important as *who* is doing what. This trait holds true for "Isis" (a relational complaint) and "Mozambique" (a relational celebration) as well. In the latter, little is said about any character in favor of descriptions of bliss and beauty on the beach; in the former, the narrator announces his marriage to Isis and departs for a failed adventure—without his wife—only to return to his wife's troublesome (nagging?) queries. Throughout all these songs, the authors display much attention to detail. They may have replaced emotional power with descriptive precision, but they did it gracefully.

The relational complaints differ in their respective strategies. "One More Cup" follows an abstract approach that emphasizes the mystical target of the narrator's affections; nothing ever happens—just more and more description. "Oh, Sister" is a simple song with a powerful sense of foreshadowing. The subject here is not a biological relative but a spiritual sibling, and the narrator longs for joint participation in His service (according to *Lyrics 1962–1985*, anyway). Finally, "Sara" is a tribute to Bob Dylan's wife. The song opens by describing the children happily playing on the beach, turns to scenes of family life, recalls a song written in her honor, and—sure enough—ends with a deserted beach and a plea for relational perseverance. Heylin's chronology cites Larry Sloman's recollection of Dylan recording this song *in his wife's presence*. There is no way to deny the intensely personal qualities of the song that carries the author's wife's name.

If nothing else, *Desire* reveals that the "discover a line, throw out an image" approach to writing had been replaced by a strategy that placed songs in a

"storytelling mode." The emphasis on scenic development, thorough characterization, and plot progression indicates the extent of Jacques Levy's influence on
Dylan's "conscious" method of songwriting. *Rolling Stone*'s Dave Marsh concurs:
"*Desire* is a very special album, although Bob Dylan's adamantly antimusical
approach keeps it from greatness. . . . On the best songs, Dylan returns to the
fantastic images, weird characters and absurdist landscapes of the Sixties. The
metaphors work on so many levels they're impossible to sift. . . . The crucial ideas
are cinematic." The *Washington Post* praises "Hurricane" ("the latest and one of
the most powerful of a long line of Dylan polemics"), acknowledges "Sara" (it "is
completely without precedent"), and condemns "Joey" (it is a "disaster"). Larry
Rohter concludes: "Because his finest songs—of which there are many—reveal
Dylan to be an incredibly astute observer of human nature and behavior, there is
a tendency on the part of his admirers to assume that he always has those
powers. It takes a failure as notable as 'Joey' to remind us that Dylan is only
human—and 'Desire' is, above all, a very human album."

Armed with a new set of songs, a new band, a stage manager, a screenwriter,
a film crew, and many old friends from the Village, Dylan returned to touring with
the Rolling Thunder Revue's vaudeville show. The biographers argue that their
subject desperately needed the medicine gleaned from "roots" music, and that
the Rolling Thunder Revue's adaptation of the Basement mentality (and its
reliance upon American Song) seemed to be the proper prescription. Moreover, by
filming the shows and staging scenes wherever through his patented "don't look
back" method of production, Dylan applied Raeben's techniques in yet another
artistic context. The *need* for expression was great, and Dylan used every means
available to satisfy that desire.

Two rounds of Rolling Thunder tours and loads of free-verse video left Dylan
with hundreds of hours of film to organize, edit, and mold into whatever artistic
statement he wanted. Meanwhile, he disbanded the Revue and organized a new
band with a new mission. This time, the vaudeville, multiartist approach was replaced by a gospel-influenced, revisionist presentation of Dylan's lifework. While
he rehearsed the band, he created *Renaldo and Clara*, after which he introduced
his new act in Japan. After releasing *Renaldo and Clara* and accepting a hard
rain of criticism, he returned to his new band, refined its act on the road, and
brought it to the studio in April 1978 to record the most negative album of his
career (at least *Tracks* had "Lily" to lighten the load).

Regarding *Street-Legal*, simply, you have your transitional statements and
you have your TRANSITIONAL STATEMENTS. Not only does this record proclaim
in bold letters "it's not working," it introduces the means through which Dylan
transcends his multifaceted dilemma and revitalizes his art. The album's gospel
sound and Revelations rhetoric say "farewell" to Norman Raeben/Jacques Levy
and "hello" to Jesus through nine songs that complain about society ("Changing
of the Guard," "No Time to Think," and "Senor") and relationships ("New Pony,"
"Baby, Stop Crying," "Is Your Love in Vain," "True Love Tends to Forget," "We Better
Talk This Over," and "Where Are You Tonight? [Journey Through Dark Heat]"). The
large band's full sound and the gospel vocals add an urgency to songs that, with-

out question, stress the negative. There are no word games, no obscure references on this record—the metaphors communicate, not obfuscate. As Dylan told Robert Hilburn, "I wanted to start off new on the album." Dylan started the new and ended the old in the same package.

Released in June 1978, the Don DeVito production involves relational complaints that run the traditional gamut from the playful pony metaphor and its recurring questions of relational stamina ("New Pony"), to the unilateral declaration of "We Better Talk" and the narrator's after-the-fact rationalizations, to the dangers of dominating relationships ("True Love Tends"), to the ever-present anxieties over absent lovers and their mystical powers ("Where Are You Tonight?"). Occasionally, songs suggest remedies, as in "Baby, Stop Crying" and the narrator's recommendation that his baby go to the river (for absolution?) or in "Is Your Love in Vain?" and the narrator's decision to give it up and try love once more or in "We Better Talk" and the narrator's conclusion that going forward without the relationship is the best way to survive. The songs' musical presentations affect their emotional impact in the same fashion as *Blood on the Tracks*, just in opposite directions. Here the repetitive lyrics and backing vocals complement the band's gospel sounds to detract from the lyrics' intensity (just as the sparse instrumentals on *Tracks* elevated the songs' emotional power).

The societal complaints introduce the "warning" theme that will dominate *Slow Train Coming*: The end times are coming, and these three songs warn of the impending doom for the unwashed. With "Changing of the Guards" Dylan presents a series of disintegrating scenes occupied by good shepherds, angels, apostate priests, and witches. As the Revelatory Fire approaches, the song warns, the idolatry will be exposed, so, if we fail to change the guards, well, it is always better to be cleansed by water than by fire. The Revelatory rhetoric continues with "No Time to Think" and its sermonic lyrics that describe contrasting character traits (e.g., humility versus materialism) in alternate verses with heavy doses of Biblical imagery tossed into the mix. The devil makes life busy, and in so doing, restricts our time for contemplating our salvation. Consequently, the song warns us to shed these earthly chains and prepare for the end times. Finally, "Senor" simplifies the story somewhat, but the ending is the same: The world, according to the narrator, is nonsensical, so, if you will, give him a moment to get himself together and prepare for the glorious end times.

This record's transitional qualities are most evident in Dylan's return to American Song and one of its richest—uniquely American—strands, gospel. The call and response, the urgency, the prescriptions for living contained in these songs do not merely foreshadow the next phase of the lifework, they introduce it. The notion that one has been "saved" suggests that some condition exists from which rescue is warranted. This album describes that condition. *John Wesley Harding* is certainly full of Biblical references and *New Morning* features a gospel sound, but this album applies those traits in a concrete manner: The slow train is coming and our first glimpse of its mission is in *Street-Legal*. As relationships deteriorate, as society devolves, as material gain is devalued, Bob Dylan issues a warning.

Once more, critical responses to the album assume opposite stances. Writing for *Rolling Stone*, Greil Marcus expresses his overall disbelief ("It saddens me that I can't find it in my heart to agree with my colleague Dave Marsh that Bob Dylan's new record is a joke. . . . Most of the stuff here is dead air, or close to it"), condemns Dylan's singing ("he's never sounded so utterly fake"), wonders why the record is so bad ("I don't know the answer, but merely not giving a damn whether a record is good enough for his audience might be a big part of the problem"), and attacks the quality of the writing. Writing for *Crawdaddy*, Jon Pareles takes the middle ground: "The Dylan I respect, though, is the free associator, the crazed doggerel genius whose songs make sense a hundred different ways. A lot of fools write love songs, but there's only one 'Highway 61 Revisited.' The best thing about *Street-Legal* is that Dylan's letting his mind ramble again, going further afield than he did on *Blood on the Tracks*, making *Desire* sound like setting-up exercises." Finally, the *Washington Post's* Robert Spitz praises the work:

> Dylan's wispy voice has never been better, his insistent phrasing building mock-serious drama at designated intervals along the way. But it is his writing, his magical blend of precise words, images and sentiments that elevates both him and this album above all others in the genre. There has never been much doubt about his dominance there, although some listeners have been put off by his self-indulgence. But for those willing to bear with the semi-autobiographical soliloquies, "Street-Legal" is Dylan's most eloquent album to date.

Now—more than at any previous point in the history of art—artists must rely on their creative instincts if they, and their art, are to survive. The diversity of art journalism not only renders a variety of media outlets for critical commentary, it facilitates the enactment of a host of journalistic priorities—agendas that may not have any relationship whatsoever to the art under review. How an artist handles these intensely subjective, instantaneous assessments could now make or break a career.

This phase of the oeuvre—this moment of stylistic crystallization inspired by the "teacher" who connected Dylan's impulse and abilities and introduced a bridge between art and craft—may not resemble innovation as much as culmination. *Blood on the Tracks'* emotional outburst seems a direction extension of "Ballad in Plain D," "Masters of War," "Positively Fourth Street," or "Like a Rolling Stone." *Desire's* orchestration seems to mirror the storytelling of the earlier satires—"Talkin' New York" or "The Ballad of Frankie Lee and Judas Priest"—minus the humor. And *Street-Legal's* transitional attributes seem to recall the Big Pink and yet another exploration of American Song, albeit in a different musical mode—a format previewed in *Harding's* lyrics and *Morning's* sounds. The evidence suggests that Dylan cultivated a narrative repertoire that he strategically applied to the creative context at hand—indeed, an old trick. The auteur also shifted from a creative orientation that stressed spontaneous innovation to one that focused on systematic application—indeed, a new trick. Thematically, the public therapy ended with "Sara." But the negativity consuming the

Street-Legal gospel show indicates that additional tensions existed as anxieties of the heart evolved into frustrations of the soul. Dylan's art now focused on the pivotal question: Could it be that the conditions that make loving relationships so difficult transcend individual lovers and families—that problems with relationships are merely symptoms of a much larger, more threatening disease; that the disintegration of society's most basic institution is just part of a greater happening? Street-Legal's Bob Dylan answered those queries with a resounding "Yes!" The slow train is coming.

the moral period

The infamous (and reportedly, contrived) 1966 interview with *Playboy's* Nat Hentoff features several insightful, humorous, and facetious moments. None of those comments contains the irony of Dylan's response to an inquiry regarding the artist's status as an opinion leader for America's youth. Hentoff asks: "Still, thousands of young people look up to you as a kind of folk hero. Do you feel some sense of responsibility toward them?" Dylan replied:

> I don't feel I have any responsibility, no. Whoever it is that listens to my songs owes me nothing. How could I possibly have any responsibility to any kind of thousands? What could possibly make me think that I owe anybody anything who just happens to be there? I've never written any song that begins with the words "I've gathered you here tonight . . ." I'm not about to tell anybody to be a good boy or a good girl and they'll go to heaven. I really don't know what the people who are on the receiving end of these songs think of me, anyway. It's horrible. I'll bet Tony Bennett doesn't have to go through this kind of thing. I wonder what Billy the Kid would have answered to such a question? (emphasis added)

"Billy the Kid"? Well, all of that changed in 1979. Dylan claimed that a fan tossed a cross onto the stage, he pocketed it, and later invited Christ into his life after a spiritual revelation in a hotel room. Why? For insight into this conversion, I consult Paul Williams's essay, "Dylan—What Happened?" (reprinted in *Watching the River Flow*). I turn to Williams because of his love for Bob Dylan, and the fact that Dylan directly confirmed Williams's observations (buying and distributing copies of the "instant book"). After witnessing seven consecutive nights of Dylan's gospel show's November 1979 opening and returning home to his storehouse of knowledge about his beloved subject, I find myself comfortable with his observations. Williams writes:

> What happened? Well, in the very simplest terms, the divorce happened. Simple terms are misleading, however. Bob and Sara Dylan were divorced in 1977, following a separation in 1974 (*Blood on the Tracks*) and a reconciliation in 1975 (*Desire*). . . . And ultimately, I think, the failure of the marriage (augmented by the frustrations of single life), led Dylan the Gemini to a painful and inescapable confrontation with the irreconcilable differences within himself. Dylan has always believed, not unreasonably, in the power of Woman. When he finally lost

faith in the ability of women to save him (and he seems to have explored the matter very thoroughly, in and out of marriage, in the years 1974 through '78), his need for an alternative grew very great indeed, and he found what people in our culture most often find in the same circumstances: the uncritical hospitality of Jesus Christ. What the man needed to save himself from, I surmise, was guilt, unendurable restlessness, alcohol, self-hatred.

Now, this is dangerous stuff. Williams realizes the troublesome nature of such conclusions and prefaces them by admitting that he is relying on "the public record; I don't have no inside line" as he concentrates on the text—the oeuvre—to trace not just an artistic evolution, but a personal revelation. Since we have consistently observed how Dylan's context affects his art, Williams's argument gains support. After all, it was Bob Dylan, not Paul Williams, who made these most personal matters public.

Interestingly, as Dylan professed his newfound beliefs in song, he endeavored to perfect that message—no more bottles of wine or overnight recording sessions. The auteur wanted a particular sound for a specific message, consequently he reached for the top shelf and Jerry Wexler. Richard Buskin describes Wexler as "the man who coined the term *rhythm and blues* to replace the title of 'race records' on the black music charts" and—through his work with Professor Longhair, Big Joe Turner, Ray Charles, Ruth Brown, LaVern Baker, the Drifters, Aretha Franklin, Wilson Pickett, and Solomon Burke—brought "black music to the masses." His work in Muscle Shoals, Alabama not only transformed the tiny studio into a "major recording center," it created a sound unique within the world of popular music. There is no way to overestimate the impact of Jerry Wexler's work. He shared with Buskin his recollections of his Dylan experiences:

> When Bob Dylan came to me and asked me to do that first gospel album . . . I had no idea what I was in for. All I knew was that the genius had done me the honor of saying that he wanted me to produce an album with him. However, it soon transpired that he wanted the structure and the sonority that he had heard in Ray Charles, Aretha Franklin, and Wilson Pickett records, as opposed to Woody Guthrie rambling and scrambling down the road with his guitar on his back and making eleven-and-a-half-bar mistakes. *He wanted that structure.* That was in 1977. Many years before, around 1972, Bob came by a session that I was doing, and we took a break and went back to my office, we lit up a cheroot, and he said to me, "Man, I've done the word thing, now I want to do the music thing." I wasn't sure what he meant, it was just idle chatter to me, but sure enough, when he came to me many years later I understood what he meant. When you listen to *Slow Train* it surely sounds different to anything else that he ever did. I'm not saying that it's better, but if Dylan hadn't gone through that Woody Guthrie/Rambling Jack Elliott phase, making mistakes on chords and going into odd meters and so on, he wouldn't have been Bob Dylan. He had to do that, but now he was saying, "I want a taste of Otis Redding." (emphasis added)

The "music thing" did not replace the "word thing" entirely. Dylan was motivated by his God to say the Right Things and by his muse to present them properly. The two albums from the Jerry Wexler/Barry Beckett/Bob Dylan creative team—1979's *Slow Train Coming* and 1980's *Saved*—are best considered together; they are cut from the same cloth. That Paul Williams reports how the initial San Francisco shows featured songs from both albums indicates the extent to which they are an integrated work. From our narrative perspective, they are best construed as a two-part presentation: Part One, "Beware, the slow train's coming," and Part Two, "Thank you, Lord!"

The biographers and Heylin's chronology indicate that the *Slow Train* and *Saved* projects are products of different creative orientations. *Slow Train's* inclusion of Dire Straits guitarist Mark Knopfler and drummer Pick Withers helped Wexler cope with Dylan's traditional recording method in a fashion that assisted the producer's efforts to layer the sound in the famous Muscle Shoals style. As the producer and the auteur negotiated a working process, the sessions came together in most respects. This was not the case for *Saved*—recorded a mere nine months later after a three-month tour (without Knopfler and Withers). The good news is that the tour featured the new songs, so the band returned to Alabama with fully formed arrangements. The bad news is that the band members were exhausted and their fatigue was evident. Thus, Heylin's chronology designates *Saved* as Dylan's "grandest failure" and the starting point for the recording difficulties that follow. Although the disparity in sound and the quality of the performances may vary, the two records' narratives capture Dylan's muse in an excited state. Once again, the "message" was flowing "through" the postman and—regardless of the sound—the mail was delivered with passion.

We start with Part One's warnings of the slow train's impending arrival. *Slow Train* (released August 1979) contains 9 tracks (running 46:44 minutes) that address four subjects: songs of warning ("Gotta Serve Somebody," "Precious Angel," "Slow Train," "Gonna Change My Way of Thinking," "When You Gonna Wake Up," and "When He Returns"), a song of commitment ("I Believe in You"), a moral prescription ("Do Right to Me Baby [Do Unto Others]"), and a celebration of God's works, the childlike "Man Gave Names to All the Animals." The album's thematic leaves little to the imagination: Worldly concerns are not going to protect you (or serve you) in the end; it is time to "change the guard." The songs are not heavy-handed in their prescriptions, just insistent in their warnings: BEWARE, secular "answers" are temporary.

These musical omens follow different strategies. The rap-list approach of "Subterranean Homesick Blues" returns with "Gotta Serve Somebody" and its overview of worldly diversity; regardless of one's position or personal tastes, service is required. "Slow Train" is more direct in its presentation of the end times and the impending doom (the American economy is controlled by hedonistic foreigners, America is disintegrating, false prophets abound, ubiquitous tribulations). "When You Gonna Wake Up" is a straightforward account of societal wrongs and warns that it is time to awaken and save what you can. This song also attacks religion's potential for hypocrisy and stresses salvation's *personal* qualities. The album closes by urging one to shed one's worldly ways and embrace the ultimate celebration "When He Returns." Even when he backs away from the

Revelatory warnings, Dylan's statement of commitment ("I Believe"), his evocation of the Golden Rule ("Do Right to Me"), and his children's tale are executed with a grace and style that reveals the artist's intense dedication to both his faith and his art.

Underneath Bob Zimmerman's senior portrait in his high school yearbook is a statement addressing his goal in life: "To join the band of Little Richard." Richard may not have been *physically* present during the recording of *Saved* in Muscle Shoals, but his *spirit* was most assuredly in Alabama. The rich, traditional gospel sounds of the Southern Black church joined a talented White wordsmith from Minnesota to scream "Praise the Lord" for 43 minutes in 1980's *Saved* (released in June). The sound may not have been perfect—the band may have been tired. Dylan and Wexler may have had difficulty communicating. But The Spirit was there and it requires little to transcend the production difficulties and share in the experience.

Saved closes with yet another warning of the end time's impending arrival ("Are You Ready"), and it is that cautionary tag that pulls the record from the clouds of celebration. From the opening cover of Hayes and Rhodes's "A Satisfied Mind" to the seven songs of sanctification that follow, the "Praise the Lord" thematic demonstrates the spiritual—not *religious*—fervor that inspired this phase of Dylan's oeuvre. Biographers and critics condemn this work for its damnation dogma but their claims are simply unfounded. This record celebrates the joy of dedication and urges the audience to join in the heavenly fun. "Saved" (co-authored with bass player Tim Drummond) is a gospel tour de force (one can feel young Elvis Presley hiding outside the church, learning his chops), "Covenant Woman" is a special thank you for the lady who paved the narrator's path to the Lord, "What Can I Do for You" is a "thanks for the Answer" statement and a request for reciprocity, "Solid Rock" and "Pressing On" are declarations of dedication, "In the Garden" is a hymn of loving recognition (plain and simple), and "Saving Grace" is a paean of thanks for the narrator's salvation. All of the celebrations constitute one big invitation—the call that comes with "Are You Ready."

When one stops and considers this two-part message, it is not difficult to imagine how the two sets of songs would work harmoniously in concert. The mixture of warning and celebration would, no doubt, establish a context for an ecclesiastical intervention and a spiritual invitation. For the altar call to be properly issued, tradition has it, it must be prefaced by testimony. And Bob Dylan was up for this task. Robert Hilburn's review of the Los Angeles shows cites this Dylan testimonial: "Christ will return to set up His kingdom in Jerusalem. . . . There really is a slow train coming you know . . . and it is picking up speed. . . . Some people call Satan the real God of this world. All you have to do is look around to see that's true. But I wonder how many of you know that Satan has been defeated by the cross. . . . [After many cheered, he replied,] Well, it doesn't look like we're alone tonight." Paul Williams reports that Dylan introduced songs with Christian slogans and sayings (e.g., "I'd like to say we're presenting the show tonight under the authority of Jesus Christ") and that as the tour advanced, he had more to say. According to Williams, Dylan issued "a rap about Satan before 'Saved,' a rap about 'a God that can raise the dead' before 'When You Gonna Wake Up,' a rap about Peter and Jesus in the garden of Gethsemane before 'In the Garden,' and an extended rap about Moses while introducing 'Ordinary People' (sung by Mona Lisa Young)." Lastly, Heylin's biography offers an example of Dylan's testimonials:

> You know we're living in the end times. I don't think there's anybody . . . who doesn't feel that in their heart. The scriptures say, "In the last days, perilous times shall be at hand." . . . Take a look at the Middle East. We're heading for a war. That's right. . . . I'd say maybe five years, maybe ten years, could be fifteen years. . . . I told you "The Times They Are a-Changin'" and they did. I said the answer was "Blowin' in the Wind" and it was. I'm telling you now Jesus is coming back, and He is! And there is no other way of salvation. . . . There's only one way to believe, there's only one way—the Truth and the Life. It took me a long time to figure that out before it did come to me, and I hope it doesn't take you that long. But Jesus is coming back to set up His kingdom in Jerusalem for a thousand years.

There were occasions when audiences became unruly (yelling for old songs and the like) and thereby angered Dylan. The media were also doubtful, as reporters speculated about conversion for profit, his Jewish heritage, and what Dylan's new orientation meant for his audience. If any of this was designed to shake this artist from his chosen path, it was certainly foolish. This is an individual who endured hostile audiences as an adolescent, confronted the status quo in Newport, combated the press on its own turf, battled hecklers around the world, rejected his followers with incoherent albums, and—in general—rebelled at every opportunity. Dylan's rebellion was not always his friend, but it was the force that supported the inspiration that invigorated the muse. If he ever wavered from his new message, it would most likely be by his own hand.

If Dylan's contention that the purpose of art is to inspire is his personal yardstick, then the *Slow Train* and *Saved* projects must represent a rousing success for the auteur. Responses were loud and diverse. Critics, fans, and a variety of partisans decried, denied, and delighted in the work. From *Rolling Stone's* glowing endorsement to the *Los Angeles Times'* seasoned praise to *Newsweek's* passive acknowledgment to the *Washington Post's* bitter condemnation, media responses to *Slow Train* were intense. *Rolling Stone's* editor, Jann Wenner, opens with the album's theme and its relationship to the artist: "Faith is the message. Faith is the point. Faith is the key to understanding this record. Faith is finally all we have. Because Bob Dylan had the power of insight and poetry early in his career, he became an article of faith himself." From there, Wenner asserts that *Slow Train* is the "most commercial" record in the oeuvre and contends that it was produced with a "care and attention to detail" unlike any other Dylan project. He claims that Dylan's "apocalyptic visions and Biblical symbolism" are not only "wholly consistent" with the lifework's topical entries, the slow train imagery is "thoroughly American" in character—"It's an affirmation of America's greatness."

The *Los Angeles Times* issued two concurring opinions. Davin Seay reports:

"Situations are viewed both objectively and compassionately; solutions, overtly Christian, are offered the listener, yet there is little sermonizing. More important, emotional intensity—the essential factor in Dylan's body of work and in the larger scope of rock music—has not been diluted. Dylan speaks in 'Slow Train Coming' with the voice of authority, a voice first raised in social protest almost 20 years ago." Robert Hilburn announces that the record is the "most musically polished album yet by the most acclaimed songwriter of the rock era." Hilburn says that the record avoids a "denominational sermon" ("You don't feel you deserve a tax deduction for the price of the LP after listening to it"); rather, it is a "stirring, elegantly designed collection that adds even further to Dylan's distinguished body of work." Other reviews staked out neutral ground, as in Newsweek's conclusion: "There is something terribly ironic about the brooding anti-ideologue taking shelter from the storm in evangelical pieties. But the times they are a-changin'—and so, once again, is Dylan." Of course, there were critics who were appalled by either the work, the artist, or both. Geoffrey Himes's review for the Washington Post is a case in point. After decrying Dylan's "self-righteous attitude" and its "grating" qualities, Himes opines: "Dylan betrays all the open-mindedness of the glaze-eyed Jesus freaks who pass out their pamphlets in public bus stations. . . . The reactionary lyrics create a civil war in each song. Dylan's condescending, nasal delivery of the lyrics grinds against the splendid Southern music like mismatched gears." The Post concludes: "Instead of hiding from his disillusionment behind a screen of religious rhetoric, he would be better off exploring the problem. He might find his situation no different from that of thousands of other divorced people. Maybe then he could recover from his debacle as he has from past mistakes."

After Saved, several critics considered the Wexler/Beckett/Dylan records as a package. For example, Kurt Loder's comments in Jann Wenner's publication demonstrate a shift in the magazine's stance:

> Abandoning the greatest of human religious quests—the intellectual pilgrimage toward personal transcendence—Dylan settled for mere religion. His art, which arose out of human complexity and moral ambiguities, was drastically diminished. With a single leap of faith, he plummeted to the level of a spiritual pamphleteer. . . . Dylan hadn't simply found Jesus but seemed to imply that he had His home phone number as well.

Loder praises Dylan's capacity to "evoke the phantom strains of traditional American music" and his ability to "conjure up the nation's historical heart with the strum of a few guitar chords" before he closes with the hope that "this, too, shall pass" into another Dylan reinvention.

Whether the critics appreciate it or not, from this point on Dylan's music would be infused with spiritual messages and, occasionally, gospel sounds. The fervor faded in the spring of 1981, however. As Dylan explained to Robert Hilburn: "I've made my statement and I don't think I could make it any better than in some of those songs. Once I've said what I need to say in a song, that's it. I don't want to repeat myself." To that end, the oeuvre's moral period closed with Shot of Love (issued August 1981). Actually, *Shot of Love* is the first part of a two-part passage: the lifework's final transition. *Shot of Love* initiates a thematic exploration of secular matters, a search for a producer who can recapture the Dylan sound from days gone by, and an era of confusion for an artist in search of creative comfort. Though relatively brief, the oeuvre's moral period provided the *auteur* an opportunity to get in touch with his American Song roots, to allow the words to flow through him (not from him), and to channel his ever-present rebellion. Now, he resolves his spiritual quest and revisits the theme that continues to haunt him.

Shot of Love contains ten songs (running 44:58 minutes) addressing six themes that are easily grouped into three categories. The record presents these topics via a variety of musical genres: gospel, blues, and reggae. Dylan briefly returns to the portrait strategy through "Lenny Bruce" and its dualistic characterization that both complains and celebrates. The song complains that Bruce was misunderstood and treated poorly as a result; it celebrates his strength and courage. It is, in every respect, an uneventful song. Dylan's storytelling improves with the four songs of relational complaint ("Heart of Mine," "Watered-Down Love," "The Groom's Still Waiting at the Altar" [apparently added to the record upon its re-release], and "Dead Man, Dead Man") and the spiritual trilogy that resolves this phase's metaphysical quest.

The relational complaints signal a return to worldly affairs by way of four, relatively uneven, songs. "Heart of Mine" is a simple, highly repetitive plea by the narrator for personal caution. The narrator just does not trust his heart to do the right thing and Dylan deploys cliché after cliché as a means of encouragement. "Watered-Down Love" communicates a struggle between a love that is pure and emotions that are of a less redeeming quality. Throughout, the narrator praises the virtues of pure love as a preface to an attack on the song's target: an *advocate* of a diluted love. With "The Groom's Still Waiting" the narrator complains about everything and the romantic interest is merely one among many targets. Several of the complaints are heavy-handed and the apparently personal qualities of the song are similar to "Property of Jesus." Although the focus is certainly on the woman, she seems to be merely a symptom of a larger problem. Joining the negativity is "Dead Man" and its relentless complaint against somebody or something that is threatening the narrator. Christian values abound as the narrator states his case in terms of good versus evil. The invective is rich, but the target is hidden.

Dylan's spiritual resolution opens with a declaration of need ("Shot of Love"), moves to a societal complaint that articulates the exigency ("Trouble"), and concludes with two songs of salvation/celebration ("Property of Jesus" and "Every Grain of Sand"). The opening salvo forcefully declares that the narrator needs not drugs, drink, government programs, popular media, revenge, or the devil—he needs love. There is no mystery: Love is the answer. Love is the antidote to the plague of tribulation that engulfs the world. With a slow musical accompaniment, "Trouble" details the problem with its laundry list of difficulties. There is trouble in our cities, on our farms, in our water, in our air, with our gov-

ernments—everywhere, there is "trouble." How, then, will "love" conquer "trouble"?
Dylan responds with the Ultimate Resolution. The Answer appears in two parts.
First, in "Property of Jesus" Dylan goes straight after those who criticized his
conversion by raising the charges brought against him, challenging his accusers
for their hard-hearted resentments, and declaring his allegiance to Jesus. The
song is powerful in its condemnation of the lifestyles of those who dwell in this
world at the expense of the next life. Dylan may have claimed that the criticism
was irrelevant, but this song recalls "Positively Fourth Street" and his musical
op-ed rhetoric. Among it all is a firm statement of spiritual perseverance. The
auteur seals the deal with as fine a metaphysical statement as anyone will find
in popular music. With "Every Grain of Sand" Dylan proclaims his pantheism.
Religious prescriptions and organizational dogma foster as much "trouble" as
any other worldly enterprise; for salvation, one need merely accept the majesty
of God's labors as they manifest in the most mundane items: grains of sand,
leaves on trees, strands of hair. Unlike those who have judged Dylan, Dylan for-
sakes worldly judgment in favor of heavenly acceptance. God is everywhere.
Praise Him. Marvel at His Work. The auteur explained his pantheism to Neil Hickey
and TV Guide years before his conversion to Christ:

> I can see God in a daisy. I can see God at night in the wind and rain. I see cre-
> ation just about everywhere. The highest form of song is prayer. King David's,
> Solomon's, the wailing of a coyote, the rumble of the earth. It must be wonder-
> ful to be God. There's so much going on out there that you can't get to it all.
> It would take longer than forever. You're talking to somebody who doesn't com-
> prehend the values most people operate under. Greed and lust I can under-
> stand, but I can't understand the values of definition and confinement.
> Definition destroys. Besides, there's nothing definite in this world.

Critics also noted the transitional qualities of the moral period's final installment. Robert Hilburn describes the record as a "frequently clumsy transitional
work in which Dylan expands his strict gospel base to include greater secular
imagery and concerns." Paul Nelson argues the album is a "churning mixture of
ultimate love (God's) and ultimate hate (Dylan's)" in which songs are "choked
with anger, rife with self-pity" and delivered by an artist who "sounds more like
an irate child who's just been spanked than a grown man who's found the answer
of answers." The Rolling Stone review closes: "If Bob Dylan is so full of God's love,
why is he so pissed off at the rest of the world?" Perhaps Dylan's retaliation was
not intended for "the rest of the world."

From Slow Train's warning to Saved's celebration to Shot of Love's transition,
this portion of the oeuvre demonstrates Dylan's ability to ply his trade. There are
no word games, no cloudy metaphors, no humor or satirical jabs, and for the
most part, no one-off recordings here. The great topical songwriter found a new
cause. The postman returned with messages of warning, then celebration. As the
spirit flowed through him, he received the message and delivered it in his particular style—a style grounded in American Song and its gospel traditions. Dylan's
mastery of the folk process extended to yet another musical genre as the

auteur co-opted a style more than suited to the creative task at hand. Dylan's 1997 comments to *Newsweek* put this period in a perspective clarified by time:

> Here's the thing with me and the religious thing. This is the flat-out truth: I find the religiosity and philosophy in the music. I don't find it anywhere else. Songs like "Let Me Rest on a Peaceful Mountain" or "I Saw the Light"—that's my religion. I don't adhere to rabbis, preachers, evangelists, all of that. I've learned more from the songs than I've learned from any of this kind of entity. The songs are my lexicon. I believe the songs.

Amen.

American song, revisited

We now enter the final and most protracted phase of Dylan's career, in which he struggled to find his artistic bearings, coped with a demanding commercial industry, endured his status as an international celebrity, and—somehow—developed a strategy that facilitated his professional survival. This period's work may be divided into four stages: 1983's *Infidels*, a long—occasionally strange—search for a comfortable professional orientation (involving 1985's *Empire Burlesque*, 1986's *Knocked Out Loaded*, 1988's *Down in the Groove*, 1989's *Oh Mercy*, and 1990's *Under the Red Sky*), two cover albums featuring "public domain" material (1992's *Good as I Been to You* and 1993's *World Gone Wrong*), and two award-winning projects, 1997's *Time Out of Mind* and 2001's *Love and Theft*. The American Song, Revisited period contains a thematic shift from the spiritual to the secular and a creative struggle with the writing/recording process through which Dylan searched for that thin wild mercury sound that disappeared somewhere in the digital, ensemble recording practices of the 1980s. As a result, the auteur employed a variety of producers and recording venues in his quest for that magical sound that releases his thoughts. Throughout this creative grind, Dylan consistently deployed an old solution to his recurrent problem: The Basement Strategy.

As we have seen, the Basement Strategy originated in Woodstock during the creative revival that accompanied Dylan's recovery from both his motorcycle accident and the celebrity mayhem that engulfed his career. The musical adventures with The Band allowed Dylan to return to his youth and the joys of musical discovery he experienced listening to late-night radio, exploring the records he obtained via those radio programs, and rummaging through his girlfriends' parents' and Dinkytown/New York friends' record collections. Dylan's relationship with American Song has always been revelatory, and it appears as though every time he found himself in a creative quandary, he returned to those musical "roots" for assistance. His entry into the New York folk scene, his adventures in impressionism, his return to music-making after the accident, his spiritual recovery from worldly ills, and now his efforts to discover his artistic balance all relied on that "inspiration behind the inspiration" for guidance.

Amidst the post-conversion struggle to discover a creative equilibrium,

Dylan invoked the Basement Strategy with regularity; for example, after Live Aid and during the prolonged rehearsals for his extensive tour with Tom Petty and the Heartbreakers (the True Confessions Tour) and, later, his brief stint with the Grateful Dead; throughout the protracted sessions with various bands at his Rundown Studios in Los Angeles in preparations for different tours and albums; with the extended musical encounters with younger musicians on his Malibu compound; via the musical therapy provided by the two cover albums; and finally, by way of the ultimate Basement exercise, *Love and Theft*. Many times in the 1980s musical colleagues reported that the unofficial music-making (i.e., rehearsals, studio warm-ups) was far superior to the official proceedings (live or recorded). To that end, Clinton Heylin quotes Tom Petty's ambition to "take the rehearsals on the stage" and Mikal Gilmore describes True Confession rehearsals with Christmas songs, gospel tunes, and stunning revisions of old Dylan tracks ("inventive versions of wondrous songs come and go and are never heard again"). That is, Dylan relished playing old songs in a spontaneous musical environment and only reluctantly recorded (or rehearsed) the material that warranted the assembly. This reliance on the Basement mentality—and the creative rejuvenation it fostered—would ultimately pull the auteur through a difficult professional reorientation.

The Basement Strategy paid off when, after the two cover albums and the discovery of a band capable of capturing the desired sound, Dylan settled into the seasoned veteran's role. No longer burdened by his past, he happily embraced it, enlivened it, and entered a phase that celebrated the music—not the musicians. At last, Bob Dylan discovered *his* secret to *his* longevity. At last, Bob Dylan released the celebrity postman. At last, Bob Dylan, the postman, could concentrate on delivering—and celebrating—that which matters to him most, his musical mail. But it would take over a decade to harvest the fruits of the Basement Strategy. Many critics will feast on, and others will cry over, the products of Dylan's prolonged search for professional sanity. It was as if the educational qualities of the folk-posturing phase returned for an extended stay as the auteur coped, once again, with external voices while he wrestled with a relentless internal drive. Here, as always, Dylan reached inside for inspiration and, once more, American Song provided the answer.

The American Song, Revisited phase opens with the second portion of the two-part transition to secular song, the *Infidels* project. With *Infidels*, Dylan shed the personal agenda associated with the moral period (especially *Shot of Love*'s counterattacks) and returned to a more diverse thematic orientation. *Infidels* (released November 1983) contains eight songs (running over 42 minutes) that address six topics: three societal complaints ("Neighborhood Bully," "License to Kill," and "Union Sundown"), a warning ("Man of Peace"), an individual complaint ("I and I"), a relational celebration ("Sweetheart Like You"), a relational plea ("Don't Fall Apart on Me Tonight"), and a flashback from yesteryear, the narrative impressionism that is "Jokerman." Heylin's chronology considers Dylan's choice of musicians "inspired," although he laments the decision to omit strong tracks such as "Blind Willie McTell" and "Foot of Pride." He dubs the work

Dylan's "great lost album" in that the inclusion of these two songs would have elevated the record's stature in the oeuvre. As released, the project most certainly prefaced the period of artistic ambivalence to come.

Much of the uncertainty was the result of the continued shift from spontaneous recording to more structured sessions. Dylan admitted to the *Los Angeles Times* that he had changed recording styles: "I decided (this time) to take my time like other people do. The extra little bit of time helped. That's going to be my pattern from now on. I'm not going to release a record until I feel it is worked out properly." For assistance, he turned to his *Slow Train* colleague, Mark Knopfler, as his producer. Dylan told the *Chicago Tribune*: "This was the easiest record I ever made because of Mark. He understood the songs so well. . . . Actually, we are soul mates. . . . He helped me make this record in a thousand ways, not only musically, which in itself would have been enough." Interestingly, once the soul mates completed their work (in May) and Knopfler departed, Dylan changed everything (in July). It is at this point, Heylin reports, that Dylan fell in love with the vocal overdub. He admitted to Paul Zollo that his songwriting on *Infidels* was overdone: "Lots of songs on that album got away from me. . . . They hung around too long. They were better before they were tampered with. Of course, it was me tampering with them." By "tampering" with the album's lyrics, vocals, and song order, Dylan communicated the uncertainty of his artistic situation. Heylin's biography concurs when he notes how "Angelina" (omitted from the final edition of *Shot of Love*) was composed via a rhyming dictionary and how "Foot of Pride" (omitted from *Infidels*) required an "unprecedented forty-three attempts" to complete. Dylan's soul mate was a brother in the studio, but the auteur desperately needed a parent, and this absence of leadership would control the next decade.

With the shift in production styles came a thematic reorientation as well. The three societal complaints—"Neighborhood Bully," "License to Kill," and "Union Sundown"—demonstrate Dylan's move from spiritual to political topics. "Bully" is a thinly veiled account of Israel's regional foreign policy, "License" articulates the self-destructive philosophies that guide governmental decision-making, and "Sundown" describes America's economic decline within the world financial community. Considered together, times are dangerous: The volatility of the Middle East, the recklessness of human nature, and the economic disorientation all point to the remedy presented in "Changing of the Guards." But there are no resolutions here, just complaints. Dylan explained his motives to the *Los Angeles Times*:

> That's the state of affairs right now. Maybe that's always been the state of affairs, but it seems especially true now. That's why I picked these particular songs for the album. I don't know if that (subject) appeals to people or not, but I felt I had to do these songs now. . . . I don't think any of my songs have been pessimistic. In every song I've written, I think, there has been a way out because that's just the nature of me.

If there is a "way out" articulated on these songs, it is—at most—implied.

The warning presented through "Man of Peace" reinforces the situations described in the societal complaints, but once more, no remedy is proposed. That all four songs are cut from the same narrative cloth as *Street-Legal* is certain. Dylan just disregarded the solution. Instead, he presents a classic relational celebration ("Sweetheart"), a standard relational plea ("Don't Fall Apart"), as well as a curious intrapersonal assessment ("I and I"—Tim Riley argues that the song "conveys the distance [Dylan] feels between his inner identity and the public face he wears") and its complement, the impressionistic "Jokerman." Why Dylan decided to omit the portrait "Blind Willie McTell" and the heavy-handed "Foot of Pride" (as well as "Tell Me," "Someone's Got a Hold of My Heart," and "Lord Protect My Child") is uncertain, although Heylin cites a Dylan remark about the predictability of music (mentioning an Eagles record) and his commitment to fight off such tendencies. Critics disagreed over the project's value, as reviews ranged from Jeff Nesin's contention that the record "is Dylan's move to grand larceny, lifting huge chunks of his former dazzling self in hopes of commercial coronation," to Christopher Connelly's, Steve Simels's, and Mark Rowland's counterpoints that the album is a "stunning recovery of the lyric and melodic powers that seemed to have all but deserted" Dylan, that it "gives us an overwhelming sense of a living, breathing, *thinking* human being at work," and that *Infidels* is "a powerful, angry, haunting, perversely beautiful record," respectively. The *Infidels* project rendered several strong songs—even if, as Heylin opines, "the reconfigured *Infidels* is a blurred Polaroid snapshot of an original self-portrait."

With that we turn to American Song, Revisited's second stage and the curious hodgepodge of albums designed, it seems, to keep product before consumers. The projects—*Burlesque* (1985), *Loaded* (1986), *Groove* (1988), *Mercy* (1989), and *Red Sky* (1990)—vary in their thematic emphases, production qualities, and level of engagement. In the mix we have Arthur Baker mixes, co-authored songs, covers, and a new songwriting strategy. At this point, Dylan is searching for his sound (among other things) and using different producers as his guide. The ever-present Basement Strategy seems to have provided his only refuge, and little of that found its way onto albums. And yet there is a distinctive rhythm present on several of these albums (*Mercy* and *Sky* are exceptions): a blend of gospel sentimentality and '50s rock and roll spirit. The gospel appears via the pensive, reflective tunes that often feature backing vocals (vocals that are sometimes good, sometimes not-so-good) that are paired with the rollicking echoes from days gone by. The search is on and Dylan's relentless drive to rediscover his rhythm will persist until he achieves that balance in 2001.

Empire Burlesque contains ten tracks (running 46:55 minutes), involves Tom Petty and the Heartbreakers (and a host of other musicians), and was produced by Baker, Dylan, Petty, and Dave Stewart (depending upon the track in question). Heylin's chronology reports that it required nine sessions to complete the thematically diverse project that features five relational complaints ("Seeing the Real You at Last," "I'll Remember You," "Never Gonna Be the Same Again," "When the Night Comes Falling from the Sky," and "Something's Burning, Baby"), two relational celebrations ("Emotionally Yours" and "Dark Eyes"), a societal complaint ("Clean Cut Kid"), a warning ("Trust Yourself"), and yet another piece of impressionism, "Tight Connection to My Heart (Has Anybody Seen My Love?)." The record is an interesting blend of production innovation and superficial lyrics (remember, this is the album that Paul Williams claims is full of movie dialogue). While "Clean Cut" (a complaint about the transformation of an average "kid" into a soldier who is ignored once his service ends) and "Trust Yourself" (an interesting song that rejects idolatry in favor of self-judgment) have something to say, most of these tunes are vacuous, contemporary pop songs.

Of the ten tracks, the relational complaints are dominant. Dylan deploys his traditional "attack the woman" strategy ("Seeing the Real You"), warns his partner that "she'll get what's coming to her" (to paraphrase "When the Night"), communicates the damage inflicted by a relationship ("Never Gonna"), and laments the passing of love ("I'll Remember" and "Something's Burning") through these first-person narratives. When combined with the two songs of relational celebration and the nebulous "Tight Connection," we enter the pop song's traditional domain—a characteristic exacerbated by Arthur Baker's production. Whether Dylan had relational matters on his mind or merely explored one of the tried-and-true pop topics, the record's thematic emphasis is without mystery. Robert Hilburn deems the album to be Dylan's "most assured and overtly commercial collection in years," while Kurt Loder proclaims it is "a blast of real rock & roll, funneled through a dense, rolling production" with lyrics that occasionally "turn out to be so obliquely insular there's no telling what they're really about," and Charles M. Young celebrates a lyrical shift: "Not a mean-spirited line on the record, and a lot about love as friendship and romance and illusion and disillusion and religion that'll ring the truth bell in your brain."

The emphasis on relational concerns continues with *Knocked Out Loaded* and its blend of covers, co-authored, and original material. Here Dylan (the album's principal producer) advances *Burlesque*'s gospel sounds via songs that say very little. The album contains eight tracks (running over 35 minutes), with five originals (three co-authored: "Brownsville Girl" with Sam Shepard, "I've Got My Mind Made Up" with Tom Petty, and "Under Your Spell" with Carole Bayer Sager), one traditional ("Precious Memories"—performed to a reggae beat), and two covers (Parker's "You Wanna Ramble" and Kristofferson's "They Killed Him"). All of the original material focuses on relational complaints (including the two Dylan songs, "Driftin' Too Far from Shore" and "Maybe Someday"). The blend of music contributes to the album's pacing. In fact, *Loaded*'s sounds are quite restless. The album features (in order) a '50s rocker, a hymn, a disco track, reggae, a pop tune, a theatrical ballad (with a gospel chorus), a Tom Petty–style '80s rocker, and blue-eyed soul. This is Dylan's original "greatest hits without the greatest hits" (his description of 2001's *Love and Theft*), because *Loaded* cruises across the American musical spectrum.

Thematically, the complaints seem to invoke all the usual images, ranging from fears that the narrator's partner is straying away ("Driftin' Too Far"), to the narrator's resignation to love his romantic interest even if they must remain apart ("Under Your Spell"), to the hope that someday the narrator's lover will understand what she had and how she lost it ("Maybe Someday"), to a relational escape in which the narrator leaves his love for everyone's favorite international destination, Libya ("Got My Mind"), to a protracted tale of love lost (the 11-minute "Brownsville"). The last entry takes us back to *Desire* and the narrative detail that Jacques Levy brought to Dylan's writing. Once more we observe that when Dylan brings his impressions to professional stage writers, these long, scene-driven, cinematic narratives emerge. Though the original material is focused thematically, the record's uneven qualities are its dominant characteristic. Critical responses seem to share that feature as well. For instance, Anthony DeCurtis argues that the record "suggests Dylan's utter lack of artistic direction," and Jon Pareles claims that it "sounds forced, using facile ambiguities to cover lack of inspiration." Other writers were more generous, such as Lennox Samuels's view that *Loaded* is "no masterpiece, it nevertheless is a generally appealing work that provides relief for fans grown weary of the singer-songwriter's lectures," and Harry Sumrall's contention that the record "is loaded with a brashness that borders on drunk and disorderly."

This creative trend advances with 1988's *Down in the Groove* (also produced by Dylan)—a ten-track piece (running 32 minutes) with six covers, two co-authored numbers (with Robert Hunter, the portrait "Silvio" and the relational celebration, "Ugliest Girl in the World"), and two originals: the celebratory "Death Is Not the End" and "Had a Dream about You, Baby." Although the inclusion of classics such as "Shenandoah" and "Rank Strangers to Me" (among others) suggests the invocation of the Basement Strategy in the recording studio, the originals appear to be uninspired. One exception, "Death Is Not," sounds as though it were a *Saved* outtake and demonstrates the moral period's lasting impact on the auteur's pen—an attribute that controls this album as much as any other. That is, the slow, respectful, gospel sound of "Death" joins the covers to provide a striking contrast to the rocking frolics of the album's other tracks. Thematically, the relational celebrations and portrait are, in a phrase, too sketchy to be meaningful. Hunter's influence is evident in the humor that makes "Ugliest Girl" and "Silvio" fun songs, with their "You bark at the moon, but you're mine" and "I'm the Man" story lines (although "Silvio" has its pensive moments). Perhaps Heylin's chronology captures *Groove*'s uneven qualities best: "The studio techniques [Dylan] had previously abhorred that 'touched-up' recordings, over-dubbed new instruments, and allowed new vocal tracks or 'punch ins,' were for the first time in full evidence." So much so that, once more, Dylan recast the record after test pressings appeared. Heylin concludes that the revised *Groove* joined the lackluster *Loaded* to confirm "in many an ex-fan's mind that the man had nothing left to say." Critics were also confused by the record, as David Fricke reports that it "zigs and zags all over the place," Ken Tucker says that it is "an eccentric but fascinating album," Holly Crenshaw argues that it "is not particularly innovative, moving or imaginative; it is merely entertaining," and Tim Holmes concludes that "Bob Dylan has finally achieved what no artist—major or minor—dreams of: the state of perfect inconsequentiality."

With that, we enter a curious point in the auteur's career during which Dylan teams with Daniel Lanois to render one of the oeuvre's stronger entries (1989's

Oh Mercy), only to return to the ambivalence of *Loaded/Groove* the following year. Dylan/Lanois achieve a sound reminiscent of Dylan/Wexler/Beckett's first entry, in that the author's sentiments are effectively conveyed in both the record's lyrical and musical dimensions. Lanois introduced his New Orleans sound just as Wexler brought Muscle Shoals to *Slow Train*, and Dylan delivered lyrics that complemented those musical platforms. Questions regarding the author's lyrical relevance were temporarily laid to rest with *Oh Mercy*.

Oh Mercy contains ten songs (running 39 minutes) that address three topics with varying degrees of clarity: six relational complaints ("Where Teardrops Fall," "Man in the Long Black Coat," "Most of the Time," "What Good Am I," "What Was It You Wanted," and "Shooting Star"), two societal complaints ("Political World" and "Everything Is Broken"), and two warnings ("Ring Them Bells" and "Disease of Conceit"). Recorded in New Orleans in just three sessions, the album demonstrates Lanois's control over his subject matter as well as the utility of leadership in the producer's chair for the occasionally wayward Bob Dylan. As we noted in the impulse section, by this time Dylan was aware of what was required to capture his sound, and his acquiescence to Lanois's direction facilitated the abandoning of the over-productions that dominated the 1980s (although the vocal overdubbing continued). Nevertheless, the omission of several strong songs (e.g., "Born in Time," "Dignity," and "Series of Dreams") indicates that the auteur's faith in his producer's decision-making was not complete.

The two songs of societal complaint articulate laundry lists of societal ills in a direct, insistent fashion. The author leaves little doubt about his stance in these quintessential examples of the Bob Dylan rap/complaint. Still, nowhere is any solution posed; instead, Dylan hammers home the consequences of secular leadership and the tenuous qualities of all things earthly. The two songs of warning—"Ring Them Bells" and "Disease of Conceit"—are not as straightforward with their specifics; however, Lanois's production contributes to Dylan's emphasis on the stories' prescriptions: The lost, incapable of distinguishing right from wrong, had better prepare for the end times ("Ring") and that conceit is a dreadful attribute that will follow you to your grave. Both songs exclaim "BEWARE" in Dylan's established style.

The heart of the album concentrates on the dominant theme of the 1980s: The relational complaint. These six songs range from the wistful angst of "Where Teardrops Fall" (a wherever-you-are-the-teardrops-follow theme), to the epic scenery of the mysterious tale of stolen love ("The Man in the Long Black Coat"), to the raw honesty and poignant emotion of "Most of the Time," to the closing song of remembrance, "Shooting Star." In every case, the Dylan/Lanois combination—well, as they say on Broadway, "It Works." And the critics agreed. Regarding the album's sound, the *Chicago Tribune* opens its review with "cancel Bob Dylan's obituary" before concluding that "here at last is an album whose musicality is as poetic as Dylan's lyrics," and *Spin* describes the Lanois/Dylan production as "high tech digital swamp music." The *San Francisco Examiner* states that "it's a recapitulation of Dylanalia: pessimistic and generalized social commentary, romantic reverie, and scathing spitefulness," the *Philadelphia*

Inquirer claims that the songs "ring with a mix of confessional vulnerability and raw power Dylan hasn't balanced as effectively since the mid-'70s," *Rolling Stone* contends that the lyrics contain "a plain-spoken directness with rich folkloric and Biblical shadings," *Stereo Review* argues that the record's "secret ingredient" is "humility," and the *New York Times* concludes: "For once in his recent history . . . *Oh Mercy* allows us to listen to a new Bob Dylan album without needing to forgive him anything. It may very well be the Bob Dylan album we want; whether it is the one we need is another matter." (What does that mean?)

What fails to work is the following record, 1990's *Under the Red Sky*. With David (Was) Weiss and Don Was as producers and an all-star cast of musicians present (e.g., Stevie Ray and Jimmie Vaughn, Elton John, Al Kooper, Slash, George Harrison, David Crosby, Bruce Hornsby), one might anticipate a rousing response to the creative momentum established by *Mercy*. This, unfortunately, was not (no pun intended) the case. The ten songs (running over 35 minutes) contain two "firsts" within its five thematic orientations. We have a romantic complaint ("Born in Time"), a celebration ("God Knows"), a societal complaint ("T.V. Talkin' Song"), and the two innovations: "Wiggle Wiggle" (a novelty song?) and six nonsense songs ("Under the Red Sky," "Unbelievable," "10,000 Men," "2 × 2," "Handy Dandy," and "Cat's in the Well"). The nonsense songs are presented in a fun, energetic manner. Their pop-song lyricism does not feature word games with playful/creative imagery or poetic impressions on a specific topic; here, Dylan's word machine is on "shuffle." To that end, the *Washington Post* observes that "part of the problem, it seems, is that Dylan arrived at the studio empty-handed." While the Newport Mod's mischievous wordplay extended songwriting's imagination, these expressions, as the *Post* suggests, take us in the opposite direction. It could have been worse: Dylan could have issued six different versions of "Little Sadie."

Heylin's biography raises several compelling points about this album and the artist's orientation during this portion of his career. One such observation appears in his interview with producer David Was: "I started to develop this unified field theory, that if something was too beautiful, if it looked like it was trying to please, then it was against his purposes. . . . It's not necessarily out of a lack of generosity of spirit. . . . It says more about . . . his inability to yield to audience-pleasing." The culprit, once again, appears to be Dylan's insistence on rewriting and overdubbing new lyrics. Reviews also raised questions about the writing, as *Musician* reports that the "lyrics often strike a somewhat bizarre but genuinely haunting balance between children's tales and biblical fables," *Rolling Stone* suggests that the record is "at best workmanlike; at worst, perfunctory" and calls *Red Sky* "a kind of Dylan-Lite," and the *New York Post* describes the lyrics as "not bad—they're ominous, pessimistic and determinedly enigmatic—but it's doubtful that today's high school students are going to use them to make the old case for Bob Dylan as great American poet." Though Heylin, Nelson, Evans, and Jeske are not so quick to condemn *Red Sky*, our narrative interpretation finds the album, in Jon Landau's term, "wanting." The Was sound and the all-stars' contributions notwithstanding, *Red Sky* suggests that the postman had, in fact, hired those Western Union boys and that their telegraphic, fragmented offerings represent a genuine anomaly within the oeuvre.

Red Sky (a reference to the Iron Range) introduced a seven-year period of reckoning; our second in the lifework. Dylan told the *New York Times* that he ceased recording new songs out of disillusionment. He explained: "Disillusion with the whole process of it. I started out when you could go in the studio and record your songs and leave. I don't remember when that changed. But I found myself spending more and more time in the studio doing less and less. There wasn't any gratification in it, really." To cope with the disillusionment, Dylan returned to the Basement Strategy to reorient as his established commercial machine issued a boxed set, greatest-hits compilations, and live performances. This time he remained on tour and refined his stage act. Heylin's biography reports that in the late 1980s Dylan experienced an "epiphany" with regard to performance and its value for him. From this point on, he approached his live shows—and the bands he employed—in a more engaging manner. Complementing that newfound orientation were the two cover albums, 1992's *Good As I Been to You* and 1993's *World Gone Wrong*. He described this invocation of the Basement Strategy to Jon Pareles: "Those old songs are my lexicon and my prayer book. . . . All my beliefs come out of those old songs, literally. . . . You can find all my philosophy in those old songs. I believe in a God of time and space, but if people ask me about that, my impulse is to point them back toward those songs."

Good As I Been was a gift to the muse by way of those "old songs" and an offering to Dylanology through its opportunity for extensive research into the thirteen traditionals that comprise the album. The auteur listed all the compositions as being in the traditional public domain, which served as a gold-plated invitation for the types of musical anthropology Dylanologists adore. More diversified music critics grasped the album's significance immediately, as the *New York Times*' Karen Schoemer proves: "Like some 1930's field recording, the album is more a document than art, more an attempt to preserve a moment than make a statement. . . . By re-examining his roots and reaffirming his past, Dylan has actually given a strange gift to the younger audience: the chance to experience, firsthand, some of the abrasive beauty and unapologetic dignity that must have jarred listeners 30 years ago. He's reintroducing himself, all over again." Peter Puterbaugh's insights are also compelling: "The album is a personal move, with Dylan endeavoring to reclaim his roots and recover his soul. Yet the signals it sends to the scene around him bear an indelible message: It's time to go back to beginnings if we hope to get back on course, not only in music but in other spheres of American life as well." *Rolling Stone*'s David Wild concurs: "This fascinating exploration of musical roots is more than a diversion for musicologists. *Good As I Been to You* shows that sometimes one can look back and find something that's both timeless and relevant." Similarly, David Hinckley maintains that the record "offers another detail for the vast canvas from which Dylan's own music came," and Larry Katz opines: "Dylan's performances of this folk material are often remarkable. His voice is crabbed, but assured. For the most part, the lyrics are clear, not mumbled. But what's most noteable [sic] is his guitar playing, which borders on masterful."

The auteur's stroll down memory lane continued with the Basement Strategy's second installment, 1993's *World Gone Wrong*. This time, Dylan contributed to the science that bears his name by including liner notes that feature musical histories and personal responses to the music contained within. The essay is a treasure, with its musical observations and distinctive writing style. This time the critics seem to focus on his performance more than anything else. *Spin's* Steve Anderson writes: "Achy but not anxious, soothing but not soporific, Dylan's vocals float across the melodies, his blurred timbre gently chafing notes instead of shredding them. . . . The result is no 'unplugged' rite of passion, where some middle-aged rocker turns reflective and avuncular in his dusking career . . . Dylan's singing is wily and nuanced enough to avoid a benign roots homage." Bill Flanagan observes in *Musician*: "Dylan demonstrates that he can say more in someone else's song than most artists can say in their own. . . . The weight of nobility and loss are as appropriate to this older Dylan's singing as anger and hunger were to the snarl of his youth." The *San Francisco Examiner's* Craig Marine reports: "These are tales of war, love gone mad, corruption, defilement, murder, redemption and longing. Dylan's attachment to this type of social documentation is evident in the intensity and effort he brings to his interpretations." And *Acoustic Guitar's* Derk Richardson places the two albums in context: "*World Gone Wrong* both illuminates *Good As I Been to You* as a necessary first step and lifts the curtain on a performer willing to express the kind of complex, ambivalent self-reflection that his best work used to enkindle in his audience." Although there were reviews that decried Dylan's singing and denounced the work as contractual filler, most critics emphasized Dylan's commitment to American Song and the album's potential for revivification.

The reorientation was almost complete as Dylan discovered a professional comfort zone that returned him to his youthful ambitions (recall his remarks to Zollo: "Being a musician was always first and foremost"). As a new century approached and Dylan neared his fortieth year in music, he finally achieved—and was comfortable with—that original aspiration. In 1997, he explained his stance to Jon Pareles:

> A lot of people don't like the road . . . but it's as natural to me as breathing. I do it because I'm driven to do it, and I either hate it or love it. I'm mortified to be on the stage, but then again, it's the only place where I'm happy. It's the only place you can be who you want to be. You can't be who you want to be in daily life. I don't care who you are, you're going to be disappointed in daily life. But the cure-all for all that is to get on the stage, and that's why performers do it. But in saying that, I don't want to put on the mask of celebrity. I'd rather just *do* my work and see it as a trade.

An artistically reborn Dylan continued his massive touring schedule throughout the mid-nineties. He paused and rejoined Daniel Lanois for an 11-song exploration (running 73 minutes) of love and loving relationships with their 1997, Grammy Award–winning work, *Time Out of Mind*. The nine romantic elegies present mature feelings about love lost and love's obsessive qualities; no word games or cavalier commentaries here as Dylan conveys an emotional depth that can only be derived from personal experience. The deep-seated irony of "Love Sick," the bouncy devotion of "Dirt Road Blues," the emotional slavery of "Standing in the Doorway," the anguish of "Million Miles," "Cold Irons Bound," and "Not Dark Yet," the rationalizations of "'Til I Fell in Love with You," and the haunting resignation of "Tryin' to Get to Heaven" communicate an unflinching honesty regarding loving relationships and life's situations. It is as if Dylan reports that irrational romantic angst is a lifelong condition—not the unique province of youthful inexperience.

Time Out of Mind also features the loving pledge "Make You Feel My Love" and a personal testimony, the 16-minute saga, "Highlands." "Make You" takes us back to the days when Dylan songs filled the airwaves as other artists did well with his material (e.g., Garth Brooks and Billy Joel). The auteur's version uses the piano–organ combination to create a romantic prayer that pledges nothing less than total subservience. "Highlands," on the other hand, is yet another extension of the satire-turned-saga narrative style initiated with "Lily, Rosemary and the Jack of Hearts." This time, Dylan wraps two extended (and thoughtful) testimonials around a "Lily"-like account of an encounter with a Boston waitress. The waitress story is rich in narrative detail, presenting simple yet poignant snippets of a typical conversation in an everyday setting. The two introspective testimonials sound like someone writing their diary after a thoughtful walk. The statements appear shallow at first and the waitress story detracts from the continuity; nevertheless, the narrator's reflections reveal something of himself and his audience. Sarah Vowell describes the song in this fashion:

> "Highlands" is so huge that it needs its very own map. If this is just a song, then a Van Eyck altarpiece is just a painting. At 16 minutes, it's a whole world; a living, breathing, mixed-up confusion of narrative, musings, wisecracks, and asides. Set atop a country blues vamp produced by Daniel Lanois to sound at least as old as the composer, its themes and allusions include nature, wanderlust, dreams, irrelevance, self-reliance, cosmetology, rock'n'roll, aging, Greek mythology, Negro spirituals, customer service, portraiture, literature, dogs, voter registration, and desire. It's at turns hilarious, poetic, and true.

Although knowledgeable Dylanologists such as Clinton Heylin dismiss *Time* for its lyrical samplings and tired demeanor, the rest of the musical world exploded in its praise. *Billboard* deems the record "a brilliant album from an artist with an endless store of genius," and the *Christian Science Monitor* maintains that "Dylan reaffirms his position as the preeminent composer and wordsmith of the rock era." *Time's* Christopher Farley writes: "Dylan seems to be haunted by an imaginary, unnamed muse who has come and gone, leaving him loveless and listless, feeling out of fashion and out of time. The situation is desperate, but the album is cathartic and ultimately hopeful: there is salvation, and it comes from within." The *Chicago Tribune* praises Lanois's efforts ("With Lanois's painterly production giving the songs a three-dimensional depth, the arrangements frame Dylan's voice as few recent recordings have") before its thematic analysis: "It is not a comforting message, but for Dylan that was never the point. He illuminates rather than sugarcoats, subverts rather than reassures, insinuates rather than preaches. And in the quiet mastery of his '90s work, he brings a new dimension to that legacy." And the *Wall Street Journal's* Jim Fusilli argues: "This is right-brain Dylan, where the source isn't Rimbaud or Verlaine, Greek mythology or the Old Testament, but Sonny Boy Williamson and the Mississippi Sheiks, and emotion lays waste to philosophy and reason." In virtually every case, reviewers praise Dylan's growth through acceptance and rejoice in his continued relevance.

It took an awful lot of experimenting and searching, but the Basement Strategy won, and the auteur reveled in American Song. Dylan's newfound comfort as a professional musician enabled a rigorous approach to touring with colleagues Larry Campbell, Tony Garnier, David Kemper, and Charlie Sexton. The year 2001 witnessed extensive tours of Japan, Australia, Europe, and the United States; and Dylanologists charted every show, logged every song, and—rest assured—cherished every moment. With his sixtieth birthday on May 24, 2001, journalists paused to consider Dylan's impact on the art form he fathered 40 years ago. CNN's Jamie Allen says that Dylan "is to modern rock music what Michelangelo or Leonardo Da Vinci was to the Italian Renaissance"; the *Washington Post's* Tim Page writes that "ultimately, Dylan is likely to be remembered as one of those defiant American originals, like Philip Glass or Georgia O'Keeffe, who follow one central vision through myriad guises with single-minded intensity"; the *Philadelphia Inquirer's* Tom Moon reports that Dylan "has undergone complete job retraining" and now "aims to be a literate Little Richard" who embraces "the musical attitudes of the blues demons he idolized"; the *New York Times'* Ann Powers claims that the auteur is "the Devil's Triangle of rock 'n' roll" and quotes Pete Townshend's view that assessing Dylan's personal impact is "like asking how I was influenced by being born"; and on the day of his birth, the *Minneapolis Star Tribune's* editors declared: "Happy birthday, man, from all your friends back home." Correspondingly, the magazine that he played some role in naming solicited comments from a variety of artists for "an appreciation of Dylan at 60." *Rolling Stone* cites U2's Bono: "No matter where you are in your life, there's a Dylan record that helps you map out the locale"; Joni Mitchell: "No one has come close to being as good a writer as Dylan"; Tom Petty: "I think he really is a kind of roving-minstrel type, like from the medieval period. . . . I most value Bob's honesty—he's a very upfront person and a true gentleman"; and author/professor Camille Paglia: "Dylan is a perfect role model to present to aspiring artists. As a young man, he had blazing vision and tenacity. He rejected creature comforts and lived on pure will and instinct. He catered to no one but preserved his testy eccentricity and defiance. And his best work shows how the creative imagination operates—in a hallucinatory stream of sensations and emotions that perhaps even the embattled artist does not fully understand." Dylan, of course, remained silent—no interviews, no comments, no public celebrations.

The most demonstrative evidence of the Basement Strategy's victory did not appear until September 11, 2001. The irony that America's poet unveiled his personal tribute to American Song on a day that forever changed the country is remarkable. Dylanologists around the globe waited in burning anticipation for *Love and Theft's* release only to have their spirits dampened by madmen with box cutters. That horror aside, Dylan described the artistic evolution that facilitated *Love* to *USA Today*:

> In the early '90s, the media lost track of me, and that was the best thing that could happen. . . . It was crucial, because you can't achieve greatness under media scrutiny. You're never allowed to be less than your legend. When the media picked up on me again five or six years later, I'd fully developed into the performer I needed to be and was in a position to go any which way I wanted. The media will never catch up again. Once they let you go, they cannot get you back. It's metaphysical. And it's not good enough to retreat. You have to be considered irrelevant.

With artistic peace of mind, a road-tested group of musical comrades (joined by famed organist Augie Meyers), and the creative momentum those two conditions generated, Bob Dylan and his band rendered a historical tribute to that all-important "inspiration behind the inspiration." Musically, Dylan deployed the various instrumental styles of American Song to his strategic ends. He explained to Robert Hilburn how the new work differed from its award-winning predecessor: "I sort of blueprinted it this time to make sure I didn't get caught without up-tempo songs. If you hear any difference on this record—why it might flow better—it's because as soon as an up-tempo song comes over, then it's slowed down, then back up again. There's more pacing." The record features rockabilly, country, blues, show tune, Tin Pan Alley pop, romantic ballad, and rock and roll sounds. In many respects, it is as if Harry Smith collected his songs, hired the tightest band he could find, and recorded their versions of his acquisitions.

Thematically, *Love* takes us back to *Highway 61* or *Blonde on Blonde* because Dylan uses these diverse American musical sounds to frame his unique form of impressionism. The Dylan-produced 12 tracks (running 57:32 minutes) feature three songs of relational complaint (*Mind* holdover "Mississippi," "Summer Days," and "Sugar Baby"), a life complaint ("Lonesome Day Blues"), a personal proclamation ("Bye and Bye"), and seven songs of narrative impressionism deploying a variety of musical styles: a traditional rocker ("Tweedle Dee and Tweedle Dum"), a Tin Pan Alley–vaudeville number ("Floater [Too Much to Ask]"), a roots tune ("High Water [for Charlie Patton]"), a 1950s rocker ("Honest with Me"), an airy pop tune ("Po' Boy"), a heavy-handed blues ("Cry a While"), and a "moon and June" show tune ("Moonlight"). That Dylan described the album to Edna Gundersen as a "greatest-hits album . . . without the hits" demonstrates his avocation of the Basement Strategy philosophy (and echoes a strategy he unveiled in *Knocked Out Loaded*).

The elegies vary in their clarity. "Mississippi" directly complains about the relational situation in question as a preface for a plea for perseverance—a "things are tough, but let's stick together" piece. "Summer Days" is a cloudy, evasive complaint that seems to focus on the struggles associated with the

relationship. "Sugar Baby" is a dreamy, wistful assessment of seasoned life lessons as they apply to current relational challenges. And "Lonesome Day" is a
litany of complaints. The narrator uses a host of negative life events (e.g., losing
his father, brother, sister, and mother) as a preface to commentary about a
relationship and its inherent difficulties. At times, these songs wander and drift
toward impressionism; however, they consistently stress the elegiac qualities of
their subject matter in a fashion that separates them from the organized wordplay that consumes the record.

When Augie Meyers was asked about the *Love and Theft* recording sessions,
he told *Rolling Stone* that Dylan would "fool around for a while with a song, then
we'd cut it. And he'd say, 'I think I'm gonna write a couple more verses,' sit down
and write five more verses. Each verse had six or eight lines. It's complicated
stuff, and he was doing it right there." Evidence of Meyers's observations exists
in the seven songs of narrative impressionism that control *Love and Theft*. Not
only did Dylan return to his beloved style of record production, he rediscovered
the spontaneous approach to writing that rendered some of his finest work. The
impressionistic portrait in "Tweedle Dee" that charts the changing nature of the
two characters' relationship, the utter chaos of "Floater" and "High Water" with
their crazy characters and scenes, the knock-knock jokes and sarcasm in "Po'
Boy," and the state-of-the-art examples of Dylan's narrative impressionism that
are "Honest" and "Cry a While" demonstrate the extent to which the auteur was
in his element, free to explore his mental impulses while anchoring his impressions by way of the songs' musical structures. How rare to observe an artist
with a 40-year career reach back to his or her cumulative experience and generate a work that so fully represents their life's work.

Critical responses to the auteur's 43rd album were, to say the least, intense.
In its five-star rating, *Rolling Stone* opines: "The music evokes an America of
masquerade and striptease, a world of seedy old-time gin palaces, fast cash, poison whiskey, guilty strangers trying not to make eye contact, pickpockets slap-
ping out-of-towners on the back." For Sheffield, the album "comes on as a musical autobiography that also sounds like a casual, almost accidental history of
the country. Relaxed, magisterial, utterly confident in every musical idiom he
touches, Dylan sings all twelve songs in a voice that sounds older than he is, a
grizzled con man croaking biblical blues and Tin Pan Alley valentines out of the
side of his mouth while keeping one eye on the exit." Falling one star behind *Rolling
Stone* is the *Los Angeles Times* (it has a four-star system) and Robert Hilburn's
view: "This is possibly the first Dylan album since 'Highway 61 Revisited' in which
the music catches your ear before the lyrics do. . . . Dylan infuses the songs with
the thoughtful, provocative and teasing wordplay that is his particular pop
genius." After noting how "individual songs are crammed with competing images
and ideas," Hilburn concludes: "For much of its 57 minutes, 'Love and Theft' feels
as if someone has gone back and applied the challenging, literary-minded, introspective elements of Dylan's revolutionary songwriting approach to the musical
settings that preceded him—and who better to do that than Dylan himself?" The

Dallas Observer reports: "Dylan untangles himself from history's suffocating roots and invents a new language—that of the post-modern troubadour-crooner-bluesman-lounge-lizard. . . . If *Time Out of Mind* was the soundtrack for the forthcoming funeral . . . then *Love and Theft* is the album meant to be put on at the wake." The *Cleveland Plain Dealer* claims: "It's a game of masks in which Dylan reprises familiar characters: the wanderer, the judge, the hobo, the workingman, the stray cat. . . . [The record] is a valentine delivered by a wounded romantic to a music he keeps on stealing from, lovingly."

Uncharacteristically, Dylan commented freely on *Love's* thematic orientation, as he told *Rolling Stone's* Mikal Gilmore: "The whole album deals with power. If life teaches us anything, it's that there's nothing that men and women won't do to get power. The album deals with power, wealth, knowledge and salvation—the way I look at it." On another occasion, he told *USA Today*: "I've never recorded an album with more autobiographical songs. . . . This is the way I really feel about things. It's not me dragging around a bottle of absinthe and coming up with Baudelairian poems. It's me using everything I know to be true." In a preview interview with the same publication he told Edna Gundersen that the "songs don't have any genetic history" in terms of his previous work; rather the music "is an electronic grid, the lyrics being the substructure that holds it all together." Dylan's comfort is evident in his music, the means through which it was created, and his public commentary. After years of struggle, the music prevailed.

The American Song, Revisited phase takes the oeuvre full circle. For a final look back, I turn to Greil Marcus's "Smithville" metaphor, for I find it instructive. If, for the sake of discussion, "Smithville" and American Song are interchangeable, and every artist who contributes to American Song's development is declared "Creator" for a day, what would Bob Dylan's "Smithville" look like? I think I know. Bob Dylan's Smithville would be a rebellious, intense little town where everybody *thinks* they know *everything* about one another, gossip is the local vernacular, and relational gamesmanship is the preferred recreational alternative. Where people share the whiskey jug on Saturday nights, cheat during card games, and drunkenly sing along to "Positively Fourth Street," "Saved," and "Highway 61 Revisited." Where people fight off their hangovers, praise their covenant women, worship their lord, and fear the slow train's approach on Sundays. Where people assemble after the Fourth of July costume parade to hear the local youth choir belt out "Desolation Row" and "With God on Our Side." Where diabolical lovers meet in local parks and serenade one another with "I Believe in You" and "Idiot Wind." Where the local college offers extension courses on musical anthropology, abnormal psychology, and relational game theory. Bob Dylan's Smithville would be *controlled* by an *uncontrollable* irony where all rules would be twisted in the ultimate game of Glissendorf: "What's the next-to-last thing to come to your mind just now? What? Alright then, I won!"

chapter four

the exemplars

We have, thus far, established the artist's biography, creative impulse, and life-work. Now we turn to the stylistic tendencies that generated that work and the exemplars that demonstrate those creative strategies in action. Here, then, are the artistic signatures that rendered the *auteur* and his *oeuvre*. To achieve this end, I merely return to the art and allow it to speak for itself. In presenting the oeuvre, I described the songs in terms of their individual narrative qualities, therefore we considered the characters, values, and plots evidenced in the respective songs and their thematic arrangement on the individual albums. I also organized those works by their creative contexts, and in turn, charted the ebb and flow of the unfolding career—a lifework intuitively dedicated to the preservation and extension of American Song. Though he occasionally wavered from his mission, in the end we observed how the "inspiration behind the inspiration" persevered and facilitated the continuation of Bob Dylan's musical career.

When we construe the individual songs, albums, and eras that comprise the lifework, five narrative strategies emerge that not only recur throughout the oeuvre, they dominate it. The narrative strategies—the *complaint*, the *celebration*, the *satire*, *narrative impressionism*, and *wordplay*—duck and weave their way through the various songs and, at times, control certain projects. *Street-Legal* is a statement of unrelenting negativity. *Saved* is a celebratory revival and a call for personal salvation. *Bringing It All Back Home* and *Highway 61 Revisited* are monuments of artistic innovation that liberated songwriters and transformed their art form. Though no single project focuses on the satire, it is the only story form to evolve systematically over time. The writer's satirical tendencies often suggest his state of mind and yield evidence regarding his professional orientation.

When considered chronologically, the lifework assumes certain rhythms of expression that embrace their creative contexts. The complaint controls the folk-posturing period and *Another Side* as it solidifies its standing as the oeuvre's bedrock story form. Whether he complains about relational or societal matters, Dylan's intensity is the defining characteristic of this storytelling strategy. Impressionistic wordplay governs the Newport Mod era as Dylan expands his art's creative boundaries. In pushing his creativity, the author also challenged his physical well-being; thus after the Woodstock respite and the transitional statements within *John Wesley Harding*, a reinvigorated Dylan explores affairs of the heart for an extended, seven-album period. There he celebrates as much as he complains (well, *almost!*) about relationships and their consequences. *Legal's* negativity introduces the moral period's three-phase spiritual journey in which Dylan forewarns, celebrates, and, afterwards, resolves his personal quest for ultimate knowledge. From that point on his stories focus on relationships, with occasional asides for social issues, celebrity portraits, or satirical commentaries.

Throughout the respective projects we note the intensity and innovation, the adaptation and cultivation, as well as the success and failure of Dylan's art. His songs complain, celebrate, satirize, and fondle the various emotions associated with life's experiences in an idiosyncratic, adventurous manner. While Dylan cultivates these feelings, he applies an American worldview that informs the content and style of his subsequent observations. To claim that Dylan is grounded firmly in American Song—and that those traditions provided signposts for his artistic journey—is supported by none other than the work itself. As he told David Gates about the religious conversion controversy, "I've learned more from the songs" than anything else in life.

From *Bob Dylan* through *Love and Theft*, the auteur has complained. The only variables involve the intensity of the emotion and the internal workings of the portrayal. The *Freewheelin'* project sets the pace for the entire oeuvre as it establishes the two domains of negativity: relational and societal issues. The romantic elegies "Down the Highway" and "Don't Think Twice, It's All Right" (and the three adaptations) complement the societal statements "Blowin' in the Wind," "Masters of War," and "Oxford Town" to inaugurate a narrative rhythm that extends for over 40 years. The momentum continues with *The Times They Are a-Changin'*, except, this time, the emphasis is clearly on social topics. "Hollis Brown," "With God on Our Side," "Only a Pawn in Their Game," "North Country Blues," and "Hattie Carroll" constitute a hallmark of topical complaint (the relational elegies "One Too Many Mornings" and "Boots of Spanish Leather" join in the fun as well). Throughout we observe the *intensity* of Dylan's pen as he not only complains, he passionately embraces the injustices depicted in his songs. *Another Side* reverses that trend and takes us into relational concerns, as Dylan's songwriting redirects his "finger-pointing" genre (e.g., "It Ain't Me, Babe," "I Don't Believe You," and the devastating "Ballad in Plain D"). These grievances fade for the next few projects as Dylan's wordplay emerges and provides a much-needed respite from this rage of negativity.

The relational complaint returns with *Blonde's* seven entries (e.g., "One of Us Must Know," "Just Like a Woman," "Most Likely You Go Your Way") and continues for seven albums (not including *Portrait* and *Dylan*). Many of these works feature a blend of complaint and celebration as Dylan concentrates on the vacillating qualities of loving relationships throughout the 1970s. Of course, *Blood on the Tracks* takes the relational angst theme to new levels of intensity, with *Desire* and *Street-Legal* echoing those emotions—each in its own way. After *Legal's* abject negativity, the complaint spawns a thematic variation with the rise of the "warning" strategy (a style that dominates *Slow Train*). These songs establish the negative as a preface to The Answer that flows from the conversion rhetoric. The "warning" theme returns in *Saved's* "Are You Ready" and reappears via *Infidels'* "Man of Peace," *Burlesque's* "Trust Yourself," and *Mercy's* "Ring Them Bells" and "Disease of Conceit." Once the spiritual shot has been fired across the worldly bow, the American Song, Revisited phase concentrates on relational concerns with dashes of societal complaint appearing from time to time (e.g., *Infidels'* "Neighborhood Bully" and "Union Sundown" along with *Mercy's* "Political World" and "Everything Is Broken"). The Daniel Lanois productions address the dark side of human relationships in a particularly relentless, moody fashion. Finally, *Love and Theft's* "Mississippi" and "Summer Days" advance the relational grievances that control *Time* just as the life complaint "Lonesome Day Blues" provides a stellar example of this foundational storytelling tactic. There is no question that the complaint is the most frequently deployed narrative strategy in Bob Dylan's lifework.

First, we consider the strategy's application as a tool of social protest. When Dylan received recognition as the voice of his generation, it was because of the anger conveyed through songs such as "Masters of War." The song's strategy is self-evident:

> Come you masters of war
> You that build all the guns
> You that build the death planes
> You that build the big bombs
> You that hide behind walls
> You that hide behind desks
> I just want you to know
> I can see through your masks
>
> You that never done nothin'
> But build to destroy
> You play with my world
> Like it's your little toy
> You put a gun in my hand
> And you hide from my eyes
> And you turn and run farther
> When the fast bullets fly
>
> Like Judas of old
> You lie and deceive
> A world war can be won
> You want me to believe
> But I see through your eyes

And I see through your brain
Like I see through the water
That runs down my drain

You fasten the triggers
For the others to fire
Then you set back and watch
When the death count gets higher
You hide in your mansion
As young people's blood
Flows out of their bodies
And is buried in the mud

You've thrown the worst fear
That can ever be hurled
Fear to bring children
Into the world
For threatening my baby
Unborn and unnamed
You ain't worth the blood
That runs in your veins

How much do I know
To talk out of turn
You might say that I'm young
You might say I'm unlearned
But there's one thing I know
Though I'm younger than you
Even Jesus would never
Forgive what you do

Let me ask you one question
Is your money that good
Will it buy you forgiveness
Do you think that it could
I think you will find
When your death takes its toll
All the money you made
Will never buy back your soul

And I hope that you die
And your death'll come soon
I will follow your casket
In the pale afternoon
And I'll watch while you're lowered
Down to your deathbed
And I'll stand o'er your grave
'Till I'm sure that you're dead

"Masters of War" is a most aggressive piece of topical songwriting. Through-out, Dylan is systematic and direct. He opens by identifying the enemy (people who provide arms and hide behind their roles), moves to the wrongdoing they foster (playing with people's lives), portrays the disregard that fosters the militarism (they load the guns for others to use while they enjoy a life of luxury), turns to the condition they have created (people fear procreation), warns of heavenly retribution, pauses—once again—to question the villain's motivation (is money that important?), and concludes with the ultimate victory and the narrator's promise to gloat over their deaths. The "Masters" are, in a word, devils: They play with people's lives, they lie, and they do it all for money. Interestingly, although the narrator promises to relish in their deaths, there is no aspiration for worldly retribution—that is left for the after life, and in so doing, confirms the belief that the villains have perpetrated the Ultimate Wrong: An evil that cannot be properly punished in this life. Tim Riley may consider the song to be "acerbic to the point of absurdity," nevertheless it is quintessential Dylan. The style holds for our next example, the relational complaint "Idiot Wind":

Someone's got it in for me, they're planting stories in the press
Whoever it is I wish they'd cut it out but when they will I can only guess.
They say I shot a man named Gray and took his wife to Italy,
She inherited a million bucks and when she died it came to me.
I can't help it if I'm lucky.

People see me all the time and they just can't remember how to act
Their minds are filled with big ideas, images and distorted facts.
Even you, yesterday you had to ask me where it was at,
I couldn't believe after all these years, you didn't know me better than that
Sweet lady.

Idiot wind, blowing every time you move your mouth,
Blowing down the backroads headin' south.
Idiot wind, blowing every time you move your teeth,
You're an idiot, babe.
It's a wonder that you still know how to breathe.

I ran into the fortune-teller, who said beware of lightning that might strike
I haven't known peace and quiet for so long I can't remember what it's like.
There's a lone soldier on the cross, smoke pourin' out of a boxcar door,
You didn't know it, you didn't think it could be done, in the final end he won
   the wars
After losin' every battle.

I woke up on the roadside, daydreamin' 'bout the way things sometimes are
Visions of your chestnut mare shoot through my head and are makin' me
   see stars.
You hurt the ones that I love best and cover up the truth with lies.
One day you'll be in the ditch, flies buzzin' around your eyes,
Blood on your saddle.

Idiot wind, blowing through the flowers on your tomb,
Blowing through the curtains in your room.
Idiot wind, blowing every time you move your teeth,
You're an idiot, babe.
It's a wonder that you still know how to breathe.

It was gravity which pulled us down and destiny which broke us apart
You tamed the lion in my cage but it just wasn't enough to change my
    heart.
Now everything's a little upside down, as a matter of fact the wheels have
    stopped,
What's good is bad, what's bad is good, you'll find out when you reach the
    top
You're on the bottom.

I noticed at the ceremony, your corrupt ways had finally made you blind
I can't remember your face anymore, your mouth has changed, your eyes
    don't look into mine.
The priest wore black on the seventh day and sat stone-faced while the
    building burned.
I waited for you on the running boards, near the cypress trees, while the
    springtime turned
Slowly into autumn.

Idiot wind, blowing like a circle around my skull,
From the Grand Coulee Dam to the Capitol.
Idiot wind, blowing every time you move your teeth,
You're an idiot, babe.
It's a wonder that you still know how to breathe.

I can't feel you anymore, I can't even touch the books you've read
Every time I crawl past your door, I been wishin' I was somebody else
    instead.
Down the highway, down the tracks, down the road to ecstasy,
I followed you beneath the stars, hounded by your memory
And all your ragin' glory.

I been double-crossed now for the very last time and now I'm finally free,
I kissed goodbye the howling beast on the borderline which separated you
    from me.
You'll never know the hurt I suffered nor the pain I rise above,
And I'll never know the same about you, your holiness or your kind of love,
And it makes me feel so sorry.

Idiot wind, blowing through the buttons of our coats,
Blowing through the letters that we wrote.
Idiot wind, blowing through the dust upon our shelves,
We're idiots, babe.
It's a wonder we can even feed ourselves.

Here the invective shifts from a societal to a relational context, but the intensity persists. The song has a straightforward rhythm in that it opens with a general complaint about the narrator's treatment in the media and the difficulty in dealing with others, pauses for the accusatory chorus, returns for more general complaint and a statement of perseverance, and then turns to the song's target. The narrator attacks the former lover for hurting his loved ones and lying, enjoys revenge (the "Rolling Stone" rhetoric about flies in the eyes and blood on the saddle), attacks once more in the chorus, and suddenly gives into personal anguish (the narrator cannot pick up the person's possessions and is confounded by memories). Dylan's character tries to muster the strength for one last attack before succumbing to the pain and accepting a measure of responsibility for the situation.

These two complaints demonstrate Dylan's confrontational pen at work. These are not causal accounts of societal subjugation or relational deterioration with an occasional insight about the situation. No. These are fierce attacks. The targets are villainous—one is a devil, the other an idiot, both are traitors. Jesus will not absolve the devilish "Masters of War" and their demise (and day in hell) is certain—it is only a matter of time. While the narrator certainly wishes ill upon the ex-lover in "Idiot Wind," we observe a shift in attitude toward the end with the story's resolution focusing on a shared responsibility. The certainty in "Masters" wanes in "Idiot" as the narrator's memories render emotional confusion. Still, not all Dylan complaints are this intense. There are songs such as "Boots of Spanish Leather" and "I Don't Believe You" that chastise their targets through the moral of the story ("Boots") or a direct complaint ("I Don't Believe") in a less vitriolic manner. And yet when Dylan turns up the intensity—as in "Dirge" or "Foot of Pride"—he takes a traditional story form to new places.

Our second strategy, the celebration, first appears in Dylan's debut work. "Talkin' New York" and "Song to Woody" initiate the "in praise of thee I sing" approach through two songs that complain about the difficulties the traveling musician endures before celebrating "the road" and its rewards in the stories' resolutions. The tactic returns briefly with "Bob Dylan's Blues" on *Freewheelin'* before shifting thematic gears from personal to societal topics in *The Times They Are a-Changin'*. There the title cut and "When the Ship Comes In" celebrate the ultimate victory achieved by the acceptance of a change in social consciousness and the benefits of perseverance, respectively. *Times* also celebrates a personal transition in "Restless Farewell" when the author bids goodbye to the folk-posturing period. After the Newport Mod's word games, the celebration strategy returns with force. Beginning with *Harding*'s two songs of relational veneration ("Down along the Cove" and "I'll Be Your Baby Tonight"), the Americana period contains a level of relational revelry unlike any other phase in the oeuvre. *Skyline*'s five songs of loving observance (e.g., "To Be Alone with You," "Peggy Day," "Lay Lady Lay," and "Tonight I'll Be Staying Here with You"), *Morning*'s six songs of romantic bliss (e.g., "If Not for You," "New Morning," and "The Man in Me"), *Waves'* six accounts of relational joy (e.g., "Tough Mama," "You Angel You," and "Wedding Song"), and later, *Desire*'s "Mozambique" convey sentiments that represent a striking balance to the relational negativity interspersed throughout those albums.

The celebration strategy reaches its peak in *Saved*. *Saved* is a testament to spiritual contentment as Dylan declares his devotion ("Saved"), praises his "Covenant Woman," and relishes his commitment to Christ ("Solid Rock" and "Pressing On"). The celebrations end with *Saved*. Although we pause for brief moments of relational veneration from time to time (*Infidels*' "Sweetheart Like You," *Burlesque*'s "Emotionally Yours" and "Dark Eyes," *Groove*'s "Had a Dream about You, Baby" and "Ugliest Girl in the World," and *Red Sky*'s "God Knows"), the celebration story form gives way to other matters. For our first example, consider the societal celebration, "The Times They Are a-Changin'":

> *Come gather 'round people*
> *Wherever you roam*
> *And admit that the waters*
> *Around you have grown*
> *And accept it that soon*
> *You'll be drenched to the bone.*
> *If your time to you*
> *Is worth savin'*
> *Then you better start swimmin'*
> *Or you'll sink like a stone*
> *For the times they are a-changin'.*
>
> *Come writers and critics*
> *Who prophesize with your pen*
> *And keep your eyes wide*
> *The chance won't come again*
> *And don't speak too soon*
> *For the wheel's still in spin*
> *And there's no tellin' who*
> *That it's namin'.*
> *For the loser now*
> *Will be later to win*
> *For the times they are a-changin'.*
>
> *Come senators, congressmen*
> *Please heed the call*
> *Don't stand in the doorway*
> *Don't block up the hall*
> *For he that gets hurt*
> *Will be he who has stalled*
> *There's a battle outside*
> *And it is ragin'.*
> *It'll soon shake your windows*
> *And rattle your walls*
> *For the times they are a-changin'.*

Come mothers and fathers
Throughout the land
And don't criticize
What you can't understand
Your sons and your daughters
Are beyond your command
Your old road is
Rapidly agin'.
Please get out of the new one
If you can't lend your hand
For the times they are a-changin'.

The line it is drawn
The curse it is cast
The slow one now
Will later be fast
As the present now
Will later be past
The order is
Rapidly fadin'.
And the first one now
Will later be last
For the times they are a-changin'.

The song rejoices in the evolution as it simultaneously issues a systematic warning to opinion leaders (media, government, families) to get with the program. Again, Dylan is methodical. First, he identifies the situation and the progress flowing from the celebrated changes. After issuing the initial warning (those who fail to swim will sink), he turns to three stanzas of application. Each stanza identifies its target, warns that a failure to embrace change is an invitation for failure, and closes with the reminder of changing times. Throughout, the song praises the underdog by constantly reiterating that today's loser will be tomorrow's winner. Dylan celebrates the ultimate victory of his generation's confrontation with the status quo though a narrative strategy that features a not-too-subtle warning that a failure to understand the situation may result in more problems. Today's underdog will be tomorrow's champion. This dualistic strategy reappears in the relational celebration "Covenant Woman" as well:

Covenant woman got a contract with the Lord
Way up yonder, great will be her reward.
Covenant woman, shining like a morning star,
I know I can trust you to stay where you are.

[chorus]
    And I just got to tell you
    I do intend

To stay closer than any friend.
I just got to thank you
Once again
For making your prayers known
Unto heaven for me
And to you, always, so grateful
I will forever be.

I've been broken, shattered like an empty cup.
I'm just waiting on the Lord to rebuild and fill me up
And I know He will do it 'cause He's faithful and He's true,
He must have loved me so much to send me someone as fine as you.

[chorus]

Covenant woman, intimate little girl
Who knows those most secret things of me that are hidden from the
*   world.*
You know we are strangers in a land we're passing through.
I'll always be right by your side, I've got a covenant too.

[chorus]

Here Dylan enjoys a double-dip as the narrator not only praises Woman, but God as well. The central value in both cases is trust. The narrator trusts the "covenant woman" to sustain her relationship with the Lord, trusts the Lord to always stand by him, and trusts his partner's knowledge of his private life. If any of this is autobiographical (beware!), Dylan uses this song to discuss one of the most significant (and elusive) values in anyone's life. Finally, the use of a standard chorus is unusual in his work and, I presume, is deployed for the reiteration that musical device serves: The auteur has a point to make here.

While songs of celebration do not enjoy the narrative status that the complaints occupy, Dylan's capacity to weave positive songs of heartfelt emotion demonstrates that his narrative sword does, in fact, cut both ways. That this narrative strategy wanes in the latter portions of the oeuvre is unfortunate and, perhaps, suggestive of the control Dylan's creative context exerts over his pen. *Saved* and the relational celebrations on *Skyline*, *Morning*, and *Waves* relate how Dylan's attention to detail may highlight the subtle nuances of positive situations just as he uses that trait to explore the dark sides of life. The author's joy—like his humor—is a welcome addition to the lifework—especially when one considers the intensity of the negativity.

Our third narrative strategy is the oeuvre's most complicated and the only approach to systematically evolve across the lifework. Dylan's satires never dominate his pen as the complaints, celebrations, or impressionism do, but nevertheless they convey his sense of humor, his moralistic storytelling, and a narrative precision unlike any other strategy. The humor first appears in the celebratory "Talkin' New York" as Dylan establishes the presentational rhythm that fuels many of the satires from the folk-posturing phase. With "Talkin' World War III," "Talkin' John Birch," and "Talkin' Bear Mountain" the auteur perfects a fun, crazy examination of life's recurrent situations, with each entry stressing a particular moral. For example, Dylan portrays the paranoid dreams of the cold war mentality ("WWIII"), the stupidity of bigotry ("Birch"), and the silliness of greed ("Bear") through narratives with similar structures: Songs that feature descriptive statements followed by short bursts of commentary. After *Another Side*'s "Motorpsycho Nitemare" (an adaptation of the traveling salesman tale) and *Back Home*'s "Bob Dylan's 115th Dream" (a revisionist view of American history), the strategy disappears among the Newport Mod's wordplay.

When the satire returns with *Harding*'s "Frankie Lee and Judas Priest" we note a difference in the strategy's application, as the comical asides (i.e., the short bursts of comments) are replaced by more detailed scenic descriptions and characterizations. At this point the satire begins to split into two new manifestations: The portrait and the saga. *Harding*'s two portraits—the title cut and "I Dreamed I Saw St. Augustine"—introduce the shift away from campfire tomfoolery; nonetheless, the stories continue the detail and moralistic messages. The transition advances with "Lily, Rosemary" from *Tracks* and its light-hearted invocation of the album's betrayal theme. With *Desire*, Dylan/Levy extend the evolution through the two portraits ("Joey" and "Hurricane") and the two sagas ("Durango" and "Diamond Bay"). At this point, narrative detail replaces satirical humor as the story form's prime mover—in short, more precision, less passion. The satire disappears during the moral period and returns ever so slightly with *Shot of Love*'s uneven portrait, "Lenny Bruce." While 1997's "Highlands" relates the satire's rich detail and moral overtones, this narrative strategy joins the relational/societal celebration in retirement. Too bad! Dylan does an excellent job with this narrative style, as evidenced in our exemplar, "Talkin' John Birch Paranoid Blues":

> Well, I was feelin' sad and feelin' blue,
> I didn't know what in the world I wus gonna do,
> Them Communists they wus comin' around,
> They wus in the air,
> They wus on the ground.
> They wouldn't gimme no peace . . .
>
> So I run down most hurriedly
> And joined up with the John Birch Society,
> I got me a secret membership card
> And started off a-walkin' down the road.
> Yee-hoo, I'm a real John Bircher now!
> Look out you Commies!
>
> Now we all agree with Hitler's views,
> Although he killed six million Jews.
> It don't matter too much that he was a Fascist,

At least you can't say he was a Communist!
That's to say like if you got a cold you take a shot of malaria.

Well, I wus lookin' everywhere for them gol-darned Reds.
I got up in the mornin' 'n' looked under my bed,
Looked in the sink, behind the door,
Looked in the glove compartment of my car.
Couldn't find 'em . . .

I wus lookin' high an' low for them Reds everywhere,
I wus lookin' in the sink an' underneath the chair.
I looked way up my chimney hole,
I even looked deep inside my toilet bowl.
They got away . . .

Well, I wus sittin' home alone an' started to sweat,
Figured they wus in my T.V. set.
Peeked behind the picture frame,
Got a shock from my feet, hittin' right up in the brain.
Them Reds caused it!
I know they did . . . them hard-core ones.

Well, I quit my job so I could work alone,
Then I changed my name to Sherlock Holmes.
Followed some clues from my detective bag
And discovered they wus red stripes on the American flag!
That ol' Betsy Ross . . .

Well, I investigated all the books in the library,
Ninety percent of 'em gotta be burned away.
I investigated all the people that I knowed,
Ninety-eight percent of them gotta go.
The other two percent are fellow Birchers . . . just like me.

Now Eisenhower, he's a Russian spy,
Lincoln, Jefferson and that Roosevelt guy.
To my knowledge there's just one man
That's really a true American: George Lincoln Rockwell.
I know for a fact he hates Commies cus he picketed the movie Exodus.

Well, I fin'ly started thinkin' straight
When I run outa things to investigate.
Couldn't imagine doin' anything else,
So now I'm sittin' home investigatin' myself!
Hope I don't find out anything . . . hmm, great God!

The song is a story with three acts: First, the problem is identified and the solution achieved; next, the search is on (Beware Commies!); and last, the resolution conveys the irony that, in the end, the paranoia turns on itself. The central character is a fool, but this fool has some famous friends. By deploying the Hitler characterization, Dylan places this foolishness in a very serious context. Remember, this is the song CBS banned from the "Ed Sullivan Show" and Columbia deleted from *Freewheelin'*. After the heavy-handed characterization, the song has fun as the narrator looks in the toilet bowl (ha, ha), behind the television's screen (what a dweeb!), and in the libraries for those evasive Reds. In the name-dropping style that recurs in Dylan wordplay, the song pauses to introduce several celebrity commies: Betsy Ross, Eisenhower, Lincoln, Jefferson, and Roosevelt. In classic satirical style, the story ends with the narrator wallowing in the idiocy.

As audience tapes of early Dylan performances indicate, the satire was an important part of young Bob Dylan's act. The humor, the topicality, and the rhythm of expression involved in these often elaborate stories were well-suited to his emerging persona. Later on, when the wordplay controlled the oeuvre, the strategy gave way to a different—yet related—narrative game. With the satire's evolution into the saga and portrait, its driving force, the humor, dissipated drastically and, in many respects, detracted significantly from the storytelling strategy. This may be the one aspect of Dylan's work to suffer from his decision to disengage from his audience and topicality. As the Traveling Wilbury's "Tweeter and the Monkey Man" (supposedly a spoof on Bruce Springsteen's narrative style) and "Highlands" indicate, Dylan maintains the capacity to write in this fashion, but—for whatever reason—this narrative strategy continues to rest in peace.

From stories that complain, celebrate, and satirize we move to Dylan's pioneering achievements in lyrical impressionism. Dylan's nonstories appear in two basic forms: organized and disorganized wordplay. We begin with the former and Dylan's narrative impressionism. Here we witness free-verse poetry married to lyrical refrains and recurrent musical structures; that is, a line or two of lyric may accompany a recurring musical figure to create the illusion of narrative coherence when, in actuality, the structure merely frames the wordplay contained within. The strategy first appeared on *Freewheelin'* via "A Hard Rain's a-Gonna Fall" and Dylan's supposedly apocalyptic portrayal of cold war politics. A closer review suggests something quite different:

> Oh, where have you been, my blue-eyed son?
> Oh, where have you been, my darling young one?
> I've stumbled on the side of twelve misty mountains,
> I've walked and I've crawled on six crooked highways,
> I've stepped in the middle of seven sad forests,
> I've been out in front of a dozen dead oceans,
> I've been ten thousand miles in the mouth of a graveyard,
> And it's a hard, and it's a hard, it's a hard, and it's a hard,
> And it's a hard rain's a-gonna fall.
>
> Oh, what did you see, my blue-eyed son?
> Oh, what did you see, my darling young one?
> I saw a newborn baby with wild wolves all around it,
> I saw a highway of diamonds with nobody on it,

I saw a black branch with blood that kept drippin',
I saw a room full of men with their hammers a-bleedin',
I saw a white ladder all covered with water,
I saw ten thousand talkers whose tongues were all broken,
I saw guns and sharp swords in the hands of young children,
And it's a hard, and it's a hard, it's a hard, it's a hard,
And it's a hard rain's a-gonna fall.

And what did you hear, my blue-eyed son?
And what did you hear, my darling young one?
I heard the sound of a thunder, it roared out a warnin',
Heard the roar of a wave that could drown the whole world,
Heard one hundred drummers whose hands were a-blazin',
Heard ten thousand whisperin' and nobody listenin',
Heard one person starve, I heard many people laughin',
Heard the song of a poet who died in the gutter,
Heard the sound of a clown who cried in the alley,
And it's a hard, and it's a hard, it's a hard, it's a hard,
And it's a hard rain's a-gonna fall.

Oh, who did you meet, my blue-eyed son?
Who did you meet, my darling young one?
I met a young child beside a dead pony,
I met a white man who walked a black dog,
I met a young woman whose body was burning,
I met a young girl, she gave me a rainbow,
I met one man who was wounded in love,
I met another man who was wounded with hatred,
And it's a hard, it's a hard, it's a hard, it's a hard,
It's a hard rain's a-gonna fall.

Oh, what'll you do now, my blue-eyed son?
Oh, what'll you do now, my darling young one?
I'm a-goin' back out 'fore the rain starts a-fallin',
I'll walk to the depths of the deepest black forest,
Where the people are many and their hands are all empty,
Where the pellets of poison are flooding their waters,
Where the home in the valley meets the damp dirty prison,
Where the executioner's face is always well hidden,
Where hunger is ugly, where souls are forgotten,
Where black is the color, where none is the number,
And I'll tell it and think it and speak it and breathe it,
And reflect it from the mountain so all souls can see it,
Then I'll stand on the ocean until I start sinkin',
But I'll know my song well before I start singin',
And it's a hard, it's a hard, it's a hard, it's a hard,
It's a hard rain's a-gonna fall.

This is, assuredly, the state of the art of the narrative impressionism strategy. The five stanzas provide a narrative context for Dylan's impressions on a host of topics that may, or may not, be related to any cold war polemic. The first four stanzas ask our blue-eyed traveler where he's been, what he's seen, what he's heard, and who he's met before the fifth stanza's inquiry into his plans *now* that he's experienced all of this. The song's final lines declare the character's intentions to take his case forward by land and sea, so that everyone may learn from his song.

Within each stanza is Dylan's free-flowing impressionism. The imagery is in turns beautiful (e.g., the young girl with the rainbow), disconcerting (e.g., the child surrounded by wolves), weird (e.g., men with bleeding hammers), ironic (e.g., the crying clown), surreal (e.g., an abandoned highway of jewels), scary (e.g., lifeless oceans), and fatalistic (e.g., wild, killer ocean waves). Through all these images Dylan hammers home the *sound* of a warning that, somehow, ties all of the "thoughts" (in the auteur's terminology) together. Each line is a starting point for its own story. This parade of images turns the theme back on the auditor and allows that individual to do what he or she will with the expression. The approach is as innovative as it is unrelenting.

Dylan previewed the strategy once more on *Another Side* by way of "My Back Pages" and "Chimes of Freedom" and their direct invocation of the "Hard Rain" strategy. Here, though, the individual stanzas begin to assume more internal coherence, although any relationship between the vignettes is thematic in the loose sense of the term. The impressionistic strategy explodes with *Back Home* and *Highway 61*. At this point the impressionism follows the complaint and celebration in its application to relational and societal contexts. *Back Home* features impressionistic accounts of societal issues ("Maggie's Farm" and "It's Alright, Ma [I'm Only Bleeding]") and relational matters ("She Belongs to Me" and "Love Minus Zero/No Limit") as well as the fantasy-filled, escapist self-exploration "Mr. Tambourine Man." The fun continues with *Highway 61* and its impressionistic portrayal of relationships ("Like a Rolling Stone," "It Takes a Lot to Laugh," and "From a Buick 6") and that harbinger of evil, "Highway 61." It sounds like superfluous hyperbole to say that the songs changed the musical world. I mean, how could a few songs on any set of albums change that much? How, indeed?

The narrative impressionism continues on one-half of *Blonde* with the song of oppression (the much-misread "Rainy Day Women #12 and 35") and four views of relational matters (e.g., "Leopard-Skin Pill-Box Hat" and "Sad Eyed Lady of the Lowlands"). At that point, the adventurous pioneering ceased. *Harding* issues pale versions of the strategy via "All Along the Watchtower" and "The Wicked Messenger" just as *Infidels* and *Burlesque* return to adaptations with "Jokerman" and "Tight Connection," respectively. Whatever prompted Dylan's rebellion toward his chosen profession—and I sense a rejection of the Western Union mentality here—it rendered a fascinating era of lyrical innovation. An impressionistic renaissance occurred with 2001's *Love and Theft* by way of the marvelous couplets contained in "Tweedle Dee and Tweedle Dum," "Floater," "High

Water," "Honest with Me," "Po' Boy," "Cry a While," and "Moonlight." *Love and Theft's* impressionism reveals the essential role that this songwriting strategy performs within the auteur's musical world. When musical confidence facilitates spontaneity, the words flow freely and imaginatively. Furthermore, *Love and Theft's* humor clearly signals Dylan's creative state of mind.

Dylan's narrative impressionism is but one part of the innovative songwriting that characterized the Newport Mod phase. The playful, free-form metaphors that were framed by recurring tag lines or musical phrases enjoyed even more freedom through songs of unadulterated wordplay. Beginning with *Freewheelin'* and "I Shall Be Free" as well as the follow-up, *Another Side's* "I Shall Be Free #10," Dylan initiated a songwriting style free of narrative structures. *Nothing* holds this surreal imagery and free-association wordplay together. Celebrity names or recurrent lines may repeat a phrase or image, but Dylan's wordplay genre, in one extreme, deploys an antilogic that invokes an antilanguage to articulate anti-narratives (see *Tarantula*, wherein the writing subverts the basic principles of communication; in other words, an inspired game of Glissendorf); in another extreme, it releases an energy with an unrestrained commitment to the author's personal objective—whatever that might be. In both cases, it abdicates any responsibility for author–audience communication; a Western Union boy would be a character—not a carrier—in these expressions.

After introducing the tactic with the "I Shall Be Free" entries, Dylan drives it home with *Back Home* and *Highway 61*. *Back Home* offers five examples of the wordplay strategy (e.g., "Subterranean Homesick Blues," "Gates of Eden," and "It's All Over Now, Baby Blue"), *Highway 61* another five (e.g., "Tombstone Blues," "Ballad of a Thin Man," "Just Like Tom Thumb's Blues," and "Desolation Row"), and *Blonde* our final two ("Visions of Johanna" and "Stuck Inside of Mobile with the Memphis Blues Again"). Nobody had ever written songs like these before and they rippled throughout the musical world. As our exemplar, we consider the song that Dylan admits was written "in the spirit," "Desolation Row":

> *They're selling postcards of the hanging*
> *They're painting the passports brown*
> *The beauty parlor is filled with sailors*
> *The circus is in town*
> *Here comes the blind commissioner*
> *They've got him in a trance*
> *One hand is tied to the tight-rope walker*
> *The other is in his pants*
> *And the riot squad they're restless*
> *They need somewhere to go*
> *As Lady and I look out tonight*
> *From Desolation Row*
>
> *Cinderella, she seems so easy*
> *"It takes one to know one," she smiles*
> *And puts her hands in her back pockets*

Bette Davis style
And in comes Romeo, he's moaning
"You Belong to Me I Believe"
And someone says, "You're in the wrong place, my friend
You better leave"
And the only sound that's left
After the ambulances go
Is Cinderella sweeping up
On Desolation Row

Now the moon is almost hidden
The stars are beginning to hide
The fortune-telling lady
Has even taken all her things inside
All except for Cain and Abel
And the hunchback of Notre Dame
Everybody is making love
Or else expecting rain
And the Good Samaritan, he's dressing
He's getting ready for the show
He's going to the carnival tonight
On Desolation Row

Now Ophelia, she's 'neath the window
For her I feel so afraid
On her twenty-second birthday
She already is an old maid
To her, death is quite romantic
She wears an iron vest
Her profession's her religion
Her sin is her lifelessness
And though her eyes are fixed upon
Noah's great rainbow
She spends her time peeking
Into Desolation Row

Einstein, disguised as Robin Hood
With his memories in a trunk
Passed this way an hour ago
With his friend, a jealous monk
He looked so immaculately frightful
As he bummed a cigarette
Then he went off sniffing drainpipes
And reciting the alphabet
Now you would not think to look at him
But he was famous long ago

For playing the electric violin
On Desolation Row

Dr. Filth, he keeps his world
Inside of a leather cup
But all his sexless patients
They're trying to blow it up
Now his nurse, some local loser
She's in charge of the cyanide hole
And she also keeps the cards that read
"Have Mercy on His Soul"
They all play on penny whistles
You can hear them blow
If you lean your head out far enough
From Desolation Row

Across the street they've nailed the curtains
They're getting ready for the feast
The Phantom of the Opera
A perfect image of a priest
They're spoon-feeding Casanova
To get him to feel more assured
Then they'll kill him with self-confidence
After poisoning him with words
And the Phantom's shouting to skinny girls
"Get Outa Here If You Don't Know
Casanova is just being punished for going
To Desolation Row"

Now at midnight all the agents
And the superhuman crew
Come out and round up everyone
That knows more than they do
Then they bring them to the factory
Where the heart-attack machine
Is strapped across their shoulders
And then the kerosene
Is brought down from the castles
By insurance men who go
Check to see that nobody is escaping
To Desolation Row

Praise be to Nero's Neptune
The Titanic sails at dawn
And everybody's shouting
"Which Side Are You On?"

And Ezra Pound and T. S. Eliot
Fighting in the captain's tower
While calypso singers laugh at them
And fishermen hold flowers
Between the windows of the sea
Where lovely mermaids flow
And nobody has to think too much
About Desolation Row

Yes, I received your letter yesterday
(About the time the door knob broke)
When you asked how I was doing
Was that some kind of joke?
All these people that you mention
Yes, I know them, they're quite lame
I had to rearrange their faces
And give them all another name
Right now I can't read too good
Don't send me no more letters no
Not unless you mail them
From Desolation Row

What a parade of images! The characters fall into two simple categories: famous people or literary characters (e.g., Cinderella, Bette Davis, Romeo, Cain and Abel, Noah, Einstein, Robin Hood, the Phantom of the Opera, Ezra Pound, T. S. Eliot) and nameless individuals identified by their role (e.g., a blind commissioner, tightrope walker, jealous monk, Dr. Filth, lovely mermaids). Occasionally, the characterizations overlap as when Cinderella assumes a Bette Davis stance, Einstein wears a Robin Hood disguise, or when the Phantom of the Opera looks like a priest. This name-as-characterization strategy throws the moniker around as the story emphasizes the expression's flow, not its contents. There is no character development.

There are hints of plot progression within the vignettes that comprise the respective verses, but any internal coherence is fleeting at best. Clearly, only the tag line "Desolation Row" holds the thing together. From our narrative perspective, the song's values are the most evasive. We never understand why anything occurs. The characters' activities are so fragmented and disjointed that depth is not only ignored, it appears to be prohibited. Throughout the madness, there are so many compelling images that one gets lost in those representations. Interestingly, the final stanza seems to break away from the imagery as if the narrator has awakened from a dream. It appears to look back on the happenings on Desolation Row with a detachment, an understanding of what it all signifies. What a journey! Dylan described the song's origins for *USA Today* in 2001: "That's a minstrel song through and through. I saw some ragtag minstrel show in black-face at the carnivals when I was growing up, and it had an effect on me, just as much as seeing the lady with four legs." Ah yes, the lady with four legs. This is the ultimate musical Rohrshach—enjoy! "Desolation Row" is more than unique—it is songwriting's *Citizen Kane*, the art form will never be the same again.

Rest assured, not all of Dylan's songs fall neatly into these five narrative orientations; however, it is remarkable how many do, in fact, fit firmly into the respective frameworks. There is a continuity of expression that is, in every respect, the hallmark of the auteur; that is, there are stylistic tendencies that are systematically applied. There is a rhythm of expression within the writings. When Dylan steps outside these structures for songs such as *Waves'* prayers (the two versions of "Forever Young"), *Slow Train's* statement of "commitment" ("I Believe In You"), *Time Out of Mind's* loving pledge ("Make You Feel My Love"), *Love and Theft's* personal proclamation ("Bye and Bye"), the nostalgia on *Freewheelin'* ("Bob Dylan's Dream"), or the nonsensical ditties on *Red Sky*, he uses language in idiosyncratic ways that also indicate his authorship (*Red Sky* pushes the envelope, though). When we pause to consider that this is forty years of work, well, the continuity evident within the lifework offers powerful evidence of Dylan-the-auteur.

To conclude this study of Bob Dylan's lifework and its contributions to American Song, I think we should return to the "impulse" section and the auteur's discussion of art's function, his artistic influences, and his creative objectives. Dylan—a man who can be more than evasive—does not hesitate in his explanations of art's purpose and his ambitions within that framework. He relates that art's purpose is to inspire audiences through emotional expressions that challenge the status quo. To achieve that end, he employs the traditions of American Song (his "roots") in an effort to generate art that pleases him. For Dylan, if the work pleases *him*, if it challenges *him*, if it inspires *him* to assess *his* situation, then his creative goal is achieved. He told *Melody Maker*: "My songs are just me talking to myself. . . . I have no responsibility to anybody except myself. If people like me—fine. If they *don't*, then maybe I'll do something else." This is not an audience-dependent artist. He neither labors over expressions, nor longs for audience approval. In point of fact, he is *exactly* the opposite. If an album sounds *too* pleasing, then Dylan shifts it around. If audiences oppose a particular innovation or idea, he confronts them and forces them to endure his perspective. He has perpetuated this attitude throughout his entire life. Bob Dylan—true to the culture that spawned him—is as rebellious as any artist who has ever worked (and "worked" is a key term: Dylan engaged the commercial world). And his artistic orientation—true to the culture that spawned him—is fiercely independent and decidedly, if not overwhelmingly, self-centered. What matters to this artist is the source of that rebellion, American Song, the "inspiration behind the inspiration."

Dylan's artistic philosophy manifests directly in his work. His emphasis on emotional inspiration is evident in his rejection of logic and, occasionally, facts. Dylan will, at any time, convolute factual evidence for the desired dramatic effect. Moreover, since he endeavors to challenge the "establishment" (whatever that may be—it could be an on-going relationship or musical tradition), he willfully subverts whatever principles are before him in service of his goal. For Dylan, who cares if he misrepresents his arrival in New York or the facts surrounding

Hattie Carroll's death or the details pertaining to Reuben Carter's case or Joey Gallo's biography or his marriage (as if *that* were anybody's business!) or any aspect of American history? Dylan is not a dialectical narrator attempting to separate fact from fiction for an audience, as in the cases of journalists or expert commentators (supposedly, even, teachers). He is not a rhetorical narrator working to persuade some audience of the merits of some specific case (like a lawyer, preacher, or salesperson). He is a poetic narrator, free to express himself as he wishes. If anyone looks to Dylan to separate fact from fiction or to persuade them toward a particular end, that individual is *using* the work in a fashion inconsistent with its creation. While in his youth, Dylan wrote topical songs as he would have written advertising jingles. He did what he felt he had to do to enter his chosen profession. Only during his spiritual conversion did he use his art in a persuasive manner (for *one* album), but that application was so straightforward as to raise no questions regarding his creative agenda. If he has ever been a spokesperson for anything, it has been for himself—the rebel's lifelong cause.

Dylan, then, has remained remarkably consistent in his pursuit of his creative goals. He has successfully expressed himself and served his inspirational American Song roots. His principal contribution is in his steadfast dedication to his musical heritage. His rededication to performance in the 1990s and his relentless commitment to "the road" demonstrate his complete allegiance to his music. Joining that offering is, of course, his innovative songwriting. For most of Bob Dylan's career he dutifully subscribed to the songwriting prescriptions of specific genres. His country, folk, gospel, pop, and early rock and roll songs all stay within the expectations of that particular branch of American Song. However, for a brief period in the mid-1960s, he took that craft into another realm. He allowed his muse to have its way and the art flowed *through* him. It was his greatest game of Glissendorf. (He won!) The satisfaction gleaned from the successful manipulation of an international audience must have been wonderfully rewarding for the Iron Range's most famous biker/poet. The postman's deliveries assumed a new, free-flowing form and the mail would never be the same again—regardless of the carrier.

part two

Bruce Springsteen

On January 20, 1988,
Bruce Springsteen induct-
ed Bob Dylan into the Rock
and Roll Hall of Fame. His speech
displayed the elocutionary grace that
typifies his oratory in situations such as *introduction*
this. Springsteen's remarks were both personal and universal. Much like his songwriting, he
probed his emotional history as a pathway to a statement that embraced far more than his individual perspective. After recalling his first experiences with Dylan's music,
Springsteen explained their significance:

> When I was a kid, Bob's voice somehow thrilled and scared me, it made
> me feel kind of irresponsibly innocent—it still does—when it reached down
> and touched what little worldliness a fifteen-year-old high-school kid in New
> Jersey had in him at the time. Dylan was a revolutionary. Bob freed your mind
> the way Elvis freed your body. He showed us that just because the music was
> innately physical did not mean that it was anti-intellectual. He had the vision
> and the talent to make a pop song that contained the whole world. He invented
> a new way a pop singer could sound, broke through the limitations of what a re-
> cording artist could achieve and changed the face of rock-'n'-roll forever.

The speech continued with a list of
songwriting innovations derived from Dylan's
pioneering work. Springsteen noted how audiences were deeply moved by the inductee's music—
occasionally to the point of interpreting his words in
intensely personal ways. To Dylan's annoyance, fans often
spoke of him (and to him) as if he were family. Still, the New Jersey
Bard declared, "I wouldn't be here without you," as he closed by telling
Dylan, "Whether you like it or not," he considered him to be the "brother" he
never had.

Whether they like it or not, big brothers pass along a variety of lessons to
their younger siblings. Many of these lessons emerge as the result of direct conversation, others are products of systematic observation, and others merely
flow from the incidental happenings of daily living. As we are about to discover,
Bruce Springsteen feels that artists leave "maps" behind for others to follow,
and he used his brother's map quite well. Just as "Bob Dylan" is an invented personality, "Bruce Springsteen" is the most orchestrated celebrity of his time. His
debt to Dylan—and many others—is considerable; nevertheless, it is to his
credit that he bothered to consult, consider, and incorporate those instructions. "Bruce Springsteen" is both genuine and contrived. We know of him what
he allows us to know. *His* mystery is genuine, but his art is without mystery.
Whereas Bob Dylan wrote around his subjects, Springsteen wrote through them.
His insights display a piercing emotional quality that make his conclusions
unavoidable. They do not play Glissendorf in New Jersey.

"Springsteenetics" is as yet an undeveloped science when compared to
Dylanology. Although known to travel across the continent to see a single show,
Springsteen fans have somehow refrained from garbology, genetic engineering,
and other Dylanological techniques. Websites feature intricate aspects of
Springsteen's career and "fanzines" such as *Backstreets* chronicle every development, but the published material pales in comparison. Springsteen's official
biographer, Dave Marsh, offers two books that focus on biography and performance commentary just as Robert Hilburn's photo/biography, Christopher Sandford's biography, Eric Alterman's personal testimonial, and Jim Cullen's historical treatise represent compelling examples of Springsteenetics. Of course,
music-industry journals and academic periodicals have had their way with him as
well. That he was spared the celebrity indignities that plagued his older brother
is a tribute to his tightly controlled operation—one of the many lessons gleaned
from all those maps he studied so carefully. To my knowledge, nobody has wished
Springsteen dead.

Springsteen's use of the sibling metaphor is instructive, since these two
artists are certainly members of the musical family that flows from the Woody
Guthrie tradition of American Song. Their portrayals of the celebrity-singer-
songwriter role extend the Guthrie prototype in everlasting—but contrasting—
ways. Throughout, a basic character trait drove each artist: Control is to Bruce

Springsteen what rebellion is to Bob
Dylan. Both characteristics emerged from
their biographies, basted in the glow of their
celebrity images, and quickly assumed command over
their artistic impulses. To the extent that Dylan rebelled
against media interviews, audience expectations, and industry
prescriptions, Springsteen endeavored to control them. Springsteen's fierce commitment to his perceived audience is the mirror image
of Dylan's unyielding dedication to himself. Though they traveled down different paths, both artists achieved standards of excellence that provided
guides for those who dared to follow in their innovative footsteps. Being a younger brother has its costs and rewards, and the following pages reveal how Bruce
Springsteen negotiated an acceptable balance between the two. Just like Dylan,
Springsteen's lifework conveys that simple but poignant fact: Excellence is
expensive.

chapter five
the artist

The April 1, 1974 edition of *Time* features a brief profile of an emerging musical personality who, in seventeen months, would grace the covers of both *Time* and *Newsweek*—simultaneously. Interestingly, the article opens with the artist's dismissal of any comparison with popular music's preeminent songsmith, Bob Dylan (saying, "The best thing anyone can do for me is not to mention Bob Dylan"), in favor of listing creative influences as diverse as Benny Goodman, Sam Cooke, Wilson Pickett, and Fats Domino. After noting the young man's "striking resemblance to Dylan," *Time's* Jay Cocks describes Bruce Springsteen's musical style: "Like rock musicians of the '60s, Springsteen dips back to the '50s for the blazing chord colors and nagging syncopations inside his walls of throbbing sound. . . . His songs are ambitious mini-operas populated by punk saints and Go-Kart Mozarts in scenarios laced with schmalz [sic] and violence. . . . Bursting with words, images rush along in cinematic streams of consciousness." The praise concludes with a cute story about Springsteen signing with Columbia Records and his subsequent telephone call to his mother. Once she heard the news, Adele Springsteen declared, "Oh Yeah? What did you change your name to?"

Mrs. Springsteen was wrong in her presumption that her son would change his identity as the result of his contractual agreement with a major record company. Bruce Springsteen would not only continue to use his birth name as his professional cognomen, he would embellish his family, their New Jersey roots, and his experiences in the Garden State to the point where he would single-handedly transform the area's image. Springsteen made it cool to be from Jersey, to accept the aftermath of adolescence in a struggling (maybe even abusive) working-class family, to seek escape from life's daily demands through frivolous—but emotionally liberating—"Saturday Nights" out-on-the-town, and perhaps most importantly, to face life and its inherent difficulties. There would be no stage names or contrived histories here; to the contrary, Bruce Springsteen immersed himself in his past, wrestled with his personal demons, and shared that experience with anyone willing to listen.

Bruce Frederick Springsteen was born on September 23, 1949 in Freehold, New Jersey to Douglas and Adele Springsteen. Bruce is the oldest child of a family that includes two younger sisters (Ginny and Pam). In 1996 Springsteen described Freehold to Karen Schoemer: "Me and my parents lived in my grandparents' house. . . . Then there was my cousin's house, my aunt's house, my great-grandmother's house, my aunt's house on my mother's side with my other grandmother in it. We were all on one street, with the church in the middle." Although the living accommodations changed over the years, the point remains: Springsteen grew up surrounded by his extended family and was grounded in their Catholicism. Douglas Springsteen worked in factories, as a prison guard, and as a bus driver; his struggle with work cast a dark shadow over the family home. Adele Springsteen—described by her son as a "Superwoman, she did everything, everywhere, all the time"—worked as a secretary for the same company throughout Bruce's youth; her stability counterbalanced her husband's volatility. Christopher Sandford captures Adele best when he claims that she could say "God Bless You" in "five languages." Assuredly, the Springsteens endured difficult times, as Bruce told *60 Minutes*: "They worked like crazy their whole lives . . . we weren't used to luck . . . that was something that happened to somebody else."

Time's 1975 cover story cites Springsteen's reflections on his formative years: "I lived half of my first 13 years in a trance or something. . . . People thought I was weird because I always went around with this *look* on my face. I was thinking of things, but I was always on the outside, looking in." Douglas Springsteen's vocational angst played a major role in that *look* and its corresponding introversion. The senior Springsteen's frustrations were all-consuming, and his relationship with his son reflected those strains. In 1981 the junior Springsteen discussed his father's anxieties with Fred Schruers by noting the contrast between a treasured photograph and the reality of Douglas's daily life: "He looked just like John Garfield, in this great suit, he looked like he was gonna eat the photographer's head off. And I couldn't ever remember him looking that proud, or that defiant, when I was growing up. I used to wonder what happened to all that pride, how it turned into so much bitterness. He'd been so disappointed, had so much stuff beaten out of him by then." That negativity inhibited young Springsteen's social development just as it eventually liberated his creative ambitions, as he explained to biographer Robert Hilburn:

> When I was a kid, I never got used to expecting success. I got used to failing. Once you do that, the rest is real easy. It took a lot of pressure off. I just said, "Hell, I'm a loser. I don't have to worry about anything." I assumed immediately that nothing was happening. But that's not the same as giving up. You keep trying, but you don't count on things. It can be a strength. Because I know some people who sweat out winning so much it kills them. So, in the end, they lose anyway. They win, but they lose. People don't realize things can often be just the opposite of what they seem.

Springsteen's elementary education at Freehold's St. Rose of Lima and his secondary schooling at Freehold Regional High School sound dreadful, and, no doubt, reinforced the unsuccessful identity established at home. Over the years, the auteur has embellished various accounts of his youth for his audiences. *Newsweek's* 1975 cover story contains this unsavory recollection: "In the third grade a nun stuffed me into a garbage can she kept under her desk because she told me that's where I belonged. . . . I also had the distinction of being the only altar boy knocked down by a priest on the steps of the altar during Mass. The old priest got mad. My Mom wanted me to learn how to serve Mass but I didn't know what I was doin' so I was tryin' to fake it." Three years later, he spun this yarn for *Crawdaddy*:

> I hated school. I had the big hate. I remember one time, I was in eighth grade and I wised off and they sent me down to the first-grade class and made me sit in these little desks, you know, little chairs. And the sister, she said, "Show this young man what we do to people who smile in this classroom"—I was probably laughing at being sent down there. And this kid, this six-year-old, who has no doubt been taught to do this, he comes over to me—him standing up and me sitting in this little desk are about eye-to-eye—and he slams me in the face. . . . I can feel the sting. I was in shock. It was always like that. I put up with it for years, but in the eighth grade I started to wise off. But even then . . . some guys would talk back and get respect, I did it and they called me crazy.

There he recalled he "didn't even make it to class clown, I had nowhere near that amount of notoriety" and acknowledged:

> By the end of high school I didn't have much to do with anybody. I almost didn't graduate because the kids in my class wouldn't let me. I was playing in bands and my hair was real long and the sister got up in front of everybody and said, "Class, don't you have any pride in yourselves? Are you going to allow this boy to embarrass you and go to graduation looking like that?" And they weren't gonna let me graduate unless I cut my hair.

Sandford contributes to this woeful history with a vignette about a class project in which Springsteen was to draw an image of Christ and responded "by showing him crucified on a Gibson" guitar. The nuns, reportedly, "went mental." Such was Bruce Springsteen's schooling.

Life outside of school was no relief, as he related to Hilburn: "Before rock and roll, I didn't have any purpose. I tried to play football and baseball and all those things . . . and I just didn't fit. I was running through a maze." When he saw Elvis Presley on the *Ed Sullivan Show* his life changed. Adele bought her son a guitar and arranged for lessons, but his hands were small and his passion faded. Later, in 1964, his interest returned and he purchased a guitar from a pawn shop—this time, the obsessive behaviors that accompany excellence assumed control. Springsteen listed the Top 20 (he kept score) with his radio under his pillow late at night, practiced his guitar without interruption for eight hours at a time, and thought, thought, thought about all the things he saw around him. In 1996, he responded to a *Mother Jones* question regarding the political aspects of his work with this poignant recollection of his youth and its impact on his art:

> No. I never start with a political point of view. I believe that your politics are emotionally and psychologically determined by your early experiences. My family didn't have a political house. We didn't have a cultural house. There was a lot of struggle in my parents' life. In Jersey, when I was 19, they traveled West to start a new life. They didn't know anybody. They had $3,000 to make it across the country with my little sister. My mother worked the same job her whole life, every day, never sick, never stayed home, never cried. My dad had a very difficult life, a hard struggle all the time at work. I've always felt like I'm seeking his revenge. My memory is of my father trying to find work, what that does to you, and how that affects your image of your manhood, as a provider. The loss of that role is devastating. I write coming from that spot—the spot of disaffection, of loners, outsiders. But not outlaws. It's about people trying to find their way in, but somebody won't let them in. Or they can't find their way in. And what are the actions that leads to? That pretty much obsesses me to this day—and probably will the rest of my life.

Despite his classmates protestations Springsteen graduated high school, entered Ocean City Community College for a brief stay (more problems with peer perceptions), failed his physical for the draft, coped with his family's move to California, and dedicated his life to his music. When Springsteen bellows "rock and roll saved my life," he does so without exaggeration. It was all he had or, at the very least, it was all he wanted. These comments to *Crawdaddy* are classic: "But rock 'n' roll, man, it changed my life. It was like, you know, the Voice of America, the real America, coming into your home. It was the liberating thing, the out, the key out of the pits. Once I found the guitar I had the key to the highway!"

Like with so many before him, Springsteen's musical life began via the generosity of others. An October 1985 *Rolling Stone* piece on Springsteen's formative years chronicles Gordon ("Tex") and Marion Vinyard's contributions to the Freehold musical scene. Tex (described as a "factory worker who loved kids and had none of his own") provided practice space, "Foodtown sodas," and Marion's tuna-fish sandwiches for local kids trying to form bands. They created one, The Castiles, and *Rolling Stone* cites "one observer" who claims that Vinyard spent $10,000 on it, and in so doing, provided musical opportunities "for kids who could never have put it together themselves." The Castiles needed a guitar player and band member George Theiss was dating a young lady whose older brother might just fit the bill. Consequently, Ginny Springsteen's brother borrowed a guitar and auditioned for Tex. After hearing a "few snatches of songs," Tex advised the youngster to learn some material and return once he had mastered it. The kid was back the next night with a five-song repertoire he acquired from his radio and "an astounded Tex" accepted Bruce Springsteen into his band.

The youngsters associated with The Castiles have similar recollections about the new guitar player. One classmate recalled: "No, he made no impression at all. . . . He was very shy—no activities, no sports, nothing like that. If he hadn't turned out to be Bruce Springsteen, would I remember him? I can't think why I would. . . .

You have to remember, without a guitar in his hands, he had absolutely nothing to say." George Theiss dated Ginny for a year and had this to say about her brother: "We were trying to be cool . . . trying to get by without carrying any books at all, or carrying one, almost like a prop. You would see Bruce, coming down the hall with an armful of books, carrying them up around his chest, like a girl. I thought he was real studious." Curt Fluhr reported: "You could tell there was something special about him. . . . You had this kid, terribly shy, not terribly attractive, but put a guitar in his hands. . . . You ever see Bill Bixby turn into the Incredible Hulk? Put him onstage with a guitar and he lit it up. It was like somebody had plugged him in." To which Vinnie Roslin added: "He just had this enormous appetite to play. . . . He'd play anytime, anywhere, for anybody. He was like a television set with one channel, and on the set was 'practice music.'" Springsteen's introversion fueled a commitment to practice guitar, and eventually, write songs. He explained his lifestyle and its impact on his art to the *Los Angeles Times* in 1992:

> That's how I learned to play the guitar, I played for eight hours a day in my room. I was not part of a clique or a group until I got into a band, and that was based around the music. I would occasionally come out and explore external things, but mostly I lived inside, probably initially because I experienced a lot of external rejection when I was growing up, which led me to create my own world. That's not unusual—everybody lives in their head, and you don't even notice it when you're young. You're out there on the road, and it even feels like a strength. It's how you have the discipline to find the time, to be alone, to think about things, writing songs.

The biographers list Springsteen's early bands (e.g., the "Rogues," "Earth," "Child"), chronicle his "coming out" via music, and discuss the growing domestic tensions surrounding his new lifestyle. Douglas Springsteen's misunderstanding of his son's appearance and misinterpretation of his interests exacerbated an already unstable relationship. Years later, the auteur used his recollections of this period to frame songs about his father, Douglas's difficulties, and their life. Hilburn's book offers one example from the *Born to Run* tour. Springsteen described how he would pull his hair back to hide its length and, generally, try to avoid his father, but confrontations—typically occurring in the kitchen—were unavoidable: "In the wintertime, he used to turn on the gas stove and close all the doors so it got real hot in there. And I can remember just sittin' there in the dark, him tellin' me, tellin' me, tellin' me. . . . And I could always hear that voice, no matter how long I sat there. But I could never, ever see his face." Springsteen told stories of a motorcycle accident, his hospitalization, and his father arranging for a barber to cut his hair while confined to a bed; of Douglas hating his radio and guitar, thinking that they were all manufactured by the same company ("goddamn radio, goddamn guitar"); of his father's belief that the army would transform his attitudes and set him straight (which Springsteen concluded by noting Douglas's relief that he failed his entrance exam and avoided service in Vietnam). When the family moved to California, the tensions relaxed, but the memories—the lasting impressions—created a foundation for the emotional autobiography that is Bruce Springsteen's lifework. The instability of the home, the insecurities of school, the intrusiveness of the religious doctrine, and the isolated mental rebellion comprise the raw materials of a psychological and sociological orientation that the auteur would explore through his chosen vocation. With time, the experience of reliving life would be liberating, but that was years away. He would gain his father's revenge and, as everyone knows, vengeance is expensive.

Springsteen's musical biography is dominated by two forms of activities: Writing and performance. The auteur's image of and relationship with his audience is *the* fundamental component of both. As he moved from bands such as "Steel Mill" and "Dr. Zoom and the Sonic Boom" (the latter featured a game of Monopoly as part of the show), Springsteen cultivated an act distinct from his Jersey shore competitors. His insistence on performing original songs, his rejection of the Top 40 cover mentality, and his commitment to his loyal following made Springsteen the bar-band king of his day. The shy, reclusive artist became the "Incredible Hulk" once onstage, and once "in character," he preferred to stay there. His inability to generate much interest in his act during a family visit to the West Coast fueled his drive further once he returned to Jersey. But he was still a provincial act—all Bruce Springsteen needed was the proverbial national "break."

In November 1971 Springsteen met Mike Appel, an ex-Marine trying to make his way in the music business. Reportedly, their first encounter left Appel unimpressed, whereas a second meeting inspired the aspiring entrepreneur (biographer Dave Marsh offers a different account of this story). Springsteen signed with Appel (supposedly, he signed the contract on the hood of his car without reading it) and the fast-talking, aggressive manager initiated the tightly orchestrated public-relations campaign that would eventually control every facet of Springsteen's career. Appel's first major achievement involved arranging an audition with Columbia Record's John Hammond, the executive who signed a talented folk singer from the Iron Range over a decade earlier.

Sources indicate that Appel sought an audition with Hammond precisely because he had signed Bob Dylan. After telling Hammond, "We wanna see if that was just a fluke, or if you really have ears" (according to the *Time* cover story), for some reason the Columbia executive granted the obnoxious manager the audition. Springsteen shared with Mark Hagen his detailed recollections of that fateful day:

> It was a big, big day for me. . . . I was twenty-two and came up on the bus with an acoustic guitar with no case. . . . I was embarrassed carrying it around the city. I walked into his office and had the audition and I played a couple of songs and he said, "You've got to be on Columbia Records. But I need to see you play. And I need to hear how you sound on tape." Me and Mike Appel walked all around the Village trying to find some place that would let somebody just get up on stage and play. . . . [They wound up at the Gaslight on MacDougal Street.] There were about ten people in the place and I played for about half an hour. . . . [Afterward they returned to Columbia for the demo tape.] Columbia

was very old-fashioned: everybody in ties and shirts; the engineer was in a white shirt and a tie and was probably fifty, fifty-five years old, it was just him and John and Mike Appel there, and he just hits the button and gives you your serial number, and off you go. I was excited. I felt I'd written some good songs and this was my shot. I had nothing to lose and it was like the beginning of something. I knew a lot about John Hammond, the work he'd done, the people he'd discovered, his importance in music and it was very exciting to feel you were worth his time. No matter what happened afterwards, even if it was just for this one night, you were worth his time. That meant a lot to me. He was very encouraging—simply being in that room with him at the board was one of my greatest recording experiences.

Hammond conveyed his recollections of that day during interviews for the two national cover stories. He told *Newsweek*: "I only hear somebody really good once every ten years, and not only was Bruce the best, he was a lot better than Dylan when I first heard him." He told *Time* that he reacted to Springsteen "with a force I'd felt maybe three times in my life" and that he considered Appel to be "as offensive as any man I've ever met." According to *Time*, contracts were signed in less than twenty-four hours.

The Springsteen–Appel team was effective, but Appel *was* offensive. His penchant for hyperbole was both an asset and an aggravation. Springsteen's account of the Hammond audition is instructive: "I went into a state of shock as soon as I walked in. . . . Before I ever played a note Mike starts screamin' and yellin' 'bout me. I'm shrivelin' up and thinkin', 'Please, Mike, give me a break. Let me play a damn song.' So, dig this, before I ever played a note the hype began." And "The Hype" became quite an issue during Appel's reign as Springsteen's handler. Appel's (and partner Jim Cretecos's) aggressive management complemented Springsteen's contagious stage act to render a formidable public-relations operation. Appel acquired the venue; Springsteen delivered the show. Unfortunately, management's skills diminished once inside the recording studio. Appel booked cheap facilities to record an act that sounded nothing like the Columbia audition, and the results introduced another edition of "Hammond's Folly." The initial Columbia release, titled *Greetings from Asbury Park, N.J.* (issued in early January 1973) featured full-band versions of Springsteen originals and generated marginal sales. The songwriting deployed Dylan's narrative impressionism in a direct, perhaps ambitious, fashion while the music followed the stage act's eclectic lead.

Springsteen backed away from the impressionism yet extended the musical style for his second release, *The Wild, the Innocent and the E Street Shuffle* (September 1973). Around the fall of 1974, Springsteen's supporting group, the E Street Band, settled into the personnel that would guide the group for the next decade and developed a sound—and an act—that provided the perfect platform for Springsteen's theater. (The band was Roy Bittan and Danny Federici on keyboards, Clarence Clemons on saxophone, Garry Tallent on bass, Max Weinberg on drums, and guitarist Steve Van Zandt floating in and out of the group.) Christopher Sandford offers this account of the band's act:

Gradually, over 1973–74, they became a showband as well as a bar-band. . . .
They were at once dark, funny and delivered with a heart that suggested many
of the yarns stemmed from deep source material. Those still thin audiences
soon learned a brand-new thing about the Boss [Springsteen's nickname]: he
was a born storyteller, whose narrative gifts came from his New York Italian
grandparents. (He also, says [ex-girlfriend] Lynn Goldsmith, practiced them
nonstop in front of a mirror.) . . . [By early 1974 Springsteen] glossed his set
into a minutely rehearsed, blocked routine that was as much Broadway as
boardwalk. He hired Louis Lahav on sound and the lighting magus Marc Brick-
man. They presented the concerts as a theatrical tapestry: It was the "spectacle" that brought the production to life. Springsteen himself was all-action.
. . . He not only flaunted his love of melodramatic soul-revue splits and slides; in
a true James Brown touch, he'd even swoon to the stage. It all followed in
the exalted tradition of the Apollo: Raunchy, horn-heavy riffs buoyed by the
breathy vocals of a sweaty frontman.

The stage act soared while the albums floundered. Hammond withstood the pressure at Columbia; a rough performance during the 1973 Columbia national convention added to the controversy. (Hammond told *Newsweek* that Springsteen "came
with a chip on his shoulder and played too long.") Hammond's Folly II entered a crucial crossroads.

Meanwhile, the third—and pivotal—album, *Born to Run*, entered production.
Springsteen has never minced words about the strains associated with the *Born
to Run* project, telling *Creem*: "That was the most horrible period of my life . . .
the most horrible period of my life. . . . I had this *horrible* pressure in the studio."
The Appel–Springsteen production team recorded the title cut (which required
six months) and vigorously promoted a pre-release version (often surreptitiously
to loyal radio stations), but the album's production stalled. Springsteen needed
more than promotion, he needed creative guidance; someone to facilitate the
artistic process, edit the results, and coordinate the promotion of the vision
behind the concept. Bruce Springsteen needed Jon Landau.

Jon Landau was a former musician, movie critic, part-time producer, and full-
time music critic when he met Springsteen in Boston in April 1974. Landau had
just reviewed *The Wild, the Innocent* for a Boston weekly when he happened upon
the musician as Springsteen stood outside a bar he was about to play in, reading the Landau review. (Predictably, Landau enjoyed the music, but not the production.) Landau recognized Springsteen, introduced himself, shared a laugh,
and entered the bar (meeting Mike Appel there). The next month Springsteen
played Cambridge again, and Landau attended the show and reviewed the event
for the same weekly, *The Real Paper*. The result was one of the most widely
quoted journalistic reviews in the history of popular music. Landau was no novice;
in fact, he ran the *Rolling Stone* record-review section and many considered him
to be the top music critic of his time. But his review of the May 9, 1974
Springsteen show—written on his 27th birthday—was personal, richly introspective, and prophetic. Jon Landau believed Bruce Springsteen to be the future
of rock and roll.

Landau's review influenced all of music journalism (in one way or another) and Columbia used the publicity to its advantage; nonetheless the third album remained unfinished. The biographers trace the difficulties with Appel's studio selection (the affordable "914 Studios" located over 60 miles away), the manager's inability to translate Springsteen's musical ideas, and the subsequent strains on all fronts. In October 1974 Springsteen encountered Landau in Boston once again, they met in New York the following month, and in February 1975 Springsteen invited Landau to a 914 recording session. Time passed, the album languished, and Springsteen formally asked Landau to join the production team. Landau moved the sessions to Manhattan's Record Plant studios and elevated the professionalism of the recording process. Since Landau's previous production credits were unimpressive, Appel did not feel threatened by the new Springsteen–Appel–Landau team. Landau brought vision, professional credibility, and focus to Springsteen's art. From then on, the albums conveyed the quality craftsmanship evidenced in the band's shows.

Born to Run was released in late August 1975. Mike Appel may have suffered from his limitations in the studio, but his promotional skills harvested an unprecedented fall crop. The Northeastern media responded to Springsteen's live act, his new album, and a formidable promotional investment by Columbia by reifying Landau's landmark observations in *The Real Paper*. Let us pause and examine the reportage, since it established the context for the remainder of Springsteen's career. First, consider *Newsweek's* description of rock and roll's future:

> The bus driver's son—who bears a striking resemblance to Dylan, sports black leather jackets like Brando in "The Wild One" and wears a gold hoop earring—was known only to a small coterie of East Coast devotees a year ago. . . . Springsteen's punk image, his husky, wailing voice, his hard-driving blues-based music and his passionate, convoluted lyrics of city lowlife, fast cars and greaser rebellion recall the dreams of the great rock 'n' roll rage of the 1950s. . . . Springsteen rarely drinks, does not smoke, doesn't touch dope and never swears in front of women.

Springsteen's response to the publicity was officially one of surprise (asking Maureen Orth, "What phenomenon?") as he pleaded innocent to all the hype ("Just gets in the way"). The article featured an array of topics ranging from record-industry promotional strategies (supposedly, the story's angle) to industry responses to the publicity, biographical matters, his audition with Columbia and Hammond's response, and the nun–trash can school story. When it turned to the inconsistencies between show reviews and record sales, enter the professional, Jon Landau. Deploying the promotional skills of a Washington spin doctor, Landau painted a silver lining to the lackadaisical sales numbers: "His first two albums' not selling was the best possible thing for Bruce. . . . It gave him time to develop a strong identity without anyone pushing him prematurely. For twelve years he has had time to learn how to play every kind of rock 'n' roll." The *Newsweek* piece was a public-relations coup: It introduced a squeaky clean hero (never swears in front of women?) with an epic commitment to his art. The Appel–Landau management team was a striking blend of aggression and reason. The marketing now transcended screaming hype at music operatives in favor of systematic positioning. The *Time* cover story pursued a different angle, but the results were similar:

> [H]e is a glorified gutter rat from a dying New Jersey resort town who walks with an easy swagger that is part residual stage presence, part boardwalk braggadocio. He nurtures the look of a lowlife romantic even though he does not smoke, scarcely drinks and disdains every kind of drug . . . he is the dead-on image of a rock musician: street smart but sentimental, a little enigmatic, articulate mostly through his music. . . . His music is primal, directly in touch with all the impulses of wild humor and glancing melancholy, street tragedy and punk anarchy that have made rock the distinctive voice of a generation.

Again, Springsteen disavowed the hype: "I don't understand what all the commotion is about. I feel like I'm on the outside of all this, even though I know I'm on the inside. It's like you want attention, but sometimes you can't relate to it." The article reviewed his background (personal and musical), his family (the name is "Dutch"), his stage act ("Springsteen has mastered the true stage secret of the rock pro: he seems to be letting go totally and fearlessly; yet the performance remains perfectly orchestrated"), his audition with Hammond (and Hammond's response to Appel), and his music's thematic (the songs, according to their author, are about "survival, how to make it through the next day"). Like the *Newsweek* piece, the story ends with an optimistic portrayal of Bruce Springsteen's "magic."

The twin covers were a state-of-the-art public-relations victory. They established a context for failure as well. *Born to Run* may have reached number one on the charts and the live show scored major victories during a well-timed West Coast tour, but the pressure the publicity placed on the artist was formidable. Appel proudly told biographer Robert Hilburn: "Hollywood couldn't have manufactured a better story. If there was any hyping, it was the press hyping itself. All I did was coordinate it. They came to us." Yet Springsteen's comments to his biographer revealed confusion: "What am I doing on the cover of *Time* and *Newsweek*? I'm not the president. I'm really just a simple guy. I got my band and my music, and I love 'em both. That's my world. My life. It always has been." Springsteen even refused to go on stage on February 15, 1977 due to stress, as he told Hilburn: "I could see how people get into drinking or into drugs, because the one thing you want at a time like that is to be distracted—in a big way." (He relented and performed.)

To combat The Hype charges, Columbia staged a series of shows in New York City, invited the music industry, and allowed the chips to fall where they may. The show delivered to the extent that the most cynical reporters/announcers expressed a newfound appreciation of the Springsteen Phenomenon. Years later, the artist explained the strategy to the *Asbury Park Press*:

The thing I always had once I had made it, and I saw myself on the cover of *Time* and *Newsweek* and people were writing that I had been invented by the record companies, was that I always had those shows to fall back on. I knew I hadn't been invented by the record company. When I was twenty-five, I had been doing it for ten years already, with nobody looking twice at us. That was good because we had time to develop, to root yourself in the community. At times when one thing or another would throw me and I would think I'd been torn apart by the things I knew, we had a tremendous amount to fall back on and it sustained us our whole career. When things got bad, I just shut up and played. Also, it was music that was provincial—not in a derogatory way. It was based on small towns and in the end, that gave me something to sing about. There wasn't a lot of that going on. Instead of finding escape, something that would free me from the things I'd known, I wanted to write about those things.

The Show certainly counterbalanced The Hype. It was also an example of Springsteen's obsessive perfectionism. Dave Marsh and *Rolling Stone* quote Springsteen's sound engineer, former Elvis Presley employee Bruce Jackson, on the performer's preparations: "At every date . . . he goes out and sits in every section of the hall to listen to the sound. And if it isn't right, even in the last row, I hear about it, and we make changes. I mean every date, too—he doesn't let it slip in Davenport, Iowa, or something." Such attention to detail grew to the point of legend and, at times, hindered the art's progress.

The down side to Springsteen's perfectionism, as Columbia Records would, no doubt, be quick to point out, was in the studio. The time required for record production severely restricted product flow, and Columbia's ability to capitalize on any media momentum was seriously hampered. When Springsteen and Landau prepared to record the fourth album, Appel obtained a court injunction to block Landau's participation in the project. Appel played a central role in the aggressive marketing that rendered the wave of *Born to Run* publicity; however, those services were no longer required. Moreover, Appel's contractual agreements with Springsteen bordered on robbery. Hilburn reports that Springsteen received 3 percent royalties while Appel's company, Laurel Canyon, received 10; furthermore, instead of the "usual 15 to 20 percent" management commission, Appel received 50 percent. Laurel Canyon also controlled all publishing to the point where Springsteen was unable to grant Dave Marsh permission to quote songs for a book project. That angered the author far more than the money. Following angry depositions, sincere artistic appeals, and extensive financial negotiations, Mike Appel and Bruce Springsteen parted ways on May 28, 1977. During a 1992 interview Springsteen was told that Appel charged Landau with stealing his client, to which he responded:

Well, that's a shame, you know, because what happened was Mike and I had kind of reached a place where our relationship had kind of bumped up against its limitations. We were a dead-end street. And Jon came in, and he had a pretty sophisticated point of view, and he had an idea how to solve some very fundamental problems, like how to record and where to record. But Mike kind of turned Jon into his monster, maybe as a way of not turning me into one. It's a classic thing: Who wants to blame themselves for something that went wrong? Nobody does. . . . But the truth is, if it hadn't been Jon, it would have been somebody else—or nobody else, but I would have gone my own way.

Christopher Sandford describes the relationship that emerged from the settlement: "Landau would introduce his protégé to a world of classic books and films which, inevitably, came to shade the music. He played something of the role of cultural tutor to Springsteen. . . . Landau, in short, became a composite father–brother type. This dual rapport was at the root of a uniquely tight bond." That "uniquely tight bond" represented one of the most formidable artistic–public-relations operations in the history of commercial art. Springsteen was an artist with an obsessive vision, and Landau understood how to work through the marketing mechanisms necessary to communicate that vision to the artist's audience.

Springsteen–Landau's first order of business was the fourth album, *Darkness on the Edge of Town* (June 1978). That Springsteen's faith had been shaken by the Appel debacle was evident in the album's tone, the live show's monologues, and his public interviews. This was no longer the optimistic youth in pursuit of his creative dreams; to the contrary, the darkness of his youth and his family's struggles now matured in the shadowy world of professional adulthood. "Trust" had always been an elusive quality in Springsteen's life; now he would share those feelings with the world.

With the *Darkness* project Springsteen–Landau initiated an artistic–public-relations program that centered around "the package" that was the album, the tour, and its corresponding spin. The *auteur* developed his vision, articulated its components by way of the album and its songs, orchestrated the vision's live presentation, and prepared a script to be followed when promoting the package during media encounters. One merely has to listen to recordings of shows and consult the corresponding media accounts to realize that Springsteen deployed a finely honed act, both on and off stage.

Once more, the key to the various projects involves their live shows. Springsteen's artistic visions are cinematic, and only the theatricality of the live show captures the expression in its entirety. Although the music contributes to the show's pacing, the between-song monologues provide a sense of narrative continuity as they invoke the rationale for the emotional outbursts that are the respective songs. During the *Darkness* tour Springsteen used his "raps" to probe his relationship with his father, to articulate the sense of hopelessness his father endured, or to celebrate life on the boardwalk and the escape it offered. With the release of his fifth album, the double-album set *The River* (October 1980), Springsteen began to explore the pleasure–pain paradox articulated on record via the live monologues. A 1984 (Baltimore) *Sun* article features a transcript of a 1981 monologue in Stockholm, Sweden:

I grew up in this little town. As I got older, I started looking around me, and it didn't seem there was any way I was going to get out of there. I looked back at my father, and the only time he got out of that town was to go to World War II.

When he came out of the Army, he got married, settled down, and went to work in a plastics factory. And his father had done the same thing. It seemed that the one thing we had in common was that we didn't have enough information; we didn't have enough knowledge about the forces that were controlling our lives. I watched my old man end up a victim, and he didn't even know it; he didn't even know of what. Now, back in the Sixties, people were asking a lot of questions about those kinds of things. The only place I ever heard it was at night when I was listening to the radio. I'd lay up in bed with the radio on underneath my pillow. It seemed that in those songs by the Drifters and in those songs by Smokey Robinson, there was a promise. There was a promise of a right to a decent life, that you didn't have to live and die like my old man did, working in some factory until he couldn't hear what you were saying to him anymore. When I go back, I see these friends of mine. When we were young, they were tough inside; they had strong hearts, and they had dreams. Slowly these days, that stuff gets beat out of you. You get run down; you get weary, and you get tired. The only thing that kept me from giving up when I was young was in the rock and roll music I heard—that there was a meaning in life, a meaning in living. But it's a promise that gets easily broken today. There's nobody but yourself, I guess, that can make that promise come true. It's been broken too many times; so you have to stay hard inside.

This was not some off-the-cuff remark used for some sort of spontaneous showmanship. These were planned, practiced, and perfected scripts. The E Street Band entered on cue and the composite of music, stage script, and theatrical lighting/sound rendered a show unlike any other in popular music. When a Springsteen family member described her relative's act as "preaching," she delivered a compelling critical observation.

Throughout their career together, Springsteen and Landau have demonstrated an uncanny sense of pacing. If a particular work strikes a certain response with the public, they rarely attempt to repeat it. It may be intuitive, it may be strategic—nonetheless it is effective. Thus, when Springsteen withdrew after *The River* tour to explore his feelings about his and his characters' situations, he provided what would prove to be another calm before another storm. The *Nebraska* album (September 1982) is a monumental work. The album's themes, its expression, its departure from the E Street wall of sound, its omission of radio-friendly material—everything about the project suggests artistic courage. (My references to a "wall of sound" involve Phil Spector's production strategy in which individual instruments—often doubled or tripled in number—are deliberately recorded and mixed to create the sense of one, huge instrumental presence.) That Columbia released what was functionally a "demo tape" of songs indicates the respect Springsteen–Landau commanded. (Springsteen prepared a home-recorded demo tape for the band to use as a song guide, but efforts to transform the originals into E Street versions failed and the tape was issued in, basically, its original form.) There were no tours in support of *Nebraska*. The work spoke for itself. In an era of American pride and nationalistic rededication, *Nebraska* dwelled on the dark side of the American Dream.

Not all of the songs from Springsteen's demo tapes were used on *Nebraska*. With Landau's and the E Street Band's assistance, several *Nebraska* leftovers were transformed into wall of sound presentations that, in many respects, betrayed their narrative content. *Nebraska's* quiet was shattered by one of the most misinterpreted works of art in modern history, 1984's *Born in the U.S.A.* (issued in June). If someone takes, say, "Mr. Tambourine Man" and explains that it describes their personal relationship with God, well, Dylan's writing style facilitated that experience. But for someone to take the lyrics of "Born in the U.S.A." as signifying a return to patriotism and domestic pride is the functional equivalent of calling an "apple" a "skyscraper." Once again, we observe the impact of the "show" on interpretations of Bruce Springsteen's art. The show sounded like a celebration, but the monologues and songs followed a different perspective.

On June 29, 1984 "460 days of Bossmania" began with a series of international arena shows, to be followed by an international stadium tour of immense proportions. (The E Street Band added Nils Lofgren and Patti Scialfa, the group's first female member, at around this time.) The media chronicled it all. *Esquire* opined: "For all this wide excellence, Mr. Springsteen has attained the highest station of American celebrity: Ubiquity. He's become time, not the watch." The *Los Angeles Times* proclaimed:

> At a time when rock music is being attacked as a corrupting influence on young people, the 36-year-old Springsteen represents the positive side of the music, exhibiting a deep-rooted love of country. His music is in no way simple flag-waving, however. Many of his best songs speak eloquently to the way American society—through governmental indifference or commercial greed—has robbed people of their aspirations.

The *Times* quotes the legendary Bill Graham: "It's like he stands for everything we were taught to believe about hard work and integrity in this country." And the *New York Times* declared Springsteen to be the best rock performer ever:

> To say Mr. Springsteen is the best rock performer ever is not to say he is the best composer, the best singer, the best guitarist or the best top-10 singles artist. . . . But for his very perseverance, his proud assertion of the values that have made rock music so beloved, Mr. Springsteen deserves our admiration. . . . Mr. Springsteen projects an almost unfailing positive vision. It is a remarkable feat: passion without enduring pain; positivism without sacrifice of power.

Journalists scrambled to gather opinions or discover unique insights regarding the surging phenomenon. For example, the *Newark Star-Ledger* interviewed Otis Blackwell, Connie Francis, Little Richard (who called him "electrifying"—now *that's* a compliment!), Frankie Valli, and Carl Perkins searching for provocative revelations, and Perkins delivered: "If Bruce had been at Sun Records in 1954, it would have been a horse race between him and Elvis to the finish. . . . If Bruce had been around in the 50s, with his image, I think it would have stopped some of the southern preachers from condemning our music." He continued: "There's not one of the pillars of rock 'n' roll that wouldn't say this boy couldn't have fit in as one of the founders of this distinctively American music form and fit in well. . . . He speaks well for America and American music. He's a super talent and human being."

Among all the commentary and publicity surrounding the *Born in the U.S.A.* tour, a provocative—and, for some, embarrassing—event occurred within another important 1984 spectacle. During a campaign stop in New Jersey, incumbent presidential candidate Ronald Reagan did what *all* public speakers do when visiting a particular area: He mentioned a local hero's name as an applause line. (I would like to think that if the campaign had taken Reagan or Walter Mondale to my native South Carolina, they would have mentioned me!) Reagan—in no way—co-opted Springsteen's views or implied any type of association; he merely dropped his name as someone *from New Jersey* who dreams from the heart and promotes hope. Neither dreaming, hoping, nor claiming that the presidency is about realizing dreams connotes partisanship, and yet a media firestorm ensued. Six years later, Mikal Gilmore remained bitter:

> It was an amazing assertion. . . . It was the art of political syllogism, taken to its most arrogant extreme. Reagan saw himself as a definitional emblem of America; Bruce Springsteen was a singer who, apparently, extolled America in his work; therefore, Springsteen must be exalting Reagan—which would imply that if one valued the music of Springsteen, then one should value (and support) Reagan as well. Reagan was manipulating Springsteen's fame as an affirmation of his own ends.

(These convoluted conclusions are embarrassing. If nothing else, Gilmore's argument demonstrates the inherent limits of syllogistic reasoning—wrong premise, wrong result.)

Unfortunately, the media's misunderstanding became Bruce Springsteen's misunderstanding and the *U.S.A.* show became increasingly politicized. Springsteen's accounts of the luckless and locked out had never been partisan; after all, which political party is responsible for poverty, war, violence, or emotional abandonment? Still, from this point on, Springsteen railed against Republicans—occasionally mentioning Reagan, George Bush, Robert Dole, or others by name—and advanced political claims in a fashion that bordered on recklessness. To donate to a food bank or support a veteran's association is not a partisan act; to tell someone to vote for or against an individual *is*—especially if such advocacy follows party lines. But none of this seemed to matter to the millions who attended his shows. Songs of intense despair were choreographed like celebrations and the audience joined in the fun. The success of Springsteen's long-awaited live album, the three-CD/five-record set, *Live/1975–85* (issued November 1986), indicated the extent to which audiences wished to embellish the experience. Several of the most celebrated concert monologues were included on the *Live* set and Springsteen appeared to use the release as a means of clarification. As we shall observe in the following section, Springsteen values artistic control more than any other facet of commercial art (far, far more than money). When audiences consistently misinterpreted his stories, he lost a lot of that control. Only time would reveal the extent of the damage from this fundamental incongruity.

On May 13, 1985 Springsteen married actress Julianne Phillips in her home state of Oregon. The groom had met his bride a mere seven months earlier after a show in Los Angeles. They divorced in March 1989. The media machinations that elevated a hokey presidential comment into a domestic political crisis had their way with Springsteen's ill-fated marriage as well. Speculations ran wide and, occasionally, deep. That his eighth album, *Tunnel of Love* (October 1987), would focus exclusively on matters of the heart led to further innuendo and assertion. In every respect (personal and professional), Springsteen needed a change, a point he related to *Rolling Stone* in 1992:

> I really enjoyed the success of *Born in the U.S.A.*, but by the end of that whole thing, I just kind of felt "Bruced" out. I was like "Whoa, enough of that." You end up creating this sort of icon, and eventually it oppresses you. . . . It's funny, you know, what you create, but in the end, I think, the only thing you can do is destroy it. So when I wrote *Tunnel of Love*, I thought I had to reintroduce myself as a songwriter, in a very noniconic role. And it was a relief.

To reintroduce his songwriting, the auteur shifted themes. A thematic change required an adjustment in the all-important show, as he indicated to the *San Francisco Examiner*: "If I wasn't going to have something different to say, it wouldn't have made sense to go out on this tour at all. . . . You can't come out and play oldies because then you're a damned oldies act." Springsteen continued: "On the last tour . . . it felt a little embarrassing. . . . It's not that I'll never play the songs again, but . . . when I went to put this show together, I said, 'Well, what were the songs that were the kind of cornerstones of what I had done?' Those are the ones I automatically put to the side." Not only did he put those "cornerstones" away, he rearranged the band's stage positioning (telling *Rolling Stone*, "The first thing I did . . . was make everyone stand in a different place") and eliminated strategic aspects of the traditional show (e.g., shifting the Springsteen–Clemons interplay to Scialfa). Springsteen explained his new plans to the *Rocky Mountain News*: "I wanted the show to be about the idea of home, of people searching for it and maybe finding it. . . . And then once you find it, how difficult it is to hold onto it, and to nurture it, and to remain in that place. And to learn how to live with love, which is very hard to do. . . . So, you get struggle, struggle, struggle." The E Street Party faded in favor of The Struggle.

The *Tunnel* tour conveyed The Struggle through a show that signaled the end of an era. Gone were the joyous antics of the Leiber and Stoller–inspired musical playlets that typified the E Street Band's act for over ten years. In its place was a more mature, slower-paced presentation of relational life. From costuming, to set design, to the scripted monologues, the tour signaled a transition that was made official shortly after its completion. With personal telephone calls and handsome bonuses, Springsteen dismissed his band. As he related to the *Los Angeles Times* in 1992: "I felt like I closed the book on a certain chapter of what I was doing. . . . I didn't think loyalty to your musicians necessarily meant always playing together." Reports indicate that various band members were either angered by, anguished with, or accepting of their band-leader's decision.

This was certainly a period of personal and professional growth for the auteur. The marital problems were merely symptoms of a much larger difficulty: An inability to adjust to life outside of music. Whereas commentators had long joked that Springsteen played four-hour shows because he had no place else to go, they were, in fact, correct. During interviews for the 1992 tour, Springsteen was quite open about his situation, as these remarks to Jim Henke indicate:

> I didn't want to be one of those guys who can write music and tell stories and have an effect on people's lives, and maybe on society in some fashion, but not be able to get into his own self. But that was pretty much my story. I tend to be an isolationist by nature. And it's not about money or where you live or how you live. It's about psychology. My dad was certainly the same way. You don't need a ton of dough and walls around your house to be isolated. I know plenty of people who are isolated with a six-pack of beer and a television set. But that was a big part of my nature. Then music came along, and I latched onto it as a way to combat that part of myself. It was a way that I could talk to people. It provided me with a means of communication, a means of placing myself in a social context—which I had a tendency not to want to do. . . . Now I see that two of the best days of my life were the day I picked up the guitar and the day that I learned how to put it down. . . . I had locked into what was pretty much a hectic obsession, which gave me enormous focus and energy and fire to burn, because it was coming out of pure fear and self-loathing and self-hatred. I'd get onstage and it was hard for me to stop. That's why my shows were so long. They weren't long because I had an idea or a plan that they should be that long. I couldn't stop until I felt burnt, period. Thoroughly burnt. It's funny, because the results of the show or the music might have been positive for other people, but there was an element of it that was abusive for me. Basically, it was my drug. And so I started to follow the thread of weaning myself.

Springsteen acknowledged that he was "really bad off for a while" and he had started "down that dark path" before he turned to therapy. He continued:

> The best thing I did was I got into therapy. This was really valuable. I crashed into myself and saw a lot of myself as I really was. And I questioned all my motivations. Why am I writing what I'm writing? Why am I saying what I'm say-ing? Do I mean it? Am I bullshitting? Am I just trying to be the most popular guy in town? Do I need to be liked that much? I questioned everything I'd ever done, and it was good.

Springsteen managed to achieve something few of his song characters ever attempt: *He changed his life for the better.*

Springsteen rebounded from his darkness through professional intervention and his relationship with Patti Scialfa. During the *Tunnel* tour, Springsteen and Scialfa grew closer and, unfortunately, endured much negative publicity in the process. In July 1990 Scialfa gave birth to the first of Springsteen's three chil-dren (Evan James, followed by Jessica Rae, and later, Sam), the couple relocated to the Los Angeles area, and were married in June 1991. Springsteen's life experienced a storybook turnaround: He grew closer to his father through his own entry into fatherhood, his domesticity allowed him to relax and enjoy life, and the tranquility of his marital relationship eased his mind. Such conclusions are not the product of idle speculations; Springsteen publicly acknowledged the changes in his life through both his interviews and his art.

With regard to the latter, he reentered the musical world through a series of spontaneous guest appearances and charity benefits in the early 1990s. One event, the 1991 Christic Benefit, featured an all-acoustic show complete with the now-standard political commentary ("When everybody starts believing those big illusions . . . you end up with a government like the one we've had for the past decade") and intensely personal songs about his father ("My Father's House") and his mother ("The Wish"). With time and the assistance of Roy Bittan, Springsteen overcame his writing struggles and generated two albums simultaneously. *Human Touch* and *Lucky Town* (issued March 1992) were both long and short in the making. Springsteen strained to assemble *Touch* and, once completed, quickly reeled off *Town* as its complement. Springsteen/Bittan auditioned and convened a new band, organized the "show" through which the new material would be presented, and initiated the *Touch/Town* tour in June 1992. He explained his new show's approach to the *Hartford Courant*: "I wanted to maintain the richness of the sound and the color, and maintain the R & B feel, and I wanted to push it out a little bit into the area of gospel music and wanted to push it out a bit in the area of harder edged rock. I just wanted to go out there and see how it felt playing with different musicians."

Loaded with family and new friends, the *Touch/Town* tour opened in Europe, traveled across the United States, and endured constant comparisons to the E Street Band's glory days. The stage act was an extension of traditional Springsteen theatrics (guitar poses and athleticism) and the wall-of-sound presentational style; however, the gospel backing vocals and mannerisms added a new twist to the show. Neither the records nor the tour enjoyed the success of the 1980s; nevertheless, Springsteen worked diligently to achieve his long-standing artistic goals. The band also appeared on MTV's *Unplugged* series that year, although Springsteen deviated from the program's format and performed with electric instruments. Columbia issued a CD of that show in Europe (as a promotion for a 1993 tour) and later in the United States. After the tour, Springsteen wrote an emotionally stirring song for Jonathan Demme's film, *Philadelphia*, titled "Streets Of Philadelphia." On March 21, 1994 he received an Academy Award for the song and offered one of the more moving acceptance speeches of that evening:

> You do your best work and you hope that it pulls out the best in your audience and some piece of it spills over into the real world and into people's everyday lives and it takes the edge off of your fear and allows us to recognize each other through our veil of differences. I always thought that was one of the things popular art was supposed to be about, along with the merchandising and all the other stuff.

Springsteen, the E Street Band, and Jon Landau (and crew) returned to the studio in early January 1995 to record a series of songs to be included in Springsteen's first greatest-hits package (released, remarkably, in late February 1995). The venture was filmed and issued in 1996 as *Blood Brothers: Bruce Springsteen and the E Street Band*. According to the film, Springsteen contacted the band on a Thursday and they assembled in New York the following Monday for the sessions. The auteur's control over his artistic environment remained complete.

One of the songs the band attempted for the greatest-hits package was titled "The Ghost of Tom Joad" (like most of *Nebraska*, the band could not work it out). Springsteen built on the song's premise and created 1995's *The Ghost of Tom Joad*. The title cut, of course, is based on the central character from John Steinbeck's *The Grapes of Wrath* and the album explores Steinbeck's themes as they manifest in contemporary America. The sparse recordings bring Springsteen's voice forward in a fashion that elevates the respective songs' emotional qualities, and the shows that accompanied the album's release extended that strategy. The tour in support of *Joad* represented a synthesis of the *Nebraska* album and the 1991 Christic Benefit in that it featured Springsteen, unaccompanied on guitar and harmonica (an off-stage synthesizer appeared on a few songs). He described the show to *Guitar World Acoustic*: "I don't know what kind of show we have. It's not quite a folk show; it's something else. It has a lot to do with cinema, maybe. It's just some different thing; I didn't know myself how different it was until I did it in front of an audience."

Part of the show's cinematic style involved Springsteen's insistence on silence during songs. Each edition opened with a speech instructing the audience to refrain from clapping along, yelling, or otherwise disrupting the silence, the mood, he was attempting to establish. Springsteen's interview with Robert Hilburn and the *Los Angeles Times* elaborates on the *Joad* tour's theatrics:

> For the music to work, you have to have silence. . . . These songs come to life in the quiet, and I knew intrusions on that quiet would chip away at the mood you are trying to convey. The show has a lot of elements. The spoken passages are as important as the songs in a way. It's theater and it's music. Ideally, I appear in between songs, but when the music starts, I disappear and the characters in the songs fill the stage with their lives and their experience.

The strategy worked. The *Joad* package may not have generated the revenue or media attention of the *U.S.A.* project, but it demonstrated the maturity and dignity of Springsteen's art. It was the record John Hammond thought he had agreed to produce.

Bruce Springsteen ushered in the new century on the road with the E Street Band. Beginning in April 1999, the group reassembled for a major reunion tour that traveled around the world to joyous receptions. Ten Madison Square Garden shows were recorded, edited, and released on CD (*Live in New York City*) as well as in various video forms. Springsteen has written for other films (receiving an Oscar nomination for "Dead Man Walkin'"), has turned down movie offers, has released a long-awaited box set of outtakes (titled, *Tracks*, a four-CD set), has issued a book of song lyrics with compelling commentary (that will prove to be more than a blessing in the following sections), has appeared on tribute albums and concerts (e.g., for Woody Guthrie and Frank Sinatra), has prepared/ performed a song commemorating the September 11, 2001 horror, and has recorded a new album with the E Street Band (*The Rising*, released in late July 2002). As it has been throughout his career, Springsteen's album projects are few and far between. But the recognition he has received from the Rock and Roll Hall of Fame (inducted in 1999), the Polar Music Award (1997), and more indicate the praise his work deserves. Springsteen's success reflects a fascinating synthesis of hard work, musical knowledge, and creative drive. For more on the creative imperative that initiated and sustained that work, let us turn to the impulse that supports Springsteen's art.

chapter six

the impulse

The synthesis of inspirational influences, artistic philosophy, and stylistic tendency that flows from the creative impulse captures the essence of the artist-as-auteur. Focus is often a prime determinant in the impulse's ability to achieve and sustain success in its creative quest. That obsession accompanies excellence is most evident in this marriage of vision and talent. Whatever inspires the artistic drive necessary to negotiate a controlling vision through the commercial minefield that is the professional art world is, indeed, a fundamental element of the creative process. The willpower required must certainly border on pathology. The claim that few artists are as focused as Bruce Springsteen appears to be supported by the evidence. Whether his mission is his father's revenge or an instinctual urge to articulate his observations, Springsteen's commitment to his art is complete. His drive for expression may well be as impressive as the art itself.

Where did such an orientation originate? What energized a shy, introverted individual to the point where he felt compelled to share his inner-most feelings with millions of strangers? Bruce Springsteen is an artist with a message, that is certain. But that message was years in the making. The music moved young Springsteen from the back of the class to the musical front row, and later, onto the public stage. The music transformed his severe introversion into a grandstanding extroversion, as he explained to Guitar World: "I came from a small town where I grew up on popular music. The subversiveness of Top 40 radio can't be overestimated. . . . I sat in my bedroom and wrote the Top 20 down religiously every Wednesday night, cheering for my heroes and hissing the villains of the day. So I wanted to play in that arena. . . . And I thought it was a worthwhile thing to risk." He continued: "The town I grew up in was very divided—racially and class-wise—yet there were songs that united everyone at some point, like the great Motown music." That Motown sound not only united a divided community, it provided Springsteen's "map" to his personal and professional future. He described soul music's influence to Time-Life video: "I think you look back and you look at all the performers that came before you . . . they make their own maps . . . and they leave them for you if you care to read them . . . there's an art to it . . . those guys were the masters . . . all the soul greats . . . they were the masters at it." Springsteen invoked his map metaphor to *Guitar World* as well:

> I'm basically a traditionalist, and I like the whole idea of a rock and roll lineage. I always saw myself as the kid who stepped up out of the front row and onto the stage—who would carry the guitar for a while, and then pass on the rock and roll flame. And you take it as far as you can and write your own map for other people to follow a little bit. You try to not make the mistakes that people who came before you made, and in some fashion you reset some of the rules of the game if you can.

Springsteen's "map" metaphor reappears throughout his public commentary. He discovered an artistic map, he followed it, and he contributed to its development. From the outset, Springsteen was in no way interested in tearing down the rules; on the contrary, he worked to understand them, to use them, to modify them when necessary, and most of all, to respect them. His map provided his professional motivation—a point he developed for the *Philadelphia Inquirer*: "I'm just doing what I feel my job is, which is to make up my own map. I've followed the people who I've admired and the music that I like, and followed those maps. . . . Now I'm trying to make my own and help other people make theirs in their lives. That's the only service my music provides." One could not be more direct in the articulation of one's professional orientation.

Initially, Springsteen's map integrated Motown's themes, Memphis' sound, and James Brown's presentational style to chart a show with a mission. The auteur confirmed the show's origins for Time-Life: "Everything we did live came out of soul music . . . the spiritual intensity . . . the idea of going for both your spirit and your gut. . . . My idea was the show should be part circus, part political rally, part spiritual meeting, part dance party—you had to go back to the physical in the end. . . . You began with the physical and end with the physical . . . get their ass moving and the spirit will follow." The show's "spiritual intensity" was its most prominent feature. The four-hour extravaganza's strategic pacing incorporated all the elements cited above—it was a physical achievement. For assistance, Springsteen modeled a performer who not only shared his intensity but also provided a contrast to the Top 40 mentality that guided most of the musical competition on the Jersey Shore band circuit. Springsteen described his role model to *Musician*'s Bill Flanagan:

> For me, James Brown was somebody I really looked to. Part of that was just learning the craft of band-leading, what you needed to know in the little bars we came up through. We weren't a Top 40 band but we played bars that had Top 40 bands play in them. So when we came on we tried to do what we wanted to do, but very often that would be met by a good part of the crowd somewhat hostilely [sic], because they wanted the Top 40 music. So you always try to

find ways to survive, and being able to focus the strengths of the band was pretty important in those days.

That focus came naturally to the intense introvert's serious nature—yet another quality he shared with Brown. He recalled his youthful intensity in a *New York Times Magazine* interview: "I took my music just about as seriously as I could take anything. I felt like I needed to. I don't know if I felt a lot of people had blown it before me. I was young and I was very intense about it. I saw it as redemptive. I was also so influenced by James Brown, and he took it real seriously, too." Christopher Sandford's biography cites a Swedish radio interview in which Springsteen acknowledged both his philosophical and functional debt to James Brown and his musical competitors:

> All the Stax stuff and Atlantic stuff, I'm very into that. . . . The band has moments when it's based a lot on those R&B bands, especially in the way I use the band. I use the band in a very similar way: If you see Otis Redding in *Monterey Pop*, the way he uses his band, the way James Brown uses his band. . . . The best band leaders of the last ten, twenty years, from what I've listened to, have been your soul band leaders. They whip them bands into shape. I tend to use mine that way.

Springsteen relied on an established musical tradition—an established American musical tradition—to articulate (and market) his show. His "mission" was more personal in nature than his carefully stylized "show."

To understand Springsteen's artistic mission, we must embrace the philosophy that supports it. There are no mysteries here. Bruce Springsteen views his profession as a job. His job is to create useful art—art that is functional for audiences. To achieve that end, he aspires to make a connection with his audience so that he may probe his emotional history and communicate insights that help his audience deal with life. He cultivated an audience, embraced its worldview, and committed himself to a message strategically designed for that constituency. With time, his commitment to be a purveyor of eternal hope waned in favor of more diverse messages, but his philosophy never wavered. His comments on these matters are remarkably consistent. We now turn to the public record and Springsteen's carefully conceived artistic philosophy.

He has given much thought to the writer's charge—in general—and to his job in particular. First, we consider this detailed account of the writer's role as conveyed to Mark Hagen in 1999:

> First of all, everybody has a memory—where do you remember, why do you remember, when you were eleven years old, and you were walking down a particular street on a certain day, there was a certain wind blowing through the trees, and the sound your feet made on the stones as you came up the drive. Everyone has memories like that, that they carry with them for no explicable reason. And these things live within you. They are an essential part of who you are. It may be that something happened. Maybe nothing happened. But for some reason on that particular day you had some moment of experience that revealed

to you what it meant to be alive. How important it is, what you can do with your life. And your life can be brought back to you by the sound of your feet on gravel at a certain moment. That's the writer's job. The writer collects and creates those moments from out of his own experience and the world that he sees around him. Then you use your imagination and put those things together, and you present that experience to your audience, who then experience their own inner vitality, their own centre, their own questions about their own life, and their moral life. Whatever you're writing about, there's a connection made. That's what you're paid for—somebody says, "Hey, I'm not alone." . . . You're just trying to bring forth experience and get people in touch with all of those things in their world. That's the real job, the job that keeps you writing. That's what keeps you wanting to write that next song, because you can do that to people and because if I do it for you, I do it for me.

Notice Springsteen's emphasis on communication and the writer's commitment to establish a connection with the audience. Fundamental to that objective is the artist's understanding of the target audience and his or her ability to probe his or her emotions as a pathway to their "inner vitality." Springsteen's objectives focus on the "connection" he must establish in order to communicate. There is very little expression for expression's sake—the job is functional. He contrasted that orientation with the "genius" associated with innovators such as Bob Dylan and Elvis Presley in this 1987 *Rolling Stone* interview:

I guess when I started in music I thought, "My job is pretty simple. My job is [that] I search for the human things in myself, and I turn them into notes and words, and then in some fashion, I help people hold on to their own humanity— if I'm doing my job right." . . . Dylan was a revolutionary. So was Elvis. I'm not that. I don't see myself as having been that. I felt that what I would be able to do, maybe, was redefine what I did in more human terms than it had been defined before, and in more everyday terms. I always saw myself as a nuts-and-bolts kind of person. I felt what I was going to accomplish I would accomplish over a long period of time, not in an enormous burst of energy or genius. To keep an even perspective on it all, I looked at it *like a job*—something that you do every day and over a long period of time. To me, Dylan and Elvis—what they did was genius. I never really saw myself in that fashion. I'm sure there was a part of me that was afraid of having that kind of ambition or taking on those kinds of responsibilities.

There Springsteen advanced a straightforward conceptualization of art's function: "What the best of art says is, it says, 'Take this'—this movie or painting or photograph or record—'take what you see in this, and then go find your place in the world. This is a tool: Go out and find your place in the world.'"

Springsteen's notion of art as a "tool"—something that is useful to his audience in its search for relevancy—shifts the creative emphasis from self-expression to functional instrument. For him to express his feelings on a given subject without placing that view in a specific context would, no doubt, seem frivolous. He labors to ground himself in his audience's worldview so that it may relate to him, his work, and the perspectives espoused within his art to the point of using that tool in some fashion. Consider these comments to New Jersey's *Asbury Park Press*:

> It's hard to see that paradox—how something can be filled with so many beautiful things and horrible things. Beauty, culture, art—it's useful. It can be a source of inspiration and strength, a way to access the grace that is in the world. I didn't grow up in a family where novels were discussed or movies or art, but you can find that beauty even if you're not exposed to culture in that way. Whether it's the way the sun feels on your face on a particular day, even if it's just—it's hard to say all this without strumming a guitar behind me . . . it's just that everybody has to find an answer to what beauty is and how it can help. These songs are my answer. I like to think, if this is useful to you, then take this as part of your journey and make use of it as you will. That's the service I provide, along with some laughs and some entertainment, I hope. I try to make something that is graceful, and reach some of that grace myself.

In order to communicate something of value for a specific group of people, a writer must formulate and maintain a mental construction of that target audience. For, assuredly, what is graceful to one audience may seem graceless to another. Springsteen, therefore, maintains a controlling image of his audience, which he described to Flanagan:

> I believe everybody who writes has an audience in his head, whether it's an imaginary audience or your real audience. . . . I always write with an audience in mind. . . . And if I feel that coming back at me then I feel like I'm doing my job. That's why people come to my music—for some emotional experience or a perspective, either on their own lives or on the world that they're living in, or on their relationships. For a perspective.

But Springsteen views his audience as more than a gathering of individuals assembled for a rock and roll show. He told Dawidoff that he considers it to be a community: "I set out to find an audience that would be a reflection of some imagined community that I had in my head, that lived according to the values in my music and shared a similar set of ideals."

In his effort to perform his "job," produce "useful" art that would "connect" with his "imagined community," and offer it a means through which it may form a "perspective" on life, Springsteen needed a story line that would evolve as he and his "community" evolved. His mission needed a narrative baseline and he explained that foundation to the *Minneapolis Star Tribune*: "When I started, I wanted to document what it felt like to grow up in America during the time that I was growing up in. And I wanted to follow those characters, not just when they were teenagers or in their 20s, but into the middle parts of their lives, into their 40s and on. The idea was to draw my own map and maybe help other people draw their maps." He elaborated on his thesis for *Newsweek* as well: "We didn't go out just to make music, we went out to make *essential* music. It was fun and entertaining and hopefully enjoyable, but at the core there was something serious and essential that tied into the experience of living in America." To produce "essential" music that would chronicle "growing up in America," Springsteen needed a narrative framework that would transcend a single song or album. He discussed that superstructure with *Rolling Stone* during interviews for his 1984 release, *Born in the U.S.A.*:

> I guess what I was always interested in was doing a *body* of work—albums that would relate to and play off of each other. And I was always concerned with doin' albums, instead of, like, collections of songs. I guess I started with *The Wild, the Innocent and the E Street Shuffle*, in a funny way—particularly the second side which kind of syncs together. I was very concerned about gettin' a group of characters and followin' them through their lives a little bit. And so, on *Born to Run, Darkness on the Edge of Town* and *The River*, I tried to hook things up. I guess in *Born to Run* there's that searchin' thing; that record to me is like religiously based, in a funny kind of way. Not like orthodox religion, but it's about basic things, you know? That searchin', and faith, and the idea of hope. And then on *Darkness*, it was kind of like a collision that happens between this guy and the real world. He ends up very alone and real stripped down. Then, on *The River*, there was always that thing of the guy attemptin' to come back, to find some sort of community. It has more songs about relationships . . . people tryin' to find some sort of consolation, some sort of comfort in each other. Before *The River*, there's almost no songs about relationships. Very few. Then, on *Nebraska* . . . I don't know what happened on that one. That kinda came out of the blue.

To provide essential music that would fulfill his job's ambition of generating a useful "body" of work, Springsteen relied on his life experiences. He discussed his approach with Charlie Rose: "I think you tend to write about things that you're trying to sort out. I think you're trying to write about things that you don't understand and you wanna understand and so you're workin' on something to help you understand what that was all about . . . writing . . . comes out of that particular fire." His goal is neither autobiographical nor polemical; rather, it involves depth of understanding. He explained his orientation to the *New York Times Magazine*:

> Look, I don't see myself as the voice of whatever. I think a lot of the motivation for the music I've written comes from my own background. I understand jobless-ness like I do because I grew up in a house with a sense of dispossession. That sort of results in frustration and anger. I didn't start out with a specific politi-cal point of view. I don't sit down and write with political intentions. It's much more internal. The things I've written about best over my entire career are things I know about. The idea of the wasted life. The idea of the pure unkindness of the world. In some fashion I always felt that I wrote about those things feel-ing a connection with my own father that I didn't have growing up. It was a way of saying, "I remember this."

On another occasion he told *Rolling Stone's* Mikal Gilmore that his views are based on "personal insights" gleaned through his life's experiences. He elaborated upon this with Neil Strauss: "The songs are not literally autobiographical. . . . But in some way they're emotionally autobiographical. As they go by, you see your own take on the world and how it's changed since you were a kid. You create a variety of characters, and the thing they have in common is some emotional thread you've tried to use to make your own way through what can feel like a particular imponderable existence." Springsteen's comments to the *Los Angeles Times'* Robert Hilburn extend his argument:

> People literalize music to me to an unrealistic degree a lot of the time. The albums do end up being some sort of emotional diary, but it's not exact. You meet a lot of people who expect you to be your music, but you're not. It's part of you, but it's never your complete self. . . . If you write really well, it is coming out of your subconscious. You are never writing as well when all you are putting down are just what your conscious thoughts are. That's not the deep water from the well. The deep water is when it becomes mystical, and it doesn't happen that often. But I think anybody who is creative will tell you, it's when you don't know how you did what you did, that's when you really did something.

From this it appears that Springsteen envisions a "community" to be served by his emotional take on a subject of relevance to that constituency; he builds a context for that expression, and after all these strategic matters are settled, he turns the articulation of his message over to his talent. In other words, he seeks a form of controlled spontaneity. Through it all, as Springsteen's commentary in Hilburn's biography indicates, he not only reaches out to his audience through his emotional diary, he uses it to come to terms with himself. He described to Charlie Rose his "psychology" as a writer:

> I didn't think I had a great talent at it. I thought that I was somebody that was gonna have to really work harder than the next guy to formulate my own ideas, my own visions. I did, when I was a kid, I did work harder than everybody else. The rest, there's a certain amount of . . . psychology that comes with what kind of person are you . . . are you a watcher . . . are you active right away or do you watch . . . do you stand back and observe . . . that was always my nature . . . my nature was I was standing back and I watched the way things interrelated . . . what was going on around me. I was too frightened to join in, I didn't know how to join in . . . observation is a part of my psychology. I think that has a lot to do with people who then go on and write or take their own thoughts and formulate them in some fashion. It's usually a result of a variety of dysfunctions that you've managed to channel into something positive and creative rather than destructive . . . and it came out of that need . . . sortin' yourself out . . . it was easier for me to observe and . . . when you're writing, in particular, with different kinds of detail, it comes in handy . . . part of it was, I think, natural and part of it I worked really hard at.

Here is where we observe the artist's risk taking when the art explores the self in pursuit of material of value to others. In an attempt to probe deeper into the self, the artist may become lost and unable to pull out of the personal turmoil that feeds the professional endeavor. As we observed in the biography section, Springsteen may have fathomed his emotional past in order to connect with his audience and its needs, but he roundly ignored his emotional well-being in the process. Subsequently, after the *Born in the U.S.A.* tour, the auteur hit an emotional wall. He addressed that personal and professional turning point in a 1988 *Rolling Stone* interview:

> I guess I used to think that rock could save you. . . . I don't believe it can any-
> more. It can do a lot. It's certainly done a lot for me—gave me focus and direc-
> tion and energy and purpose. . . . But as you get older, you realize that it is not
> enough. Music alone—you can take some shelter there, and you can find some
> comfort and happiness, you can dance, you can slow-dance with your girl, but
> you can't hide in it. And it is so seductive that you want to hide in it. And then
> if you get to the position of somebody like me, where you can if you want to, you
> really can. . . . Well, you *think* you can, anyway. In the end you really can't, be-
> cause no matter who you are, whether it's me or Elvis or Michael Jackson, in
> the end you really can't. You can use all your powers to isolate yourself, to sur-
> round yourself with luxury, to intoxicate yourself in any particular fashion that
> you so desire. But it just starts eating away inside, because there is some-
> thing you get from engagement with people, from a connection with a *person*,
> that you cannot get anyplace else. I suppose I had a moment where I kinda
> crashed into that idea, before I was married.

He goes on to point out that even when he makes an "enormous" connection for the three hours of his show, "you can't live there," and he would be wise to come to grips with the other 21 hours of that day. Springsteen recovered from his rock idealism and his story continued by incorporating his recovery into his emotional autobiography. As *his* story evolved, so did his art. His intensity was in no way diminished; he merely refocused his drive so that his imagined community could follow his progress and do with his heartfelt diary what it wished. At this point, a large portion of Springsteen's constituency departed for another "party" and dutifully ignored the more mature observations emanating from his creative work.

Throughout his pursuit of his "job" and its goals, Springsteen developed sty-listic tendencies that flowed naturally from his stated artistic objectives. A "body" of work requires "continuity" if the creative outcome involves charting an identifiable cast of characters' activities across time. Central to the notion of narrative continuity is the auteur's foremost professional attribute: Control. Springsteen cultivated an unusual level of control: Control over himself, control over his craft, and control over his art's dissemination. My earlier comments that Bruce Springsteen was the "most orchestrated" celebrity of his time is a direct consequence of this systematic control of his public image, his art, and its distribution. The Mike Appel debacle threatened Springsteen's need for con-trol, and Appel's replacement, Jon Landau, not only restored the desired order, but his contributions to this artistic/commercial phenomenon have played a major role in maintaining Springsteen's intense need for control over his profes-sional existence. One gains the impression that Springsteen's treasured "maps" must have indicated the importance of gaining—and sustaining—control over all matters professional.

Springsteen's self-control and artistic independence are the pillars upon which his creative life rest, as he related to *Musician's* Chet Flippo:

That's why I started this. For the independence. I'm telling my story out there. I'm not telling somebody else's. I'm saying what I want to say. That's the only thing I'm selling. I had a few small jobs before I started playing but when I picked up that guitar, that was when I could walk down my own path. That's just the way I like it. It's a lucky feeling, you know, because how many people get to set their own standards and kind of run their own circus?

As early as 1978 he told Dave Marsh that his need for control was his motive for playing in the first place. Little doubt his father's lack of control over his vocational life inspired Springsteen—perhaps to the point of overcompensation. Nevertheless, his external control does not ensure internal tranquillity. While he may struggle to fend off external influences over his art's formulation and distribution, his creative work is the product of an—at times—uncontrollable internal battle. He described the situation in a 1975 *Crawdaddy* interview:

Well, like at one time I wrote everything in a few minutes, you know, ten minutes. And then once I took six months to write one song, "Born to Run." And then I sort of went back, this album, to like three, four days working on something. Plus, I was fighting myself all the time, you know. Always do that. Everybody's hard on themselves, well I take it to an extreme sometimes, where it starts like being self-defeating. In a way it's good, because I think in the end you do pull out the best stuff, but it's really a mind-breaking project. It'll freak you out. You get frustrated and you go nuts. . . . I get this inner tension, you know, that is like really unbelievable. It's something that builds up in you that has no particular release. And if you get stuck on something you just go nuts! You go crazy. You wanna [strangle] somebody. You wanna, you know, run into the street.

Here we observe one of the principal contributors to Springsteen's need for control: His artistic drive. True to his blue-collar background, Springsteen believes that the source of his art is not divine inspiration or natural talent—rather, he considers his "job" nothing less than hard work. He told Charlie Rose that he is a "miner" and that when he writes, he is "down there mining." Our miner does not sit and wait for inspiration to strike, but digs for his ideas and struggles with their articulation. As he related in the Time-Life video: "I didn't see myself as some gifted genius type of guy, I thought I was a hard-working guy . . . I worked really hard at learning to play . . . learning to write and sing." He elaborated on that point in another interview with Bill Flanagan in 1992:

I just thought I was gonna be a guy who was gonna have to . . . work *really* hard. . . . I wanted to have my own vision and point of view and create a world of characters, which is what the writers I admired did. It was a world unto itself, a world you slipped into, and yet a world that felt connected to the real world in some very important ways. I knew when I was very young I wanted to do that. Dylan's writing—that's just what felt exciting. So I took off in that direction. Hey, everybody shoots for the top! You don't know where it's gonna lead you. I

just took it a day at a time. I had a real serious dedication to it, but I always
felt I'd have to really sweat it out, to work really hard at it. I think I wrote ambi-
tiously. From the beginning I wrote wildly big with the idea of taking the whole
thing in and being definitive in some fashion. I think the show took on that approach also. I was ambitious. . . . I was shooting for the moon. And I guess
somewhere inside I felt like I could hit it.

And he did. Springsteen's first two album's lyrical content reflect in an unquestionable fashion his "ambitious" writing style and Dylan's influence. Although
they were the products of hard work, the imagery projected through *Greetings
from Asbury Park, N.J.* and *The Wild, the Innocent and the E Street Shuffle*
reminded critics of Dylan's spontaneous, "in the spirit" writings, hence the round
of "New Dylan" publicity that threatened Springsteen's control over his artistic
direction. In response, he shifted songwriting orientations, as he explained to the
New York Daily News: "After my second album, I started trying to get to the subject as straight as possible . . . I was finding my own style. Well, that flood of
images on the first two records was my style, but it was also associated with
Dylan. There are still a lot of images on 'Born to Run,' but at least from 'Darkness,' I was trying to write the way people speak as simply as possible." On another occasion, he told Flanagan: "I just felt like I wanted to speak more directly
. . . like people telling stories and talking about themselves, as if you were sitting
on the couch. So I started to go in that direction. In the end I'm not sure what
difference it makes in communicating, but at the time it was something I wanted
to pursue and I've gone that way ever since. I tend to opt for simplicity and clarity. I like the images to be clear."

As early as his third album, Springsteen settled into the narrative style that
would guide his pen for the rest of his career. While he returned to his impressionism briefly in 1992's *Lucky Town,* Springsteen established a strategy and
worked diligently to create believable characters who talked in provincial ways
about their recurrent life situations. In support of this he did two things: He
refined his writing and expanded his repertoire of narrative influences. Regarding
the former, Sandford claims that Springsteen "groomed" his lyrics "like a show-
dog" with songs going "through thirty, forty, and, in one case, fifty-six drafts."
Sandford and Nicolas Dawidoff observe how Springsteen's notebook, dictionary,
and thesaurus were his "constant companions" in his workmanlike approach to
songwriting. Regarding the latter, Springsteen expanded his artistic maps to
include other musical forms, cinema, and nonmusical writers. One new influence,
country music, added depth to his unfolding story and his efforts to mine more
mature subject matter, as he described to Dawidoff:

But there was a point where some of the issues rock-and-roll addressed
stopped. You've got your Saturday night, but you're gonna have to wake up the
next morning, pal, and you'll have to face the consequences of the choices you
make. Rock had been mainly about avoiding those choices. Country musicians
like Hank Williams and Merle Haggard asked the hard questions I was beginning
to ask myself. . . . Country was concerned with how you go on living after you

reach adulthood. I said, well why can't rock ask those same questions. Because the audience is going to be asking those questions real soon. Then, at a certain point, the questions country music was asking seemed to stop, so I moved into listening to a lot of Woody Guthrie. He seemed to me to have a bigger, broader canvas.

Contributing to that "broader canvas" were writers such as Flannery O'Connor and filmmakers such as John Ford. Springsteen admired O'Connor's attention to detail and Ford's dedication to continuity. In all cases, Springsteen—the craftsman—is more than willing to consider anything that facilitates the achievement of his strategic ends.

All the while that the auteur struggled to control the inner battles that rendered the art and to combat the outside influences that could hinder the work, he maintained steadfast control over the final product's dissemination. Once he regained control over his career from Mike Appel, Springsteen never relinquished it again. All indications are that his microscopic management of his art sets the standard for creative control. That he actively pursued litigation regarding the illegal distribution of studio outtakes by bootleggers demonstrates his commitment to control his art's dissemination. The rationale behind his drive for artistic control flows naturally from his creative philosophy and his efforts to orchestrate useful art for his audience. Since the auteur's messages are strategically conceived, he fights any attempt to disrupt the continuity of his musical prescriptions. As a result, studio outtakes are carefully guarded and songs that get "off message" are withheld. In fact, Springsteen's creative output is severely inhibited by his rigid stance on quality control. He discussed that trait with Dave DiMartino:

> I don't want to just take up space on the shelf, ya know? Or worry that if you don't have something out every six months, or even a year, that people are going to forget you. I was never interested in approaching it in that way. I've never been, from the beginning. I just have a feeling about the best I can do at a particular time, ya know? And that's what I wanted to do. And I don't come out until I feel that that's what I've done. Because there's so many records coming out, and there's so much stuff on the shelves. Why put out something that you don't feel is what it should be? And I don't believe in tomorrows, that "Oh, I'll put the other half out six months from now." You may be dead, you just don't know. You make your record like it's the last record you'll ever make.

He may approach each project as if it is his last, but that endeavor will never see the light of day if, in Springsteen's estimation, it drifts off message. These remarks to Neil Strauss pull the artistic philosophy and the resulting musical product together into a coherent whole:

> In some way I was trying to find a fundamental purpose for my own existence. And basically trying to enter people's lives in that fashion and hopefully maintain that relationship over a lifetime, or at least as long as I felt I had something useful to say. That was why we took so long in between records. We made

a lot of music. There are albums and albums worth of stuff sitting in the can.
But I just didn't feel they were that useful. That was the way that I measured
the records I put out.

Whether or not one appreciates Bruce Springsteen's art, the orchestration
of his creative output is impressive. This is an artist with a *coherent* plan of
action. Remarkably, he devised his strategy at an early age and has exercised
considerable discipline over a commercial process that contains a variety of
divergent, even competing, imperatives. While he may espouse an artistic orientation that sounds so simple on the surface, the realization of that ambition is
anything but pedestrian or easy. His interview with Ed Bradley for CBS's *60
Minutes* yields a splendid example of his creative worldview: "Basically, I started
out to try and tell a good story. One that will hold interest. One where something
is revealed, where something happens. Where I create characters that come to
life. That are real, that are recognizable, that could be you, that could be me in
a certain circumstance . . . and I ask the listener to walk in those shoes." And
his remarks to the *Asbury Park Press* about his lifework appear to be so uncom-
plicated: "It's my ongoing novel, if you will." Yet, the creative discipline, the philosophical commitment, and the physical energy necessary to keep his art on message may very well separate Bruce Springsteen from his songwriting peers.

The key to it all is the work's continuity. Springsteen not only admired John
Ford's cinematic continuity, but he directly incorporated that trait, as these
comments to Chet Flippo reveal:

> I was always very interested in keeping a continuity in the whole thing. Part of
> it for me was the John Ford westerns, where I studied how he did it, how he car-
> ried it off. And then I got into this writer, William Price Fox, who wrote *Dixiana
> Moon* and a lot of short stories. He's just great with detail. . . . But I was just
> interested in maintaining a real line through the thing. If you look just beneath
> the immediate surface, it's usually right there.

When Flippo inquired if he consciously writes in terms of scenes and images,
Springsteen responded: "Oh yeah, I always loved the movies. And, after all, music
is evocative. That's the beauty of it. . . . That's what I always want my songs to
do: To kind of just pan out and be very cinematic. The *Nebraska* record had that
cinematic quality, where you get in there and you get the feel of life. Just some
of the grit and some of the beauty."

In order to tell a "good story" and sustain the internal unity of his cinematic
"ongoing novel," Springsteen had to complement his scenic detail with a characterological coherence uncommon in the world of popular music. He may have been
motivated by the soul masters' performance skills, but his songwriting departs
from the traditions associated with popular music. Though he uses song structures in his writing (e.g., choruses, bridges), his attention to character development, scenic continuity, and narrative coherence borrows extensively from fiction
writing and cinema. The auteur's commentary on character development demonstrates the extent to which he departs from songwriting tradition. When the

New Music Express inquired if Springsteen had to "know" a character in order to portray that personality, he replied:

> No, you're not trying to recreate the experience, [you're] trying to recreate the emotions and the things that went into the action being taken. Those are the things that everyone understands, those are things that everyone has within them. The action is the symptom, that's what happened, but the things that caused that action to happen, that's what everyone knows about—you know about it, I know about it. It's inside of every human being. Those are the things you gotta mine, that's the well that you gotta dip into and, if you're doing that, you're going to get something central and fundamental about those characters.

The emotional depth of a song is Springsteen's narrative litmus test, as these comments to Flippo indicate: "That's the hardest thing to do, the very hardest . . . if you don't have that underlying emotional connection that connects the details together, then you don't have anything. . . . That's the trickiest thing to do and that was my only test of songs: Is this believable? Is this real?" His commentary about his art—like the art itself—achieves a tranquil simplicity that misrepresents the enormous depth conveyed through both.

The Springsteen Legacy in the History of American Song is an innovative synthesis of the various "maps" left by his predecessors. Many of Springsteen's influences are musical, several are not—all are American. Woody Guthrie's pen, James Brown's theatrics, John Steinbeck's values, John Ford's scope, Bob Dylan's imagery, Flannery O'Connor's precision, and the entire State of New Jersey provided the raw materials of Springsteen's art. As we are about to discover, his contributions to the development of American Song demonstrate a level of commitment and sacrifice rare in the world of commercial art. But that dedication and drive came naturally to this artist; he was born with an impulse to do through his art what he could not approach otherwise. The connections that were so difficult to achieve in his personal life became the centerpiece of his "job." And yet, Springsteen was not satisfied by a single evening of communication. He wanted to build—and sustain—a *relationship*. That ambition separates Bruce Springsteen from his musical peers. *Relationships* require work, and this artist readily embraced that job.

chapter seven

the oeuvre

I opened our discussion of Bob Dylan's lifework by noting his professional status and suggesting how that influenced the content and style of his lifework. Bruce Springsteen is not only a professional artist with creative and commercial factors to negotiate, he is an artist on a mission. His mission is to connect with his audience so that they, together, may come to terms with living in contemporary America. The oeuvre is, in every respect, by an American, for Americans, and tailored to represent a strategic take on the American way of life. The lifework's symbolic prescriptions are not, however, for *all* Americans. Springsteen's work speaks to a specific demographic group—not a demographic based on racial, ethnic, gender, or even socioeconomic variables; no, his work speaks to an *emotional* demographic. Springsteen writes about the emotional struggles of daily living for working Americans. No grandiose tales of the rich and famous or vituperative expositions on worldly happenings here; just poignant accounts of the emotional consequences of life's everyday events.

Flowing naturally from the artistic ambition of creating useful accounts of life's recurrent situations for an evolving community is the stylistic pursuit of narrative continuity. In service of that objective, Springsteen deployed a "soap opera" storytelling strategy though which he articulated melodramatic portrayals of everyday events in a systematic—occasionally prescriptive—manner. The story's plot hinges on life-cycle "struggles" as characters negotiate the pleasures and pains of work and recreation; peer, romantic, and familial relationships; as well as the ebb and flow of that delicate balance between dreams and actualities. Springsteen's soap opera, "The Worker's Elegy," unfolds in three phases across the lifework: The story's "dreaming, reckoning, and acceptance" phases conclude with 1995's *Greatest Hits* compilation and return via the reprise that is Springsteen's 1995 studio release, *The Ghost of Tom Joad*. The narrative opens with the introduction of Springsteen's fun-loving, urban cast of characters and their adolescent "dreams" of a better life. Characters play with cars and switchblades (as well as the occasional gun), anxiously plan their nights and weekends, and ponder life's bountiful offerings through carefree scenes of adolescent recklessness. These individuals—many are from the wrong side of the proverbial tracks and are determined to stay there—display a firm belief in their resilience and their ability to transcend their parents' mundane, uninspired lifestyles. The story turns with its second phase and the characters' realization that their youthful ambitions may falter. Marrying young and for the wrong reasons; locked into jobs with little-to-no chance of advancement (if they *have a* job); trapped in a frivolous lifestyle of hot rods, Saturday nights, and wasted paychecks; and devoid of any apparent motivation to end this vicious cycle of their own making, these characters face a darkness full of emotional turmoil that inspires violence, rebellion, and failure. Dreams of escape fade, never to return. With a growing recognition of life's conditions, Springsteen's characters enter the "acceptance" phase in which a shift of emphasis occurs. At this point, characters turn away from external sources of gratification toward more mature, internally motivated rewards; that is, they realize the value of loving relationships and, consequently, turn their energies toward new challenges. The story ends with the *Human Touch/Lucky Town* package, features a brief flashback with the original material prepared for the *Greatest Hits* album, and returns via the poignant vignettes of *Tom Joad*.

The Worker's Elegy unfolds in chronological order. The auteur's aspiration to render a body of work is achieved through the soap opera's three phases. The "dreaming" period extends from Springsteen's debut work, 1973's *Greetings from Asbury Park, N.J.*, to 1973's *The Wild, the Innocent and the E Street Shuffle*, and concludes with the transitional statement that is 1975's *Born to Run*. The new Springsteen–Landau creative team introduced the "reckoning" phase with 1978's *Darkness on the Edge of Town* and advanced the story line through 1980's *The River*, 1982's *Nebraska*, and 1984's blockbuster, *Born in the U.S.A.* The story closes with the "acceptance" phase's introductory meditation, 1988's *Tunnel of Love*, and 1992's twin releases, *Human Touch/Lucky Town*. Throughout the story's development, Springsteen's carefully orchestrated tours—and their offspring, the all-important "show" and corresponding media interviews—drive home the soap opera's thematic, using all available means to connect with his target audience. Like an effective political campaign, the program is message-driven and Springsteen–Landau deploy a host of theatrical and public-relations tactics that enable the tour to stay on message. Springsteen's talent complemented Landau's knowledge to choreograph the Worker's Elegy's every detail. It is an impressive feat.

Springsteen's 1992 tour featured media interviews that offered several seasoned takes on his story, its presentation, and their consequences for the author. His comments to *Rolling Stone*'s Jim Henke are instructive:

> All I try to do is to write music that feels meaningful to me, that has commitment and passion behind it. And I guess I feel that if what I'm writing about is

real, and if there's emotion, then hey, there'll be somebody who wants to hear it. I don't know if it's a big audience or a smaller audience than I've had. But that's never been my primary interest. I've had a kind of story I've been telling, and I'm really only in the middle of it. . . . I can't contrive something that doesn't feel honest. I don't write demographically. I don't write a song to reach these people or those people. . . . I want to sing about who I am now. I want to get up on-stage and sing with all of the forty-two years that are in me. . . . I'm a lifetime musician; I'm going to be playing music forever. I don't foresee a time when I would not be onstage somewhere, playing a guitar and playing it loud, with power and passion. I look forward to being sixty or sixty-five and doing that.

Whatever stories Springsteen weaves for his audience when he turns sixty-five will, no doubt, build upon the Worker's Elegy. Although he claims he does not write "demographically," Springsteen's envisioned audience—his imaginary "community"—involves a specific segment of the American way of life. There are no Ivy League graduates, no Southern farmers, no Western cowboys in Springsteen's soap opera. The auteur's emotional autobiography is firmly situated on the Jersey Shore, in the Big Apple's shadow. And it is a fascinating account of working-class life in that part of the United States.

the dreaming phase

Since many of America's pioneers traveled to these shores in pursuit of religious freedom, perhaps the Worker's Elegy should begin in church. Often, dreams are solidified in church as individual aspirations assume a communal quality when shared in society's principal venue for spiritual contemplation. For instance, the Black American church embraces the hopes and fears of its constituency through an, at times, rollicking, emotional, joyous (and occasionally, extremely *long*) service that allows participants to transcend the vicissitudes of daily living, envision a better way of life, and share a temporary escape through a sense of community unavailable elsewhere. In particular, the Southern Black church not only married Afro-rhythmic musicality to White, Western religious doctrine, it provided the musical foundation for the art form we call "rock and roll."

Bruce Springsteen's tale of American working life begins in an offspring of that Southern Black church: The soul-inspired, physically demanding, and spiritually uplifting escape that is his "show." That his musical inspirations were, themselves, one step from the pulpit sets the tone for the spiritual experience his show represents. Springsteen's concerts—in particular, his club shows—established the narrative foundation for the Worker's Elegy in that the characters introduced in his first two albums flow directly from his audience. The youngsters in *Asbury Park* and *The Wild, the Innocent* who cope with street life, mingle with gangsters, and live to party attended Springsteen's club shows—therefore we open there. Nowhere is Springsteen's artistic philosophy more evident than in his live performances, where he stood in his pulpit, stared into his congregation's eyes, and played the role of the hardest-working White man in show business.

Springsteen's "Rock Church" did not go unnoticed by the media, especially the Northeastern media. For example, during the media hype surrounding *Born to Run* and the *Time/Newsweek* cover stories, the *New York Times* reported: "Mr. Springsteen has it all—he is a great lyricist and songwriter, he is a wonderful singer, guitarist and piano player, he has one of the best rock bands anybody has ever heard, and he is as charismatic a stage figure as rock has produced." Two weeks later, the *Times* ran another piece, this one also by John Rockwell: "Mr. Springsteen's gifts are so powerful and so diverse that it's difficult even to try to describe them in a short space. . . . And Mr. Springsteen's themes perfectly summarize the rock experience, full of cars and love, street macho and desperate aspiration. Hearing these songs is like hearing your own life in music, even if you never lived in New Jersey or made love under the boardwalk in Asbury Park." Whether the journalistic fraternity was simply overwhelmed by the live shows, showing an allegiance to one of its own (Landau), responding to the dearth of musical inspiration in the mid-1970s, or some combination thereof, the publicity surrounding Springsteen was nothing less than incredible.

These shows represent the essence of the dreaming phase's story. Young characters fight their way through their individual workweeks or endure life on the street in anticipation of the weekend and the communal escape provided by rock shows, street races, and teenage street frolic. And Springsteen gave life to that story through his live crusade and its music, monologues, and theatrics. The congruity between the live show and the subsequent records lends credibility to both forms of expression. At this point in his career and its story, Bruce Springsteen was most definitely part of the cast.

The narrative impressionism that dominates *Greetings from Asbury Park, N.J.* (released in January 1973) reveals the sort of mindless atmosphere that controls the dreaming phase. Of the album's nine tracks (running just over 37 minutes), seven involve the impressionistic writing style pioneered by Bob Dylan and two weave more coherent stories: "Spirit in the Night" and its escape/party theme and the portrait, "It's Hard to be a Saint in the City." Although nowhere near as abstract as Dylan's wordplay strategy, "Blinded by the Light" and "Does This Bus Stop at 82nd Street" reflect Dylan's narrative impressionism through their use of recurring tag lines and musical structures. The remaining songs display a lighter version of Dylan's style that fall somewhere between a story and impressionism ("Growin' Up," "Mary Queen of Arkansas," "Lost in the Flood," "The Angel," and "For You"). "Growin' Up" conveys a sense of rebellion through its portrayal of the central character's insistence on rejecting whatever is requested by authority figures (it is a barrage of images—the words come in droves). "Mary" relates a need for escape through scenes featuring circus acts, rhyming crazed metaphors, and dark imagery. "Angel" and "For You" present character portraits: The former, an uneven account of a bicycle-riding youngster who endures city life; the latter, a rhyming litany of abstractions that, in its own way, reveals the narrator's commitment to his woman (a suicide victim). And "Flood" is a three-part musical: part one, an aggressive account of pregnant nuns and weird street life; part two, a more coherent vignette about a street racer and his

demise; and part three, a story about a street shooting. Each installment gen-
erates emotional takes on these young people's situations. The relentless
rhyming structures evident in these songs suggest the ambitious qualities of
Springsteen's early songwriting. In *Songs*, the auteur reports that *Asbury Park*
is the only album in which he "wrote the lyrics first," and that those words came
from a "very unself conscious place."

The wall-of-sound production (again, a recording strategy in which the various instruments are shaped into one huge sound) involved in songs such as
"Blinded" and "Hard to be a Saint" must have shocked John Hammond. This was,
in no way, the acoustic troubadour of Springsteen's Columbia audition. Instead
of a lone voice articulating impressionistic poetry, Hammond got a party. The
joyous sounds of "Blinded" with its guitar-driven, saxophone-laced account of
crazy-named characters doing strange things that just happen to rhyme (it is
an overwhelming parade of images), and "Spirits" full-band escape to an aptly
named lake where reckless teenage friends do what reckless teenage friends do,
communicate the partying atmosphere that a Bruce Springsteen show represented. There is little doubt that if you had never attended a Springsteen show,
you would gain a different feel for these songs. The songs introduced the
Worker's Elegy's carefree cast of characters and provided rich material for the
party environment of the heralded Springsteen show.

The festivities continue with *The Wild, the Innocent and the E Street Shuffle*
(released September 1973) and the album's seven songs of teenage street life
(running almost 47 minutes). Here the street is a tough, relentless place.
Although "love" exists in this world, the atmosphere is aggressive and appears
to establish the need for an escape to a more nurturing environment. The
impressionism continues with "The E Street Shuffle" (a wall-of-sound account of
crazy-named characters going about their adolescent business—it is all a
party) and lighter versions of the strategy: "Kitty's Back," "New York City Serenade," and "Wild Billy's Circus Story." The record also features two songs of
romantic escape ("4th of July, Asbury Park [Sandy]" and "Rosalita [Come Out
Tonight]") and a relational portrait ("Incident on 57th Street").

The lighter forms of impressionism are wide-ranging in their musical presentations. For example, the ten minutes of "Serenade" features a lovely two-and-
a-half-minute piano introduction that sets the scene for a musically evocative,
lyrically evasive account of New York City street life. The song recalls "Lost in the
Flood" in that it contains two independent vignettes that are woven together by
the street-life theme. The track's theatricality is its strength; again, this was,
no doubt, great material for the live show. Joining that strategy is "Kitty" and
its cute cat metaphor about a tom cat, his wayward lover, and her eventual
return. The track's musical punctuation contributes to the song's pacing in a
fashion that, once again, feeds the live act's theatricality and the album's party
atmosphere. Lastly, "Wild Billy" conjures images of Dylan's "Desolation Row"
through its slow carnival sound (tuba, accordion), circus characters (e.g., a man-
beast, a fire-eater, a sword-swallower, a midget), and its general, lighthearted,
craziness. The story posits an escape that just might raise life's weirdness by a

notch or two. In any event, the rhythmic word choice suggests that this is one well-groomed "show dog."

The romantic escapes and relational portrait preface Springsteen's song-writing future as the auteur's provincial language, scenic descriptions, and strategic characterizations demonstrate the narrative side of his pen (not that there is *anything wrong* with internal chaos!). The marvelous detail of "4th of July" and its portrayal of the boardwalk, the street characters, the mindless activities, and ultimately, the narrator's decision to leave the street life behind paints an insightful account of the emptiness that inspires the search for a better life (as well as the impact of breaking up with a girlfriend). That theme is extended by the show-stopper "Rosalita" and its wall-of-sound presentation of crazy-named street urchins pursuing weird but rhythmic street activities while the narrator pleads with Rosalita to step through that door and join him in a better life. Once more, the song's theatrical pacing enlivens an already raucous account of the narrator's budding musical career and his effort to use his new-found livelihood to lure Rosalita away. Their proposed destination is anything but substantive as the narrator just wants to sit around and listen to music all day and night. Finally, the relational portrait of Hispanic lovers featured in "Incident" combines romance and street life as the song embellishes the youngsters' love while exploring the switchblade lifestyles of ethnic gangs on urban streets. The song is long on description—Springsteen's detail sharpens the story's emotional qualities. These songs reinforce Tom Waits's observation in Bill Flanagan's book on songwriting that Springsteen songs are like "little black and white films" with their attention to narrative detail and pacing.

Critical responses to the second album invariably opened with references to the first, as reviews compared the initial installment's wordiness with *The Wild's* tamer, more musical approach. *Creem's* Ed Ward conveys his excitement: "It's either a flawed work of genius or else a work of flawed genius. It's irregular as hell, inconsistent, annoying sometimes, but once you've listened to it a couple of times and start to see what's going on, you forgive all that and just GET OFF." *Crawdaddy* shares the enthusiasm: "Springsteen lets loose here with aural authority, apparently trading in his Divine Right to sit at the throne of Dylan for a less lyrically ambitious but more musically mature and eclectic rock 'n' roll Boss sound." After *Rolling Stone* described *Asbury Park* as "'Subterranean Homesick Blues' played at 78," the review notes the new record's style: "Like *Greetings,* the new album is about the streets of New York and the tacky Jersey Shore, but the lyrics are no longer merely zany cut-ups. They're striking amalgams of romance and gritty realism." Ken Emerson continues: "Springsteen is growing as a writer of music as well as of words. The best of his new songs dart and swoop from tempo to tempo and from genre to genre, from hell-bent-for-leather rock to luscious schmaltz to what is almost recitative."

Asbury Park and *The Wild, the Innocent* complement Springsteen's live shows to create the narrative baseline for his lifework's investigation of his slice of the working American's pie. Workers in the Deep South, industrial Midwest, rural

Southwest, and urban West Coast also sought relief from their respective situations; however, their brand of ethnic diversity, group violence, frivolous escape, and teenage mayhem was probably substantially different from the Jersey Shore version. But the underlying emotions behind those acts—Springsteen's characterological "deep water"—are universal. Springsteen is exploring what he knows here and his depth of emotional understanding directly informs his writing. At times, the attention to detail is overwhelming; moreover, it conveys a sense that this writer truly is in touch with his subject matter. Although the impressionism seems forced at times (almost overwritten), the emotion flows naturally and enables a shared experience that might otherwise prove difficult.

With 1975's *Born to Run* the party stops long enough for Springsteen's characters to assess their situations. In *Songs*, Springsteen reports that this project was a "turning point," as his characters became "less eccentric" ("they could have been anybody and everybody") and his scenes lost some of their provincialism ("you're not necessarily on the Jersey Shore anymore"). He told his biographer, Robert Hilburn, that the songs "really dealt with faith and a searching for answers" and *Crawdaddy*: "But most of the songs are about being like *nowhere*. Just being out there in the void. Every song on the album is about that, I think. About being, like, nowhere and trying to make heads and tails out of it, you know, trying to figure it out? It's such a personal album." Everything changes with *Born to Run* (released August 1975). Springsteen's details shift from overt references to New Jersey as his characters focus their energies on the hard choices emerging before them. This characterological "struggle" will henceforth control the oeuvre. And this struggle—as well as the means through which Springsteen's characters cope with it—is quintessentially *American*. If American Song rests on the principles of simplicity, mobility, and hope, this album evokes those traits in a straightforward fashion. Furthermore, the use of the automotive-escape story line brings forth the uniquely American relationship between young men and their cars. The false sense of mobility and the unshakable belief in the proverbial promised land drive these characters from their delusional party atmospheres toward the day of reckoning awaiting up around the bend. The album's wall-of-sound production style reinforces the expression's emotional impact as well. Like Dylan's *Blood on the Tracks*, there is only one *Born to Run*.

The record's eight tracks (running 39:28 minutes) fall into three narrative categories: A musical celebration ("Tenth Avenue Freeze-Out"), the struggle theme and its two orientations (the relational struggle, "She's the One" and the sociological struggles, "Backstreets," "Meeting Across the River," and "Jungleland"), and the escape theme's two manifestations, the relational/car tales ("Thunder Road" and "Born to Run") and automotive worship ("Night"). The struggle thematic is central in that characters go beyond complaining about their respective situations; they are trying to work their predicaments out. This implied sense of hope is, no doubt, the rationale behind Springsteen's claim that these songs are about a search, not an escape. Perhaps critics should refrain from arguing with authors; nevertheless, the lack of any destination or direction, along with the songs' emphasis on the conditions that warrant the action portray what these people are running away *from* far more than what they are running *toward*. On the other hand, this may be just a distinction without a difference.

We open with the songs of struggle and the narrator's internal battle over the woman of his dreams in "She's the One." Springsteen's ability to articulate universal emotions is evident in this account of the embattled narrator's efforts to come to grips with his fear of and devotion to his woman. She plays with his emotions, lies to him, and tries to dominate him, but he—somehow—resists, at least for the moment. The passion is poignant—the dilemma is compelling. The character is bitter about his life's situation and she may be the answer to his perceived predicament, and yet, her actions generate doubt. That doubt recurs in the sociological struggles as well. In "Backstreets" we observe characters wrestling with maturity and wondering if teenage pacts are going to hold up against the strain daily life brings. They may question their relationship, but they do not doubt the seriousness of their situations—the city is dying and they are fearful of going down with it. The decaying urban jungle provides the context for more switchblade theatrics in "Jungleland" and Springsteen's return to "Incident on 57th Street." Urban gangs and street urchins do their things in a world so bleak that the poets' pens remain silent—they just watch in dismay. Our final installment of the urban-struggle theme takes us deeper into *West Side Story* and Springsteen's adaptation of that Broadway classic in "Meeting Across the River." This song builds upon "Backstreets" and "Jungleland" via a straightforward account of two aspiring criminals' efforts to pick up some action in the big city. The narrator's desperation is evident in his insistence that his partner remain cool when they meet their connection later in town; besides, he needs the money so that he may retrieve his girlfriend's radio from the pawnshop. These are the kind of friends *nobody* needs.

The escape theme gains momentum from the songs of urban struggle in that we obtain a clear picture of the conditions that inspire the exodus. "Thunder Road" and "Born to Run" are, essentially, the same story. The character from "Rosalita" purchased a car with the record company's advance and he is trying to convince Mary ("Road") and Wendy ("Run") to take a chance on him. "Run" spends more time than "Road" with its portrayal of the urban decadence that supports the urge to escape; however, both songs plead for faith—faith in the vehicle and its driver. The destination? The always-sunny promised land, of course. The passion, the belief, the commitment that Springsteen's characters convey make these songs anthems for the dispossessed. Finally, for those without a woman by their side, there is always her replacement, the burning bush of American mythology: The car. In "Night," Springsteen shares the bliss of chrome worship through this tale of the working-man's respite, his automobile. The use of second-person pronouns signifys that this song is for you, as Springsteen describes the slavery and abuse of work, the joy that racing in the streets holds, and the continued belief that "she" is out there, somewhere, waiting for "you."

Born to Run was not only a breakthrough for Springsteen's characters, it provided the turning point for his career. Run's reviews are stunning. Critics wrestle with all of the Hype, search for reasons to resist the public relations, and succumb to the music. *Rolling Stone's* Greil Marcus—a proud resident of the West Coast—casts a dim view of the "new Dylan" rhetoric and all the praise emanating from the East Coast (leaving him feeling "somewhat culturally deprived, not to mention a little suspicious") as he poses the question, is "the kid" as good as his publicity? Marcus responds: "Springsteen's answer is *Born to Run.* It is a magnificent album that pays off on every bet ever placed on him— a '57 Chevy running on melted down Crystals records that shuts down every claim that has been made. And it should crack his future wide open." For Marcus, the record's strength lies in Springsteen's "extraordinary dramatic authority" as he recasts old stories in a powerful, meaningful fashion: "No, you've never heard anything like this before, but you understand it instantly, because this music . . . is what rock and roll is supposed to sound like." *Creem's* Lester Bangs concurs in every respect. He too rejects the Hype (saying, "Out here in the Midwest, where at this writing Springsteen has not even toured yet, you can smell the backlash crisp as burnt rubber in the air") and he, too, yields to the music:

> Springsteen can withstand the reactionaries, though, because once they hear this album even they are gonna be ready to ride out all cynicism with him. Because, street-punk image, bardic posture and all, Bruce Springsteen is an American archetype, and *Born to Run* will probably be the finest album released this year. Springsteen is not an innovator—his outlook is rooted in the Fifties; his music comes out of folk-rock and early rock 'n' roll, his lyrics from 1950s teenage rebellion movies and beat poetry as filtered through Sixties songs rather than read. Springsteen's gifts lie in the way he has rethought traditional sounds and stances, coming up with a synthesis fresh enough to constitute a minor renaissance. After all, what's more old-fashioned than the avant-garde?

Bangs concludes that the record evokes "an American moment . . . bursting with pride." Although the Hype would rebound with the twin covers, Springsteen would kill it off with live shows in New York and, thank goodness for Greil Marcus, Los Angeles. Springsteen's subscription to American Song paid off. Simplicity, mobility, and hope—if mixed properly—make good stories.

From the party to the predicament, the "dreaming" phase of the Worker's Elegy establishes the cast of characters, their values, and their situations in a fashion that sets the stage for a lifetime's work. Furthermore, it establishes why the story is, in fact, an "elegy." Through all the partying, street racing, dancing, and revelry, an underlying complaint has been established: The American way of life may not be all its cracked up to be for these characters. The steadfast belief in the American Dream may be displaced. Springsteen's characters had better fill their tanks for their drive to the promised land. A day of reckoning may be just over the horizon.

the reckoning phase

The word is that the church will never fail you, but *individuals* surely can. When Mike Appel's relationship with Bruce Springsteen began to deteriorate and examinations into their contractual arrangements indicated that the auteur did not have legal control over his oeuvre, Appel threatened what Springsteen valued most—artistic control—and Springsteen experienced firsthand the emotional trauma that engulfed his characters. When Springsteen faced that moment of realization that all of his carefully conceived plans *might not work*, he experienced that empty feeling of staring failure right in the face and acknowledging that dreams—in and of themselves—just might not be enough. That Appel had abused his client financially was one thing, but the loss of control over his art was another for the idealistic songwriter. Insider Dave Marsh captures the situation well:

> Bruce was willing to forgive whatever financial wrongdoing might have been done, but the moment he realized that he did not own his own songs, he realized that he was fighting for his creative life. The notion that he could be denied rights to his work incensed Bruce, and he fought ferociously to regain control of his career, which he saw slipping away. Everything he had done in contravention of record business formula had been designed to insure the integrity of his songs and his music, and when he saw that the litigation threatened that integrity, he hit back, hard.

Our biography section overviewed the financial controversies, the creative tensions that resulted from Jon Landau's successful intervention into Springsteen's professional world, and the artist's view that—regardless of whether it was Landau or Santa Claus—the Appel–Springsteen team had run its course. Of relevance here are the emotional scars that these events inflicted on the author and how he would incorporate those feelings in his "imagined community." A guy who *could not drive* might place all those characters in all those cars through impeccable descriptions that fall outside the purview of his direct experience, but the depth of emotions associated with his loss of control over his work would feed the "deep water" from which Springsteen extracted his characters.

Springsteen admits that his experiences with his mother and father, his troubles with Appel, and his newfound interest in country music and "American noir" (i.e., American B films) fueled the songwriting for *Darkness on the Edge of Town* (released June 1978). In *Songs*, he reports that the songwriting was "difficult" and recalls "spending hours trying to come up with a single verse" as he searched for a "tone" that was "somewhere between" *Born to Run* and 1970's "cynicism." He also pursued a sense of "struggle" that "steered away from any hint of escapism" and placed his characters in a "community under siege." Springsteen claims he discovered his "adult voice" through *Darkness* by infusing the record with his "own hopes and fears." He discussed the connection between *Born to Run* and *Darkness* in another *Crawdaddy* interview:

All people do their whole lives is they try to get free, essentially, of all the bull-shit that was laid on them coming up. They can't get out, they don't know how to get out. Even my own father, he never broke free. You look for someone to blame, something to blame, there is nobody to blame. Nobody specific. And I grew up with that. On *Born to Run* there was the hope of a free ride. On *Darkness*, there ain't no free ride—you wanna ride, you gotta pay. And maybe you'll make it through, but you ain't gonna make it through 'til you been beat, you been hurt, until you been messed up. There's hope, but it's just the hope of, like, survival. It couldn't be a warm, innocent album like *Born to Run* because it ain't that way, it wasn't that way for me anymore. That's why a lot of pain had to be there, because it's real, because it happens. But still, I came out of it—you can see it onstage, I wasn't stopped. . . . I had a big awakening in the past two, three years. Much bigger than people would think. Learned a lot of things, saw a lot of things. Realized a lot of things about my own past. So it's there on the record.

Springsteen told *Rolling Stone's* Dave Marsh that the album signifies a "certain loss of innocence" for his characters as they face "all the betrayals . . . all the imperfections [that] surround [people in] whatever life you lead." Christopher Sandford concludes that Springsteen's characters are "blunt, forthright, broke and screwed-up, luminously 'real' and piercingly American." These are the people who populate the community on *Darkness*.

The ten tracks on *Darkness* (running 43 minutes) fall into three narrative categories: The struggle ("Racing in the Street," "The Promised Land," and "Darkness on the Edge of Town"), a two-part societal complaint featuring a rebellion theme ("Badlands" and "Adam Raised a Cain") and an acceptance dimension ("Something in the Night," "Factory," and "Streets of Fire"), and the emerging avenue of hope, the relational celebration ("Candy's Room" and "Prove It All Night"). The auteur establishes his story in the record's first three tracks: "Badlands" identifies the scene, its problems, and the narrators willingness to fight; "Adam" conveys the sociological inheritance before the narrator, the futility of it all, and a not-too-subtle hint of forthcoming violence (after all, we all know what Cain *did*); and "Something" articulates the unsavory realization that one is better off never having anything because the world robs people of their treasured possessions. This is the story. The relational songs provide a brief respite, yet there is struggle there as well. The music is, in a word, operatic: It is so emotional, so theatrically paced, and so convincing. Springsteen's character development runs deep.

The reckoning phase's theme that life has reached a critical turning point—that the community is under "siege"—is established by the "Badlands"/"Adam" opening salvo and its blend of hope and understanding. Yet, the songs of "acceptance" tip the balance in a new direction. In "Something," the narrator submits to his situation—there is no fight left in this individual. Everything he seems to care for has not just been threatened, it has been taken away—it is gone. He is drunk on bitterness. "Factory" lightens the tone by presenting the walking dead who somehow manage to make it through the working day, only to go out at night and beat up one another. Again, the suggestion that all of this is going to result in violence is gaining momentum. A community under siege either capitulates or resists and, unfortunately, this story is trending toward a form of self-defeating self-mutilation. "Streets of Fire" seals the narrative deal: The narrator readily admits that he is a loser in a world of strangers—the community itself has disintegrated. There is no hope in these songs.

"Racing in the Street" acknowledges the choice between giving up and hanging on. Now, hanging on does not appear to be that attractive, but it is an improvement over total resignation. The characters either have the look of death or else they hate—I mean *hate*—their lives. This is grim stuff, even if it is traveling 90 miles an hour. Our second song of struggle, the album's title cut, "Darkness," features a narrator with desire. Even though he lost his wife and his finances are in ruins, he is still willing to suck up his bitterness (who *wouldn't* be bitter!) and go out fighting. Why? Springsteen supplies the motivation in "Promised Land." This anthem states its case in no uncertain terms: The fight must continue. In the face of all the hardships, all the disappointment, the narrator states the case for belief. It is the only thing Springsteen's community under siege has left.

Or is it? The two songs of relational celebration suggest that there may be hope after all. "Prove It All Night" presents a hard-working narrator who gives it all to his beloved. The societal dreams may not materialize, but that does not mean life ends for this character: There is hope in love and he is committed to prove that to his lover. This narrative logic holds true for "Candy" as well. The narrator's love is powerful; it is a commodity that cannot be bought. Springsteen seems to suggest that all of the trappings associated with the American Dream may just be window-dressing after all. Love and commitment are what matters. (Interestingly, Eric Alterman claims that Candy is a "prostitute," which adds a distinctive, darker twist to the song.)

Yet, at their best, these two songs of relational joy are sidebars to a tale of intense, relentless struggle. Critics disagree on this point. *Rolling Stone's* Dave Marsh contends that the record is a unified message ("Ideas, characters, and phrases jump from song to song like threads in a tapestry, and everything's one long interrelationship"), but claims that the album's title is misleading: "Despite its title, it is a complete *rejection* of despair. Bruce Springsteen says this over and over again, more bluntly and clearly than anyone could have imagined. There isn't a single song on this record in which his yearning for a perfect existence, a life lived to the hilt, doesn't play a central role." *Creem's* Mitch Cohen argues that "the emphasis on father—son conflict and Catholic checks-and-balances make Springsteen too much a James Dean character as seen by Martin Scorsese . . . the LP isn't much fun," before he concludes:

> Darkness sounds like the record it's supposed to be: A tough, exhaust-fumed hymn to feverish desire, a dissection of internal wounds that can be healed not by compromise but by conquest. Bruce Springsteen matters because he knows there is a vision worth pursuing: To find the dark glow of possibility in a beautiful woman's eyes, seize it, and run like hell as far as it will take you. Put your foot to the floor and, darling, don't look back.

Finally, *Crawdaddy's* Peter Knobler appears to take the middle ground between these two interpretations. First, he discusses the extent to which Springsteen's professional problems have affected this record and how the unabashed joy he once brought to his trade has been severely diminished. From there he considers the record's strengths and weaknesses. Knobler considers the reiteration of urban scenes, melodramatic vocal "howls," and the writing's word choice ("settling for words rather than choosing them") to be weaknesses. Its strengths overcome those concerns as the record's "raw emotion" is enough "to make you shake" as Springsteen shares his character's "pain" as a means to overcome it: "The power of Bruce Springsteen has always been that he writes what he knows, and that he's so in touch with it that he makes you feel it too."

When the Worker's Elegy concludes we will appreciate Cohen's wisdom. Perhaps Marsh envisioned a narrative turn that never materializes or focused on the dire conditions that inspired the "yearning" he describes. In any event, Knobler's assessment that the auteur *knows* despair is compelling, but it is his intuitions about loving relationships that may be the real news from this record. That understanding is, at this point, tentative. The infatuation over "Candy" and the blind commitment of "Prove" suggest the same emotional state evidenced in his teenage characters from the dreaming phase. Their naiveté drives their situation. As the curtain falls on the American Dream, Springsteen's characters' anticipations of "Something in the Night" assume a new direction, and *Darkness on the Edge of Town* sets the scene for that narrative turn.

Before the soap opera's characters channel their despair into senseless violence and relational demolition, the story pauses for a mixed bag of intense emotions. In *Songs*, Springsteen observes that *The River* (released October 1980) was both a "reaction to and an extension of" the themes presented on *Darkness*. He explains that he wanted to introduce a greater "emotional range" on the album by incorporating the "fun" associated with his live show with the narrative turn established by *Darkness*. Steve Van Zandt joined the production team's efforts to capture that "live" sound (they succeeded). Thematically, Springsteen articulated his ambitions to *Creem*: "When I did *The River*, I tried to accept the fact that, you know, the world is a paradox, and that's the way it is. And the only thing you can do with a paradox is live with it. . . . I saw it as romantic. It's a romantic record—and to me 'romantic' is when you see the realities, and when you understand the realities, but you also see the possibilities." His comments to Fred Schruers support that position, and in turn, reinforce Cohen's astute observations:

> Everybody seems to hunger for that relationship, and you never seem happy without it. . . . It just got to a point where all of a sudden these songs about things of that nature started coming out. I think you do tend to think about that particular thing around thirty. But even up till then, when I was writing all the earlier songs, "Born to Run" and stuff, they never seemed right without the girl. It was just part of wherever that person was going, that guy was going. It wasn't gonna be any good without her.

All of these strategic elements converge in *The River*—a 20-track double album (running 83:46 minutes) that uses a garage-band, live sound to present ten songs of relational/lifestyle celebration as well as ten songs of relational/societal complaint/struggle. The ten negative songs extend the emotions established in *Darkness*, while the ten positive tracks build on the party atmosphere that dominated the dreaming phase. As usual, Springsteen accomplished his goals: The record runs the emotional gamut. The songs of celebration fall into two camps: Relational themes ("Sherry Darling," "Two Hearts," "Crush on You," "I Wanna Marry You," "Drive All Night," and "Wreck on the Highway") and lifestyle statements ("Cadillac Ranch" and "I'm a Rocker"). Complementing the fun are two songs of escape, "Out in the Street" and "Ramrod." *The River's* songs of complaint address relational matters ("Hungry Heart," "Fade Away," and "Stolen Car") and societal conditions ("Jackson Cage," "The River," and "Point Blank"). Lastly, the album offers an account of relational struggle ("The Ties that Bind"), a mix of relational and societal embattlement ("Independence Day"), and the social struggles, the cloudy "You Can Look (But You Better Not Touch)" and "The Price You Pay." Springsteen's characterological "deep water" yields frivolous, irresponsible, heart-felt, dedicated emotions that are portrayed through musical structures that are occasionally deceiving—what sounds like a party, may actually be a funeral.

The songs of celebration provide a welcome reprieve from the previous album's psychological and sociological darkness. The stories range from "Sherry's" fun-filled romp around town (nothing could be finer than cruising with a six-pack and your girlfriend's mom as you take her to collect her unemployment check—everybody's dream come true), to "Two Hearts" and its wall-of-sound statement of belief in the search for love, to "Crush" and its boyish commitment to chase the little girls, to the promise of love and its redeeming values in "I Wanna Marry," to "Wreck" and its poignant recognition of what truly matters in life and how it may all suddenly disappear. The lifestyle celebrations and tales of escape complement the relational parties through their tried-and-true articulations of the immense rewards of owning a hemi-powered hot rod, hanging out on the street, dancing the night away, or gazing at that mechanical marvel of American ingenuity, the Cadillac. Several songs toss about media characters (from James Bond to Columbo, Kojak, Burt Reynolds, and James Dean) in fun-loving ways that reinforce the songs' emphasis on the life-is-a-party theme. These songs are a clear return to the dreaming phase; only "Wreck" conveys any sense of emotional progress.

On the flip side of the narrative coin, we have the return-to-darkness portion of *The River's* program. That "Hungry Heart" will never find its way onto a Promise Keeper's crusade is certain (the character just drops his *family* and runs off—his *family*!). "Fade Away" and "Stolen Car" chart the heartbreak of losing love and embracing desperation. "Jackson Cage" and "Point Blank" depict what society has done to the narrator's girl, her sense of resignation and despair, and his effort to muster the strength to save them both. And "The River" posits the central notion: Is an unfulfilled dream a relentless, abusive lie? The four songs of struggle build on this negativity, but they manage to interject a small bit of hope into the story: "Independence Day" and its suggested transition revisits "Adam Raised a Cain" in no uncertain terms, "The Ties" and the narrator's belief that he can save his girl from herself, and "You Can Look" with its three, unrelated vignettes that appear to suggest life's limitations through a raucous-party sound. Of these songs, "The Price You Pay" provides the narrative link between *Darkness* and *The River*. There Springsteen dispels the notion of a promised land and its mythical yield in favor of a more realistic understanding of the costs dreams may exact from dreamers. No more blind faith—everything has a price (i.e., you wanna ride, you gotta pay).

The River's reviews are mixed. Many reviews—such as *Time's* and *Newsweek's*—simply chart the record's contents and praise Springsteen's commitment. Other commentators pursued more detailed analyses. *Rolling Stone's* Paul Nelson, for example, offers a mixed response. He claims that the album is a "contemporary, New Jersey version of *The Grapes of Wrath*, with the Tom Joad/Henry Fonda figure—nowadays no longer able to draw upon the solidarity of family—driving a stolen car through a neon Dust Bowl." For Nelson, this is the final edition of a "trilogy" that began with *Born to Run* that is, at times, "downright brilliant," and at others, tiresome: "Springsteen has lost some of his naturalness and seemed more than a bit self-conscious about being an artist." Although he considers the work to be a "milestone," Nelson hopes the story ends here. Steve Simels concurs: "It's a question of focus, Springsteen has narrowed his vision to the point that all the larger-than-life quality has gone out of his work." Although Simels worries that Springsteen may be "degenerating into overripe self-parody," *Creem's* Billy Altman just attacks: "I can't think of any other major star in the whole history of pop music whose range of thought and whose expression of those thoughts has been as limited as Bruce Springsteen's." He continues:

> One gleans no insights whatsoever from *The River*; it is all just more trapped-in-my-one-place-of-sanctuary-the-car mentality, and by the time the record's through, you kinda wish that Bruce's car was buried in the middle of the Cadillac Ranch in Texas, or that someone would revoke his driver's license and tell him that all the songs for his next album should be about planes or boats or skateboards or some other means of "metaphorical" transportation.

The review concludes with an interesting account of a letter that accompanied the record's promotional copies for radio stations and how Columbia requested that DJs refrain from playing extended portions of the album in order to prohibit home-taping. Altman's outrage is sincere.

The River is, in many ways, a deceiving record. To be sure, it retreads old material, yet the live, party sound often hides an underlying current of impending doom. "Love" may be in the house and that is news, but there is some business to attend to first. Life out in the street, mindless rocking, or the stately beauty of a freshly waxed Cadillac may offer an emotional respite, yet that escape is frivolous to begin with and fleeting at best. The album's title cut captures the situation best: It conveys the *initial* response to the fact that dead-end jobs or unemployment, a lifeless marriage, or the sudden loss of youthful ambition is hurtful. Springsteen provides the details and allows us to share in these *initial* emotions that accompany the loss of one's lifelong dreams. With time, those *initial* responses fade; the gravity of the situation hits home; the emotions are building. *The River* charts that growth, and the darkness is about to seek retribution.

In the interview with Kurt Loder cited earlier, Bruce Springsteen reviewed his "body" of work and noted that *Nebraska* just "kinda came out of the blue." I disagree. The *Nebraska/Born in the U.S.A.* writing period signifies that potentially terrifying moment when irrational dreams evolve into the arational realities that evoke irrational responses. Springsteen's characters were bursting with emotion and these feelings were going to manifest themselves somehow, someway, someplace. That his characters were often trapped in dead ends of their own making added fuel to these violent eruptions that were hell-bent on shifting responsibility to external entities or punishing innocents for self-inflicted wounds. Many of Springsteen's characters were *not* responsible for their situations, since they were victims of paranoid foreign policies, failed economics, or untrustworthy lovers. The author deals with these characters and their emotional responses to their situations through the two-part story that emerged from the *Nebraska/U.S.A.* writing sessions. Those with self-inflicted wounds would now seek external retribution (i.e., *Nebraska*), and the institutional victims would lodge their complaints and live with the consequences (i.e., *U.S.A.*). Although he may claim that these stories came "out of the blue," they represent a logical resolution to his unfolding narrative: Victims must be avenged. What is illogical is the public's response to his complaint.

Springsteen's views on the *Nebraska* project are, as always, instructive. *Songs* reports that the record connects to his "childhood" more than any other project (again, that "emotional autobiography") and how he was influenced by Flannery O'Connor and cinema (he notes Terrence Malick's *Badlands* in particular). His emphasis was on detail, in that he "wanted to let the listener hear the characters think, to get inside their heads, so you could hear and feel their thoughts, their choices." He continues:

> These new songs were narrative, restrained, linear, and musically minimal. Yet their depiction of characters out on the edge contextualized them as rock and roll. If there's a theme that runs through the record, it's the thin line between stability and that moment when time stops and everything goes to black, when the things that connect you to your world—your job, your family, friends, your faith, the love and grace in your heart—fail you. I wanted the music to feel like a waking dream and the record to move like poetry. I wanted the blood on it to feel destined and fateful.

He elaborated on this in a 1984 *Rolling Stone* interview: "*Nebraska* was about that American isolation: What happens to people when they're alienated from their friends and their community and their government, and their job. Because those are the things that keep you sane, that give meaning to life in some fashion. And if they slip away, and you start to exist in some void where the basic constraints of society are a joke, then life becomes kind of a joke. And anything can happen." Almost 20 years later, he told *Mojo*: "I had no intention of recording *Nebraska* in that fashion, whatsoever. It was—not a mistake—an accident, let's say, and, anyhow, at the same time I recorded *Nebraska* I was recording *Born in the U.S.A.* in the studio in New York, so I had these two extremely different recording experiences going." Two different recording experiences—one story operating on two narrative planes. We open with the recognition and retaliation of *Nebraska*.

Nebraska (released September 1982) contains ten tracks (running 40:49 minutes) that portray three sets of stories: There is the now-standard, two-pronged complaint featuring a relational episode ("My Father's House") and five societal installments ("Atlantic City," "Mansion on the Hill," "Johnny 99," "Used Cars," and "Reason to Believe"). There are three portraits that reinforce the complaint themes through their focus on the central character's condition: The relational complaint of "Highway Patrolman" and the individual tales of unadulterated evil ("Nebraska") and utter despair ("State Trooper"). The relational celebration "Open All Night" revisits the respite love provides. The recording is minimalist, the music stark and repetitive, and the tone is dreary beyond belief. While this record is not for everyone, it is a fundamental element of the unfolding soap opera—its melodrama is its centerpiece.

The portraits are revealing in that they convey how humans can rationalize anything. Blood is so much thicker than anything else that a police officer will abdicate his sworn duty in order to support his sense of family. "Highway Patrolman" demonstrates how Springsteen's characters think. There is more than a little bit of self-indulgence here and that grants license for these people to do anything. In the present case, the officer allows his brother to get away with, literally, murder—all in the name of family loyalty. Speaking of murder, "Nebraska" charts Charles Starkweather's and Caril Fugate's insanity (according to the story, they murdered ten people for fun) and his testimony at trial in which he merely chalks it up to malevolence. The implication here is that society can drive people to do the unspeakable. This is, assuredly, self-indulgence to the extreme. Finally, "Trooper" and "Open All Night" take the same lyrics (at times, virtually identical) to weave two stories with slightly different spins. In the former, the narrator speeds down the turnpike without a license or any other mandatory identification in the apparent hope of getting caught; in the latter, the narrator speeds away from his empty job to his baby's waiting arms.

The complaints shed additional light on these characters' worldviews. In "Mansion" and "Used Cars" we witness the unabashed materialism that drives these individuals. The narrator in "Mansion" is consumed by jealousy and implies that wealth is, somehow, wrong. The character in "Used" describes (in wonderful detail) the family out together purchasing a used car and that young narrator's conviction to never buy one again. (Should this character win the lottery, any guess what the first purchase will be?) Here we witness the values that have guided these characters' decision-making throughout this continuing story. The materialism, the greed, and the corresponding jealousy that embody these individuals' worldviews are pathetic. Consider the characters in "Atlantic City" where a failure to live within one's means results in deserting the home and embracing crime.

Whereas the characters in "My Father's House" and "Reason to Believe" are sympathetic, characters such as "Johnny 99" provide case studies for a pro-death-penalty argument. The view that a loss of job and inability to pay debts is a rationale for random murder is disturbing. The narrative logic is not distressing because Springsteen's art chronicles such debasement; it is unsettling because people do, in fact, think that way. The frivolity of street life and its avoidance of responsibility have matured into a sociological monster. The claim that society—or a particular political orientation—spawns such an outlook and should, therefore, share the responsibility for antisocial behavior is preposterous. To accept such a position is to trivialize the honest victimization of characters such as those in "Reason to Believe" and, later, in "Born in the U.S.A." and "Downbound Train." The sympathy Springsteen inspires in Darkness teeters on the brink during The River and leaps over the edge in Nebraska. To suggest—in any way—that "society" created these monsters is to abdicate any sense of individual responsibility. There are victims in these stories, but they are not the central characters.

Critical responses to Nebraska address the project's artistic and commercial orientations. The San Diego Union focuses on the art and the record's "downbeat, working-class meditation on the failed but spiritually undead nature of the American Dream . . . [Springsteen's] gloomy narrative resonate like low-pitched tuning forks struck on the bedrock of hard times." The Los Angeles Times claims that the album "speaks with unflinching immediacy and compassion" as Springsteen focuses on a "message that couldn't be ignored." The Trouser Press argues that the auteur "may have scaled down his attack, but [he] hasn't diminished his ambition one bit. . . . Springsteen still treats life as a big deal, full of high drama with inner meaning for those intent on finding it." Rolling Stone reports that this is Springsteen's "bravest record" in terms of its commercial risks and thematic tone: "Nebraska comes as a shock, a violent, acid-etched portrait of a wounded America that fuels its machinery by consuming its people's dreams." Creem observes: "Its singular gloom seems appropriate to the times and its underlying compassion is restrained and moving, tho I suspect that most people will find it more admirable than likeable." Musician considers the record to be as "bleak and unyielding as next month's rent" and the Los Angeles Herald Examiner contends: "Springsteen achieves a simplicity of language and directness of expression of the highest literary order. It's also a definitionally American style of language, uttered about American lives and truths, hopes and ends." And Steve Simels extends the argument he advanced about The River in that he finds the record "boring," with a style that "sounds like it was written for rock critics rather than people." He concludes: "As much as it pains me to say it, I think what we have here is a classic case of a 'primitive' artist corrupted by 'intellectuals' (well, ex-rock writers, such as his producer, Jon Landau, and official biographer, Dave Marsh)."

Whether critics liked Nebraska or not, responses were intense. No writer treated these stories lightly. While the suggestion is that Springsteen had thoroughly mined this particular narrative vein, the fact remains that this was merely part one of a two-part story. *Born in the U.S.A.* completes the package with its blend of the Worker's Elegy soap opera and pop singles. While the pop singles stay on message, the symbolic prescriptions that emerged from the *Nebraska/U.S.A.* package are about to get lost. In an effort to reach a mainstream audience, Springsteen is about to do the unthinkable: He is about to lose control of his message. The mass party of his concerts, the diluted imagery of his videos, and the All-American Boy publicity campaign will enrich everyone's bank accounts while they simultaneously rob the auteur of his most treasured possession: His ideas.

In *Songs*, Springsteen equates the "Born in the U.S.A." debacle with Woody Guthrie's frustrations over the "This Land Is Your Land" misinterpretation. He bemoans: "A songwriter writes to be understood. Is the way you choose to present your music its politics? Is the sound and form your song takes its content?" There Springsteen conveys his "ambivalence" over the songs that were added to the *Nebraska/U.S.A.* writing material. He included "No Surrender" at Steve Van Zandt's insistence, he wrote "Dancing in the Dark" in response to Landau's request for a single, he used a song composed for Donna Summer ("Cover Me") for some unknown reason. The result was Springsteen's greatest commercial success, greatest artistic compromise, and perhaps, his greatest creative regret. That the album sold over eighteen million copies worldwide (according to official biographer Dave Marsh) and contained seven Top Ten singles no doubt soothed the auteur's creative pains. (In fact, during the 1996 *Tom Joad* shows he laughingly made this very clear as he tipped his hat to misinterpretation and its financial rewards.)

The record that inspired an entire nation to stand and cheer itself is a statement of abject negativity. *Born in the U.S.A.* (released June 1984) contains twelve tracks (running almost 47 minutes) that *complain*. There are eight songs with varying degrees of societal complaint ("Born in the U.S.A.," "Cover Me," "Working on the Highway," "Downbound Train," "No Surrender," "Glory Days," "Dancing in the Dark," and "My Hometown"), two songs of relational complaint ("Bobby Jean" and "I'm Goin' Down"), a lifestyle celebration that ends up in one character's imprisonment ("Darlington County"), and a relational plea for adultery ("I'm on Fire"). Springsteen's characters and their value orientations range from the sublime to the ridiculous as several of the auteur's characters portray the values that the nuns in Freehold preached against. At the time, though, none of that seemed to matter because the musical world embraced *U.S.A.* as a kind of patriotic musical Rohrshach, forcing preconceived notions upon a body of work that was anything but malleable. And Bruce Springsteen stood in front of the E Street Band and led the rally.

We begin with the real victims from the *Nebraska/U.S.A.* story. The central characters in "U.S.A.," "Downbound," "No Surrender," "My Hometown," and "I'm Going Down" are experiencing problems in living that are not the results of their foolishness, but come rather from life's public and personal tragedies. The Vietnam veteran in "U.S.A." experiences the senselessness of a war that was a product of governmental paranoia and endures the rejection that national embarrassment brings. The lover in "Downbound" fights through the marital rejection he incurs as the result of the loss of his job and his personal economic downturn. "Hometown" charts the demise of the character's town and the communal hardships economic shifts bring. "Goin' Down" chronicles yet another case of relational deterioration. And "Surrender" articulates how friends face disintegrating situations and embattled dreams through statements of perseverance. Although the soldier entered the service because he broke the law, these characters are, assuredly, victims. There is no evidence of self-inflicted wounds as these individuals endure the emotional turmoil of their respective situations. The "gloom and doom" is stifling.

"Cover Me," "Glory Days," "Dancing," and "Bobby Jean" deal with negative situations through relational pleas for help, nostalgia, or escape. Their underlying complaints are washed over by musical structures that mask the characters' emotional situations. "Glory Days" is particularly sad. Characters relish their past as a means of hiding from their present as they gather in bars or share drinks at day's end to cope with the emptiness of their lives (like Johnny Rotten, they have no future). The remedy in "Dancing" complements the glory days nostalgia party as they return us to the dreaming phase's logic and its insistence on avoidance as a coping strategy. As always, the more things change, the more they remain the same. The plea-for-adultery scenario joins the fear and loathing in Darlington storyline to advance the scenario further. Well, at least nobody got killed.

Critical responses to *U.S.A.* are generally positive. The *Cincinnati Enquirer* explores the *Nebraska* connection: "*Nebraska* was a proving ground. . . . The stark melodies on the solo album swept the cobwebs from Springsteen's head. He heard things differently after that. The sameness that produced so many forgettable and unsingable tunes on his earlier albums . . . was absent on *Born in the U.S.A.* As a result, Springsteen delivered the most tuneful album of his career." Such was the typical response to the album's mixture of depressing stories and celebratory sounds. In that vein, *Musician* claims that "[w]ith its hard, exultant music and its hard, desperate lyrics, *Born in the U.S.A.* is both a grim portrait and a strong-willed celebration." The *Los Angeles Times* views the album as "a richly absorbing and highly accessible album" that charts how the "American Dream is slipping away because of [our] own indifference." There, Hilburn notes that Springsteen "recorded five songs for every one that he ended up using," to which the *New York Times*' Stephen Holden adds that the artist "wrote more than 60 songs" in a project that represents his "most comprehensive vision of American life to date." In its five-star review, *Rolling Stone* contends "you get such a vivid sense of these characters . . . because Springsteen gives them voices a playwright would be proud of." Finally, the nation's newspapers offered views as varied as the *Salt Lake Tribune*'s conclusion that the record is "full-fledged Americana . . . chock full of images, events, situations and experiences relating to life in America," the *San Diego Union*'s opinion that the work "suffers from a somewhat narrow artistic vision, but that doesn't prevent it from being a rich, vital work that both challenges and entertains," and the *Phila-*

delphia Inquirer contends that it is "an album of emotional complexity expressed in the simplest, most realistic terms," before closing with this astute observation: "Beyond all the stories of ruined lives and wild times, what *Born in the U.S.A.* is really about is growing old, with rock 'n' roll, making the music expansive enough to accommodate new concerns and more complicated emotions, taking responsibility for yourself and a loved one in an increasingly impossible world. In other words: commitment."

With Ken Tucker's wily observation as our exit point, we reach the end of the Worker's Elegy's reckoning phase. But first, the Springsteen economic machine paused to capture a moment and share it with the world. The tours that accompanied the reckoning phase's albums involved some of the musical world's more memorable shows, and the Springsteen camp reviewed those performances, weighed their merits, and assembled one of the era's most anticipated live recordings, *Bruce Springsteen & The E Street Band Live/1975–85* (released November 1986). This five-record/three-CD package contains 40 tracks from ten years of concerts. Moreover, the Return-of-The-Hype publicity that surrounded its release sustained the intense commercial momentum established by the *U.S.A.* tours and that record's chart success (remember, there were seven Top Ten singles released from that album). Although the record did not sell as well as anticipated, it provides an unanticipated service for music history in capturing for posterity the E Street Band's work with Springsteen. These were grand shows that featured a crack musical outfit operating at its peak. *Live/1975–85* is an outstanding historical artifact.

Critical responses to the boxed set consistently focused on two attributes: What should have been included on the albums (there were many complaints about the overuse of *U.S.A.* songs), and the records' inclusion of several examples of the famed Springsteen "raps." The *Dallas Morning News* expresses the sentiments that typified the reviews: "Bruce Springsteen is one of the finest performers alive, perhaps the best exponent of rock 'n' roll at the moment—a man whose performances leave you dazzled, overwhelmed, exhilarated, a believer. But you have to be there, because the key is participation. No matter how far back you are, you get a sense of community at Springsteen's shows—a feeling that there's no distance between performer and audience." From there Lennox Samuels doubts the project's ability to convey that experience, yet he concludes that "it comes very close." *Creem* agrees and energetically argues that "the album reminds us that there is no more thrilling sound in modern rock than that of The Boss roaring . . . like all ten of the ten Mightiest Soulmen in History of the Heroism of Little Guys." *Musician's* Bill Flanagan backs off the hyperbole and writes: "In some critical quarters there is a case being made for this album as a sort of aural novel, a thematically united American epic . . . maybe it's self-indulgent to wish that it captured a little less of Bruce the legend and a little more of Bruce the friend." *Time's* Jay Cocks claims: "That is what makes *Live/1975–85* unique: It is a concert as well as a confessional. Springsteen makes everyone accomplices in the shared experience of a common emotional life." And *Rolling Stone* appreciates the between-song raps ("Two of the album's finest moments aren't even musical") as it, too, praises the project's ability to capture "Springsteen's vision."

Live/1975–85 is a fitting capstone to the reckoning phase's enactment of the Springsteen Vision and its blend of poignant observation, confused party, and emotional diversity. Unlike the youthful simplicity of the dreaming phase, this portion of Springsteen's unfolding soap opera features wide-ranging emotions extending from *Darkness'* understanding, to *River's* embellishment, to *Nebraska's* reaction, to *U.S.A.'s* acquiescence. This is a dark story about a narrow segment of America's working world. The narrative continuity sustained throughout these works is impressive. The depth of character development, the scenic precision, and the story's pacing are as artistically uplifting as the tale's value orientation is frightening. Springsteen mined the American psyche and his yield—though, on its own terms, accurate—reveals the types of self-indulgence that gives "America" a bad name abroad. And yet not all working Americans respond to economic downturns or unemployment by killing women and children. Not all American teenagers are stuck in a postadolescent time-warp expecting something for nothing. Many Americans—like Douglas and Adele Springsteen— saved what they could, took serious chances (often relocating), and worked diligently with what they had to improve their situations. Now that the characters on "Nebraska" and "Johnny 99" are tucked safely away on death row, Springsteen's imagined community focuses its energies on longer term issues, and that is our next topic.

the acceptance phase

The Worker's Elegy now turns away from street life, postadolescent angst, self-indulgence, and senseless retribution toward the equally complicated emotional world of adulthood. At this point we observe a shift in expectations away from external sources of gratification to internal rewards as characters deal with domestic issues and the challenges they pose. Characters embrace adulthood, complicated emotional relationships, relational joy, parenthood, and, of course, relational deterioration through songs that back away from wall-of-sound musicality. The E Street Party is over. The endless string of Saturday nights is finished. Springsteen parks his metaphorical car in the metaphorical garage and turns his attention to the loving relationships that have proven so hard for him as well as his imagined community. That this portion of the oeuvre contains a song entitled "Better Days" deploys understatement as a literary device.

Tunnel of Love (released October 1987) introduces this radical move away from bombastic musical portrayals of vocational, economic, and relational anxieties. Instead, Springsteen uses softer, more subtle musical platforms to support his tale of societal acceptance and its attention shift toward home life. As with every facet of his lifework, Springsteen carefully crafted his narrative strategy and *Songs* presents that rationale. There the auteur reports that he had no interest in continuing the mass momentum established by *U.S.A.* and its supporting tours. Rejecting the superficiality that accompanies mass appeal, he focused on a new topic that he had yet to explore: male–female relationships. Springsteen notes that the songs emerged quickly and the recording followed suit, but he denounces any suggestion that the work is autobiographical. The writer's emotional tour of his imagined community yields accounts of adults exploring their identities, struggling with self-destructive tendencies, and searching for relational security. Springsteen concludes that for twenty years he depicted "the man on the road" and that now he portrays the "hopes and fears of the man in the house."

Of course, Springsteen explained his narrative shift during the media interviews that supported the record and its subsequent tour. For example, he told the *Rocky Mountain News*: "It's not that the record has any answers . . . but I felt that it's a reflection of the doubts and fears and mistakes that most people will experience in a real relationship." He continued: "I mean, romantic love is wonderful. I feel that there are definitely songs on the record that are romantic. But at the same time, they're pretty straight-ahead. They're not pulling any punches. If you're expecting your wife or girlfriend to be some sort of fairy-tale princess, that doesn't last long. . . . You have to experience the whole thing, the stuff that hurts and the stuff that feels real glorious. And that's where the richness of life and experience lies." On another occasion, he identified to Steve Pond the emotional autobiography that supports *Tunnel*:

> I wanted to write a different kind of romantic song, one that took in the different types of emotional experiences of any relationship where you are really engaging with that other person and not involved in a narcissistic romantic fantasy or intoxication or whatever. . . . I wanted to make a record about what I felt, about really letting another person in your life and trying to be a part of someone else's life. That's a frightening thing, something that's always filled with shadows and doubts and also wonderful things and beautiful things. . . . It's difficult, because there's a part of you that wants the stability and the home thing, and there's a part of you that isn't so sure. That was the idea of the record, and I had to change quite a bit to just get to the point to write about that stuff. I couldn't have written any of those songs at any other point in my career. I wouldn't have had the knowledge or the insight or the experience to do it.

Armed with Springsteen's newfound experience, the Worker's Elegy enters the acceptance phase with *Tunnel of Love* and its 12 songs (running 46:25 minutes) of personal and relational maturation. The album presents five narrative forms that pivot around the record's centerpiece, "Brilliant Disguise." As the auteur acknowledges in *Songs*, "Disguise" is a synopsis of the project's themes in that it questions everything about the narrator's relationship: Who is she, what is her motive, what is his motive, are they doing the right thing, and ultimately, who is he? The doubt—the utter lack of trust—and the despair this trait inspires provide the superstructure for the songs that examine those agonizing sentiments. *Tunnel* features four "pleas" that portray intrapersonal uncertainty ("Walk Like a Man") and relational matters ("Ain't Got You," "Tougher

Than the Rest," and "Valentine's Day"), a portrait ("Cautious Man"), a relational celebration ("All That Heaven Will Allow"), an intrapersonal struggle ("Two Faces"), and five relational complaints ("Spare Parts," "Tunnel of Love," "One Step Up," "Brilliant Disguise," and "When You're Alone"). The album unfolds spatially in that emotions are introduced and allowed to float in and out of various contexts. Characters question themselves and their individual values as a preface to questioning others and their worldviews. Distrust is ubiquitous, longing is universal. There are times when these people are not having nice days; still, once more, at least nobody gets murdered.

The intrapersonal anxieties that abound in this record crystallize in the three-song combination of "Cautious Man," "Walk Like a Man," and "Two Faces." In "Walk," the narrator prays for abilities first observed in his father as he recalls the simple yet poignant memory of a child walking in a parent's footsteps on the beach. He just wants to be the best man he can be, but he is confronted by fear. That fear is examined in "Cautious" as Springsteen tells the tale of an experienced, wise man whose approach to life's decisions is pragmatic and thoughtful—until love came to town, that is. Now he wrestles with his instincts, resigns himself to newfound luxuries (no Cadillacs here though), and wrestles with a new fear: The loss of it all. The major threat to it all is that Old Devil, the self. Springsteen considers that emotional struggle in "Two Faces" in which the narrator copes with being the narrator. This character has two competing personalities—they wage war, and he fears the damage that internal battle is having on his treasured relationship. "Two Faces" is powerful. Its honesty and sincerity are jarring. While "Brilliant Disguise" extends this scenario to a broader context, I contend that "Two Faces" is the narrative foundation for *Tunnel of Love*. It is a story of a man at war with himself.

The relational themes on *Tunnel* predictably explore good and bad romances. On the good side, we witness the relational pleas in "Ain't Got You," "Tougher," and "Valentine's" and their loving portrayals of dedication. The relational celebration "All That Heaven" communicates why these narrators are so committed to their women; they are idyllic. A guy could have everything in the world, but he has nothing in her absence ("Ain't Got"). A guy may not be the best-looking or the smoothest in town, but his commitment is complete ("Tougher"). And the song that ties the soap opera together, "Valentine's Day," in which the narrator accepts the fact that his dreams did not materialize, expresses his love for his home, worries about his relationship, and urges his partner's commitment. These songs work in harmony to communicate the newfound value of loving relationships and how they—like life's dreams—cannot be taken for granted.

Contrasting these heart-warming scenarios are the songs of relational complaint. "Disguise" raises the doubt, "Tunnel" and "One Step" discuss the struggle, "When You're Alone" portrays the results failure will bring, and "Spare Parts" flashes back to "Hungry Heart" and the kind of man who inspired the Promise Keeper's crusade. Although the internal struggle in "Disguise" is foreboding, the "Tunnel" metaphor and literalism in "One Step" convey the sense of struggle and potential failure that is readily available from this risky endeavor. It is as if the record praises relationships, warns of the internal battles and the interpersonal struggles associated therein, and offers the rationale for why everything is so difficult: People can be jerks. On "When You're Alone" we observe the old axiom, "When the going gets tough, your baby leaves" (once again), as Springsteen warns his lover that she will be sorry one day. Demonstrating his utter lack of sexism, the auteur places the shoe on the other foot in his portrayal of the abandoned teenage mother in "Spare Parts." Here, girl gets pregnant and boy deserts her in a guiltless act of selfishness. The girl longs for her old life and struggles with the baby, but she perseveres while, hopefully, her old boy friend burns in hell. *Tunnel* is, without question, a well-rounded bit of storytelling that conveys the shift of emphasis in the Worker's Elegy.

Critical responses share this observation. *Rolling Stone's* Steve Pond writes: "Springsteen is writing about the promises people make to each other and the way they renege on those promises, about the romantic dreams we're brought up with and the internal demons that stifle those dreams. The battleground has moved from the streets to the sheets, but the battle hasn't changed significantly." Jay Cocks describes *Tunnel* as "an album about love that is not about exaltation or passion but about the doubt and fear, longing and uncertainty that shadow every deep feeling, every tender gesture." Jon Pareles notes that the record "extends Mr. Springsteen's fatalism even further, dousing the last glimmer of unexamined hope and blocking the last escapist fantasies." The *Seattle Times* argues: "Some artists could fake such an album, but not Springsteen. This is as genuine a statement as any rocker has ever made and one of the most truthful LPs in rock history. . . . It may not be Springsteen's masterpiece, but it is a masterly work by a true artist." *Creem* suggests that the record "occupies a stretch of Everyman's land between more-than-a-bunch-of-demos and less-than-a-great-album" before concluding with a swipe at Dylan: "So OK, Bruce Springsteen has taken the plunge off the pedestal. He hasn't printed a masterpiece this time around; but fortunately, he hasn't painted his *Self Portrait* either." Perhaps the last word on *Tunnel* should go to the auteur who used an interview with *Newsweek* to explain his latest work and take a now-customary jab at Ronald Reagan:

One of the things I want the record to be about is, we live in a society that wants us to buy illusion every day. That happens on a national scale, like Reagan telling us there are no hungry people here, just people who don't know where to go to get the food. There's that will to pretend that everything is OK. That I'm OK, and you're OK. That it's morning again in America. That happens on a personal level also. People are sold this every day: you're gonna live happily ever after. So when you do begin to feel conflict—the natural human conflict that comes with any human relationship—people have a tendency to repress it, make believe it's not there, or feel guilty and ashamed about it. I wanted the record to be against that. Against that illusion. You just can't live like that, and people shouldn't be asked to. It's a cheapening of your own real experience, things that you *know* inside. People deserve better. They deserve the truth. They deserve honesty. The best music, you can seek some shelter in it momentarily, but it's essentially there to provide you something to face the world with.

Springsteen's passions not only run deep, they run consistently. His views that art is a tool that people may use to appreciate all facets of life, his commitment to share his views, and his intense—I mean *intense*—need to be understood remain constant. His work may shift surface contexts, but the underlying content holds steady: Do not run from your emotions, embrace them, and they will pave the road to personal understanding.

With that, we reach the end of the Worker's Elegy and achieve the auteur's personal and professional goal: Personal understanding. At this point we depart from the logic of most soap operas in that melodrama rarely makes room for closing scenes of eternal happiness, and yet that is exactly the narrative bucket of gold Springsteen provides at the end of the story's rainbow. Everybody loves a happy ending and Springsteen does not disappoint. The story comes full circle in that the joyous accounts of street life now shift to the home and the bliss that accompanies a family, domestic tranquility (and the challenge of sustaining that condition), and an *acceptance* of life's conditions. The lifework comes full circle as well as the writer returns to the soul-inspired, gospel-influenced sounds that originally emanated from his Rock Church; moreover, the final entry features a return to the impressionistic writing style last seen on his first two albums. It is hard to imagine that Springsteen *planned* this resolution to his unfolding story. As he and his imagined community matured, the story evolved as well.

In *Songs*, Springsteen outlines the two records' histories and his motivations for the work. After his move to the West Coast and a two-year break in writing, he initiated *Human Touch* in an effort to get back to work. He struggled and, for the first time in his career, he worked with another writer (Roy Bittan). With a new band and an old sound in his head, Springsteen labored to tell his tale of loving acceptance. After writing *Touch's* original final track, "Living Proof," he experienced a three-week burst of creativity that led to the second album, *Lucky Town*. He reconfigured the songs and rendered a dual message about the "blessings and the unanswerable questions" that accompany "adult life, mortality, and human love." Springsteen described his feelings about the new music to *Rolling Stone's* James Henke:

> I believe in this music as much as anything I've ever written. I think it's the real deal. I feel like I'm at the peak of my creative powers right now. I think that in my work I'm presenting a complexity of ideas that I've been struggling to get to in the past. And it took me ten years of hard work outside of the music to get to this place. Real hard work. But when I got here, I didn't find bitterness and disillusionment. I found friendship and hope and faith in myself and a sense of purpose and passion. And it feels good. I feel like that great Sam and Dave song "Born Again." I feel like a new man.

Springsteen's passion is evident in the 24 tracks that comprise the *Human Touch* and *Lucky Town* package (released March 31, 1992). *Touch* contains 14 tracks (running 58:49 minutes) that address relational matters in a systematic, calculated fashion. The album features a prescriptive life lesson ("With Every Wish"), eight installments of the "relational plea" strategy ("Human

Touch," "Soul Driver," "Cross My Heart" [written with Sonny Boy Williamson], "Roll of the Dice" [with Bittan], "Real World" [with Bittan], "All or Nothin' at All," "Man's Job," and "Real Man"), a life complaint ("The Long Goodbye"), three relational complaints ("57 Channels [And Nothin' On]," "Gloria's Eyes," and "I Wish I Were Blind"), and closes with the traditional children's song, "Pony Boy." *Town* offers ten songs (running 39:38 minutes) that follow three strategies: The relational pledge "If I Should Fall Behind," three relational celebrations ("Better Days," "Leap of Faith," and "Book of Dreams"), and six songs of impressionism that present varied accounts of life's lessons ("Lucky Town," "Local Hero," "The Big Muddy," "Living Proof," "Souls of the Departed," and "My Beautiful Reward"). Both records use backing vocals to create a gospel atmosphere reminiscent of Dylan's *Street-Legal* with its call-and-response musical style. The albums work in harmony to issue a capstone statement to the Worker's Elegy story line.

The "relational plea" strategy that dominates *Touch* conveys the view that although love is in the house, it cannot be taken for granted. First, Springsteen issues the guiding life lesson that is "With Every Wish" in which he uses two vignettes (one about a young boy fishing, the other about a jealous lover) to demonstrate that one had better be careful about what one wishes for because your wish may be granted and you may mishandle it. The story ends with the narrator's commitment to wish away anyhow, to cast his fate to the wind, and hope for the best. This is the narrative foundation of the eight relational pleas in which Springsteen advances a "c'mon baby we can do it, can't we?" scenario with slightly different spins. In the title track, the narrator assesses the two lovers' sorry states and the difficulties of living in a merciless environment as a preface to the plea to not give up and keep believing in each other. "Soul Driver" paints a picture of uncertainty and urges faith; "Cross My Heart" is a, well, promise to persevere; "Roll of the Dice" uses gambling metaphors to communicate the narrator's romantic risk-taking; "All or Nothin'" issues the prescription for a successful love: full commitment; the commitment theme returns in "Real World" and Springsteen reprises "Tougher Than the Rest" with "Man's Job" and "Real Man." The reiteration is direct and abundantly clear: There are certainly better men in this world, but the narrator's commitment will make the difference in the long run. The narrator is up for his job.

Balancing these statements of loving perseverance are our final installments of the relational complaint narrative strategy. The life complaint "The Long Goodbye" offers a cloudy account of the narrator's inability to break away from his present situation. The song is an apparent statement of futility in which our narrator seems to be stuck in the "Glory Days" bar, unable to muster the resources to move along. The relational complaints are more direct in their portrayals of deteriorating or dead relationships. "57 Channels" uses a media metaphor to communicate the end of a failed relationship, "Gloria's Eyes" takes us back to "I'm Goin' Down" and the sadness of watching it all go away, and "I Wish" is a poignant account of the pain the narrator endures every time he sees his ex-lover with another man. The last number does a brilliant job of contrasting the joys of sight (images of springtime, birds, summer nights, stars) with the agony of his confrontation with failure. Springsteen's message is oh so clear: Fight for that relationship—it may well be all you have left to fight for.

Having brought closure to a story twenty years in the making, the auteur offers the final look back that is *Lucky Town*. Few bodies of work enjoy the joyous capstone statement conveyed through "Better Days." The narrator describes his sorry life and how everything was fading away until he met the woman who became his friend and lover. Springsteen interjects a touch of impressionism to relate wealth's limitations as a preface to a cry of unbridled joy over his relationship. With "Leap" the narrator communicates what must occur in order to jump start love: Simply, no guts, no glory. The blissful scenes of "Book of Dreams" relate the narrator's peaceful joy over his situation (his lover is the apple of his eye) and the relational pledge; "If I Should Fall Behind" conveys what must occur to sustain that condition. Relational partners must help each other along, be patient, and together they can make it through a demanding life.

Springsteen closes the Worker's Elegy with a series of impressions that follow the same rhythm of expression. The six impressionistic accounts of life's lessons offer a vignette or two to establish a point, move to a bridge that anchors that message, and close with the moral of the story—again, presented through a vignette. "Lucky Town" looks back on life, "Local Hero" describes the irony of celebrity, "Big Muddy" portrays life's challenges and the need to get your hands dirty, "Living Proof" relates the emancipation that childbirth brings, "Souls" revisits "Wreck on the Highway" with impressions about life's tragedies and the narrator's intense desire to protect his son, and "Beautiful Reward" offers closure through a message of perseverance. Here Springsteen occupies the "Mansion on the Hill" and it does not mean a thing. Ultimately, the search is the reward. With this final look over his shoulder, Bruce Springsteen closes one of the most evocative, coherent, and committed bodies of work in the history of popular music. You may not *like* the story, but you have to admire the dedication.

Critical responses to the *Touch/Town* package were generally positive, although there were those writers who reject the notion that maturity and rock music can coexist. The *Los Angeles Times* searches for the connection that joins the two albums and concludes: "The common bond is a theme that Springsteen has resisted for most of his career: happiness. . . . This is mature rock 'n' roll with an edge—a gateway in Springsteen's career and a significant step in the evolution of rock." *Rolling Stone*'s review opens with *Tunnel*, its theme of deception and the relational difficulties that accompany distrust in the self (much less the other), and how the two albums resolve that scenario. For Anthony DeCurtis, *Touch* explores "the movement from disenchanted isolation to a willingness to risk love and its attendant traumas again" while *Town* "examines [Springsteen's] life as a family man, negotiates a truce with his demons and achieves a hard-won sense of fulfillment." The *Hartford Courant* considers that all-important relationship between the auteur and his audience: "Fatherhood has changed Springsteen, but in that he's not so different from his audience. It might not interest kids who have been more interested in rap or dance music all along, but Springsteen remains a central figure for rock's aging fans, providing timeless songs with an enduring moral force." And Seth Rogovoy offers proof of Catlin's point regarding Springsteen's message and younger audiences: "If Springsteen's two new albums break little, if any, new ground in his own career, they bear no relevance at all to popular music circa 1992, except, perhaps, as a footnote to Springsteen's own considerable legacy as the heir to Presley's throne. If Nirvana smells like teen spirit, then Springsteen smells like mid-life crisis."

The acceptance phase of the Worker's Elegy takes the emotional turmoil of an embattled life and channels that energy into a more positive context. Springsteen's emotional autobiography and its application within his imagined community yield mature insights that do not back away from life's disappointments; rather, characters apply negative lessons in productive fashions. The failure of their life's dreams provides the understanding that they can take nothing for granted. Therefore they work in their relationships. They fight off the negative consequences of unfulfilled ambitions, personal insecurities, and relational difficulties by constantly rededicating themselves to the interpersonal tasks at hand. The self-destruction, the emotional lashing out, and the useless nostalgia give way to the kind of hard work that, if applied earlier, could have saved the lives of innocent victims and avoided the needless self-mutilations associated with the reckoning phase. Maturity, in a word, is the central concept here.

A fitting way to conclude the Worker's Elegy is with a greatest-hits package, and that is exactly what Springsteen–Landau did. In so doing, the auteur followed his manager's lead in the selection of various cuts from the oeuvre to be included and worked to produce several new tracks for the record. For this, the E Street Band reassembled in New York for a feverish recording session that yielded several new songs, some of which made the final cut, some of which found their way onto Tracks. The new songs included the Academy Award–winning "Streets of Philadelphia," a romantic song from the film Jerry Maguire ("Secret Garden"), a remnant from days-gone-by ("Murder Incorporated"), and the songs "Blood Brothers" and "This Hard Land." Each song evokes a special slice of the pie that is Springsteen's lifework: The sociology of "Hard Land," the communal spirit of "Brothers," and the boardwalk braggadocio of "Murder." The rationale for including "Murder" is hilarious and suggestive—once again—of Springsteen's relationship with his audience. He told the New York Times:

> For years, there's this guy that's been following me around with a "Murder Incorporated" sign. . . . I see him in the audience like every five shows. I have never played the song, ever, in concert and would have no intent to do so, and yet this guy follows me around with this sign and flashes it during the entire show. So it was he who I had in mind when we put the song on the album. We said, "Let's put this on for that guy, whoever he is."

Springsteen revisited the raw materials from which the Worker's Elegy was formed with his 1998 boxed set, Tracks. The four discs span Springsteen's career, ranging from the John Hammond audition through each of the projects we have discussed thus far. Scholars of Springsteenetics drooled over the outtakes just as much as they lamented omissions about which only they are aware.

The live show-stopper "Thundercrack," the fabulous B-side "Pink Cadillac," the original *Nebraska*-drenched "Born in the U.S.A.," the heartfelt tribute to his mother "The Wish," and the *Greatest Hits* outtake "Back in Your Arms" are but a few of the insightful numbers featured on *Tracks*. Several songs contain lyrics that were shelved and reappeared years later, revealing the "work in progress" aspects of the unfolding oeuvre. And yet, to the extent that these songs shed light on various aspects of the lifework, they remain sidebars to the Worker's Elegy. Springsteen's *intense* commitment to stay on message throughout his lifework resulted in decisions that—for one reason or another—cast these songs aside. Had the oeuvre yielded albums that were merely assemblages of songs, then we would be wise to reassemble the work, place these songs in their respective contexts, and contemplate their contributions to the story. But that was—in no way—the case. The auteur labored fastidiously over each install-ment of his unfolding story; hence we stand by those decisions, avoid peeking into his narrative closet, and examine the work "as intended." Springsteen's court battles with bootleggers and other unofficial releases indicate the extent of his desire to shape *his* message *his* way. His commitment indicates the con-tractual qualities of his relationship with his imagined community—a bond that is quite unique within the world of popular music.

the worker's elegy, a reprise

With 1995's *The Ghost of Tom Joad* Bruce Springsteen applies the Worker's Elegy to new, more diversified contexts. The auteur expands his "imagined com-munity" as he explores the struggles of daily living for those not being blest by living on the Jersey Shore. Continuing his deep-seated fascination with John Steinbeck's *The Grapes of Wrath*, Springsteen opens with Tom Joad and his tale of sociological struggle before applying that notion to more contemporary set-tings. He does not totally forsake his emotional autobiography. Although many of the situations are products of research, the emotional depth of understand-ing transcends a newspaper account of immigrant youth in San Diego, photo-graphs of abandoned steel mills in Ohio, or news accounts of drug factories in California. Springsteen's intimacy with psychological suffering informs and enlivens this exploration of Another America and its citizenry.

A seasoned songwriter approached his task with the knowledge necessary to build his case. In *Songs*, Springsteen describes his inventive strategy in consid-erable detail. Following *Nebraska*'s lead, the auteur labored to give life to char-acters through his voice. For the author, narrative precision is the key: "The cor-rect detail can speak volumes about who your character is, while the wrong one can shred the credibility of your story. When you get the music and lyrics right . . . your voice disappears into the voices of those you've chosen to write about. Basically, I find the characters and listen to them." Once Springsteen discovers his characters, he probes himself for the song's "emotional center." There he reports how he researched his subjects, returned to 1978 and the reckoning phase's narrative details, and applied that knowledge to people of different ethnicity enslaved by the identical "brutal circumstances" as the characters portrayed in the Worker's Elegy. Joad is, then, "the Worker's Elegy, a Reprise."

In Joad's liner notes, Springsteen credits the sources of his materials: Dale Maharidge and Michael Williamson's Journey to Nowhere; Morris Dees's A Season for Justice; Sebastian Rotella's Los Angeles Times piece, "Children of the Border"; another Los Angeles Times article by Mark Arax and Tom Gordon, "California's Illicit Farm Belt Export"; and John Ford's version of Steinbeck's book. Sandford's biography notes how Springsteen contacted reporters and other sources to seek details about the respective stories. He searched externally for the particulars, whereas he turned inward for the work's "emotional center," as he explained to Fred Schruers: "[Tom Joad] wasn't that different from the legacy of my own family. My parents struggled a lot. The material followed ideas that I started out with—things that bothered me, and I wrote about them. You've got to find your own isolation, your own sense of being between the road and the void. . . . After that, what else does a writer do? He looks around."

Armed with personal and factual knowledge, Springsteen pursued his creative ambitions, which he shared with Guitar World Acoustic:

> I want to make a record where I don't have to play by the rules. I won't have any singles or any of that kind of stuff. . . . I hadn't done that in a real long time; I guess I wanted to see if I could do it again. You don't really choose the voice you follow; you sort of follow the voice that's in your head. You're lucky if you find it. And once you've found it, you're supposed to listen to it.

The spirit of rule-breaking extended to the studio, as he explained: "It's a little unusual; we tried to mix it, tried to master it—and every time we did something to it, it made it sound more like a record and less like a living thing. We had kind of a variation of [Nebraska] going on. I guarantee you, [Tom Joad] will be the only record released this year that has no eq [equalization] and absolutely no master." By forsaking the commercial and production prescriptions associated with the recording industry's ironclad rules of procedure, the auteur was in a position to achieve the creative objectives he articulated for the New York Times Magazine: "I had an interest in writing about the country—all of it. I was creating intimate portraits of individuals that you can draw back from and look at them in the context of the country they live in. You have to find circumstances where those characters resonate with psychological, emotional and, by implication, political issues."

To fully comprehend Springsteen's intimate portraits and his characters' plights, once more we return to the "show." The album presents the respective vignettes in its carefully designed way, but the show tells the whole story. As mentioned previously, the Joad tour presented a show with an established set of audience rules that Springsteen introduced at the beginning of each performance (e.g., no yelling, no singing along, "silence" was required). Once the rules were announced, the auteur used his tried-and-true song introductions to provide the complete details of the individual songs. Several of these monologues were rather long; their detail leaving absolutely no doubt about the song's message and—in Springsteen's view—allowing the characters to emerge and speak for themselves. Though one should hesitate to suggest that the introductory monologue was *better* than the song itself, the listening experience would surely be incomplete in its absence. The *Joad* tour was—in every respect—the state of Springsteen's art.

The Ghost of Tom Joad (released November 1995) contains 12 tracks (running 50:18 minutes) that address three topics. One song, "My Best Was Never Good Enough," according to its author is a parody of the cliché-ridden simplicities that dominate the evening news. Another song is a longing for dreamy escape to yet another promised land, "Across the Border." And ten songs enact the "struggle" theme: Two sociological struggles ("Tom Joad" and "Galveston Bay"), one relational struggle ("Dry Lightning"), and seven lifestyle struggles ("Straight Time," "Highway 29," "Youngstown," "Sinaloa Cowboys," "The Line," "Balboa Park," and "The New Timer"). Within the various conflicts we observe combinations of societal or relational complaint, relational longing, victimization, or intrapersonal turmoil; in each case, the struggle the characters endure with that particular situation is the centerpiece of the story.

Springsteen's characterological "deep water" yields compelling insights regarding the internal battle to stay on the straight-and-narrow path that a seasoned ex-con endures ("Straight"), the failed attempt to gain a sense of freedom through crime ("Highway 29"), the sense of pride and loss steelworkers experience as they watch their livelihood disappear ("Youngstown"), the misguided efforts of immigrants who seek their fair share of the promised land's bounty only to be victimized by drug and sex merchants ("Sinaloa" and "Balboa," respectively), the lonely life of a widower who works for the border patrol, his confusion over his job, and his intense desire for what he once had ("The Line"), and the abusive lifestyle of a traveling laborer who is confronted with violence and deceit ("The New Timer"). These are emotional portraits that use their various situations as a vehicle to explore the respective characters' psychological states. Springsteen gives them life on record and in performance. Their feelings come through him. The results are a tribute to Bruce Springsteen's talent.

The two sociological struggles display this trait as well, yet their emphasis is on the specific situation more than the characters' emotional response. "Joad" sticks to the Ford/Steinbeck script as it describes the conditions under which these dispossessed people live as a preface to Joad's pledge to his mother to fight such conditions wherever they appear. It is, in every respect, a thematic overture. "Galveston" is a more complicated tale of post-Vietnam bigotry and economic struggle as two characters from the same war (one Vietnamese, the other American) turn on each other and wage an economic battle in the Texas fishing industry. The story ends positively (Springsteen claims he changed the original version) as a planned act of violence is rejected, the competition accepted, and love of family renewed. It is as if the drunken character from "Johnny 99" had simply had his fill and returned home to his family instead of needlessly gunning down innocents in a blind act of violence. A kinder, gentler auteur yields to his evolving artistic impulse.

The Grammy Award–winning *Joad* is a masterful piece of storytelling from one of America's foremost storytellers. The attention to characterological and scenic detail, the depth of the emotional portrayals, the internal coherence, and the performer's commitment to his message make *Joad* an exemplar of the narrative style that guided a 30-year career. Springsteen's ability to crystallize his talent and experience into a work of art that seizes the respective signatures and applies them to new subject matter demonstrates his *control* over his creative instincts. The synthesis of art and craft that rendered the auteur's oeuvre is on display in *The Ghost of Tom Joad*. Such comprehensive statements are rare events in the history of art.

Critics seized on this logic as well. *Time's* Karen Schoemer observes: "In the most obvious sense, 'Tom Joad' is a sequel to 'Nebraska.' It follows similar skeletal arrangements, and it explores themes of displacement and despair. . . . [Springsteen] seems to be reconnecting with himself and his artistic past." *Musician* reports:

> Of the adjectives to describe Bruce Springsteen and his music, one clearly leads the pack: American. . . . And as always, his songs convey the possibility, if not the realization, of salvation through love. What drives his cast of luckless losers, and lends spirit to even his most depressing lyrics, is the need to belong to someone, be it God, family, or that girl down at the local bar. In this respect, Springsteen's American landscape is one that the whole world can relate to.

Stereo Review states: "Springsteen's map of the U.S. shows the paths of twelve disenfranchised characters walking the backroads and pot-holed streets of America. . . . [The record] stands as a deeply affecting narrative about men and women driven to desperate deeds in desperate times." The *Philadelphia Inquirer's* Tom Moon is tired of Springsteen's "downcast narratives that ramble down one blue highway, then another, spitting out the usual road-as-wisdom, road-as-escape tropes like spent chewing tobacco on the median strip." Lastly, *USA Today's* Edna Gundersen cites Springsteen's response to critics like Tom Moon, and the overall view that his records no longer chart as they once did: "I just wanted it out there. I'm very, very sure about what I'm doing. When the record was finished, I knew it was good. I didn't have any fantasies about it getting an enormous amount of airplay. I couldn't care less what number it comes in this week or next week or the week after. . . . I'm going to be on that stage playing my songs, giving whatever I've got to the audience. That's my job."

That last statement—in all its glorious simplicity—sums up Bruce Springsteen's career: His art is his job; its mission is to connect with audiences and give them something useful in their daily struggles with life's recurrent situations. The means through which he pursues his job have evolved across the years; yet his mission has never wavered. All of which leads me to wonder just what Bruce Springsteen's version of Greil Marcus' "Smithville" would be like. Having applied that notion to conclude our discussion of Bob Dylan's work, perhaps we should try it here as well. Aside from being in New Jersey, what would that "imagined community" look like? How would people act there? I think I know. Springsteen's Smithville is a mill village where all the churches are lined up neatly on Church Street, and all the families assemble there on Sunday, their only day of rest. In Smithville, everybody buys groceries from the company store where credit is always available to company employees and is needed to pay the outlandish prices the store charges for its merchandise. There are no unions, Rotary Clubs, Masonic Lodges, or even Boy or Girl Scout troops in Smithville. Just work, church, and a strip of pool halls and fast-food restaurants on Main Street where workers cruise on Saturday nights (gas is also available from a company store). Fights break out in the alleys, girlfriends roam from car to car, beer is the drug of choice, and Memphis soul is the preferred musical form in Smithville. Few kids go to college in Smithville; instead, they follow their parents' legacies in the mills. It is a dreadful life, but it is all American. Yet none of it *really* matters because Smithville is a short drive from the Jersey Shore, and *all* of life's pleasures await there.

chapter eight

the exemplars

Once more, having established the auteur and his oeuvre, we turn to the stylistic tendencies that rendered that work. Just as in the Dylan study, that task is achieved merely by allowing the art to speak for itself. Few artists in the history of popular music have labored so intensely to devise and advance a systematic account of a specific, evolving situation as Bruce Springsteen. Not only did he create an imagined community and chart its maturation over time, he maintained a rigid system of quality control that ensured his work remained "on message." To achieve that end, the auteur deployed a soap opera storytelling strategy to weave melodramatic portrayals of his imagined community's life events. That Springsteen used the technique to successfully articulate useful accounts of life's struggles for his audience is clear. That the Worker's Elegy makes a unique contribution to the development of American Song is certain. The oeuvre is a remarkable body of work.

The Worker's Elegy unfolds chronologically, just as the author planned it. I characterize Springsteen's lifework as a "soap opera" for two reasons: The work is continuous and stresses melodrama. The writer's accent on the emotional "deep water" from which he draws his characters places characterization at the forefront of the story. Scenic conditions, of course, are central as well, yet the use of characterization as a means of communicating the story's value orientation represents Springsteen's narrative focus. Moreover, the concentration on a specific cast of characters facilitates an examination of life's impact on these individuals at certain points in time. As scenic conditions evolve, the story emphasizes how the characters respond to the challenges of the moment, and in so doing, relates how their value structures affect those responses. Such a strategy allows for a narrative depth that may very well be unprecedented. Whether one identifies with these portrayals is fundamentally irrelevant—what is relevant is the storytelling strategy's successful implementation.

As we have seen, the Worker's Elegy charts the lifecycle struggles of a specific segment of working Americans. From youthful dreams of escape to uncertain destinations through the fateful recognition of an inescapable situation to the acceptance of their lives and the new challenges of maturity, Springsteen's characters depict the emotional qualities of the American experience. The mindless—and at times, irresponsible—activities of American adolescence and the impact of the American Dream dogma on these characters' worldviews reveal the American psyche's emphasis on external, occasionally materialistic, reward systems. The American Dream's failure to deliver the desired goods inspires a host of responses ranging from anger, to jealousy, to sullen disillusionment. Nowhere do we observe young people in pursuit of individual growth; instead, we witness the consistent emphasis on material gain. While these characters stare at "mansions" and detest used automobiles, their jealousy grows. The story is a sad testimony to American materialism.

Once these characters realize that nobody is going to give them the key to the city (or more accurately, the bank), they grow embittered and contemplate revenge. Youthful fantasies fly out the car window as Springsteen's characters attempt to run without realizing their inability to hide. *The River* represents a significant turning point in the story in that the record's blend of partying and disillusionment articulates the American crossroads at which these people stand. They do not know whether to party or wind their watch. Since they have rarely thought about anything, they have no resources to draw upon. They grow angry. They grow resentful. Few of these characters inspire sympathy; there are no war veterans or abandoned mothers at this point in the story. With *Nebraska*, we consider an adaptation of an old axiom: When the going gets pathetic, the pathetic get going. And yet, with "My Father's House" and "Reason to Believe" the narrative tide turns. The characters in these stories are not victims of their own materialism; rather, they *have* been emotionally abandoned. Their pain is innocent, not self-inflicted, and genuinely sympathetic. *Born in the U.S.A.* extends the trend with its blend of victimization and self-abuse. Rest assured, the guy from "Downbound Train" is not going to hang out at the "Glory Days" bar. The Vietnam veteran and the character contemplating his hometown's demise are totally different people from the pedophiles and the party animals. Springsteen is about to finish these characters off and send them to jail. Perhaps a co-authored piece with Johnny Cash could trace these characters' lives in prison, where community life assumes an entirely new meaning.

Although irresponsibility continues to raise its irreverent head from time to time, the soap opera's acceptance phase leaves these people behind as the auteur moves from the "man on the road" to the "man in the house." With an occasional reference to bygone dreams, these older characters face the challenges of relational development and parenthood with the lessons of failure firmly in mind. *Tunnel of Love's* characters are truly sympathetic. Their ambitions to come to terms with themselves, to be mature and virtuous—in general, to be better people—represent a major shift in characterization. Even after the male character in "Spare Parts" deserts his lover and leaves her with child, the story charts her struggle (and victory) and reveals her ex-lover to be the loser that he, in fact, is. These types of cowardly characters are about to exit Springsteen's imagined community forever. (The *Tom Joad* reprise revisits all personality types and is, therefore, the exception.) From this point on, the Worker's Elegy presents the domestic struggle, its victories and defeats, and the challenging nature of contemporary American life.

The story coherently displays certain characteristics that should be discussed before moving into the respective exemplars. The characters' self-victimization, their responses to that condition, the inherent anxieties, and the soap opera's resolution are noteworthy attributes of the auteur's oeuvre. First, the self-victimization these characters endure is striking: Notice how these people are prisoners of their own acts. These characters rarely, if ever, take measures to better themselves or their conditions. Ensnared in a cycle of frivolous escapes (cars, "Saturday nights," boardwalks), their lack of ambition makes them easy prey for institutional enslavement. The residents in Springsteen's "Smithville" will gladly pay the company store twenty dollars for a six-pack of beer (on credit) and indenture themselves for another month just for *that night's* pleasure. Nobody goes to night school nor works two jobs nor sells their car nor delays any gratification whatsoever. Such traits dilute their sympathetic appeal just as our second attribute—their response—reinforces that feeling. The loss of faith and the corresponding loss of trust that accompany these characters' realizations about their situations take them deeper into this emotional abyss of their own making. Subsequently, we witness an *increase* in frivolity and *more* fast cars, cheap women (and men), inane violence, and materialistic disillusionment. Nevertheless, these characters have been seriously affected by their experiences. They will never be the same again—which takes us to our third attribute and the characters' intense anxieties. When Springsteen takes "the man" out of his car and places him in his house, he enters the home, baggage and all. In other words, we witness an "anxiety shift" in which these characters take all of their emotions about the perceived injustices they have experienced thus far to their relationships. The insecurities garnered from years of (perceived) societal and institutional victimization create a set of expectations for similar (perceived) happenings in other contexts. We have, then, victims consumed by their victimization. The distrust is intoxicating. And these people have one prodigious emotional mountain to climb—but climb they do, and the story ends with positive scenes of relational acceptance, a newfound commitment to continue the struggle (i.e., loyalty), and Springsteen's impressionistic look back at the events of the previous 25 years (i.e., *Lucky Town*). The anxieties never go away; however, they are more positively channeled and therefore become useful. These characters may forgive, but they will *never* forget.

Springsteen's "ongoing novel" is a remarkably systematic work of art. One reason why the work sustains its coherence is the auteur's reliance on certain story forms to convey his message. Throughout all the scenes of street life, violence, victimization, domestic struggle, and familial turmoil, Springsteen deploys four narrative structures to portray those conditions. Interestingly, these structures really do not control the oeuvre until the third album, *Born to Run*. The first two albums—*Asbury Park* and *The Wild*—rely on impressionistic accounts of vacuous street happenings more than any other strategy. The tactic is effective in that it depicts the emotionally haphazard existence these characters' treasure. Although we gain a glimpse of these forthcoming story forms in the first two albums (principally the "escape/search" structure's application in "Spirit in the Night," "Rosalita," and "4th of July"), the E Street Party dominates the story in a useful, insightful fashion. With *Born to Run*, the four structures—the *struggle/plea*, the *escape/search*, the *celebration*, and, of course, the *complaint*—assume control. These four narrative structures shape the value-laden characterizations of the Worker's Elegy into a coherent soap opera and its continuous portrayal of characterological melodrama.

Just as certain narrative structures controlled specific Dylan albums, this trait manifests itself within the Worker's Elegy as well. For example, *Born to Run* is dominated by the struggle/plea and escape/search narratives. *Darkness on the Edge of Town* introduces and focuses on the complaint strategy. *Nebraska* extends that storytelling trend and adds the "portrait" as a means of articulating those sentiments. *Born in the U.S.A.* is a paragon of complaint. *Human Touch* focuses on the relational struggle/plea. And *Tom Joad* is a monument to lifestyle, relational, and sociological struggle. Often, these story forms appear in their pure state; on other occasions, they blend their internal strategies into narrative alloys of the respective storytelling formulas. For instance, the relational struggle depicted in "She's the One" involves more than a little bit of relational complaint, even though the thrust of the message focuses on the narrator's internal conflict. "Born to Run" uses a state-of-the-art version of the escape/search strategy, although it also communicates the societal complaint that supplies the urge to move on. "Born in the U.S.A." is, most assuredly, a societal complaint, and yet the narrator's internal struggles directly inform the dirge. Such overlap signifies the narrative depth of Springsteen's work.

Before exploring the four narrative structures that weave in and out of the lifework, we should pause to consider Springsteen's impressionism. Though modeled after Dylan's work, Springsteen's wordplay assumes a more structured format in that his language is typically less imaginative than Dylan's (no Glissendorf here) and his framework is more focused. Still, the images rush by in droves. Often, the technique conveys the hyperactive context that is street life—especially *New York City* street life—in an insightful fashion. The expression's rhythm serves the narrative superstructure well. Our example, "Blinded by the Light," is a tidal wave of images:

> *Madman drummers, bummers and Indians in the summer with a teenage diplomat*
> *In the dumps with the mumps as the adolescent pumps his way into his hat*
> *With a boulder on my shoulder, feelin' kinda older, I tripped the merry-go-round*

With this very unpleasing sneezing and wheezing the calliope crashed to
   the ground
Some all-hot half-shot was headin' for the hot spot snappin' his fingers,
   clappin' his hands
And some fleshpot mascot was tied into a lover's knot with a whatnot in
   her hand
And now young Scott with a slingshot finally found a tender spot and
   throws his lover in the sand
And some bloodshot forget-me-not whispers "Daddy's within earshot save
   the buckshot, turn up the band."

And she was blinded by the light
Cut loose like a deuce, another runner in the night
Blinded by the light
She got down but she never got tight but she'll make it all right.

Some brimstone baritone anticyclone rolling stone preacher from the East
He says "Dethrone the dictaphone, hit it in its funny bone, that's where
   they expect it least"
And some new-mown chaperone was standin' in the corner all alone
   watchin' the young girls dance
And some fresh-sown moonstone was messin' with his frozen zone to
   remind him of the feeling of romance.

Yeah he was blinded by the light
Cut loose like a deuce, another runner in the night
Blinded by the light
He got down but he never got tight but he's gonna make it tonight.

Some silicone sister with her manager's mister told me I got what it
   takes
She said "I'll turn you on sonny to something strong if you play that song
   with the funky break"
And go-cart Mozart was checkin' out the weather chart to see if it was
   safe to go outside
And little Early-Pearly came by in her curly-wurly and asked me if I needed
   a ride
Oh some hazard from Harvard was skunked on beer playin' backyard bom-
   bardier
Yes and Scotland Yard was trying hard, they sent some dude with a calling
   card, he said "Do what you like but don't do it here"
Well I jumped up, turned around, spit in the air, fell on the ground
Asked him which was the way back home
He said, "Take a right at the light, keep goin' straight until night and then
   boy you're on your own"
And now in Zanzibar a shootin' star was ridin' in a sidecar hummin' a
   lunar tune

Yes and the avatar said blow the bar but first remove the cookie jar, we're
gonna teach those boys to laugh too soon
And some kidnapped handicap was complainin' that he caught the clap
from some mousetrap he bought last night
Well I unsnapped his skullcap and between his ears I saw a gap but figured
he'd be all right.

He was just blinded by the light
Cut loose like a deuce, another runner in the night
Blinded by the light
Mama always told me not to look into the sights of the sun
Oh but mama that's where the fun is.

Whew! To read these lines is one thing, but hearing Springsteen belt out his firestorm of images is certainly another. The internal rhyming structure is more reminiscent of a Broadway musical lyric than a Bob Dylan song. Whereas Dylan's in-the-spirit impressionism seizes and explores fleeting images, this is, assuredly, one finely groomed "show dog." Our characters—a "fleshpot mascot," a "bloodshot forget-me-not," a "brimstone baritone anticyclone rolling stone preacher from the east," a "new-mown chaperone," a "fresh-sown moonstone," a "silicone sister," a "go-cart Mozart," a "hazard from Harvard," "the avatar," and more—engage in strange (but rhyming) activities that go nowhere via scenes of varying clarity. And yet, the chorus seems to anchor the collage of uneven images as these "runners in the night" make it through whatever it is they are attempting to do. Besides, who cares anyway? It is *all* a party. Never again would Springsteen write in this fashion. When he deploys his impressionism in *Lucky Town* it is a much tamer version that facilitates the connection with the song's moral.

From maddening images of urban craziness we turn to Springsteen's struggle/plea narrative strategy. This storytelling structure first appears in *Born to Run* and immediately establishes the two contexts of its application: The relational and societal domains. The relational struggle in "She's the One" complements the societal conflicts in "Backstreets," "Jungleland," and "Meeting Across the River" to establish the embattled worlds in which Springsteen's characters live. The trend continues with *Darkness* and "Racing in the Streets," "Promised Land," and the title cut in which the choice is presented: Fight or resign. The narrative pause that is *The River* revisits the choice through the relational strife in "The Ties That Bind" and "Independence Day" as well as in the broader picture presented through "The Price You Pay." The strategy is absent in *Nebraska* (where characters no longer struggle—they act) and returns briefly via the relational plea, "I'm on Fire" in *U.S.A. Tunnel's* reliance on the strategy is apparent in the relational pleas that are "Ain't Got You," "Tougher Than the Rest," and "Valentine's Day" as well as in the fierce internal struggle portrayed by "Two Faces." Six of *Human Touch's* 14 tracks use the relational plea (e.g., "Human Touch," "Soul Driver," "Cross My Heart," "Man's Job," and "Real Man") and *Joad's* reliance on the "struggle" story form is complete. This is, indeed, a steady storytelling staple in Springsteen's oeuvre. First, consider the societal struggle presented through the landmark work, "The Promised Land":

On a rattlesnake speedway in the Utah desert
I pick up my money and head back into town
Driving 'cross the Waynesboro county line
I got the radio on and I'm just killing time
Working all day in my daddy's garage
Driving all night chasing some mirage
Pretty soon, little girl, I'm gonna take charge.

[chorus]
    The dogs on Main Street howl
    'Cause they understand
    If I could take one moment into my hands
    Mister, I ain't a boy, no I'm a man
    And I believe in a promised land.

I've done my best to live the right way
I get up in the morning and go to work each day
But your eyes go blind and your blood runs cold
Sometimes I feel so weak I just want to explode
Explode and tear this whole town apart
Take a knife and cut this pain from my heart
Find somebody itching for something to start.

[chorus]

There's a dark cloud rising from the desert floor
I packed my bags and I'm heading straight into the storm
Gonna be a twister to blow everything down
That ain't got the faith to stand its ground
Blow away the dreams that tear you apart
Blow away the dreams that break your heart
Blow away the lies that leave you nothing but lost and brokenhearted.

[chorus]

The song uses straightforward language and clear imagery to tell a story of an embattled man who is not quite ready to give up his quest for a better life. He works, he plays, he believes. His steadfast belief in hard work is threatened by a longing for something better, and that desire is on the verge of inspiring violence. At this point, Springsteen's metaphors are rich in their communicative power as he presents a "dark storm" brewing ahead and the narrator's willingness to confront it. This individual is not afraid to test his faith; in fact, he warns that without that faith, the "storm" will be all-consuming. For him, however, the storm may contain cleansing powers that rid life of broken dreams and their consequences. Faith is the key—faith will provide the fuel that ensures that the struggle will yield victory. Faith provides the path to the promised land.

The faith conveyed through "The Promised Land" is a recurrent theme in Springsteen's tales of struggle and pleading. Without that trait, resignation is the only option. The battle must continue or else the characters know they will fade into the darkness. Through it all, a sense of optimism remains. These attributes appear in relational contexts as well, as we observe in "Two Faces":

> I met a girl and we ran away
> I swore I'd make her happy every day
> And how I made her cry
> Two faces have I.
>
> Sometimes, mister, I feel sunny and wild
> Lord I love to see my baby smile
> Then dark clouds come rolling by
> Two faces have I.
>
> One that laughs, one that cries
> One says hello, one says good-bye
> One does things I don't understand
> Makes me feel like half a man.
>
> At night I get down on my knees and pray
> Our love will make that other man go away
> But he'll never say good-bye
> Two faces have I.
>
> Last night as I kissed you 'neath the willow tree
> He swore he'd take your love away from me
> He said our life was just a lie
> And two faces have I
> Well go ahead and let him try.

"Two Faces" moves beyond the superficial struggles that threaten relationships to the *real source* of the conflict for this particular character: His embattled personality. The narrator's manic-depressive tendencies create a roller coaster of emotion (presented through more meteorological metaphors) that stifle his ability to make his relationship work. He treasures his vow to provide eternal happiness and laments his failure to sustain that condition. His inner turmoil is all-consuming; he prays for help. Yet, hope remains through his faith in his love. When that "other man" denounces the relationship as a "lie" the narrator rises to the occasion with a resilient "Well go ahead and let him try." The song is masterful in its portrayal of the most fundamental ingredient for relational success: self-trust. In the absence of internal harmony, the chance for relational concordance diminishes considerably. Furthermore, Springsteen's character displays the maturity that emerges as the Worker's Elegy enters its final stages, in that he does not blame external factors for his inability to achieve his goals. He stares squarely at himself and accepts the challenge posed by this ultimate struggle.

Springsteen's "struggle/plea" narratives join the complaint as the bedrock forms upon which the Worker's Elegy is built. As characters fight their perceived conditions and issue pleas for help, they fend off the resignation that would, assuredly, guarantee their failure. Often—as with "The Promised Land," "Two Faces," and most of Joad—we do not know how the story ends. We are presented with the context, the character's assessment of the situation, a statement of commitment, and are left to ponder the story's resolution. Hence, the story form shies away from epic accounts of relational or societal victory in favor of an emphasis on the struggle itself. At the heart of that struggle is the character's emotional response to his or her condition. The stories do more than merely complain, they engage the situations that inspire the complaint.

Without the complaint there would be no struggle, therefore our next narrative structure invokes one of the oldest forms of popular music storytelling. Complaints about love, work, society, and everything else one can imagine dominate the history of popular music—and that trait is evident in the Worker's Elegy as well. Interestingly, the story form does not appear until Springsteen's fourth album, *Darkness on the Edge of Town*. There we observe conflicting responses to the complaints lodged, in that characters rebel against ("Badlands" and "Adam Raised a Cain") and accept their situations (e.g., "Something in the Night," "Factory," "Streets of Fire") in varying degrees. In either case, the complaint itself is the thrust of the story. The story form gains momentum in *The River* with its blend of relational (e.g., "Hungry Heart," "Fade Away," "Stolen Car") and societal (e.g., "Jackson Cage," "The River," "Point Blank") complaints. The negative dominates the *Nebraska* project as it uses the sentiment as a springboard to violence (e.g., "Atlantic City," "Mansion on the Hill," "Johnny 99," "Used Cars," and more) and *U.S.A.* is consumed by the strategy (ten of the twelve tracks deploy the tactic). The complaint assumes a relational emphasis with *Tunnel* (e.g., "Spare Parts," "Brilliant Disguise," "One Step Up") and echoes into *Touch* via "Gloria's Eyes," "I Wish I Were Blind," and "57 Channels." There the complaint dies. *Joad* uses the sentiment to articulate its struggles and, once more, demonstrates the interdependence between the two forms. A compelling example of the complaint–struggle interplay reflects one of the prime motivations for Bruce Springsteen's lifework; that is, the father–son relationship as portrayed in "Adam Raised a Cain":

> In the summer that I was baptized
> My father held me to his side
> As they put me to the water
> He said how on that day I cried
> We were prisoners of love, a love in chains
> He was standin' in the door, I was standin' in the rain
> With the same hot blood burning in our veins
> Adam raised a Cain.

All of the old faces
Ask you why you're back
They fit you with position
And the keys to your daddy's Cadillac
In the darkness of your room
Your mother calls you by your true name
You remember the faces, the places, the names
You know it's never over, it's relentless as rain
Adam raised a Cain.

In the Bible Cain slew Abel
And east of Eden he was cast
You're born into this life paying
For the sins of somebody else's past
Daddy worked his whole life for nothing but the pain
Now he walks these empty rooms looking for something to blame
You inherit the sins, you inherit the flames
Adam raised a Cain
Lost but not forgotten
From the dark heart of a dream
Adam raised a Cain.

This is powerful imagery in and of itself, but when one pauses to consider Springsteen's relationship with his father it assumes a haunting presence. The Biblical analogy notwithstanding, the song conveys the biological transference of emotional conditions that render a difficult life. Enter the Biblical qualities and we note the evil—guilt-ridden—aspects of the story. Springsteen's character wrestles with a situation beyond his control. His fate is in the cards; his hand has been dealt long before he entered this world and now he must cope with the consequences. The story hinges on the relationship, for without the relationship and all of its trappings, the complaint is empty. The lines are evocative: "You know it's never over, it's relentless as rain" (yet another meteorological reference), "You're born into this life paying / For the sins of somebody else's past," and "You inherit the sins, you inherit the flames." The narrator has been "cast" into a situation merely by the chances of his birth and his biological relationship with his father is the culprit. The complaint is clear, the consequence is certain, the victimization is complete. Such conditions emerge in other contexts as well, as our next example indicates:

Born down in a dead man's town
The first kick I took was when I hit the ground
You end up like a dog that's been beat too much
Till you spend half your life just covering it up
Born in the U.S.A.
I was born in the U.S.A.
I was born in the U.S.A.
Born in the U.S.A.

Got in a little hometown jam
So they put a rifle in my hand
Sent me off to a foreign land
To go and kill the yellow man.

Born in the U.S.A.
I was born in the U.S.A.
I was born in the U.S.A.
I was born in the U.S.A.

Come back home to the refinery
Hiring man says "Son if it was up to me"
Went down to see my V.A. man
He said "Son don't you understand now"

Had a brother at Khe Sahn fighting off the Viet Cong
They're still there, he's all gone
He had a woman he loved in Saigon
I got a picture of him in her arms now.

Down in the shadow of the penitentiary
Out by the gas fires of the refinery
I'm ten years burning down the road
Nowhere to run, ain't got nowhere to go.

Born in the U.S.A.
I was born in the U.S.A.
Born in the U.S.A.
I'm a long gone daddy in the U.S.A.
Born in the U.S.A.
Born in the U.S.A.
Born in the U.S.A.
I'm a cool rocking daddy in the U.S.A.

Just as one may be victimized by birth, one may suffer injustice through other, uncontrollable conditions. (How this song was misconstrued to be a patriotic anthem is mind boggling—regardless of its musical characteristics or performance.) Here Springsteen's plain-spoken lyrics paint a clear picture of social prejudice. Whatever this character did to warrant his "sentence" in the military, surely his debt to society was paid in full. The auteur captures one of the unique facets of the Vietnam experience in that—for the first time in American history—war veterans returned home to an unappreciative citizenry. A bad thing was made worse through a public backlash at both the decision-makers who perpetuated the war and the victims of their narrow-minded poli-cies. Never before had veterans returned "home" and been refused their old jobs or been denied the services of the Veteran's Administration. Springsteen's sym-bolism communicates that the narrator stands within the shadows of jail and near the afterproducts of his old job, waiting. This is the classic complaint: It raises the situation, explores it, and leaves us to contemplate the consequences.

Springsteen's capacity to identify with the emotional qualities of his characters is evident in his complaints. Whether he explores the ups and downs of loving relationships, the empty feelings of loss that accompany the failure to realize one's dreams, the downtrodden spirits of the luckless and locked out, or the frustrations of familial situations, his songs of complaint ring true with an emotional depth that suggests more than an identification with his characters' plights. Springsteen appears to display a compelling ability to empathize as he walks in his characters' shoes and participates in their lives. Little doubt that such a skill could lead to serious problems in living. The more "faces" one has to cope with, the more difficult the coping process.

One means of coping with life's struggles and the conditions that foster recurring anxieties is through escape, our next narrative structure. Although the auteur asserts that several of these songs stress a "search" more than mere "escape," a close examination of the text suggests that the songs' emphasis on the characters' motives speaks more about what they are running _from_ than anything else. Still, why not accommodate Springsteen with an escape/search category? In any event, the escape/search story structure was the first of our four approaches to appear in the oeuvre and the first to depart. Beginning with _Asbury Park_'s "Spirit in the Night" and moving into _The Wild_'s "4th of July" and "Rosalita," Springsteen's tales of adventurous escapades at a nearby lake and his romantic appeals for a joint exodus from the boardwalk scene represent his first departure from the impressionistic writing that controls the first two records. The tactic reaches its peak via _Born to Run_'s anthems "Thunder Road" and the title song (with a dash of "Night" tossed in). The urge returns in _The River_'s transitional accounts (e.g., "Out in the Street" and "Ramrod") and disappears. While hints of the escape/search story creep into songs from time to time, the strategy ceases until _Joad_'s "Across the Border" and its romantic portrayal of a dreamy promised land just over the hill. Our exemplar, "Born to Run," reveals why the escape/search story structure is a powerful entry in the Springsteen canon:

> In the day we sweat it out on the streets of a runaway American dream
> At night we ride through mansions of glory in suicide machines
> Sprung from cages on Highway 9
> Chrome-wheeled fuel-injected
> And steppin' out over the line
> Baby this town rips the bones from your back
> It's a death trap, it's a suicide rap
> We gotta get out while we're young
> 'Cause tramps like us, baby we were born to run.
>
> Wendy let me in, I wanna be your friend
> I want to guard your dreams and visions
> Just wrap your legs 'round these velvet rims

And strap your hands across my engines
Together we could break this trap
We'll run till we drop, baby we'll never go back
Will you walk with me out on the wire
'Cause baby I'm just a scared and lonely rider
But I gotta know how it feels
I want to know if your love is wild
Girl I want to know if love is real.

Beyond the Palace hemipowered drones scream down the boulevard
The girls comb their hair in rearview mirrors
And the boys try to look so hard
The amusement park rises bold and stark
Kids are huddled on the beach in the mist
I wanna die with you out on the streets tonight
In an everlasting kiss.

The highway's jammed with broken heroes
On a last chance power drive
Everybody's out on the run tonight
But there's no place left to hide
Together, Wendy, we can live with the sadness
I'll love you with all the madness in my soul
Someday girl, I don't know when, we're gonna get to that place
Where we really wanna to go
And we'll walk in the sun
But till then tramps like us
Baby we were born to run.

This is one of rock music's great anthems. The story—told in clear, plain language—opens with a concise picture of the dreaded lifestyle that signifies a "runaway American dream." To cope, characters mount "suicide machines" of splendor and hit the highway. Why? Because their lives are caught in a "death trap" and bound for "suicide" unless they get out while the getting is good. From scenic conditions, Springsteen turns to the relationship and the narrator's pledge to protect Wendy in their fight to escape. Here we see Springsteen's "search" in that the narrator's desire to test "love" complements his sheer will to get the hell out of town. Our next scene depicts the happenings around town—kids posing in cars, youngsters hanging out on the beach—as a preface to yet another pledge of commitment. The story closes with more scenes of hot rods, another pledge, and a final push to escape. The song has it all: cars, love, street life, the boardwalk, the beach. And yet, we know nothing about these characters. Do they have jobs? Are they in school? Our only insights are confined to the street, the boardwalk, and the beach. This is quintessential adolescent reasoning: "We gotta get out of this place."

And that is the essence of Springsteen's escape/search narrative strategy.

"Thunder Road" is—in virtually every respect—the same story as "Born to Run." "Spirit in the Night," "Night," "4th of July," "Out in the Street," and "Ramrod" follow similar logic. Lots of scenic descriptions, minimal characterization (often restricted to name only—and there are some interesting names, indeed), and the ever-present sense of urgency are the raw materials of this narrative structure. Only "Rosalita" offers any insight into the characters and their situations as a prelude to the escape pitch issued toward the song's end. The escape/search theme is so important to the Worker's Elegy. When the entire oeuvre is considered in its totality, the escape/search structure occupies but a few songs; however, the theme is an essential element in songs of complaint, struggle, and occasionally—our final strategy—the celebration.

The Worker's Elegy does not celebrate that often, but when it does, a great time is had by all. The party-celebration theme is a central ingredient of Springsteen's impressionistic accounts of street life that control the initial albums. With "Tenth Avenue Freeze-Out," the accounts assume a bit more structure. *Darkness* shakes off the gloom and doom to celebrate "Candy" and love ("Prove It All Night"), before the celebratory explosion that occurs in *The River*. Ten of the record's 20 tracks speak to one form of celebration or another and therefore demonstrate *The River's* transitional qualities. The car party in "Sherry Darling," the relational praise in "I Wanna Marry You," the commitment in "Drive All Night," and the lifestyle celebrations in "Cadillac Ranch" and "I'm a Rocker" offer compelling examples of the Elegy's party theme. Even the unending dirge that is *Nebraska* takes time out to celebrate ("Open All Night"). After *U.S.A.'s* raucous "Darlington County," the celebrations confine themselves to relational matters with *Tunnel's* "All That Heaven Will Allow" and *Town's* "Better Days," "Leap of Faith," and "Book of Dreams." Still, when all the votes are counted, there is no better example of the celebration story line than *U.S.A.'s* "Darlington County":

> *Driving into Darlington County*
> *Me and Wayne on the Fourth of July*
> *Driving into Darlington County*
> *Looking for some work on the county line*
> *We drove down from New York City*
> *Where the girls are pretty but they just want to know your name*
> *Driving into Darlington County*
> *Got a union connection with an uncle of Wayne's*
> *We drove eight hundred miles without seeing a cop*
> *We got rock and roll music blasting off the t-top singing*
>
> *[chorus]*
>   *Sha la la*
>   *Sha la la la la la la*
>   *Sha la la la la la la la.*
>
> *Hey little girl standing on the corner*
> *Today's your luck day for sure all right*

Me and my buddy we're from New York City
We got two hundred dollars, we want to rock all night
Girl, you're looking at two big spenders
Why the world don't know what me and Wayne might do
Our pa's each own one of the World Trade Centers
For a kiss and a smile I'll give mine all to you
Come on baby take a seat on the fender
It's a long night and tell me what else were you gonna do
Just me and you, we could sha la la

[chorus]

Little girl sitting in the window
Ain't seen my buddy in seven days
County man tells me the same thing
He don't work and he don't get paid
Little girl, you're so young and pretty
Walk with me and you can have your way
And we'll leave this Darlington City
For a ride down that Dixie highway

Driving out of Darlington County
My eyes seen the glory of the coming of the Lord
Driving out of Darlington County
Seen Wayne handcuffed to the bumper of a state trooper's Ford.

[chorus]

This song—originally written for the *Darkness* album—captures the devil-may-care attitude of Springsteen's party-animal characters. The characters take a holiday joyride down South as they use the search for work as an excuse to cut loose. Springsteen's imagery gives life to the scene as the rollicking road party enters South Carolina with fifties-style "sha la las" echoing the joy. The carefree attitude dominates the story. They invite "little girls" to join in the fun and promise prime real estate in return for affection. The city slickers—Southern women story turns in the final stanza as the absent Wayne is finally found. What he did or what happens—well, it is beside the point. Let's Party!

Springsteen's songs of celebration are an integral part of the Worker's Elegy. Their presence—or absence—signals the emotional tone of that particular installment of the soap opera. Not all celebrations are parties, however. "Prove It All Night" and "Better Days," for example, concentrate on either the joys of relational commitment or the deep satisfaction that accompanies the Worker's Elegy's resolution. In many respects, the life-is-a-party mentality that dominates the younger characters early in the soap opera creates part of their emerging problems in living, in that the party's inability to sustain itself on a continuous basis provides a basis for the subsequent disillusionment. As "Sherry Darling" relates, one need not have a "job" (or a future, for that matter) in order to have a good time (we can always cash the unemployment check and party down). Finally, the E Street Party Sound that enlivens the songs of celebration also accompany many negative portrayals and, subsequently, bury the struggle or complaint conveyed therein (e.g., "Born in the U.S.A."). In all cases, the celebratory sounds and stories from the auteur's oeuvre represent a fundamental component of his art.

With that, we have the Worker's Elegy. A 30-year body of songwriting that takes the concept of narrative continuity to new heights in the world of popular music. From his enterprising impressionism to his heart-felt excerpts from his emotional autobiography, Bruce Springsteen has charted the ebb and flow of his imagined community's lives as they passed through the various stages of their particular lifecycles. Will Springsteen continue his story? Will he describe what his characters endure as they enter the sunset of their lives, welcome grandchildren into their world, and cope with the fixed-income existences that so many people from their socioeconomic milieu endure? I think not. The impressionistic look back on life's lessons in *Lucky Town* and the emotional reprise in *Tom Joad*, in my view, signal an intuitive end to the story. And intuition has played a compelling role in the development of Springsteen's art. He may plot and build, but his work displays an emotional continuity that evades even the finest writers. He feels his story. His emotional intuitions are central. The curtain has fallen on the Worker's Elegy. It is, in every way, a "job" well-done: The connection was established, the tool was honed, the relational bond was honored.

When we opened this journey into Bruce Springsteen's lifework we noted his consistent use of a "map" metaphor to communicate what he learned from other artists (including the brother he never had, Mr. Dylan), his desire to understand—and perhaps modify—that "map," and in turn leave a richer "map" for subsequent artistic siblings to follow. Bruce Springsteen achieved that goal through the Worker's Elegy. Other "public writer number ones" may have left behind extended treatments of their Huck Finns, Nick Adamses, or Jay Gatsbys, but no popular songwriter has ever created an imagined community and followed their activities over an extended period of time in the fashion that Springsteen mastered. Like Finn, Adams, or Gatsby, Springsteen's characters personified a particular slice of the American pie; nevertheless, the depth, insight, and continuity achieved make an undeniable contribution to American Song and—in more general terms—American culture. To fully appreciate our culture, we must embrace our darker qualities as well as celebrate our finer attributes. The light and dark meet everyday: Their encounter defines our existence. Bruce Springsteen's art explores the darkest part of the day, that moment just before the darkness gives way to light. The emotional deep water associated with that fleeting moment offers a bountiful yield, and the Worker's Elegy represents quite a harvest.

part three

Hammond's folly, revisited

chapter nine

the auteurs

Conventional wisdom has it that a musician/band's third album project is a defining moment. Should the first two albums be critically or commercially successful, the third record indicates whether the achievement was genuine. If the first two records received mixed responses, the third suggests the artist's professional direction and level of industry support. And if the first two albums fail, well, the third project could be the last shot. Third albums define recording artists: Creative philosophies are usually in place, procedural practices are typically developed, commercial relationships are probably established. Take your favorite musical acts and examine their third album—trends tend to crystallize at this point in the commercial lifecycle. No other performing art seems to have such a decisive occasion.

Bob Dylan's third album of original material was actually his fourth release for Columbia Records. Nevertheless, *Another Side of Bob Dylan* was—in every way—the pivotal moment of his professional career. More than the protest songs, the Newport publicity, the 1966 craziness, the 1974 comeback, the 1980s morality, or the musical renaissance of the late-1990s, *Another Side* defined "Bob Dylan." The auteur dropped his artistic anchor on June 9, 1964. Recorded in a single evening, *Another Side* introduced an intensity of expression that was not only startling, it cemented the creative foundation for the lifework. The depth and vitriol of his commentary on loving relationships ("It Ain't Me, Babe" and "Ballad in Plain D"), the simplistic poignancy of his satirical writings ("Motorpsycho Nitemare"), and the idiosyncratic gamesmanship of his innovative wordplay ("Chimes of Freedom" and "My Back Pages")—the songwriting signatures that guided the postman along his enigmatic route for over 40 years—were in clear evidence in this third original work. Whenever Bob Dylan deviated from the immediacy and spontaneity of the *Another Side* creative process, his art suffered. *Another Side* is quintessential Dylan in its writing, performance, and production qualities.

Bruce Springsteen's third album represents a crucial development in his career as well. After two critically acclaimed but commercially disappointing albums, the *Born to Run* project had the potential to make or break Springsteen's national reputation, his relationship with Columbia Records, and the internal dynamics of his emerging operation. Springsteen built a theatrical troupe with a tenacious musicality that made the resulting "show" an unmitigated critical and commercial success. But his inability to transfer his stage magic into the studio raised the stakes for his third record. Here, too, we witness another defining moment in that Springsteen also dropped anchor and would consistently revisit the writing, performance, and production techniques that emerged during the *Born to Run* marathon. This would be the Springsteen Method: Forever "grooming" those beautiful "show dogs" that are his lyrics, laboring through take after take in the studio (often for songs that would never see the light of day), and thinking, thinking, thinking about the message, its usefulness, and viability. Fortunately, *Born to Run* delivered. The escapist anthems ("Born to Run" and "Thunder Road"), the musical revelry ("Tenth Avenue Freeze-Out"), the romantic struggle ("She's the One"), and those "little black and white films" ("Backstreets," "Meeting Across the River," and "Jungleland")—the stylistic signatures that provided the narrative baseline for the Worker's Elegy—were the controlling factors of Springsteen's artistic statement, *Born to Run*. Control, precision, perfection. These were the dominant characteristics to emerge from the *Born to Run* sessions, and they would guide the auteur's every public activity.

Both albums make significant contributions to American Song's development as well. *Another Side* marries idiosyncrasy and intensity, and in so doing, liberates songwriting—songs would never be the same again. *Born to Run* solidifies the Worker's Elegy as it unveils an unprecedented continuity—systematic storytelling entered a new musical frontier. These are two fundamental developments in American songwriting history. Furthermore, consider these two records' productions and their revelations about their respective authors. The postman is at his best when he delivers his mail in spontaneous, in-the-spirit settings—reducing creativity to instinct. The preacher is at his best when his strategically conceived theatrics are systematically molded into a field-tested statement—controlling creativity through orchestration. Dylan's "it's time to make a record" philosophy would spawn victories, defeats, and the occasional suspension. Springsteen's functional approach would render coherent musical prescriptions that are deep in emotion, narrow in scope. Self-expression versus communication. "My Back Pages" and its impressionism versus "Thunder Road" and its clarity. The vitriolic conviction of "Ballad in Plain D" versus the anguished uncertainty of "She's the One." Two artists with two totally distinct visions, philosophies, procedures, and, in the end, contributions to American Song. John Hammond's wisdom is impressive.

Just as Dylan's enigmatic imagery and Springsteen's narrative continuity contribute to American Song's evolution, they demonstrate the power of creative initiative within the world of commercial music. Commercial art is a dynamic context controlled by an unyielding uncertainty. *Negotiation* is ubiquitous. Agendas continually clash; art and commerce frequently wage war. Just look at the serious conflicts surrounding Dylan's and Springsteen's careers: Both men sued their original managers, both men battled the Hype, both men endured career-long struggles in the studio (albeit for different reasons), and both men survived because of their creative resolve. Bob Dylan and Bruce Springsteen are testaments to artistic perseverance. The art that emerged from these fiercely individualistic artists is a product of specific stylistic choices that flowed from their guiding creative philosophies. That creative worldviews differ, and, occasionally, define artists is evident in these two examples.

These two careers point to the difficulties associated with structural or ideological interpretations of commercial art as well. There is no controlling force in evidence here. Everywhere there is negotiation; subsequently, relativity abounds. Dylan's wild mercury sound may explode inside his head, but his struggle to capture that musical quality in the studio was constant. Springsteen's ability to manage every nuance of his professional life is formidable, but his inability to control his audience's interpretations of his carefully crafted messages was frustrating. Music journalism, marketing science, corporate cultures, technological expertise, sociological environment, creative inspiration, and more converge, negotiate—and somehow—deliver commercial art. In one instance, celebrity hype may sway the critics and produce a result. In another, a technological innovation may encounter a unique performance style and produce a result. In yet another, a creative force may overpower an international corporation or a societal constraint and produce a result. Commercial art is the product of such diverse, dynamic influences that the individual motivation that enables the successful implementation of a creative vision—that force of artistic willpower—may be a work's defining characteristic. If nothing else, these qualities require that we construct our arguments about commercial art on a case-by-case basis—unless, that is, we seek to create yet another critical singularity that yields only what we place into it.

When Bruce Springsteen first entered the public consciousness, journalists often cited his physical resemblance to Bob Dylan as a starting point for their observations. Such reporting invariably referenced the two artists' allegiances to American Song as well—tracing Dylan's extension of Guthrie's vision and Springsteen's integration of Motown and Memphis. True, Dylan's personification of Guthrie's freedom and rebellion themes joined Springsteen's synthesis of pop theatrics and gut-level social commentary to revise and extend their respective musical maps. Still, to the extent that these two Americans share any trait whatsoever, they also represent radical creative departures. This concluding chapter explores these fascinating contrasts. We open with definitions.

Bob Dylan claims that songs are artistic attempts to capture moods—perhaps, subversive moods—that inspire audiences in some fashion. A song is more than a commercial product: It is a sentiment with a history. Understanding a song's musical heritage is the key to unlocking its potential passion, and, in turn, focusing its ability to move the listener. To achieve that end, Dylan writes for himself, producing sound stages that appeal to his musical roots and deploying lyrical structures that suit his expressive objectives. If the song pleases him, the auteur reasons it is suitable for others. He is, in David Hajdu's estimation, not a "communicator."

Bruce Springsteen claims that songs are tools that audiences may use to structure and understand their lives. In order to produce useful, functional art for his imagined community, Springsteen explores himself and fathoms the emotional deep water that yields universal insights into the human endeavor. These emotions provide the narrative raw materials that are systematically shaped into symbolic prescriptions for living. To achieve that end, the auteur created a body of work that forcefully hammers home his message. He is a communicator. He is, in Dave Marsh's estimation, an "actively antiironic artist."

Stylistically, Dylan's writing is apolitical and multidirectional: A musical Rohrshach that represents the Ultimate Game of Glissendorf. The joke may very well be on you: You lose! I won! On the other hand, this is the progenitor of the "finger-pointing" song through which the author either castigates a subject for personal reasons or propagates a view for a particular audience. His ability to discover an emotional rhythm and apply it to a strategic storytelling end is as impressive as his propensity for gamesmanship. With the exception of his moral period, however, to ascribe any motive to any portion of Dylan's work is risky business. He may *seem* to stand behind a particular song, but you *never* know. The auteur is artist and audience, all rolled into one. To suggest that Bob Dylan is doing anything for anybody other than himself is a critical conceit that may lend itself to embarrassment.

Springsteen's "antiirony" is political and directional: A Norman Rockwell view of an emotional autobiography that leaves nothing in doubt. Every scene is massaged. Each detail is groomed. This is not a game—this is serious work. Better yet, this is a job. A vocation that demands precision and control. The author is on a mission: A communicative quest to provide useful accounts of life's recurring situations (stories that, by the way, jibe with his worldview). His commitment to his job is all-consuming. And half the world thinks his most disillusioned political statement is the opening salvo of a patriotic pep rally. "Antiirony" loses.

Yet both oeuvres unfold chronologically in direct relation to their creators' lives. In some ways, they are diaries: Introspective accounts of two sets of life experiences. The extent to which a work's context impacts its eventual content and form is always revealing. Although through differing styles and with contrasting motivations, these two writers explore what is before them in their individual lives as a pathway to public commentary on the same. Rare is the work that departs from this trend. Bob Dylan, I am sure, has no desire to write another "Desolation Row," and Bruce Springsteen, I am certain, holds no wish to write another "Born to Run." The times, the auteurs, and the oeuvres evolve. Such conclusions indicate the utility of auteur theory and its emphasis on "the lifework" that represents a convergence of biography, talent, motivation, and skill. Like the commercial art world itself, no single characteristic controls the work. Relativity is the key concept here—and "relativity" is a contextually bound concept.

A second trait the two men share involves an intense commitment to their public images. Dylan's image represents an overt effort to actively personify his lifelong rebellion. From day one, it appears, Bob Zimmerman/Dylan has fearlessly rebelled. Every aspect of his public life was tailored to meet the needs of the *image de jour* and its unique spin on the rebellion persona. From tall tales about musical contacts, to motorcycles and leather jackets, to the adaptation of the Dylan name, to the Newport Mod and more, the artist used his music to feed his controlling image. At times, the image overpowered the art. On the other hand, Springsteen's image represents a more subtle manipulation. Whereas the physical appearance that inspired all the hassling from his father, teachers, and schoolmates must have been radical, his introversion counterbalanced that presence—until he stepped onstage and the Incredible Hulk appeared, that is. As time passed—and Jon Landau officially entered the Springsteen camp—the image grew sharper in its focus and the Landau-inspired public-relations operation controlled all facets of a persona that occasionally failed to jibe with the art. These two songwriters are as image-conscious as any artist, anywhere. They are direct descendants of the Woody Guthrie celebrity-singer-songwriter tradition of American Song.

A third trait the two writers share involves a "currency versus continuity" tension that weaves and bends its way throughout the respective works. The creative struggle over writing for the moment and writing for the oeuvre recurs with considerable frequency. For example, Dylan's acquiescence to the protest movement slowed his natural progression into electric expression. Springsteen's internal battle over the articulation of the *Nebraska* and *Born in the U.S.A.* material confused everything. Dylan's efforts to write "consciously" about his domestic life threatened his traditional mode of "unconscious" expression and its intuitive flow. Springsteen's commitment to take the man out of the car and place him in the house separated him from his musical roots and creative influences. On countless other occasions as well, the "moment" seemed to work against the "oeuvre" and generated creative friction for the auteur. The resolution of that particular conflict generally indicated that individual's professional future, for good or ill. The "minstrel's dilemma" is a recurrent phenomenon in the commercial art world.

For further insight into the respective writings, we turn to four qualities that control their enactment as well as providing a basis for comparison. Earlier, we used narrative synthesis to capture the characters, values, and plots of the individual albums and the creative phases that rendered them. With those findings in mind, an examination of Dylan's and Springsteen's uses of language, their narrative styles, their methods of music production, and their performance orientations yields additional knowledge of their artistic individuality and contributions to American Song. Like twins born into and raised by the same family, their differences can be as startling as their similarities. We begin with all writers' basic tool, their use of language.

the language

The gamesmanship that accompanies Bob Dylan's writing is a manifestation of a lifelong personality trait. From the outset, the evidence suggests, Dylan has toyed with words, ideas, and people. His creativity is laced with a mischievous quality that wavers between playful invention and systematic deception. Nowhere is this characteristic more evident than in his use of language. Dylan's word choice often subverts the basic principles of communication to an extent where the result is nothing more than idiosyncratic (or straightforward) gibberish. The ultimate presentation of this linguistic folly is Dylan's self-described book of "words," *Tarantula*. *Tarantula* is a marvelous example of Glissendorf—everybody is excluded from the author's private world and its secret nuances.

The most satisfying quality of a victorious game of Glissendorf is the personal gratification that accompanies the victim's demise. The unabashed joy that flows from a target's mental dissection is too great to share, so, by rule, it must be suppressed. Glissendorf, you see, is a private game. Two players may align and prey upon a potential victim, but the victory is never celebrated—at least not in public. It takes a special type of personality to relish a successful game of Glissendorf: Silent victories are not for everyone.

Mass Glissendorf—now that is an extraordinary game! When the individual player has the wherewithal to confound an entire group of people, well, the victory is exhilarating. Imagine the skill involved as the player pulls the semantic wool over an entire population's eyes—leading them down a symbolic path that only the player knows goes nowhere. The power! Moreover, what if the game involved *critics* who endlessly decipher what is functionally indecipherable. The thrill of reading Ivy League–educated interpretations of utter nonsense must have been intoxicating. I heard a story about a man with a bad drug habit who was about to go to jail until he started attending Pentecostal tent meetings and speaking in ceremonial tongues as the elders dutifully interpreted his junk-inspired gibberish. He laughed, he avoided jail, and he soon died (taking his private victory with him). Now there was one mighty fine game of Glissendorf! The Newport Mod spoke in his own brand of tongues and the musical elders had their way with their interpretations as well—much to the chagrin of the innovative, mischievous young wordsmith. In many respects, Dylan picked a fight that he could never win—unless he withdrew, that is.

As a case in point, let us return to that wonderful game of Glissendorf that is "Desolation Row." The imagery and detail lure us into a place that only the author understands. To make sense of the various characters is inviting, but utterly useless (and very much in Rohrshach country). Characters appear and do strange—maybe even outrageous—things only to disappear, never to return. The perspective changes with every other line. The insistent madness prohibits any value development or plot progression. The images come in waves. The song represents more than a wild-and-crazy stream of consciousness: It is an Alice in Wonderland parade that follows rules of which we are not privy. One may only conclude that "Desolation Row" is as chaotic and fantastic as its author and his unrestrained gamesmanship. To suggest that it is more than a game is to fall prey to the game itself. You lose.

Glissendorf is an art form. Its relationship to Surrealist or Beat poetry is one of mutual coexistence. It is the product of an irreverent attitude, a talent for wordplay, and a topical flexibility. It should be appreciated on its own terms and not confused with other, established forms of expression. It is the heart of Bob Dylan's art, and it is the one part of his creative repertoire that he *did not* acquire from somebody else. Glissendorf is intuitive. It is seductive. And it is the auteur's unique brand of anticommunicative poetry. Dylanologists may *think* they can unlock the meanings to these expressions, but guess who that joke is on.

Dylan discussed this facet of his art with Robert Shelton during a 1966 interview that appears in Shelton's biography. A tired but reflective Dylan addressed his writing in the clearest of terms: "There is not a person on the earth who takes it less seriously than I do." Dylan explained that his writing would not pave his way to heaven or prohibit his entry into hell; furthermore, he conveyed that little joy results from his labors. When Shelton inquired if Dylan purposefully breaks the established rules of songwriting, the auteur responded unequivocally: "I don't break the rules, because I don't see any rules to break. As far as I'm concerned, there aren't any rules." The interview continued with Shelton asking if Dylan thought himself to be a poet. The rebellious author answered by pointing out the irony that anyone who calls him- or herself a poet is certainly not one. Dylan declared he wound not cast himself as a poet anymore than he would call himself a protest singer. Simply, he despised definitions, although he offered this revealing statement: "I would really like to think of myself as a poet, but I just can't because of all the slobs who are called poets." (He shared similar sentiments about protest singers as well.) That Dylan's lifelong rebellion offered complete freedom from the constricting definitions that others placed upon him is evident in this exchange. Bob Dylan was doing *his* thing and he refused to trivialize it through labels that served other people's agendas—especially if he cared neither for the people nor their priorities.

Complementing Dylan's symbolic gamesmanship are two equally important dimensions that directly impact a given work's language: The "Basement Strategy" and the "topicality" consideration. The Basement Strategy is a product of Dylan's lifelong dedication to American Song—one last time, that "inspiration behind the inspiration." No matter what vernacular was deployed to create the desired affect, the music (and, sometimes, the lyrics) paid homage to the auteur's enduring dedication. From those late-night radio shows drifting up the Mississippi River full of exclusive musical knowledge to be shared only with social intimates, to the "care packages" of musical revelation purchased via the same radio programs that brought the music from the airwaves onto the Hibbing record player, to the youthful odysseys to Jim Dandy's musical library and the disc jockey's seminars on blues and jazz, to all those hours listening to friends' music collections and rummaging through the Folklore Center, Bob Zimmerman/Dylan immersed himself in music history. It seems as if everywhere he turned, someone offered a music lesson. The movies may have fed the image, but the music satisfied the soul (and then fed the image as well). American Song provided the rhythm that was the pathway to Dylan's unique form of expression. For instance, Bob Spitz discusses the educational impact of Sunday gatherings that Bob and Sidsel Gleason sponsored for Woody Guthrie at their home in New Jersey in which folk singers such as Cisco Houston, Pete Seeger, Jack Elliott, and others played for their dying colleague. Dylan hitchhiked to the event with regularity. Spitz explains their significance for the budding auteur: "For Bob Dylan, they were perhaps the most educational days of his life. If it could be said that he'd gotten his primary schooling from Gatemouth Page's radio show, his bachelor's degree in Dinkytown and Denver, and his master's on the street in Greenwich Village, then the Gleasons certainly provided him with the resources to fulfill his Ph.D. requirements." Subsequently, whenever the auteur was lost or in need and the search for his creative bearings was underway, he turned to his "education" for a musical inspiration or that famous first line of a song. Glissendorf is a natural extension of his personality, whereas the "Basement Strategy" represents a cultivated reservoir of musical knowledge. These two elements mixed and matched to give the world a new type of song.

The "topicality" dimension of Dylan's songwriting supported the wordplay and music in that he did, occasionally, write to be understood. For Dylan, there is always an agenda—a public or private rationale for a given course of action. If, for instance, writing advertising jingles had been the path to success, he would have excelled. Dylan did what he felt he had to do. Whenever he assembled his musical paintings, he considered his creative context and dutifully responded to those conditions. The folk singer used an Oklahoma twang and slang to weave authentic tales of the dispossessed. The rebellious voice of his generation used Glissendorf strategies to manhandle the self-imposed idolatry that threatened his creative freedom. The rebellious voice of his generation used country music as his reentry into an international musical scene dominated by orchestrated, arty theatrics. A converted Christian used all available means of musical persuasion to appeal to the lost and warn them of their impending doom. The rebellious voice of his generation purposefully distorted his work, pulled his finest songs off albums at the last minute, and dissolved himself into the musical woodwork in order to regain his creative equilibrium. Everywhere, there are controlling agendas that organized the lyrical and musical dimensions of the work. Never does a work appear without a specific purpose. And a contractual obligation is a "specific purpose."

The linguistic techniques that emerge from Dylan's gamesmanship, musical allegiances, and contextual considerations have their limits. A traditional tune or an evocative topic may inspire some innovative but factually inaccurate wordplay that is the stuff of lawsuits. Who cares if Dylan distorted Hattie Carroll's case or convoluted the occasional news report in order to achieve his artistic ends? But when he twisted the events of Hurricane Carter's case to fit his writing scheme, he paid the price (literally). When he wanted to publicly align the John Birch Society with Adolf Hitler, his record company (and the Ed Sullivan Show staff) balked. And when he publicly dissected his relationship with Suze Rotello ("Ballad in Plain D") and his marriage (Blood on the Tracks), the musical world cringed. I must conclude, then, that it is possible to *lose* a game of Glissendorf. When nobody knows what you are saying, you may say what you wish; yet, when the words focus and resonate, limitations may appear.

Dylan's language is the epicenter of his art. It is his principal source of originality. Still, the wild juxtapositions, the crazed metaphors, the incongruent imagery, the emotional precision, and the unrestrained passion of Dylan's language were shaped by his artistic image and professional/personal context. The auteur met the creative needs of the day through traditional American sound platforms that supported his cryptic or calculated wordplay. The wordplay may involve traditional blues or folk lyrics, lines from movie dialog, overheard comments from a street corner, or linguistic insanity; whatever the case, it was applied systematically. Such is the music of Bob Dylan and his contribution to American Song's language.

Bruce Springsteen's language use follows a different strategy. Whereas Dylan played with words within strategic contexts, Springsteen shaped his words as carefully as any other facet of his creative operation. On and off stage, Springsteen worked from carefully crafted scripts that ensured his message would be delivered in the desired fashion. The song lyrics, the between-song monologues/theatrics, the media interviews—any public utterance—was a product of the intense control that characterized the Springsteen operation. There is no doubt that the maps that young Springsteen read as he prepared himself for his vocation complemented his personal experiences with his father's struggles to generate an acute need for control. His command over his perceived situation begins with the linguistic means through which he articulates his strategic stances. After listening to the songs, witnessing the shows, and reading the interviews, there is little question that Bruce Springsteen selects his words carefully.

In his oeuvre section, I opened our treatment of Springsteen's lifework by describing his early club shows as a form of "Rock Church." There I argued that his blend of spirituality, theatricality, and musicality was a direct extension of the Southern Black church and its long, joyous, liberating communal rituals. Allow me to extend the analogy in this discussion of Springsteen's language as well. You see, one of the most fruitful—and provocative—communicative environments is this type of church. Participants explore their personal anxieties in light of universal pieties in an attempt to make the "ultimate connection" and discover relief from their worldly concerns. The utility of these ritualistic exercises is most evident in their continuity, as practice—in both word and deed—is the pathway to redemption. In church, the preacher is the living personification of this spiritual search for relief. The preacher embodies the message and will, most assuredly, be effective only as long as his congregation can gaze into the pulpit and see themselves. The identification is crucial. The struggle for redemption is real. That these symbolic rituals are serious business may be observed in the passion that engulfs their enactment.

A dominant characteristic of these ritualistic ceremonies involves the preacher's reliance on the local vernacular. While the proceedings may be anchored in sacred text, the process through which the "word" is given life for the immediate audience is through language and stories tailored to that context. From there, the emotion carries the day. I once worked in a factory with a Black minister who maintained a day job in order to purchase the clothes, car, and other materials that he felt were essential to his image (his church was poor, so additional funds were required). He wanted his congregation to look up on stage and see "success," so he worked quite hard to generate that image. One day, we were talking about his service (which he dutifully recorded each week and played for me on Monday during lunch) and the passionate manner in which he sang his sermon. He assured me that if you stood in the pulpit and announced "the dog, he crossed the street," nobody would do anything. But, if you scream (in his best James Brown voice) "THE DOG, HE CROSSED THE STREET," somebody will yell "Amen."

That Bruce Springsteen's congregations scream "Amen" with all the passion and gusto of their spiritual leader is undeniable. Springsteen-the-preacher uses working-class stories that are articulated though a working-class vernacular that probes his emotional autobiography in an attempt to invoke universal principles of use to his constituency. The mundane—that "dog crossing the street"—may provide a starting point for an emotional exploration far more significant than the playful example indicates. More often than not, the "rap" that introduces the musical rejoinder sets the tone. For instance, Springsteen's recollections of his parents' attempts to persuade him to forsake his music for more suitable vocations set the scene for "Growing Up" and its account of teenage rebellion. The moral in this sermon relates that "rebellion" may prove to be the road to salvation; you have to resist the metaphoric chains that confine ambitions. On another occasion, Springsteen recalled his constant battles with his father and his father's belief that the army would provide the much-needed discipline to straighten out his son's life. Suddenly, Springsteen recounted the experience of his army physical, how he failed, and how his father was pleased by the fact that his son would *not* have to go to Vietnam. The moral? That Vietnam was such a travesty that his father reversed a lifelong opinion. Springsteen followed the story with "The River" and its ironies. These theatrical portrayals are, in every way, sermonic.

Within the songs themselves, we observe the working-class language and imagery through which the auteur prescribes his symbolic medicine. In "The Promised Land" Springsteen's character declares, "I've done my best to live the right way / I get up in the morning and go to work each day," as a preface to his account of his anxieties about a potentially dead-end life in which "your eyes go blind and your blood runs cold." Springsteen forewarns of impending violence ("Sometimes I feel so weak I just want to explode / Explode and tear this whole town apart") unless we acknowledge the situation and follow his prescription to "Blow away the dreams that tear you apart / Blow away the dreams that break your heart / Blow away the lies that leave you nothing but lost and broken-hearted." The symbolic rhythm is unequivocal: Your efforts to live the "right way" may enslave you and require you to muster the resources to "blow away" those constricting parameters and refocus your life. The language is clear, emotional, and sermonic. This is not a lighthearted or fuzzy account of an unfortunate social condition; it is a prescription for personal action. The preacher identifies with the congregation through a story that sets the scene for the prescribed response; an act that involves nothing less than the auditor's salvation.

Reconsider our exemplar section and the poignant examples of Springsteen's language in the "Adam Raised a Cain" parable, the "Born in the U.S.A." societal complaint, the "Born to Run" anthem, and the "Darlington County" lifestyle celebration. Characters harvest the sorrowful inheritance of their parents' failures, find themselves in "foreign lands" because they got themselves in "hometown jams" with no other remedy available (other than jail), describe themselves as "tramps" as they muster the emotional resources to escape a "runaway American dream" and its chrome-infused posturing, and laugh at themselves as they celebrate a decadent lifestyle that is going absolutely nowhere. Simple, systematic stories told through plain language in understandable settings that are designed for a specific audience. The language presents the tone, the feel, the emotions that are organized through the soap opera narrative strategy. The language used to articulate the hopes and fears of the auteur's "imagined community" represents an impassioned work of art.

The postman and the preacher. The former receives the mail and delivers it in his own idiosyncratic way, the latter uses sacred rituals as the springboard for emotional portrayals of life's situations. One drops the missive off and allows the recipient to do as he or she wishes; the other orchestrates every aspect of the sermon in order to maximize the lesson's impact. The language used in both instances reveals the differences in these two orientations. For the postman, he may choose to illuminate or to obfuscate: The choice is his and his alone. For the preacher, his job requires precision; therefore he strives for communicative perfection—anything less fails his divine calling. The two folk singers John Hammond signed for Columbia Records traveled down two fundamentally different creative paths. What guided these two writers was their respective philosophies—artistic worldviews that dictated every word of every song.

the narrative styles

With Dylan's enigmatic and Springsteen's systematic uses of language established, we turn to the second factor in our comparative analysis and their narrative styles. Dylan's narrative style—a fine blend of Glissendorf wordplay and Basement musicality—is controlled by the topicality variable. Again, the creative context dictates the storytelling strategy. When viewed in its totality, the oeuvre's narrative flow is discontinuous. The independent vignettes that comprise the respective album projects serve specific functions at certain points in time. These narrative "missions" pursue their own objectives, and the writer's artistic impulse works within that creative boundary. Predictably, these missions follow the career's chronology and its various quests involving discovery, rejection, recovery, repentance, and prosperity.

Dylan's early storytelling involved a concentrated application of the folk process. His legitimate use of previously established song structures and lyrics fits firmly within the folk music songwriting tradition. Consequently, we observe Dylan's evolution from Guthrie juke box, to Greenwich Village magpie, to king of American protest music during this time frame. From his initial album's covers of traditional death songs and musical tributes; his second album's blend of romance, protest, and satire; and his third record's total concentration on the protest genre, the auteur's march toward self-expression progressed. What began with Little Richard–inspired versions of a standard coffee-house folk repertoire assumed a distinctive character as the simplicity of "Blowin' in the Wind" evolved into the stark vitriol of "Masters of War" and the cryptic "verbal binge" of "A Hard Rain's a-Gonna Fall" quite quickly. Throughout that rapid progression, Dylan's playful satires floated in and out of the musical framework, enlivening live performances while largely remaining off record. Our exemplar section features two examples of Dylan's storytelling from this era that demonstrate his emotional range: The anger of "Masters" is a real contrast to the playful sarcasm of "John Birch." The imagery, the simplicity of expression, and, of course, the intensity of both stories capture Dylan's unique co-optation of the folk narrative style. Simply, this period features a talented wordsmith in pursuit of a job. This "mission" required Dylan to absorb every possible influence, allow that contribution to assimilate itself, and subsequently emerge via Robert Shelton's "distinctive song stylist" that was the emerging auteur. At this point, no doubt, Dylan's artistic philosophy of writing for himself took a back seat to writing for the market.

All of this soon changed. With acceptance came expectation, and for Bob Dylan, with expectation comes rebellion. The songs that followed contain some of his most defiant songwriting as Dylan not only shied away from message music, but avoided communication altogether. Dylan's wordplay parades about unrestrained, free to dash here and there, following inspirational whims that often have no relationship to one another. The muse is at rebellious play and everything else is irrelevant. This journey into abstraction officially opened with Dylan's public announcement that he no longer wished to write for "others" and that he would now write only for himself. And that is exactly what he did with the spontaneous production that was Another Side, as the writer's finger-pointing shifted contexts from the societal to the personal. Another Side's blend of sharp personal attack, satire, and impressionism is a fine bookend to its companion piece, the narrative portion of Blonde on Blonde. In between we witness the anticommunication of Back Home and Highway 61 in which the rebellion runs wild through interesting mixtures of Basement musicality and Glissendorf folly. The results were original, unprecedented, and the perfect response to his pugnacious quest to reject the constricting demands that surrounded him. That Bob Dylan could have easily hired those Western Union boys and filled the airwaves with messages is certain. That Bob Dylan refused to do so is historic.

The rebellion was costly. The celebrity histrionics that accompanied his Newport Mod persona exacted a serious toll on the young wordsmith's health. Through it all, the muse also suffered. The "accident" provided the opportunity and a new mission emerged: recovery. This enterprise represents the apex of the Basement Strategy as the auteur immersed himself in the Americana that birthed him for his creative convalescence. From the Basements themselves, to the countrified tales of loving relationships (i.e., *Harding* and *Skyline*), to the Americana on Parade of the Rolling Thunder extravaganza, Dylan explored American Song's narrative traditions as he recovered from the various abuses of celebrity. Gone were the cryptic wordplay, the evasive imagery, and the cavalier attitude that characterized the Newport Mod. In its place came lyrical sincerity, traditional musicality, and homespun wisdom about love, life, and, gradually, worldly deterioration. Although there were pauses in Dylan's creative rehabilitation to deal with irresponsible fanatics and irrepressible executives, the writer's pursuit of revitalization was steady and sincere. His lessons with Norman Raeben demonstrate the enormity of Dylan's struggle with his instincts and his intellect as he sought to do consciously what had heretofore been an unconscious process. This assignment was no moment's task—in fact, it would take over 25 years to complete this recovery.

The converted take missions seriously. The drive associated with a spiritually inspired quest to use one's talent to serve is, in every way, unrelenting. Dylan's selection of Jerry Wexler says everything about his narrative commission: Present the Message through the Sound, and serve the Lord. Dylan's writing at this juncture—foreshadowed via the much overlooked *New Morning*—is clear, purposeful, and stylistically grounded in an established American musical genre, gospel music. Stories focus on the two-pronged tale of warning and celebration. Trusting the audience to do the right thing and accept Christ, the warning wasted little time on admonitions, yielding instead to celebration. The gospel show that accompanied *Slow Train* and *Saved* contained an orchestrated blend of the warning–celebration thematic with pauses for testimony and invitation. The King of American Protest experienced little difficulty in his evolution into a messenger for the Prince of Peace as the auteur's topicality merely shifted subjects and musical genres. With *Shot of Love*'s look back, Dylan judged what is not to be judged—his detractors (here the admonitions flow), and in so doing, completed his mission. His public commentary is straightforward on this matter: He said what he had to say and moved on. This fascinating period in Dylan's career reveals the breadth of his songwriting talent. One gains the impression that this writer could ply his trade to any occasion with success.

Dylan's quest for professional equilibrium—and artistic prosperity—was a long, winding search for creative security. Unable to record the elusive sound in his head, he compromised his creative method, accepted the compositional strategies of the 1980s recording industry, and lost his bearings. The more he wrote, the less he said. The Lanois productions were productive compromises, but they failed to satisfy the auteur's principal audience, himself. Arthur Baker, Don Was, Don DeVito, or whomever assumed the producer's chair (including Dylan) was, for some inexplicable reason, unable to record that wild mercury sound. Subsequently, Dylan's stories ran hot and cold, ranging from the sublime to the ridiculous. The sound evaded Dylan, and only *it* could unleash the words.

There were flashes of brilliance during this musical expedition, but Dylan's ulti-mate dissatisfaction is evident in his ever-changing modes of operation. *Infidels'* vigor was followed by *Burlesque's* tired return to Muscle Shoals. *Loaded* and *Groove* limped along in a songwriting malaise that seemed to cease with *Mercy*, only to return with *Red Sky*. In an admirable demonstration of determination, Dylan remained on tour; refining his act and rediscovering his rhythm. The two cover albums of roots music placed him in the proper frame of mind, but the late 1990s, in Dylan's estimation, found him alone with that music. With time and perseverance, he found the rhythm that had evaded him for so long. After *Time Out of Mind's* universal success (which pleased everyone, it seems, but Dylan), the road show sharpened, Dylan's animosity toward his early works lightened, and the music prevailed, thanks to Larry Campbell, Tony Garnier, David Kemper, and Charlie Sexton. The musical security provided by his band allowed the post-man's instincts to return. He trusted his *band* as he once trusted *himself*. The results, once again, support the essential argument that the context controls the muse.

Love and Theft uses the band's rhythmic dexterity to provide musical plat-forms for Dylan's heralded impressionism. Until this point, rare indeed was that flash of Glissendorf that characterized the auteur's more rebellious writings. Not until the musical camaraderie of his road-tested ensemble provided the cre-ative safety net of the Basements did Dylan cut loose and allow the mail to once again flow through him. He focused on the tried-and-true topic of relational issues and the Basement musicality and instinctive wordplay responded. This mission was, finally, victorious.

Dylan's celebrations, complaints, satires, and wordplay weave their way in and out of the respective narrative missions depending upon the storytelling needs of that day. The narrative strategies used to organize Dylan's language and convey his moods were subject to his creative context, since some moods require articulation and others do not. As the mission changed, the impulse fol-lowed. Such a narrative vacillation is quite a contrast to Dylan's "little brother" (self-proclaimed by Springsteen) and his diehard dedication to the single task that was the Worker's Elegy.

Writing a soap opera is a quite different narrative charge from writing the television movie of the week. Soap operas require continuity to be effective. Characters must be developed and cultivated. The characters also embody the story's values as the soap opera's changing scenes provide the narrative pacing necessary to keep the story alive. This is a difficult storytelling task that was mastered by early filmmakers (and their Saturday serials) and radio writers, serial fiction writers, and, more recently, by television scriptwriters. Songwriters have never entered the melodramatic world of the continuous soap opera—that is, until Bruce Springsteen.

The Worker's Elegy is a testament to narrative continuity. The auteur's abil-ity to stay "on message" is as impressive as any other feature. Not only does Springsteen's level of narrative continuity make a unique contribution to Amer-ican Song's development, it may never be replicated. Writers may dabble with

Dylan's wordplay (as Springsteen did) or approximate his intensity, but it is doubtful that *anyone* will assemble a body of work such as did emerge from Bruce Springsteen's pen. There are two key elements to Springsteen's writings: His characterological coherence and his use of melodrama. The melodrama's heightened emotionality places Springsteen's characters in situations that prompt their value-laden responses. Everything is a Big Deal. Springsteen's characters cannot go for a drive without a spiritual revelation, cannot look at a beautiful house or a new car without an emotional response, cannot go on a date without considering the long-range impact of the relationship, nor accept their lot in life without contemplating violent revenge. The same cast of characters (and their values) move from scene to scene in an excited state of anxiety. Why? Because the Worker's Elegy is a tale of trust. Characters can no longer trust the American Dream—nor can they trust their parents, friends, employers, government, and, most of all, their lovers. When Springsteen's characters finally accept the self-imposed limitations of the American Dream, they simply experience an anxiety shift, as the worries of the man in the car become the worries of the man in the house. *Trust* is the emotional prime-mover in Springsteen's soap opera, and the issue is *never* resolved.

Springsteen faced several obstacles in his battle to stay on message with the Worker's Elegy, and we should spend a moment discussing these pivotal points where the focus could have easily been lost. While the auteur never abandoned his creative charge, it seems as if everybody else did. There were times when Springsteen's outward focus appeared confused as well, but his intuitive commitment never wavered. These creative "battles" set formidable hurdles for Springsteen's muse, and its victory gave the world the Worker's Elegy.

Without question, the first battle involved the *Born to Run* marathon. Wallowing in the aftermath of his Dylanesque impressionism and the commercial labels it imposed, coping with the Hype and its creative pressures, and enduring the technological limitations of his managers' inexperience in the recording studio, Springsteen fought his way through draft after draft, take after take. His comments to journalists leave little doubt about the utter agony associated with the endurance test that was the *Run* sessions. The budding auteur's intuitive search for his story line—as well as the musical means through which he would articulate that account—were *totally* lost until Jon Landau's arrival. Landau brought professionalism to the recording process, stability to Springsteen's creative urges, and accountability to the entire Springsteen operation. *Born to Run* is, ultimately, an uneven exposition of Springsteen's emerging vision; however, Landau's presence facilitated Appel's departure, and, afterwards, *Darkness on the Edge of Town's* emergence. As a result, Landau's first major contribution to Springsteen's development (journalistic rhetoric aside, of course) may not have been in *Run's* completion, but rather in *Darkness'* appearance. Springsteen's initial battle within himself, with Appel's studio leadership and hyperbole, and with the content and style of his emerging narrative, was resolved—that is, his artistic future was secured—by the very writer who deemed him to be the future of rock and roll.

But Springsteen's battles were, in no way, over. After settling into the Worker's Elegy with *Darkness* and its reiteration, *The River*, the writer struggled with his unfolding story's next step. Springsteen, his celebrity, his characters, and their story worked themselves into the narrative corner that generated the *Nebraska* and *Born in the U.S.A.* material. A second battle ensued—here Springsteen both won and lost. He *won* in that the emotional deep water that yielded *Nebraska* washed over the Springsteen commercial machine to the point where his initial demo tape of that material was released (thanks to Chuck Plotkin's ingenuity). The world experienced the auteur in the raw. The story's compelling particulars aside, the writer conveyed his depth of emotion in an unadulterated, focused fashion. Commercial risks were cast aside. The impulse was afforded the freedom it needed to do what it needed to do. Springsteen *lost* in that the very commercial machine that stepped aside to facilitate *Nebraska* stomped all over the rest of the material that emerged along with it. Both records represent branches from a dark, introspective, agonizing narrative tree; one branch was allowed to live on its own, the other was transformed in a commercial celebration that betrayed everything. As Dave Marsh suggests, the "Dancing in the Dark" video featuring a smiling, dancing Springsteen lip-syncing lyrics that suggest anything but a happy-go-lucky moment on the dance floor says everything about the *U.S.A.* project. The message was buried. The control was gone. The "460 days of Bossmania" must have seemed like 460,000 days in hell for the idealistic auteur. The preacher lost control over his sermon's meaning, yet somehow he stepped aside and allowed the service to continue without missing a beat; in essence, the congregation was allowed to have its way.

To suggest—as fans and journalists have—that Springsteen "sold out" with *Born in the U.S.A.* is more than a little bit naïve. The pressures to follow *Nebraska* with a more commercially viable product must have been considerable. Springsteen's acquiescence to Landau was warranted, although creatively disruptive. His bitterness remains evident to this day through his constant explanations about "Born in the U.S.A." in concerts over the years. Nevertheless, it is fascinating how a Norman Rockwell painting of death, despair, and detachment was transformed into a patriotic Rohrshach. That people hear what they want to hear must be frustrating for artists like Bruce Springsteen, and amusing to artists like Bob Dylan.

Everything changed after *U.S.A.* and the *Live* boxed set, including Springsteen's unfolding story. The preacher revised the sermon (shifting from societal to relational concerns), the service was adjusted (shifting the performance interplay and dismissing the "E Street Party"), and a new battle was enjoined. This conflict lasted longer than the *Born to Run* situation in that it would take years for Springsteen to officially end the E Street Party, reconcile his personal demons, and to discover the domestic bliss he had longed for his entire life. After the *Tunnel of Love* tour, the divorce from Julianne Phillips, and the band's official dismissal, Springsteen struggled with his musical ideas for quite some time. Eventually Roy Bittan helped him assemble his thoughts (the first co-authored material in the canon) and recruit a new band. The *Human Touch/Lucky Town* dual release provided the Worker's Elegy's resolution. *Tom Joad* revisits the elegy's sentiments and communicates the depth of the soap opera's emotions, but for all intents and purposes the story ends here. There is nothing like it in all of popular music.

The auteurs' language and storytelling styles embody their respective approaches to art. An artist that writes for himself uses words that only he understands. A writer striving for a connection with his audience uses words that facilitate that objective. A narrator that uses idiosyncratic idioms to arouse emotions in himself either allows the wordplay to frolic or molds it according to the writing charge at hand. A storyteller interested in sermonic prescriptions subscribes to narrative structures that enable the lesson to be understood, time and again. In both cases, the creative philosophy dictates the content and style of the artistic offering. In both cases, significant contributions to American Song's development resulted. But our comparison does not end here. To fully grasp the contrasting philosophies of these two narrators, we must consider two more variables: Their methods of musical production and performance.

the production methods

Dylan's and Springsteen's production methods parallel their creative strategies: One is spontaneous, the other is methodical. But music production requires more than the performing artist. At this point in the creative process the industry enters into play with a host of nonmusical personnel. The plot, as they say, thickens quickly. The creative philosophy that guides the work now extends to the studio, and eventually to the corporate board room. What happens when the auteur encounters the industry? In the studio, does he or she receive the assistance of creative collaborators or sterile technicians? Does he or she experience challenge or sycophancy? Is the guiding objective one of quality or quantity? These are some of the issues associated with music production, and the means through which an artist negotiates *them* is just as important as the creative challenges that enable the process in the first place. Wonderful songwriters who failed to negotiate industry matters play every night in coffeehouses around Peoria.

What kind of relationship do you think Bobby Zimmerman of Hibbing, Minnesota would have with his employers? Do you think he would report to work on time, assume the duties for which he had been contracted, toe the company line and cooperate with peers, and loyally serve his benefactors? I think maybe *those* expectations might fall just outside the range of Mr. Zimmerman's acting ability. Throughout all of his images—each and every mask—the subsequent persona embodied the artist's unrelenting, controlling creative motivation: rebellion. From screaming in the faces of the Jacket Jamboree's patrons, to Newport 1965, to staging tours without publicity, to releasing records designed to alienate faithful audiences, to reconsidering completed projects just as they enter production, to—well—mocking every conceivable convention of communication, Bob Zimmerman/Dylan has rebelled. It has been a controversial habit.

We have spent much time chronicling the spontaneous qualities of an effective Bob Dylan recording session. Initially, these attempts to capture lightning
in the studio centered on Dylan, the lone musician, as in the *Another Side* experience. Eventually, he expanded his musical aspirations and enlisted more musicians, although sessions continued their lightning-grabbing, impulsive methodology. While Clinton Heylin disputes Al Kooper's claims that the fabled "Like a
Rolling Stone" session was a one-take divination in which Kooper sat in on the
organ (he had never played the instrument before), the fact that Dylan encour-
aged such studio folly is unquestionable. The Nashville musicians employed for
the *Blonde* sessions concur in their recollections of a variety of studio idiosyncrasies: Writing songs as the sessions unfolded and recording them *immediately*
afterward, promoting unconventional instrumental techniques, and—in the case
of "Rainy Day Women"—encouraging general craziness as a pathway to a pure,
uninhibited extemporaneous performance. Dylan's unrelenting rebellion inspired
him to tear down the established recording protocols and invite that thin wild
mercury sound to emerge. The "it's time to make a record" commercial philosophy required Dylan to assemble his "thoughts" (often, on scraps of paper or in
incomplete versions), enter the studio to search for a musical vibe to convey
them (often, visualizing the *sound* to the musicians), and allow the musical gods
to have their way. This "don't look back" method of music production was certainly unorthodox; nonetheless, it presented an artist who views his work as
"art," not "craft." That Bob Dylan actually considered himself to be a medium is
evident in these practices.

David Hajdu offers a useful example of Dylan's creative method that reflects
on all facets of the production process. He describes a writing session in which
Dylan "laid out dozens of photographs torn from newspapers and magazines
in a montage on the floor and sat down amidst them with his guitar." Hajdu
continues:

> Bob would start with a simple musical framework, a blues pattern he could
> repeat indefinitely, and he would close his eyes—he would not draw from the
> pictures literally but would use the impression the faces left as a visual model
> for kaleidoscopic language. He appeared to sing whatever came to him, discon-
> nected phrases with a poetic feeling. When something came out that he liked,
> he scrawled it down hurriedly, so as to stay in the moment, and he would do
> this until there were enough words for a song. . . . He was not pursuing refine-
> ment, sophistication, and clarity of expression, those ideals of the Cole Porter
> generation of songwriters, but their near opposites: kinetic energy, instinct,
> and ambiguity.

The Glissendorf master toyed with rhythmic patterns of words until lightning struck and he had recorded the occurrence dutifully, continuing until he had
"enough words" to stop (a revealing approach to closure). The visuals inspired a
mood—Dylan tried to ride that vibe, and the rest was magic (remember, not all
magic is *good* magic). Now this may be a fine way to capture a "thought" on
paper, but it makes for one chaotic—and potentially expensive—recording ses-

sion. Dylan's refusal to recognize the difference stymied his efforts with professional producers (T-Bone Burnett was probably right) and fueled his renaissance with *Love and Theft*. In 2001 Dylan's band facilitated that inspirational vibe that enabled the auteur to write additional verses on the spot and then record them with the assistance of a responsive engineer. Augie Meyers's amazement is justified, but for Bob Dylan it was the return of creative business as usual.

Our narrative "missions" did weigh in, however. When Dylan wanted musical precision, he turned to established professionals capable of generating that sound—if he followed their instruction. The Nashville crew reassembled for the patented country rhythms used to present the *Harding* and *Skyline* material. While Dylan was searching for his creative bearings in the mid-1970s he solicited the input of writers, musicians, and performers of different orientations for various recording sessions and the Rolling Thunder/*Renaldo* extravaganza (the auteur's return to the Village is instructive as well). In service of his Lord, Dylan turned to the state-of-the-art soul sound that was the Muscle Shoals tradition and Jerry Wexler's expertise. After the moral period, as the mission lost its focus, so did everything else. The rehearsals returned to the Basements, but that magic could not be transferred to the studio or stage. Adrift in a sea of commercial and creative pressures, Dylan tried a host of solutions ranging from employing established producers, celebrity musicians, and accomplished co-authors. Sometimes that lightning was harnessed; oftentimes it was not. Heylin's session chronology is invaluable in this regard, which notes the specifics of each recording and how the various tracks were approached. His book captures Dylan's struggles as no other work does. (Is it possible that "Foot of Pride" required 43 takes?)

Dylan's rebellion certainly made a bad situation worse. It restricted his ability to evolve with the technological times, it debilitated his capacity to co-author, and it impaired his postproduction decisions. Ensemble recording, methodical writing, and systematic sequencing violated that first principle of the Dylan creative creed: Spontaneity. All of Dylan's "postman" and "medium" metaphors accurately communicate the necessarily extemporaneous qualities of the *entire* inventive process. As a result, Dylan works best when he works alone. Producers *do* get in his way. After all, he is both author and audience; therefore a third party merely muddies the process. His early producers did nothing more than "make him smile" as he left the studio, and that is exactly what he needed. Dylan's method of musical production requires an engineer who can follow instructions; anything else is a distraction.

The production process could be characterized as this creative genius's Waterloo except—unlike Napoleon's Waterloo—this story has a happy ending for the genius. The perfect manifestation of Dylan's production philosophy emerged when he discovered his "E Street Band." The Campbell, Sexton, Garnier, and Kemper ensemble facilitated Dylan's return to his natural recording style and its spontaneity. The auteur trusts his band's instincts as much as his own and he dutifully allows it the freedom to express itself. The band's relentless performance schedule created a crack musical unit that transferred to the studio with ease. *Rolling Stone* reports how Dylan built *Love and Theft* through a song-a-day, workmanlike process. With his trusted musical imagery in place, Dylan's words roamed about in couplets of expression reminiscent of the Newport Mod's unbridled heyday. If he needed a few lines to round off an idea, to Augie Meyers's amazement he merely sat down and they appeared. After years of struggling with all facets of the music-production process, Dylan finally found creative comfort through a band who could capture that wild mercury vibe—regardless of musical genre—which, in turn, allowed that "kaleidoscopic language" to emerge. All of this is, once more, a testament to Bob Dylan's artistic perseverance: A weaker artist would have given up, released old music or concert recordings, and gone to the bank. Through all the changes and challenges, the rebellion and its allegiance to American Song prevailed.

Spontaneous rebellion and instinctual urges have nothing to do with Bruce Springsteen's art. A writing style that deploys a dictionary, a thesaurus, and a perfectionist's determination demands the functional equivalent throughout the other facets of the process as well. For soap operas—especially for sermonic melodramas—continuity is everything since, in the absence of continuity, narrative chaos may emerge. And there is no room for creative chaos in Bruce Springsteen's artistic world. Everywhere there is precision; an unrelenting, potentially subversive control that produces music that either stays on message or stays in the studio. This is, in every way, quality control to the maximum level.

Unlike his older brother, Springsteen's art has always involved collaborators. Whether these creative colleagues were in his audience, backstage between sets at the Upstage in Asbury Park, in his band, in the stage crew, or in management, Springsteen consistently worked with other people. Along the way, he assembled a creative team that has remained remarkably consistent across a 30-year career. From Steve Van Zandt to Jon Landau, Roy Bittan, Chuck Plotkin, Toby Scott, Bob Clearmountain, and the road/stage crew that lights, amplifies, and transports his musical troupe, Springsteen has worked with a select group of people who occupy crucial roles in his organization. With a few highly publicized exceptions, Springsteen stands by his professional colleagues and he expects them to return the loyalty. Such an orientation yields a level of control and continuity unavailable otherwise.

Perhaps the role of senior collaborator belongs to longtime friend Steve Van Zandt. Dave Marsh cites Van Zandt's role in maintaining musical and personal harmony between Springsteen and his band during the pivotal *Born to Run* tour (a crucial period featuring new band members Bittan and Weinberg), his role in *The River*'s recording (for which he received a production credit), his participation in the *U.S.A.* decision-making (convincing Springsteen to include "No Surrender" while recognizing "Dancing in the Dark" for what it was), and his general understanding of the band leader's style gleaned from years of experience. Van Zandt's independence required him to leave, and then return to, the band many times—but he is always available for Springsteen. Van Zandt reflects the essence of Springsteen's professional orientation: A loyal subservience that cuts two ways in that Springsteen asks nothing that he is unwilling to give himself. Such an opinion is not the product of idle speculation—there is an abundance of factual support for the claim.

The *Blood Brothers* film offers this dynamic as its driving theme. Called on a Thursday to assemble in New York the following Monday to record several songs for a greatest-hits package, the band and production team promptly reported on time. Everyone dropped everything else in response to Springsteen's call (Van Zandt, it appears, was the exception, as he arrived a bit later). The film is a Springsteen Family home movie. Love is everywhere. The video presents the band discussing the new songs (Springsteen describing them, the band dutifully taking notes), rehearsing them (more discussion after playbacks), recording them through a familial interplay of loving personalities (there is a scene in which the band actually votes on an issue), posing for photographs, and making a video (loads of backstage love shots on the joys of music-making). The message is unequivocal: This is a *team*. Everyone involved participates in decisions, although always with Springsteen (he never speaks to the camera). Throughout, commentary from Landau, Plotkin, and Clearmountain explains exactly what the team is doing (from Landau on press releases, to Plotkin on the band's studio magic, to Clearmountain on how the band "arranges" itself as it records) as we see rapid cuts of studio footage intermixed with video tomfoolery. The film demonstrates Springsteen's work ethic through its clever portrayal of the title cut's recording. Dividing the process into "three takes," the movie charts the work involved in the song's development. Springsteen is relentless in his pursuit. The victorious final take represents the film's climax; afterward, our musical family gathers for a sing-a-long and rides off into the sunset, mission accomplished. With children playing in the studio, smiles on every face, and loving affection dripping from every tongue, this is a film that celebrates a musical family; the music is incidental. Moreover, it is a musical family with leadership: Landau, Plotkin, and Clearmountain are every bit as important to the process as the musicians. With Landau's logic and Springsteen's creativity at the helm, *Blood Brothers* communicates how the Springsteen family works together to make records.

There is no Jon Landau in Bob Dylan's world. If there were, perhaps Dylan's 30-year search for creative equilibrium could have been avoided. On the other hand, Dylan's rebellion is the central ingredient of his art, so steady guidance may have proven debilitating, or more likely, impossible. In contrast, Bruce Springsteen needed Jon Landau. Since his creative aspirations involved nothing less than perfection, someone needed to tell him when to stop. Dylan may stop when he perceives that he has "enough words" for a song, but Springsteen will groom and groom his work until somebody intervenes and calls a halt to the process. This is Jon Landau's job. Springsteen's job is to present useful art for his imagined community; his manager's job is to keep him from going crazy in the process. Since his acceptance into the Springsteen organization, Landau has performed at least three major roles for his artist: Teacher, creative arbiter, and professional collaborator. We would be wise to take a moment and explore this relationship.

The biographers cite the educational impact of Jon Landau's tutorage. Christopher Sandford and Dave Marsh independently describe how music critic/

Boston musician Landau introduced his protégé to blues, country, gospel, folk, and other musical genres that he had read about, but never heard. Their personal—and professional—relationship grew as the two men spent hours together listening to and discussing music. Marsh reports that "Bruce reacted to such musical encounters as though given a key with which to tap the memories of his ancestors." The results were immediate as Springsteen modeled "The River" on Hank Williams's "Long Gone Lonesome Blues" and expanded his list of musical influences. Landau also taught Springsteen about other art forms and inspired an interest in cinema and American literature. As noted earlier, John Huston's and John Ford's films as well as Flannery O'Connor's and John Steinbeck's books had considerable impact on Springsteen's artistic maturation. To that end, Marsh cites Springsteen's comments to a Parisian audience: "I was lucky, too, because I met this guy when I was in my middle twenties who said you should watch this or you should read this. And most people, where I come from, never have someone try and help them in that way." Dylan, too, enjoyed the instruction of a variety of knowledgeable musical and literary tutors, but no individual stood by his side as Jon Landau supported Springsteen. By all accounts, it is a rare relationship in the commercial art world. Landau not only saw the future the night before his birthday, he helped shape it.

Landau's leadership did not end with educational or public-relations matters in that his involvement in Springsteen's creative methods was crucial as well. Insider Marsh (he is married to Landau's assistant, so his knowledge is intimate) describes Landau as the creative arbiter between Springsteen's self-described two personalities: The "rock and roll natural" and the "thinkin' fool." When Springsteen was hung up over the Nebraska/U.S.A. material, enter Landau-the-arbiter who nurtured his artist and supported the compromise that rendered the two totally different expressions. Once the Nebraska material was released and troubles over the U.S.A. sequencing emerged, enter Landau-the-creative collaborator who wrote a detailed letter to Springsteen suggesting a song order to remedy that problem as well. From rescuing Springsteen from the Born to Run marathon, to enabling the Darkness record, to supporting the Nebraska diversion, to coordinating the U.S.A. explosion, Jon Landau has played a central role in the articulation of his client's art. When Springsteen's perfectionism consumes him, Landau brings him back to reality. Marsh cites Paul Nelson's observations in the Village Voice: "If Landau was somewhat in awe of the kind of instinctual genius who could resolve esthetic problems by compounding them, Bruce had no less respect for someone who invariably got to ten by counting out nine individual numbers, one at a time. It was the ideal artistic marriage of creative madness and controlling method." One has to wonder if the Worker's Elegy would have evolved without Landau's participation.

Just as word choice and narrative style determine the art's enactment, so do the methods through which artists negotiate their ideals and their realities. How artists manufacture their work says as much about the oeuvre as any individual project. It is as precise a manifestation of creative philosophy, biography, and stylistic tendency as the subsequent art itself. As the Dylan example reveals, the art may easily get lost in the production process. As the Spring-steen story indicates, the art may be systematically controlled by the production process. The dynamics vary from artist to artist. In all cases, however, production methods are central to the creative process as artists encounter the industry that sustains them. This domain of activity may make or break a career. The same principle holds true for our next consideration, the work's performance.

the performance orientations

How could two artists be more different? One catches a vibe, rides it, and walks away from it; the other stews over word choice, frames the results according to his master plan, and carefully manages the final product. One, historically, works alone; the other, historically, works with an established team—literally, a professional family. Our final point of comparison yields yet another distinction between these two pioneering musicians. The performance philosophies that guide their stage work reinforce what we have observed thus far. Dylan's detachment is to Springsteen's engagement what the two ends of a magnet represent: Polar opposites who feed off of the same field of action to different ends. Once more, creative philosophy dictates the result, as the postman delivers the mail and walks away while the preacher drives home the sermon and worries about his congregation's salvation. If the postman walked his route well, it was a good day. If the preacher gave his all and saved just one soul, it was a fine service. American Song's two siblings appear to cover both ends of the performance spectrum in a manner totally consistent with their creative worldviews. We have, then, yet another example of artistic individuality.

Bob Dylan's performance orientation has, most assuredly, evolved throughout his 40-year career. Like his language use, narrative style, or production methods and their mission-oriented applications, Dylan's performances—on and off stage—vary according to the creative agenda. From the self-effacing young folk apprentice, to the combative Newport Mod, to the reclusive resident genius, to his commercially defiant vaudeville act, to his pious gospel show, to the confused indifference of his 1980s tours, to his heartfelt musical renaissance of the mid-1990s, Dylan's performance style has been—to coin a phrase—"blowing in the wind." Just think about these radical stylistic differences and what they say about the volatile qualities of Dylan's career. The laughing, playful, Chaplinesque entertainer from the Greenwich Village period suddenly turns cold, aloof, and mysterious. An aesthetic war ensues, artist–audience battles follow, and the motorcycle accident brings to a halt what surely had to end, somehow. Afterward, a warmer but still mysterious performer appears. He acquiesces to commercial pressures and returns to touring via a state-of-the-art production that leaves him empty and disillusioned. He feels used. In response, he proposes Tour '74's photo negative, The Rolling Thunder Revue. This also plays out and Dylan is left unfulfilled. To the rescue comes none other than the Lord and a return to the confrontational style of the Jacket Jamboree and the Newport Mod; this time, the Word fuels the performance. This also plays out and Dylan is left unfulfilled. Now, a long, debilitating struggle engulfs the auteur. He tries everything, to no avail. He distorts, contorts, and vilifies his music, but he never stops trying. The media write him off as a relic, but he persists. Finally, with Campbell, Garnier, Kemper, and Sexton, Dylan discovers a performance peace of mind that, somehow, someway synthesizes all of his previous experiences into a positive outcome. What a story!

Throughout this musical maturation we observe various mixtures of the Glissendorf, Basement Strategy, topicality creative cocktail. If Dylan is in a positive frame of mind, we may witness earnest musicianship and a cessation of the musical gamesmanship. Should he perceive the need to confront his circumstances, we may observe a variety of lyrical and musical revisions or innovations that distance the auteur from his oeuvre. And should he, for some reason, feel antagonistic toward the situation, we may see outright hostility. Always, however, there is distance. It is merely a matter of degree: A warm disengagement, a cool aloofness, or a cold confrontation. The context dictates the act, but never does he engage an audience, never does he empower an audience—his distance enables him to control the performance situation.

There are so many examples of performance variations in response to contextual considerations that one could do as Paul Williams and Betsy Bowden have done and write book-length expositions on that topic in and of itself. Bowden offers this interesting rationale for her work: "But it is not Dylan's lyrics alone, nor his guitar and harmonica, that sent our parents clutching their ears and climbing their respective suburban walls in the sixties. It was that voice—that whining, grating, snarling voice that can drip scorn or comfort, can stretch or snap off words in disregard of their meaning or in fulfillment of it, can say for the listener what she has not quite yet said for herself." From there Bowden examines selected songs performed on different records and argues how the variations in performance yield variations in interpretation. For her, performance dictates meaning. One case in point is Dylan's "Just Like a Woman" in which Bowden concludes that the 1966 version (on *Blonde*) and the 1974 version (on *Before the Flood*) "portray two narrators with different attitudes—regretful in 1966, gleefully sadistic in 1974." Thus we have one song with two meanings. Maybe so, but as a critic, Bowden steps into her own Catch 22: Whether the object under consideration is the word-written or the word-spoken, its meaning is subjective. What a given song means to a listener is subject to that individual's experience with that song. Just ask Bruce Springsteen about that potential incongruity. Dylan recognized this at the outset; that is why he writes and performs for himself. Ultimately, and for Springsteen ironically, it is the only way in which "control" may truly be achieved. (By the way, one can only imagine Bowden's response to the *Budokan* or *Hard Rain* radical revisions in the 1980s.) These performance studies shed much light on the varied styles through which Dylan presented his art; nevertheless, they seem to end up in that maze of meaning that is so attractive for critics. For some reason, critics have a god-awful time accepting ambiguity.

One performance context that has not changed over the years is Dylan's work off stage. Here the auteur performs for his public in yet another clever manifestation of the Glissendorf strategy. From the outset, Dylan's performances before the media have pursued private agendas. What started with celebrity fabrications quickly evolved into the combative confrontations we discussed previously. Such antics have inspired knowledgeable writers such as Robert Shelton to conclude that *everything* Dylan does is a performance; that there is, indeed, no time in which he removes his mask to engage the public. Just as he obliterated his songs in their *Budokan* incarnations, he may trivialize a crucial biographical point—or fabricate a replacement—in an interview. Of course, a favorite strategy is to merely turn the question around on the interviewer ("Well, how have you changed since the sixties?" Dylan often fires back in response to the question that refuses to go away). Bob Dylan is the poster boy for the "trust the art, not the artist" critical philosophy.

Besides, from a performance perspective, it was all downhill after the Jacket Jamboree anyway. Bob Zimmerman knew *then* who he was playing for and it has never, ever changed. Even when his creative motives seemed most obvious (during the moral period), Dylan served a personal function (testimony). This loyalty to self—this commitment to the muse—is Dylan's saving grace as an artist. Had he allowed "outsiders" to dictate his writing or performing styles or had he endeavored to "communicate" with a specific audience, he could have fallen prey to their wishes and, my friends, *that* is *not* how you play Glissendorf. The control Bruce Springsteen craves—the control that is so elusive for that idealistic artist—has never troubled Bob Dylan. He writes for himself, he plays for himself—I only wonder if he ever applauds himself. Nobody knows better than Dylan that an audience should always be polite to a performer.

Would it shock you if I suggested that Bruce Springsteen maintains a slightly different performance orientation? First and foremost, we must understand that the Worker's Elegy is Springsteen's bible—a reference text that allows the patron to pick and choose which story shall serve that day's spiritual need. It is a *useful* text that may be used as a *tool* in one's personal search for emotional stability. It is unique in that Springsteen's bible is hymnal and scripture all rolled into one. In service, the preacher calls out a number or recites a passage from that bible as a preface to the participatory act that is worship. Bibles are great for personal reflection and spiritual gratification, but they are no substitute for church and the public affirmation of the private conviction. In church, the worldview is ratified and celebrated; it is the ultimate symbolic act, the heart of salvation.

Bruce Springsteen's "show" is everything, as he explained to Charlie Rose: "The writing, it's the blueprint of what you're gonna do . . . it's the essence of your idea that you're gonna try to communicate to your audience. The show is takin' that thing and you expand . . . performing it and performing it well sorta expands its boundaries and its power and you flush it out and entertain people with it. . . . [Performing the song and making that connection] is the fulfillment of the whole process in some fashion." Springsteen even went as far as to tell Rose that that is why he writes songs, to perform them for somebody. The tedious preparations of his pre-show routine (sound and light checks, and so on), the tightly scripted musical choreography of the show itself, the orchestrated post-show encounters with journalists and local interests—every facet of Spring-steen's appearance is coordinated to achieve maximum communicative impact. He is the ministerial Wizard of Oz of the rock world, projecting larger-than-life images through state-of-the-art mechanisms that are designed specifically for his audience. This wizard, however, readily admits passage backstage where he steps out from behind his curtain and continues his act. No one will ever pull the veil back and discover the real, disarmed Bruce Springsteen. This wizard's map draws a radical out-of-bounds marker that severely restricts passage into this portion of his life. That 60 Minutes aired Ed Bradley asking personal questions of Springsteen that he refused to answer demonstrates the extent of the artist's resolve. And so be it.

The auteur's marriage of prescriptive symbolicity and musical theatricality renders an act—a Reverend Oz—with a specific take on his congregation's con-dition. The passion of a fundamentalist preacher, the staging of a Broadway the-ater production, and the public-relations coordination of a presidential election campaign all rolled into one, the Springsteen show aspires to new heights each and every night. Big shows or small shows, football stadiums or Jersey Shore clubs, each venue and its corresponding staging feeds the message. Before tours begin, the Springsteen organization contacts local charities that are con-sistent with that tour's theme and coordinates meetings for donations. Spring-steen devises standard responses to anticipated journalistic inquiries that, again, stay "on message." Between-song monologues and song introductions are choreographed to provide dramatic pacing. Everything is subservient to the tour's message. The show moves the patron and he or she returns home to con-sult the bible and its reiterations of the show's symbolic medicine.

Springsteen's performance philosophy echoes the job description we consid-ered in the impulse section, as his remarks to Kurt Loder indicate: "I believe that the life of a rock and roll band will last as long as you look down into the audi-ence and can see yourself, and your audience looks up at you and can see them-selves—and as long as those reflections are human, realistic ones." He elabo-rated on this perspective three years later to Mikal Gilmore: "When I go onstage, my approach is 'I'm going to reach just one person'—even if there's 80,000 peo-ple there. Maybe those odds aren't so great, but if that's what they are, that's okay. . . . My idea was that when I went on a stage, I wanted to deliver my best to pull out the best in you, whatever that may be. But sometimes you don't do that. Sometimes you just pull out someone's insanity—you don't know what you're going to pull out or what will come to the surface." While he cannot con-trol his congregation's responses, Springsteen can control his service. A Spring-steen show is anything but a song list—it is a theatrical statement. His inter-view with Mojo outlined the show's tactical pacing and how songs perform certain "jobs" for the act (he specifically addressed how "Thundercrack" and

"Rosalita" served a "show-stopper" function). Like virtually every aspect of his career, Springsteen crusades are choreographed; they are orchestrated to achieve a strategic effect.

The auteur's commitment to his craft assumes an extraordinarily personal tone when he describes his attitude as a performer. This statement from a 1980 *Rolling Stone* article is a prime example:

> The audience brings a lot, even when you think you have nothing left within you. You know, tonight is *tonight*, and what you do tonight, you don't make up for tomorrow, and you don't ride on what you did last night. I always keep in my mind that you only have one chance. Some guy bought his ticket, and there's a promise made between the musician and the audience. When they support each other, that's a special thing. It goes real deep, and most people take it too lightly. If you break the pact or take it too lightly, nothing else makes sense. It's at the heart of everything; I'm not sure how . . . [the musician–audience relationship is] no different than if you stood with this person and shook his hand.

Springsteen extended his "handshake" metaphor in a 1996 interview with the *Asbury Park Press*: "Buying a ticket—that's a handshake. And I like to say, 'Thank you for supporting me. I'm gonna be the best I can.' That ticket is your bond. And meeting with the fans is maintaining that connection. It's something I did for myself. I didn't want to get lost. Isolation has always come very easy to me. That's what I do to combat that. I put myself out there so I'm not isolated." Remarkably, the commitment to his show is so passionate that he reportedly has difficulty leaving a venue once the performance ends. A 1997 *New York Times Magazine* piece cites Terry Magovern's (deemed Springsteen's "aide de camp") observation that his employer's "mental adrenaline" is so acute that he develops a relationship *with the building*: "He begins to feel a deep closeness to the building. He really feels the place, and he can't easily tear himself away." (With two-to-three hour sound checks, three- to four-hour shows, and an unwillingness to leave the venue, well, a Springsteen show *must* have been a full day for those involved.) The art's true focal point, then, is not the music, the words, or individual performances, but the *show*—a theatrical event that synthesized song, performance, and audience reciprocity into a narrative account of the "American Experience." A 1984 *Los Angeles Herald Examiner* review captures this phenomenon with compelling clarity:

> As someone here noted recently, if rock 'n' roll had never existed Bruce would have been a great showman in some other field—a world-shaking evangelist, or a great filmmaker, or a novelist, or the only white stand-up comic who could hold a candle to Richard Pryor. . . . I'm sure Springsteen scholars will consider this an elementary observation, but after my first experience of Bruce live, it's clear that his medium is not the song or the album, but the *show*. Ultimately, the songs achieve fulfillment as the building blocks of his live set and can be fully appreciated only in that context, framed by his dexterous spoken introductions. . . . The result is a rock show that really does have the amplitude of a big

novel and the stirring theatricality of an epic movie; that's as sprawlingly imaginative and inseparably American as "Leaves of Grass"—another unwieldy vision
of this country that just kept accumulating in its creator's lifetime, as each
new building-block poem was added.

David Chute's observation is widely shared. An artist–audience "connection"
is achieved by the service and the preacher's "handshake" agreement with individual audience members. Springsteen's comments to Q restate his perspective:

> I always want my shows to be a little bit like a circus, a touch of political rally,
> a little touch of a lot of different things. Really, in the end I want people to go
> away feeling more connected to each other and connected in their own lives
> and to the whole world around them, and to accomplish that you got to be
> connected. . . . These are people you have a relationship with like you have a
> relationship with your wife, your family and friends.

In this rock crusade, the "family" metaphor runs deep.

Unlike with his musical big brother, there is no emotional variance involved
with the performance dimension of Springsteen's art. The passion that characterized his early club shows advances through each tour. The staging may shift,
the actors may change places, the Reverend Oz may even appear solo, but the
underlying passion never fades. There is no period of detachment or disillusionment evident in Springsteen's shows. The "tonight's the night" mentality never
ceases. The musicians may recast a song, but the revision is in service of the
show's theatricality or pacing. Bruce Springsteen read those Soul Master's
maps very, very carefully, pilfered what he felt was necessary (always extending
credit), and, consequently, created the hardest-working White man in show business. The effort, as Springsteen explained to VH1, is considerable:

> The hardest thing about the show is I wake up in the morning and I know I gotta
> turn myself into a hysterical, raving lunatic later that evening . . . it's the pres-
> sure I enjoy the least. There's something about it that makes you slightly un-
> comfortable, but at the same time, that's what I do. To make it real, you have
> to go there . . . the trick every night is to get there and get as far into that as
> you can. It's part of your guarantee is, you know, that you're gonna reach that
> point for your audience.

Like with his musical big brother, writers of various orientations focus on the
performance qualities of Springsteen's art. Early on, journalists practically
embarrassed themselves with their glowing reviews of the live act (recall those
New York Times reviews and their accolades). A publication as formal as the
Times shuns publicity as a matter of editorial policy, yet these reviews gush with
praise. For Rolling Stone to call Springsteen the "greatest rock performer ever"
is one thing, but the New York Times? Official biographer Dave Marsh uses
Springsteen's performances as the organizing principle for his two-volume chronology. The heart of the performance, in the biographer's view, is the between-song
"rap" that delivers the show's message: "All of them have a point to make about

the music—or, rather, the music has a point to make about the stories." He also notes how the raps and songs evolve together, in that a story used to introduce a song in 1981 may shift to another tune in 1984 that elaborates on that theme. Everywhere there is continuity in Bruce Springsteen's art.

From the art's language, to its storytelling style, to the means through which it is produced, to its public performance, these two sons of American Song have taken their musical inheritance and had their way with it. One finds refuge in music history as he undertakes a variety of creative missions that serve the artistic needs of the day. The other mounts a symbolic crusade that focuses— I mean *focuses*—on his imagined constituency's plight in the hopes of providing emotional relief for its recurrent problems. One artist ascertains his creative mission and dutifully shapes his words and music, their sound, and his perform-ance accordingly. In service of that mission, he satisfies himself. His control is complete. His resolve is unshakable. The other artist is a tribute to stability. Since his function never varies, he assembles a musical methodology that matures as his crusade unfolds and ensures the continuity necessary for a pro-tracted work. His purpose is to communicate—to establish a connection and sustain it. His resolve, too, is strong, yet the incongruities between his message and its interpretation are exasperating. His efforts to reinvigorate the message confound his problem and in the end may have killed his crusade's potential for symbolic growth. How odd: One uses irony to service personal ends, the other suffers from the irony of service!

When discussing Bob Dylan's and Bruce Springsteen's oeuvres, I closed with Greil Marcus's idea of "Smithville" and his portrayal of a typical American town that embodies the worldview communicated within Harry Smith's *Anthology of American Folk Music*. Marcus is clever in his analogy's ability to interpret both Smith's *Anthology* and the *Basement Tapes* from Dylan's Woodstock respite. To suggest that a lifework embraces a worldview and that the respective projects that comprise that body of work represent individual elements of that worldview captures the essence of auteur theory. The synthesis of biography, artistic phi-losophy, creative impulse, and stylistic tendency renders the auteur. The negoti-ations that occur when the auteur encounters a commercial industry render the art. It is a fluid—at times wildly uneven—process. And yet when we stand back, the dust of a given moment fades. As we back up to consider a broader view, a clearer picture comes into focus and Bob Dylan's "Smithville" stands in stark contrast to Bruce Springsteen's "Smithville." Though they exist in the same country—perhaps the same county—and they function under the same legal system, life in each town follows its own distinctive rhythm.

Dylan's Smithville is an ironic place where individual agendas prosper and fre-quently clash. No worries though, the town feeds off its conflicts. Through rebel-lion, Dylan's Smithville prospers. Its instability is its prime source of stability. Change is Smithville's only constant. Not everybody can live in Dylan's Smithville, but those who do are never, ever bored. The rumors are too rich, the intensity is too strong to ever allow anyone the luxury of boredom. Citizens check their daily planners not to see what they will *do* tomorrow, but rather who they will *be* tomorrow. Relationships are hell in this Smithville. The conflict, the instability, the changing personalities, and the intensity that make the town so intriguing are debilitating when applied to loving relationships. The power games are maddening. Love is an all-consuming passion in Bob Dylan's Smithville—it is a game without end.

Springsteen's Smithville is a serious little mill town. The "haves" have done a fine job of keeping the "have-nots" in their place. In fact, the "haves" in Springsteen's Smithville never appear; they leave town (no doubt on permanent vacation) and only their mansions and brand-new, shiny, luxurious Cadillacs remain behind in full public view. For the "have-nots," the drudgery of daily living inspires an unhealthy belief in fantasies and dreams. But nobody ever *does* anything constructive about their situation. Their only relief comes from attending church. The respite, though, is temporary. Clueless and determined to stay that way, citizens accept their lot in life, undermine through frivolity their capacity to improve their situations, and contemplate their revenge. Violence is commonplace in Springsteen's Smithville. Nothing ever changes. Distrust is ubiquitous. Bruce Springsteen's Smithville is the dark underbelly of the American Dream.

Two artists, two worldviews, two Smithvilles. One fueled by rebellious conflict, the other stymied by its perceived limitations. Yet both are American. They share the same heritage, the same language, the same myths, the same freedoms. Each would benefit from exposure to the other. Springsteen's Smithville could use a little constructive rebellion and individual initiative, while Dylan's Smithville would benefit from the negative example and a little highway time. Two completely different takes on America. Two fundamentally different extensions of American Song. Both signed to Columbia Records by the same man. Hammond's Folly, indeed!

Woody Guthrie and American song

Joe Klein closes the 1999 edition of his Woody Guthrie biography by discussing his subject's two principal attributes: Rebellion and independence. Klein contends that Guthrie is "one of the patron saints of American rebelliousness," but his "most enduring quality has turned out to be his wild, heterodox and overpowering sense of freedom." He continues: "It is a deeply American trait, made possible by the vastness of the land and the stability of the political system. If Woody could be said to have had an ideology, it was a uniquely American one: He was militantly informal." From there, Klein takes issue with a remark Guthrie scribbled below his "This Land Is Your Land" lyrics: "You can only write what you see." Klein challenges Guthrie by arguing,

> You can write about things you've never seen, things you can only imagine—
> there are no limits. And that is Woody's gift to his descendants: The freedom
> to walk away, go off to some other town or just some different place inside your
> head; the freedom to come back home again and do what you were doing in the
> first place. The freedom to try any old thing; the freedom to start over. There
> is nothing more American than that.

This is the Woody Guthrie tradition of American Song: A militantly informal exploration of personal freedom and rebellion.

With Klein's observations as our starting point, we close with the questions posed at the outset. What does auteur theory tell us about Bob Dylan, Bruce Springsteen, and their contributions to American Song? How do these two writers build upon the Guthrie tradition of American songwriting? How do the rebellion and freedom themes manifest themselves within these two writers' fiercely independent worldviews?

Guthrie's two descendants personify different points of emphasis regarding the Dustbowl Poet's rebellion and freedom themes. For Bob Dylan, the rebellion embodied the freedom in that by rejecting everything, one may have anything. For Bruce Springsteen, the perceived lack of freedom suppressed the rebellion in that the individual initiative necessary for insurrection proved to be his greatest challenge. Dylan's rebellion took him down a path of self-indulgence that yielded art of historic proportions. When his innovations crowded him, he rebelled yet again, leaving himself free "to start over" and "try any old thing." His rebellion guaranteed his freedom. But rebellion did not come easily for Dylan's musical little brother. Springsteen's freedom was constricted not by socioeconomic status or environment, but by a fundamental lack of trust. Rebels, you see, must trust themselves. In the absence of self-trust, there is no freedom. Through music, Springsteen transformed his self-concept and discovered personal faith. As he shared his emotional autobiography in song, he worked through his problems, channeling his feelings in a productive fashion. With his art being his only refuge, he developed his musical church and worshiped passionately for hours upon hours at a time. His source of freedom slowly became his prison. Eventually, he mustered the "freedom to walk away" from that situation—a liberty that provided the inspiration to "come back home again" a dozen years later. The Worker's Elegy chronicles a genuine search for trust through metaphors that enable his audience to do the same. Springsteen's search for security and Dylan's confident rebellion come from opposite sides of the metaphorical railroad tracks, and it shows in their art.

The essence of these two stories may be found in that fascinating intersection of biography and art that yields the auteur. Consider these two scenarios: First, a middle-class kid from a sterile Midwestern environment absorbs the popular media of his day (his socioeconomic status enables consumption) and feeds a rebellious personality. His heroes—Brando, Dean, Little Richard, Elvis—step out and challenge the status quo. They are bold, passionate, and clever. They are, in a word, inspirational. He assimilates their perceived personalities into his own. He has the resources to own motorcycles, cars, and the necessary gear. These antisocial orientations inspire a disregard for societal structures and their reward systems. Remember, for the fifties' rebel, property, possessions, rules (even cleanliness)—all of these traditional "things"—were worthless and therefore devalued. Relationships emerge as a focal point. Since rebels, by their very nature, are self-absorbed, relationships prove challenging, always threatening, and occasionally rewarding. The conflict makes for a wonderful game. It spawns a lifework.

Second, a lower-class kid from an industrial, working-class environment grows up without "things" and covets them. He watches his parents work diligently to provide life's necessities, but luxuries are out of the question. In fact, for one parent, keeping a job is a struggle in and of itself. Subsequently, "things"—and the conditions that render them—become vitally important. Family relationships are strained due to a general instability. Emotional support is more than difficult to come by; as a result, isolation emerges as the kid's personal strategy. He discovers the guitar, isolates himself until he masters it, and uses it to obtain external gratification: Not money, but applause, acceptance, personal significance. For subject matter, he writes about the societal subjugation that he observed growing up—a social condition shared by many in his audience. He creates a melodrama about a vacuous existence that harbors empty, materialistic fantasies—an emotional dead end without a resolution. It births a lifework.

These two biographical scenarios provide the foundation of these writers' art. Dylan's rebellion fueled his professional decision-making, his creative worldview, and eventually his thematic orientation. It is his artistic currency and probably his personal hell. He served himself; rebellion engendered freedom. Springsteen's emotional insecurity inspired an intense need for control—control over his life, his art, his professional development. To massage his anxieties, Springsteen wrote about them. He built a body of work that offers for others that which he developed for himself: A means through which to cope, an avenue of hope. True to his blue-collar background, he conceived his art as a job. His job assumed a ministerial aura that informed his attitude toward performance (his church) and his recordings (his bible). As time passed and his life unfolded, he chronicled those events for his congregation and offered testimony for the cause. He served others as he would have them serve him. It is his artistic lifeblood and probably his personal hell.

These two artists contributed to the Guthrie tradition of American Song through their extensions of Guthrie's celebrity-singer-songwriter image and their stylistic responses to their respective situations. As we have seen, in our contemporary musical world the artistic image is often as important as the art itself. Guthrie—along with his contemporaries in cinema, radio, journalism, and fiction—pioneered this phenomenon. He quickly became an American icon: A living symbol of the rebellion and freedom portrayed in his songs. Hence, a song was more than a song, it was a message from Woody Guthrie. This was not Frank Sinatra loaning his image to the words of an unseen writer. This was a voice with a face, a style, a look, and a message. There would be no journalistic concerns over "public writer number one" without the cult of personality that accompanied the rise of media celebrities during the mid-twentieth century. The artistic image became a driving force that inspired the rebellious voice of his generation to forever rebel and the American worker's spokesperson to keep his offerings "on message." In many respects, the image subsumes the art. This is the Guthrie tradition, and the postman and the preacher each extended it in his own, militantly informal fashion.

   Complementing that development are Dylan's and Springsteen's respective innovations within American Song's continuing maturation. The iconoclastic wordplay and the systematic continuity of the two oeuvres make significant songwriting contributions that transcend musical genres. Like the country itself, American Song is a mix and match of musical influences that either stand on their own or merge into hybrids that revise and extend the respective traditions. Whether the music embraces America's blues, country, folk, or pop traditions (to name but a few), Dylan and Springsteen have influenced that songwriting. The language and emotional depth of the art form have been forever changed by these two innovators. John Hammond's wisdom is historic.

   The year 2001 found Dylan and Springsteen hard at work touring, actively engaging the musical world by plying their distinctive trades. Inspired by young fans' requests to see him perform with the E Street Band (as well as his own desire to allow his children a glimpse of the same), Springsteen initiated a two-year tour in 1999. The Springsteen commercial operation captured the event for posterity by filming/recording the tour's ten-night closing at New York's Madison Square Garden (released on CD, DVD, and via Home Box Office and VH1 specials). Dylan's continuous touring also carried on with a brief pause in the spring of 2001 to record *Love and Theft* in New York. Both tours were moving examples of showmanship that seemed to capture the state-of-the-artists at this point in their respective careers. Allow me to close with an overview of the two performances.

   Bruce Springsteen and the E Street Band's tour was an opportunity for everyone to celebrate "the show" and its players. From beginning to end, this production was a tribute to the performers. For example, the show opened with the band taking the stage two members at a time. Each couple slowly strolled on stage, accepting the applause of their adoring fans. Bittan and Federici, Tallent, Van Zandt and Scialfa, Lofgren and Weinberg sashayed onstage and assumed their positions as the crowd exploded upon Clemons and Springsteen's appearance. Church was officially in session. The service revisited all of the old theatrics. Although the between-song raps dissipated somewhat, Springsteen's athleticism and clowning as well as the band–audience interplay picked up where they had left off 15 years earlier (he even dusted off his old invitation, "Is anybody alive out there?"). As "Tenth Avenue Freeze-Out" geared up on the HBO version, Springsteen jumped on Bittan's piano and revved the crowd, the song opened and the service entered into a higher gear. Springsteen initiated a call-and-response routine by shifting the song to "Take Me to the River" as he screamed about his search for "the river of life," "the river of love," "the river of faith," "the river of hope," and "the river of transformation" (as he paced from side-to-side, confronting his congregation). He invited the audience to join him at "the river of sanctification," but he warned them that "You got to work at it." Springsteen declared, "You just don't stumble onto those things . . . you can't get to those things by yourself." "That's why I'm here," the preacher assured his followers, "I'm here for a rock-and-roll baptism . . . a rock-and-roll bar mitzvah." The long segment continued with band introductions (via fever-pitched histrionics), the audience raising their hands in the air like an old-time fundamentalist revival, and Springsteen's tightly choreographed call-and-response routines. On the VH1 special, "Light of Day" also recalled the preacher's heyday through yet another call-and-response routine. The New York version extended this bit as Springsteen teased his audience about New Jersey—claiming that he understands their envy—and, at one point in his preaching, he reached over to "lay hands" on Nils Lofgren who instantly fell to the floor in response. It was an old-fashioned tent service; salvation was in the air, but "you got to work at it." The crowd sang along, Springsteen fed their enthusiasm with his antics (he moved from one camera pose to another), and the band reveled in its glory. The show ended in a telling fashion. With the song "If I Should Fall Behind" as the backdrop, various band members stepped to the microphone to sing a verse or a few lines, the spotlight being focused on that individual. Each singer had their moment: Springsteen, Van Zandt, Lofgren, Scialfa, Lofgren and Scialfa duet, Clemons on sax and then singing, back to Springsteen, and on to a choral closing. The tone was somber. The service dutifully acknowledged its ministers and closed. Testimony was offered, the invitation was issued, everyone was sanctified.

Bob Dylan and his band followed a fundamentally different performance strategy. We move from "church" to a "concert." Using a standard recorded introduction, the band appeared onstage and opened each show with a traditional (e.g., "Duncan and Brady," "Roving Gambler," "Somebody Touched Me," "I am the Man, Thomas" or "Hallelujah, I'm Ready to Go") before venturing into a blend of acoustic and electric versions of old and—after the September 11th release of *Love and Theft*—new material. The set list changed with every venue, although certain songs (e.g., "Tangled Up in Blue," "Blowin' in the Wind," "Forever Young") seemed to find their way onto most shows (Dylanologists dutifully posted each play list on the Internet immediately after the show, occasionally with reviews). Dylan never addressed his audience other than an occasional "Thank You." (On some nights he did not even introduce the band.) The music carried the day. The musicianship was extraordinary. Dylan's singing was clear, exact, and emotive. Songs featured extended solos with Campbell and Sexton complementing Dylan's guitar work to create a wall of acoustic or electric sound that was anchored by Kemper and Garnier's timekeeping. In particular, Campbell's work on the pedal steel and mandolin was exemplary. The lighting was spare, but the sound was immaculate; it was a concert, plain and simple. When finished, Dylan and his band faced the audience to receive its applause without facial expression, arms hanging by their sides. No bows, no congratulations, no response whatsoever. The show was not about the musicians. They did *everything* imaginable to downplay their role in the proceedings. This show was about the music and *nothing* interfered with its presentation. Dylan's image was nowhere in sight. He was just another musician.

The preacher and his church, the postman and his mail. The preacher may age, his bible has not been revised in years, but he assembled his deacons for a service that displayed the vigor of his passionate youth. The absence of new material is irrelevant; it is, after all, the service that matters—a timeless enactment of spiritual commitment and a vehicle for his parishioners' journeys through their individual lives. Indeed, "Is anybody alive out there?" After the service, everybody returns home to consult their bibles. It also is timeless. On the other hand, the postman has walked many routes in his day: Some routes he traveled alone, using the maps left behind for his use; some routes were wacky innovations that rattled the entire postal system; no one knew where they stood in relation to the postman—he was doing his own thing. Once, the postman even delivered the Lord's mail with passion and grace. Other routes were, well, confused. The day's mail was floating about, unsure of its destination or content; occasionally, just mail for the sake of mail (dare I say "junk mail"?). In a world where "going postal" has become commonplace and rebellious postal workers seek revenge, this postman has assimilated the lessons from years of experience and, somehow, settled down and accepted his role. He is at peace with his job. And through it all, the preacher and the postman have advanced American Song's range and depth. And through it all, the preacher and postman have remained true to the Guthrie tradition. Throughout the ebb and flow of their respective careers Bob Dylan and Bruce Springsteen have, assuredly, remained militantly informal. Hammond's Folly—like Seward's—was a historic purchase.

references

general

Clarke, D. (1995). *The rise and fall of popular music.* New York: St. Martin's.

Crawford, R. (2001). *America's musical life: A history.* New York: W. W. Norton.

Davis, F. (1995). *The history of the blues: The roots, the music, the people from Charley Patton to Robert Cray.* New York: Hyperion.

Emerson, K. (2001, May 27). Songs of ourselves. *Los Angeles Times* <LATimes.com>.

Ewen, D. (1972). *Great men of American popular song.* Englewood Cliffs, NJ: Prentice-Hall.

Flanagan, B. (1986). *Written in my soul: Rock's great songwriters talk about creating their music.* New York: Contemporary.

Furia, P. (1992). *The poets of Tin Pan Alley: A history of America's great lyricists.* New York: Oxford University Press.

Gillett, C. (1996). *The sound of the city: The rise of rock and roll.* New York: Da Capo.

Guralnick, P. (1986). *Sweet soul music: Rhythm and blues and the southern dream of freedom.* New York: HarperPerennial.

————. (1989). *Feel like going home.* New York: Perennial Library.

————. (1989). *Lost highway: Journeys and arrivals of American musicians.* New York: HarperPerennial.

The history of rock 'n' roll. (1995). Time-Life Video.

Jasen, D., and G. Jones. (1998). *Spreadin' rhythm around: Black popular songwriters, 1880–1930.* New York: Schirmer.

Klein, J. (1980). *Woody Guthrie: A life.* New York: Delta.

Malone, B. (1985). *Country music USA.* Austin: University of Texas Press.

Palmer, R. (1978). *Baby, that was rock & roll: The legendary Leiber & Stoller.* New York: Harcourt Brace Jovanovich.

Pollock, B. (1975). *In their own words.* New York: Macmillan.

Rock 'n' Roll. (1995). Public Broadcasting System. Boston: WGBH.

Santelli, R., H. George-Warren, and J. Brown. (Eds.). (2001). *American roots music.* New York: Abrams.

Smith, L. (1999). *Pete Townshend: The minstrel's dilemma.* Westport, CT: Praeger.

Taylor, G. (1989). *Reinventing Shakespeare: A cultural history from the Restoration to the present.* New York: Oxford University Press.

Webb, J. (1998). *Tunesmith: Inside the art of songwriting.* New York: Hyperion.

Wilder, A. (1972). *American popular song: The great innovators, 1900–1950.* New York: Oxford University Press.

Bob Dylan

Allen, J. (2001, May 23). Bob Dylan at 60: Timeless and transcendent <CNN.com>.

Anderson, S. (1994, January). Bob Dylan: *World Gone Wrong. Spin*, pp. 77–78.

Back to the roots. (1969, April 11). *Time*, pp. 70–71.

Basic Dylan. (1968, January 12). *Time*, p. 50.

Bauder, D. (1985, June 21). Two '60s legends who won't fade away. (Stamford, CT) *Advocate* (NEWSBANK).

Bernstein, J., and S. Daly. (1990, December). Platter du jour. *Spin*, p. 83.

Bob Dylan: The 1965 interview. (1997). *The Baktabek interview collection*. London: Baktabak Recordings.

Bob Dylan: The American troubadour. (2000). *Biography*. New York: A&E Television Networks.

Bowden, B. (1982). *Performed literature: Words and music by Bob Dylan*. Bloomington: Indiana University Press.

Bream, J. (1986, January 19). Bob Dylan. *Minneapolis Star Tribune* (NEWSBANK).

Buskin, R. (1999). *Inside tracks*. New York: Avon.

Carlin, P. (1997, November 3). Song: *Time Out of Mind. People*, p. 25.

Catlin, R. (1993, October 24). Dylan's other side plays others' songs. *Hartford Courant* (NEWSBANK).

———. (2001, September 11). Dylan plumbs depths of heart and soul in new gem. *Hartford Courant* <ctnow.com>.

Champlin, C. (1978, January 25). Two views of Dylan's "Renaldo and Clara." *Los Angeles Times*, pp. IV: 1, 12.

Cocks, J. (1985, June 10). Here's what's happening, Mr. Jones. *Time*, p. 84.

———. (1985, November 25). Hellhound on the loose. *Time*, p. 122.

———. (1992, October 26). Bringing folk back home. *Time*, p. 73.

Cohen, J., and H. Traum. (1972). Conversations with Bob Dylan. In Craig McGregor (Ed.), *Bob Dylan: A retrospective* (pp. 263–92). New York: William Morrow.

Cohn, N. (1996). *Awopbopaloobop alopbamboom: The golden age of rock*. New York: Da Capo.

Coleman, R. (1965, January 9). Beatles say—Dylan shows the way. *Melody Maker*, p. 3.

Connelly, C. (1983, November 24). Dylan makes another stunning comeback. *Rolling Stone*, pp. 65–66, 69.

Considine, J. D. (1991, March 27). "Bootleg Series" plays out the bluesy, rough-edged steps of Dylan's development. *Baltimore Sun* (NEWSBANK).

Cott, J. (1975, March 13). *Blood on the Tracks*: Back inside the rain. *Rolling Stone*, pp. 43, 45–46.

———. (1978, January 26). Standing naked: Bob Dylan. *Rolling Stone*, pp. 38–44.

———. (1978, November 16). Bob Dylan: The "Rolling Stone" interview, part II. *Rolling Stone*, pp. 56–62.

Crenshaw, H. (1988, July 2). Dylan's "Down in the Groove" entertaining, not innovative. *Atlanta Journal* (NEWSBANK).

Crowe, C. (1985). Interview with Bob Dylan. *Biograph*. New York: CBS.

Cusimano, J. (1975, April). Records: Dylan comes back to the wars. *Crawdaddy*, pp. 67–68.

Damsker, M. (1994, April 7). Books: The way we were. *Rolling Stone*, p. 25.

Davis, F. (1999, May). Napoleon in rags. *Atlantic Monthly*, pp. 108–17.

Day, A. (1988). *Jokerman: Reading the lyrics of Bob Dylan*. Oxford: Basil Blackwell.

DeCurtis, A. (1986, September 11). Records: *Knocked Out Loaded. Rolling Stone,* pp. 92–93.

———. (1989, September 21). Dylan and the Stones: The shock of the old. *Rolling Stone,* pp. 115–16.

———. (1991, April 4). Bob Dylan's blue highway. *Rolling Stone,* pp. 53–55.

DiMartino, D. (1993, February). History lessons. *Musician,* pp. 89–90.

Dr. Bob sums up. (1970, June 22). *Time,* p. 61.

Dylan. (1974, February 11). *New Yorker,* pp. 32–33.

Dylan, B. (1994). *Tarantula.* New York: St. Martin's Press.

Dylan in conference: I just hope to have enough boots to be able to change them. (1968, January 20). *Melody Maker,* p. 9.

The Dylanologist. (1971, April 12). *Newsweek,* p. 123.

Ebert, R. (1998, May 1). Blood on the tracks: Documentary shows Dylan as cruel twirp. *Chicago Sun-Times,* p. 37.

———. (2001, September 13). Bob Dylan plays a winning hand. *Dallas Morning News* <DallasNews.com>.

Erlewine, S. (1997). *All music guide to rock.* San Francisco: Miller Freeman.

Evans, P. (1990, October 4). Records: *Under the Red Sky. Rolling Stone,* pp. 160–61.

Evearitt, D. (1976, December 3). Bob Dylan: Still blowin' in the wind. *Christianity Today,* pp. 29–30.

Ewen, D. (1972). *Great men of American popular song.* Englewood Cliffs, NJ: Prentice-Hall.

Faris, M. (1980, June 22). What's Bob Dylan up to of late? Just ask A.J. *Chicago Tribune,* p. 6: 30.

Farley, C. (1997, September 29). Dylan's lost highway. *Time,* p. 87.

Favorite son: Birthday wishes to Bob Dylan. (2001, May 24). *Minneapolis Star Tribune* <Startribune.com>.

Flanagan, B. (1986). *Written in my soul: Rock's great songwriters talk about creating their music.* New York: Contemporary.

———. (1986, February). Record reviews: Two decades of poetry and hard truth. *Musician,* pp. 114–16.

———. (1988, September). Reviews: Bob Dylan: *Down in the Groove. Musician,* pp. 110–12.

———. (1993, December). My back pages. *Musician,* pp. 85–86.

The folk and the rock. (1965, September 20). *Newsweek,* pp. 88–90.

Folk singers. (1963, May 31). *Time,* p. 40.

Fong-Torres, B. (1974, February 14). Knockin' on Dylan's door. *Rolling Stone,* pp. 36–41, 44.

Fricke, D. (1981, August 8). And what makes Bob sick. *Melody Maker,* p. 3.

———. (1985, December 5). Dylan's dilemma. *Rolling Stone,* pp. 51–53.

———. (1988, July 14). Records: *Down in the Groove. Rolling Stone,* p. 142.

———. (1990, February 3). The tour of no return: Dylan on the road in the eighties. *Melody Maker,* p. 36.

———. (1997, December 25). The year in recordings: *Time Out of Mind. Rolling Stone,* p. 156.

———. (2001, September 27). The making of Dylan's "Love and Theft." *Rolling Stone,* pp. 11–12.

Fusilli, J. (1997, October 9). Bob Dylan: Never out of mind. *Wall Street Journal,* p. 4.

Futterman, E. (1994, April 7). Times they are a changin' . . . Dylan speaks. *St. Louis Post-Dispatch,* p. 1G.

Gates, D. (1989, March 13). Bob Dylan. *Newsweek,* p. 67.

———. (1991, April 8). Notes from underground. *Newsweek,* p. 63.

———. (1997, October 6). Dylan revisited. *Newsweek,* pp. 62–68.

Gill, A. (2001, September 6). Bob Dylan: *Love and Theft. Independent* <independent.co.uk>.

Gilmore, M. (1985, November 10). Behind the glasses, Dylan at 44 looking scruffy but ready. *Chicago Tribune*, pp. 13: 5, 8.

———. (1986, July 17). Positively Dylan. *Rolling Stone*, pp. 31–34, 135–36.

———. (1991, May 30). Bob Dylan at fifty. *Rolling Stone*, pp. 56–60.

———. (1998). *Night beat: A shadow history of rock & roll.* New York: Doubleday.

———. (2001, November 22). The *Rolling Stone* interview: Bob Dylan. *Rolling Stone*, pp. 56–69.

Gleason, R. (1968, December). Bob Dylan: Poet to a generation. *Jazz & Pop*, pp. 36–37.

———. (1975, March 13). The blood of a poet. *Rolling Stone*, p. 22.

Glover, T. (1975, October). Records: The ultimate underground record sees the light of day. *Creem*, pp. 64–65.

Goldberg, J. (1979, September). Dylan digs the diamond mine. *Creem*, p. 52.

Graustark, B. (1979, December 17). The (new) word according to Dylan. *Newsweek*, p. 90.

Gray, M. (2000). *Song & dance man III: The art of Bob Dylan.* London: Cassell.

Gundersen. E. (1998). Dylan on Dylan: "Unplugged" and the birth of a song. In C. Benson (Ed.), *The Bob Dylan companion: Four decades of commentary* (pp. 223–25). New York: Schirmer.

———. (2001, May 18). Forever Dylan. *USA Today*, pp. 1–3E.

———. (2001, May 18). Times change, but Dylan leaves a lasting imprint. *USA Today*, pp. 1–4A.

———. (July 16, 2001). "Love" takes Dylan in different direction. *USA Today*, p. 1D.

———. (2001, September 10). Dylan is positively on top of his game. *USA Today* <USA Today.com>.

Hajdu, D. (2001). *Positively 4th street: The lives and times of Joan Baez, Bob Dylan, Mimi Baez Fariña and Richard Fariña.* New York: Farrar, Straus and Giroux.

Hampton, W. (1986). *Guerrilla minstrels.* Knoxville: University of Tennessee Press.

Hansson, N. (2001, September). The Rome interview. *La Repubblica* <Expectingrain.com>.

Happy birthday Bob: An appreciation of Dylan at 60. (2001, June 7). *Rolling Stone*, pp. 48–52, 122.

Harrington, R. (1985, June 28). Dylan finally sheds himself of old religious trappings. *Cleveland Plain Dealer* (NEWSBANK).

———. (2001, September 16). Dylan's American gamut <Washingtonpost.com>.

Helm, L. (2000). *This wheel's on fire: Levon Helm and the story of The Band.* Chicago: Acappella.

Henahan, D. (1967, September 7). The screen: Bob Dylan and company. *New York Times*, p. 50.

Hentoff, N. (1964, October 24). Profiles: The crackin', shakin', breakin' sounds. *New Yorker*, pp. 64–90.

———. (1966, March). Playboy interview: Bob Dylan. *Playboy*, pp. 41–44, 138–42.

Heylin, C. (1995). *Bob Dylan: The recording sessions [1960–1994].* New York: St. Martin's Griffin.

———. (2001). *Bob Dylan: Behind the shades revisited.* New York: William Morrow.

Hickey, N. (1976, October 16). Dylan today. *Melody Maker*, pp. 32–33.

———. (1998). Bob Dylan (1976). In C. Benson (Ed.), *The Bob Dylan companion: Four decades of commentary* (pp. 150–56). New York: Schirmer.

Hilburn, R. (1978, January 25). Two views of Dylan's "Renaldo and Clara." *Los Angeles Times*, pp. IV: 1, 12.

———. (1978, May 28). Bob Dylan opens up on Bob Dylan. *Los Angeles Times*, pp. C: 1, 66.

———. (1978, November 17). Dylan returns to the Forum. *Los Angeles Times*, pp. IV: 1, 26.

———. (1979, August 18). Dylan's stirring "Slow Train." *Los Angeles Times*, p. II: 10.

———. (1979, November 6). Bob Dylan: Fundamental light still shineth. *Los Angeles Times*, pp. V: 1, 16.

———. (1979, November 18). Dylan's new furor: Rock 'n' religion. *Los Angeles Times*, p. C: 82.

———. (1979, November 20). Dylan's evangelicalism goes on. *Los Angeles Times*, pp. V: 1, 14.

———. (1980, November 11). Bob Dylan on his own terms. *Los Angeles Times*, pp. C: 1, 4.

———. (1981, August 30). "Shot of Love": Buried gems. *Los Angeles Times*, p. C: 73.

———. (1983, March 13). Looking back: Dylan at pop storm center. *Los Angeles Times*, p. C: 54.

———. (1983, October 30). Bob Dylan at 42—rolling down highway 61 again. *Los Angeles Times*, pp. C: 3–4.

———. (1984, August 5). Dylan: The view from route '84. *Los Angeles Times*, p. C: 54.

———. (1985, June 9). Dylan brings it all back home again. *Los Angeles Times*, p. C: 57.

———. (1985, November 17). Bob Dylan—still a-changin'. *Los Angeles Times*, pp. C: 56, 62–63.

———. (1992, April 12). With no direction known: Dylan on tour. *Chicago Sun Times* (NEWSBANK).

———. (1998). "I learned that Jesus is real and I wanted that." In C. Benson (Ed.), *The Bob Dylan companion: Four decades of commentary* (pp. 161–67). New York: Schirmer.

———. (2001, September 9). This year's Dylan is a sonic dynamo <LATimes.com>.

———. (2001, September 16). How does it feel? Don't ask <LATimes.com>.

Hill, G. (1993, October 18). Dylan: Fans an inspiration for "World Gone Wrong." *Boston Herald* (NEWSBANK).

Himes, G. (1979, September 19). Self-righteous Dylan. *Washington Post*, p. C4.

Hinckley, D. (1985, May 29). Bob Dylan's "Empire Burlesque." *New York Daily News* (NEWSBANK).

———. (1992, November 3). "Good" old Bob. *New York Daily News* (NEWSBANK).

Holden, S. (1989, October 1). A "new Dylan" crosses paths with the old. *New York Times*, p. H29.

Holmes, T. (1986, January 16). Dylan: A life in music. *Rolling Stone*, pp. 43–45.

———. (1988, September). Bob Dylan: *Down in the Groove*. *Spin*, p. 86.

Humphries, P. (1995). *The complete guide to the music of Bob Dylan*. New York: Omnibus.

Infusino, D. (1986, July 30). Less than top Dylan is still very good. *San Diego Union* (NEWSBANK).

Jacobson, M. (1995, April). Hero with 1,000 (gnarly) faces. *Esquire*, p. 147.

———. (2001, April 12). Tangled up in Bob. *Rolling Stone*, pp. 64–74, 151.

Jennings, D. (1974, October). Records: *Before the Flood*. *Creem*, pp. 64–65.

Jeske, L. (1990, September 10). Bob Dylan revisited. *New York Post* (NEWSBANK).

Jones, A. (1990, February 3). Blood on the tracks: The legend of Bob Dylan. *Melody Maker*, pp. 29–36.

Jones, M. (1964, May 23). If you want to do it—then do it! *Melody Maker*, p. 12.

———. (1995, March 20). A primitive's portfolio. *Newsweek*, pp. 60–61.

Joyce, M. (1989, September 20). Bob Dylan, brooding but clear. *Washington Post*, p. D7.

———. (1990, September 16). The times keep on a-changin'. *Washington Post*, pp. G1, 9.

Katz, L. (1991, March 25). New "Bootleg Series" tracks musician from folk to rock. *Boston Herald* (NEWSBANK).

————. (1992, November 1). Dylan's new release is as "Good as" it gets. *Boston Herald* (NEWSBANK).

————. (1993, October 26). Album gives insight into Dylan's "World." *Boston Herald* (NEWSBANK).

Keller, M. (1983, September 11). Religion, politics, a new record: What's up with Bob Dylan. *Chicago Tribune*, pp. 12: 5–6.

Kilday, G. (1978, January 22). Film-maker Dylan: A peek behind the mask. *Los Angeles Times*, pp. C: 1, 43.

King, P. (1988, June 26). "Groove" is a downer for Bob Dylan. *Pittsburgh Press* (NEWS-BANK).

————. (1989, October 8). Dylan, newcomer turn out fine albums. *Pittsburgh Press* (NEWSBANK).

Kleinman, B. (1998). Dylan on Dylan (1984). In C. Benson (Ed.), *The Bob Dylan companion: Four decades of commentary* (pp. 30–40). New York: Schirmer.

Kot, G. (1989, September 24). Dylan delivers. *Chicago Tribune*, p. 5: 3.

————. (1992, October 25). He may not have all the answers, but he always asks the right questions. *Chicago Tribune*, pp. 13: 16, 21.

————. (1993, August 15). Casting giant shadows. *Chicago Tribune*, pp. 13: 6–7.

————. (1997, September 28). Like a rolling stone. *Chicago Tribune*, p. 7: 17.

Kotkin, J. (1978, January 20). Bob Dylan, alone. *Washington Post*, pp. D1, 2.

Landau, J. (1968, May). *John Wesley Harding*. *Crawdaddy*, pp. 11–17.

————. (1975, March 13). *Blood on the Tracks*: After the flood. *Rolling Stone*, pp. 43, 47–51.

Levy, J. (1989, October). Bob Dylan: *Oh Mercy*. *Spin*, p. 98.

Lewis, G. (1970). The pop artist and his product: Mixed-up confusion. *Journal of Popular Culture*, 2, pp. 327–38.

Lingeman, R. (1971, June 25). Bob Dylan, I'm writing to you. *New York Times*, p. 32.

Loder, K. (1980, September 18). God and man at Columbia. *Rolling Stone*, p. 48.

————. (1984, June 21). The *Rolling Stone* interview: Bob Dylan. *Rolling Stone*, pp. 14–18, 23–24, 78.

————. (1985, February 14). Records: Bob Dylan: *Real Live*. *Rolling Stone*, pp. 46–47.

————. (1985, July 4). Records: Bob Dylan rocks again. *Rolling Stone*, pp. 48–49.

————. (1987, November 5). Bob Dylan. *Rolling Stone*, pp. 301–3.

————. (1992, October 15). The *Rolling Stone* interview: Bob Dylan. *Rolling Stone*, pp. 110–13.

MacDonald, P. (1986, July 25). Tried true confessions. *Seattle Times* (NEWSBANK).

Marcus, G. (1978, August 24). Records: "Street Legal" a misdemeanor. *Rolling Stone*, pp. 51–53.

————. (1997). *Invisible republic: Bob Dylan's basement tapes*. New York: Henry Holt.

Marin, P. (1972, February 20). With the help of electricity the young could hear themselves speak. *New York Times Book Review*, pp. 4–5.

Marine, C. (1993, October 28). Bob Dylan revisited. *San Francisco Examiner* (NEWSBANK).

Marsh, D. (1976, March 11). Records: Desire under fire: Mythic images of women and out-laws. *Rolling Stone*, pp. 55–59.

————. (1976, October 21). "Hard Rain," hard rock, hard sell. *Rolling Stone*, p. 39.

Maslin, J. (1979, July 12). Bob Dylan: Brave new world at Budokan. *Rolling Stone*, p. 72.

Mayer, I. (1986, July 16). Dylan's new disc only a partial knockout. *New York Post* (NEWS-BANK).

McClure, M. (1974, March 14). The poet's poet. *Rolling Stone*, pp. 33–34.

McGregor, C. (1972). *Bob Dylan: A retrospective.* New York: William Morrow.

———. (1972, May 7). Dylan: Reluctant hero of the pop generation. *New York Times*, p. 15.

McKeen, W. (1993). *Bob Dylan: A bio-bibliography.* Westport, CT: Greenwood.

McLeese, D. (1988, June 6). Dylan album offers a bit of everything. *Chicago Sun Times* (NEWSBANK).

———. (1989, October 1). Dylan finds "Mercy" in Louisiana. *Chicago Sun Times* (NEWSBANK).

———. (1990, November 29). Recordings: Traveling Wilburys, vol. 3. *Rolling Stone*, pp. 105–6.

Meehan, T. (1965, December 12). Public writer No. 1? *New York Times*, pp. 44–45.

Milano, B. (1997, December). Positively Bob Dylan. *Stereo Review*, p. 106.

Miller, J. (1985, December 9). The two lives of Bob Dylan. *Newsweek*, pp. 93–94.

———. (1986, June 23). The minstrel in middle age. *Newsweek*, p. 80.

Mitchell, G. (1975, October). Records: *The Basement Tapes. Crawdaddy*, pp. 65–66.

Mitchell, R. (1989, September 27). Mercy, Dylan LP is good. *Houston Chronicle* (NEWSBANK).

Moon, T. (1988, June 13). The latest from Dylan: An easy, bluesy album. *Miami Herald* (NEWSBANK).

———. (1989, September 19). Dylan album reflects New Orleans sojourn. *Philadelphia Inquirer* (NEWSBANK).

———. (1991, April 4). Bootleg adds luster to the Dylan myth. *Miami Herald* (NEWSBANK).

———. (2001, May 20). If it's a milestone time for Dylan, 60 isn't why. (Philadelphia) <Inquirer.com>.

Morgan, J. (1985, April). Bob Dylan: *Real Live. Creem*, p. 50.

Morley, J. (1991, July). Blue Light Special: Bob Dylan (Or, what Bob Dylan can teach you about the unfinished war in Iraq). *Spin*, pp. 84–85.

Morse, S. (1993, October 24). "World Gone Wrong" is Dylan gone right. *Boston Globe* (NEWSBANK).

———. (1997, September 26). Dylan explores his dark side. *Boston Globe*, p. D15.

———. (2001, September 7). King of hearts. *Boston Globe* <boston.com>.

Nelson, P. (1975, September 11). Records: The basement tapes caper: A new/old mystery. *Rolling Stone*, pp. 50–54.

———. (1981, October 15). Records: The politics of sin. *Rolling Stone*, pp. 59–61.

———. (1990, October). Bob Dylan: *Under the Red Sky. Musician*, p. 121.

Nelson, P., and J. Pankake. (1998). Flat tire. In C. Benson (Ed.), *The Bob Dylan companion: Four decades of commentary* (pp. 20–23). New York: Schirmer.

Nesin, J. (1984, February). Keep the faith, Bobby! *Creem*, p. 51.

Nicholaus, C. (1975, April). Dreck in the groove. *Creem*, pp. 60–61.

O'Hare, K. (1991, March 24). New bootleg Dylan recalls the genius. (Springfield, MA) *Sunday Republican* (NEWSBANK).

Olsen, B. (2001, September 17). Bob Dylan, joker. *New Zealand Herald* <nzherald.co.nz>.

Orth, M. (1974, January 14). Dylan—rolling again. *Newsweek*, pp. 46–49.

———. (1975, February 10). Constant lover. *Newsweek*, pp. 65–66.

———. (1975, November 17). It's me, babe. *Newsweek*, p. 94.

Page, T. (2001, May 24). Bob Dylan, not ready for to fade. *Washington Post* <Washington post.com>.

Pareles, J. (1978, September). Untangling from the blues. *Crawdaddy*, p. 65.

———. (1986, July 17). Music: Bob Dylan and Tom Petty. *New York Times*, p. 15.

———. (1986, August 10). Bob Dylan and Neil Young face life in the 80's. *New York Times*, pp. 20, 30.

———. (1989, January 29). With concert disks, is it live or memories? *New York Times*, p. 28.

———. (1997, September 28). A wiser voice blowin' in the autumn wind. *New York Times*, pp. 1, 28.

Perry, C. (1991, April 3). Dylan in rare form. *Houston Post* (NEWSBANK).

———. (1993, October 26). Dylan's irritating brilliance shines on edges of album. *Houston Post* (NEWSBANK).

Petkovic, J. (2001, September 11). You won't be cheated by Bob Dylan's latest. (Cleveland) *Plain Dealer* <Cleveland.com>.

Poet's return: "It's what I do." (1969, September 12). *Time*, pp. 80–81.

Pond, S. (1979, May 13). Dylan: Still a mystery. *Los Angeles Times*, p. C: 83.

Pousner, H. (1985, November 30). Almost definitive Dylan. *Atlanta Journal* (NEWSBANK).

Powers, A. (2001, May 11). Dylan keeps a-changin', making him a hard act to follow. *New York Times* <Nytimes.com>.

Puterbaugh, P. (1990, January). Dylan's vision. *Stereo Review*, p. 111.

———. (1993, February). Bob Dylan: *Good as I Been to You. Stereo Review*, p. 120.

Rachlis, K. (1976, December 2). Records: Rolling Thunder's downpour. *Rolling Stone*, pp. 91–92.

Ransom, K. (1990, November 17). Dylan's new hard edge may surprise old fans. *Ann Arbor* (Michigan) *News* (NEWSBANK).

Richardson, D. (1994, May/June). Dylan's folk revival. *Acoustic Guitar*, pp. 91–93.

Richardson, S. (1993, September 16). Bob Dylan: The 30th Anniversary Concert Celebration. *Rolling Stone*, p. 72.

———. (1994, December 15). Performance: Bob Dylan. *Rolling Stone*, p. 38.

———. (1995, May 4). Recordings: His back pages. *Rolling Stone*, pp. 63, 65.

Riegel, R. (1982, March). More of an outlaw that you ever were? *Creem*, pp. 42–43, 57–58.

Riley, J. (2001, July 9). Dylan talks pops. *Liverpool Echo* <icLiverpool.com>.

Riley, T. (1999). *Hard rain: A Dylan commentary*. New York: Da Capo.

Robbins, P. (1998). Bob Dylan in his own words (1965). In C. Benson (Ed.), *The Bob Dylan companion: Four decades of commentary* (pp. 48–57). New York: Schirmer.

Rockwell, J. (1976, January 25). Are the times a-changin' too much for Dylan? *New York Times*, pp. D1, 17.

———. (1985, November 24). Bob Dylan sums up a life in music. *New York Times*, p. B1.

Rodnitzky, J. (1976). *Minstrels of the dawn: The folk-protest singer as a cultural hero*. Chicago: Nelson-Hall.

Rohter, L. (1976, January 5). Dylan's "Desire": Baring his soul after all these years. *Washington Post*, pp. D1, 3.

Rose, D. (1975, December). For whom the tribute tolls. *Crawdaddy*, pp. 26–27.

Rosenbaum, R. (1978, March). Playboy interview: Bob Dylan. *Playboy*, pp. 61–90.

Rowland, M. (1983, December). Record reviews: Bob Dylan: *Infidels. Musician*, p. 104.

Saal, H. (1968, February 26). Dylan is back. *Newsweek*, pp. 92–93.

———. (1969, April 14). Dylan's country pie. *Newsweek*, pp. 102–4.

Samuels, L. (1986, July 30). This time, the music's the message from Dylan. *Dallas Morning News* (NEWSBANK).

Scaduto, A. (1971). *Bob Dylan.* New York: Grosset & Dunlap.

————. (1971, November 28). Won't you listen to the lambs, Bob Dylan? *New York Times Magazine,* pp. 34–40.

Scheck, F. (1997, November 7). Bob Dylan, rock's preeminent wordsmith, makes a comeback. *Christian Science Monitor,* p. 15.

Schoemer, K. (1992, December 6). Bob Dylan revisits his roots and finds a gift for the young. *New York Times,* p. 2: 26.

Seay, D. (1979, September 23). Dylan and the musical ministry. *Los Angeles Times,* pp. C: 82, 84.

Selvin, J. (1997, September 28). Dylan's best new songs in ages. *San Francisco Chronicle,* p. 46.

————. (2001, September 9). Dylan is brilliant on "Love and Theft." *San Francisco Chronicle* <sfgate.com>.

Sheffield, R. (2001, September 27). Recordings: Love and Theft. *Rolling Stone,* pp. 65–67.

Shelton, R. (1965, August 27). Pop singers and song writers racing down Bob Dylan's road. *New York Times,* p. 34.

————. (1965, August 30). Dylan conquers unruly audience. *New York Times,* p. 20.

————. (1978, July 29). How does it feel to be on your own? *Melody Maker,* pp. 27–30.

————. (1986). *No direction home: The life and music of Bob Dylan.* New York: Ballantine.

Shuster, F. (1992, May 16). A night with Dylan? What did he say? *Los Angeles Daily News* (NEWSBANK).

Simels, S. (1984, January). Dylan lives! *Stereo Review,* p. 80.

Singer, D. (1980, January 4). Not buying into subculture. *Christianity Today,* p. 33.

Smith, A. (1991, May 5). Dylan's buried treasures. (Providence, RI) *Journal-Bulletin* (NEWSBANK).

Smith, R. (1997, October 21). Sick of it all. *Village Voice,* pp. 69–70.

Snyder, M. (1989, October 22). Bob gives a peek at real Dylan. *San Francisco Examiner* (NEWSBANK).

Sounes, H. (2001). *Down the highway: The life of Bob Dylan.* New York: Grove.

Spitz, B. (1989). *Dylan: A biography.* New York: W. W. Norton.

Spitz, R. (1978, June 28). "Street Legal" Magic. *Washington Post,* p. E4.

Stookey, N. (1980, January 4). Bob Dylan finds his source. *Christianity Today,* p. 32.

Sumrall, H. (1986, July 18). Dylan cooks like a summer day. *San Jose Mercury News* (NEWSBANK).

Tempest, M. (2001, September 11). If music be the food of love, play on. *The Guardian* <guardian.co.uk>.

Thomson, E., and D. Gutman (Eds.). (2001). *The Dylan companion.* New York: Da Capo.

Trakin, R. (1986, September). Record reviews: Bob Dylan: Knocked Out Loaded. *Musician,* pp. 104–6.

Tucker, K. (1988, June 8). Bob Dylan's new album: Perverse and pretty good. *Philadelphia Inquirer* (NEWSBANK).

————. (1997, October 3). Tombstone blues. *Entertainment Weekly,* pp. 80–82.

Van Matre, L. (1974, February 3). Mellow Dylan makes a few weak "Waves." *Chicago Tribune,* p. 11.

————. (1985, November 10). Still compelling: A long look back at two decades of Dylan. *Chicago Tribune,* pp. 13: 4–5, 8.

————. (1986, July 22). Dylan back again, but latest album is no KO. *Chicago Tribune,* p. 5: 3.

Varga, G. (1989, September 20). "Mercy!" Dylan in top form. *San Diego Union* (NEWS-BANK).

———. (1991, March 25). A look back at Dylan's best years. *San Diego Union* (NEWS-BANK).

Verna, P. (1997, October 4). Reviews and previews: *Time Out of Mind. Billboard*, p. 89.

Vowell, S. (1997, December). Bob Dylan: *Time Out of Mind. Spin*, p. 154.

Walls, R. (1988, October). Bob Dylan: *Down in the Groove. Creem*, pp. 26–27.

Welles, C. (1964, April 10). The angry young folk singer. *Life*, pp. 109–14.

Wenner, J. (1969, November 29). The *Rolling Stone* interview: Dylan. *Rolling Stone*, pp. 22–33.

———. (1979, September 20). Bob Dylan and our times: The slow train is coming. *Rolling Stone*, pp. 94–99.

Wild, D. (1992, November 26). Come gather round, people. *Rolling Stone*, pp. 17, 19.

———. (1993, January 7). Recordings: *Good as I Been to You. Rolling Stone*, p. 45.

Williams, P. (1991). *Bob Dylan performing artist: The early years 1960–1973.* Novato, CA: Underwood-Miller.

———. (1992). *Bob Dylan performing artist: The middle years 1974–1986.* Novato, CA: Underwood-Miller.

———. (1996). *Bob Dylan: Watching the river flow.* New York: Omnibus.

Williams, R. (1990, September 23). The calm after the storm. *New York Times*, p. H28.

Willis, E. (1974, February 18). Rock, etc.: Dylan and fans: Looking back, going on. *New Yorker*, pp. 108–10.

———. (1975, April 7). Rock, etc.: After the flood. *New Yorker*, pp. 130–32.

Wilonsky, R. (2001, September 6). Bob Dylan: *Love and Theft. Dallas Observer* <Dallasobserver.com>.

Wissolik, R., and S. McGrath. (1994). *Bob Dylan's words: A critical dictionary and commentary.* New York: Eadmer.

Worrell, D. (1985, November 25). It's all right in front. *Time*, p. 123.

Worthington, R. (1988, July 31). The town of Bob Dylan's youth leaves his past blowing in the wind. *Chicago Tribune*, p. 5: 5.

Young, C. (1985, August). Record reviews: Bob Dylan: *Empire Burlesque. Musician*, pp. 96–97.

Zito, T. (1974, January 16). Greeting the guarded voice of a generation. *Washington Post*, pp. B1, 10.

Zollo, P. (1997). *Songwriters on songwriting.* New York: Da Capo.

Bruce Springsteen

Altman, B. (1981, January). Records: Born to stall. *Creem*, pp. 50–51.

Bangs, L. (1975, November). Bruce Springsteen: Hot rod rumble in the promised land. *Creem*, pp. 82–83.

Barol, B. (1985, August 5). He's on fire. *Newsweek*, pp. 48–54.

———. (1987, November 2). Myths keep us strangers. *Newsweek*, pp. 76–78.

Bream, J. (1985, August 1). See Springsteen open tour in Ireland. *Rolling Stone*, p. 20.

———. (1992, October 25). Springsteen has change of style. *Minneapolis Star Tribune* (NEWSBANK).

Bruce Springsteen. (1987, February). *Musician*, pp. 32–33, 43.

Bruce Springsteen and the E Street Band: Live in New York City. (2001, May 27). New York: HBO.

Bruce Springsteen: The Rolling Stone files. (1996). New York: Hyperion.

Castro, J. (1986, December 15). The Boss's thunder road to riches. *Time,* p. 60.

Catlin, R. (1992, March 30). The Boss shows his bright side. *Hartford Courant* (NEWS-BANK).

———. (1992, August 14). Bruce is not "boss" he used to be, but he's still at the top. *Hartford Courant* (NEWSBANK).

Charlie Rose: The music interviews. (1999, October 2). Bruce Springsteen. New York: VH1.

Chute, D. (1984, November 6). Boss' message not reflected in fan antics. *Los Angeles Herald Examiner* (NEWSBANK).

Cocks, J. (1974, April 1). Along pinball way. *Time,* p. 80.

———. (1980, December 22). The River. *Time,* p. 90.

———. (1986, November 10). There's magic in the night. *Time,* p. 113.

———. (1987, October 12). Songs for the witching season. *Time,* p. 92.

———. (1992, April 6). Reborn, and running again. *Time,* p. 64.

Cohen, M. (1978, September). Records: The Boss hoss heads into oblivion. *Creem,* p. 59.

Connelly, C. (1982, October 14). Springsteen LP draws mixed reactions. *Rolling Stone,* pp. 61, 69.

Corcoran, M. (1995, February 26). The Boss' new compilation is timed to cash in on the awards. *Dallas Morning News* (NEWSBANK).

Corn, D. (1995, December 11). Guthrie's ghost. *Nation,* p. 733.

———. (1996, March/April). Bruce Springsteen tells the story of the secret America. *Mother Jones,* pp. 22–25.

Cotter, K. J. (1996, November 27). Springsteen's life, music inextricably entwined. *Asbury Park Press.*

———. (1996, November 27). To his 6-year-old, Bruce Springsteen is "Barney for adults." *Asbury Park Press.*

———. (1996, December 1). After hours with the Boss. *Asbury Park Press.*

Cullen, J. (1997). *Born in the U.S.A.: Bruce Springsteen and the American tradition.* New York: HarperCollins.

Curry, B. (1992, November 26). A wiser boss. (Raleigh, NC) *News and Observer* (NEWS-BANK).

Dalton, J. (1985, October 10). My home town. *Rolling Stone,* pp. 20–28, 78–80.

Damsker, M. (1982, October 10). Bruce Springsteen, Billy Joel: Now big enough to be inspired. *San Diego Union* (NEWSBANK).

Davis, M. (1988, February). Records: What's love got to do with it? *Creem,* p. 24.

Dawidoff, N. (1997, January 26). The pop populist. *New York Times Magazine,* pp. 27–33, 64, 69, 72, 77.

DeCurtis, A. (1991, January 10). Springsteen returns. *Rolling Stone,* pp. 15–17.

———. (1992, April 30). New Bruce: Lose your illusions. *Rolling Stone,* pp. 53–56.

———. (1992). Bruce Springsteen. In Jim Miller (Ed.), *The Rolling Stone illustrated history of rock & roll* (pp. 619–25). New York: Straight Arrow.

DiMartino, D. (1981, January). Bruce Springsteen takes it to the river: So don't call him "Boss," OK? *Creem,* pp. 24–29, 60.

Dougherty, S. (1992, April 6). The Boss is back. *People Weekly,* pp. 67–68.

Duncan, R. (1976, January). Bruce Springsteen is not god (and doesn't want to be). *Creem,* pp. 33–35, 73–74.

Emerson, K. (1974, January 31). Springsteen goes gritty and serious. *Rolling Stone,* pp. 49–50.

Farley, C. J. (1995, December 4). Border music. *Time,* p. 83.

Flanagan, B. (1987, January). Records: Bruce Springsteen and the E Street Band Live/ 1975–85. *Musician*, pp. 84–85.

———. (1992, November). Ambition, lies, and the beautiful reward. *Musician*, pp. 58–76.

———. (1995, July). Frontman: Bruce Springsteen. *Musician*, p. 7.

Flippo, C. (1984, September 3). Blue-collar troubadour. *People Weekly*, pp. 68–74.

———. (1984, November). Bruce Springsteen: A rock 'n' roll evangelist for our times crusades for patriotism and puritanism of a different stripe. *Musician*, pp. 52–58.

Ford, R. (1985, December). The Boss observed. *Esquire*, pp. 327–29.

Fricke, D. (1987, January 15). Bruce looks down the long road. *Rolling Stone*, pp. 50–52.

Frith, S. (1976, March). Casing the promised land. *Creem*, pp. 26, 72.

Gardner, E. (1996, February). Records: Okie from New Jersey. *Musician*, pp. 89–90.

Gelman, D. (1975, November 3). Doubleheader. *Newsweek*, p. 93.

Gilmore, M. (1982, September 24). Springsteen's "Nebraska": One from the heartland. *Los Angeles Herald Examiner* (NEWSBANK).

———. (1987, November 5). Bruce Springsteen. *Rolling Stone*, pp. 23–26.

———. (1990, November 15). Bruce Springsteen. *Rolling Stone*, pp. 82–88, 174.

Goldberg, M. (1992, March 5). Double dose of Springsteen. *Rolling Stone*, pp. 21, 24.

Graff, G. (1996, Issue 17). Working-class hero. *Guitar World Acoustic*, pp. 25–28.

———. (1996, October 17). A quiet night in the darkness. *San Diego Union-Tribune* (NEWSBANK).

Gundersen, E. (1995, December 1). In "Joad," Springsteen answers ghost of his past. *USA Today*, p. 16D.

Hagen, M. (1999, January). The midnight cowboy. *Mojo*, pp. 70–89.

Henke, J. (1992, April 16). Bruce's lucky touch. *Rolling Stone*, pp. 15, 23.

———. (1992, August 6). Springsteen: The *Rolling Stone* interview. *Rolling Stone*, pp. 38–44, 70.

Hepworth, D. (1992, August). Springsteen—The Q interview. *Q*.

Hewitt, P. (1981, May 9). Not the me-me-me-me. *Melody Maker*, pp. 23–27.

Hilburn, R. (1982, September 19). Springsteen: Brooding over the American dream. *Los Angeles Times* (NEWSBANK).

———. (1984, June 3). Springsteen still blows them away. *Los Angeles Times* (NEWSBANK).

———. (1985). *Springsteen*. New York: Scribner's.

———. (1985, September 27). Springsteen: The power of idealism. *Los Angeles Times* (NEWSBANK).

———. (1988, May 1). On latest tour, an older and wiser Boss says he has "something new to say." *San Francisco Examiner* (NEWSBANK).

———. (1992, March 29). The Boss feels good. *Los Angeles Times* (NEWSBANK).

———. (1992, June 7). How Bruce got a life. *Los Angeles Times* (NEWSBANK).

———. (1996, January 28). Reborn in the U.S.A. *Los Angeles Times* (NEWSBANK).

Himes, G. (1984, August 26). Springsteen's music is mature, personal. *The (Baltimore) Sun* (NEWSBANK).

Hinckley, D. (1992, August 16). Hometown boy. *New York Daily News* (NEWSBANK).

Holden, S. (1984, May 27). Springsteen scans the American dream. *New York Times*, pp. C19, 24.

Homecoming: Bruce Springsteen and the E Street Band. (2001, December 16). New York: VH1.

Humphries, P. (1996). *The complete guide to the music of Bruce Springsteen*. London: Omnibus.

Knobler, P. (1975, October). Running on the backstreets with Bruce Springsteen. *Craw-daddy*, pp. 35–43.

————. (1978, August). Records: Wounded in the badlands. *Crawdaddy*, pp. 67–68.

————. (1978, October). Bruce Springsteen's rites of passage: You want it, you take it, you pay the price. *Crawdaddy*, pp. 48–54.

Kot, G. (1992, August 23). Springsteen chases the spirit. *Chicago Tribune*, pp. 13:4–5, 22.

Landau, J. (1974, May 22). Growing young with rock and roll. *The Real Paper*.

Leland, J. (1992, April 6). Baby, we were born to last. *Newsweek*, p. 65.

Loder, K. (1984, December 6). The *Rolling Stone* interview: Bruce Springsteen. *Rolling Stone*, pp. 20–22, 70.

Lombardi, J. (1988, December). St. Boss: The sanctification of Bruce Springsteen and the rise of mass hip. *Esquire*, pp. 139–54.

MacDonald, P. (1987, October 11). Springsteen's new album explores the trials, riches of love. *Seattle Times* (NEWSBANK).

McCarthey, T. (1984, June 22). Summer brings a new crop of vinyl to the record bins. *Salt Lake Tribune* (NEWSBANK).

McLeese, D. (1988, April 18). Springsteen shows dark side. *Rocky Mountain News* (NEWS-BANK).

Marcus, G. (1975, October 9). Springsteen's thousand and one American nights. *Rolling Stone*, pp. 74–75.

Marsh, D. (1978, July 27). Records: The Boss' triumphant return. *Rolling Stone*, pp. 57–58.

————. (1978, August 24). Bruce Springsteen raises Cain. *Rolling Stone*, pp. 36–40.

————. (1996). *Born to Run: The Bruce Springsteen story*, vol. I. New York: Thunder's Mouth.

————. (1996). *Glory Days: The Bruce Springsteen story*, vol. II. New York: Thunder's Mouth.

Mendelssohn, J. (1987, March). Records: Ten years after. *Creem*, pp. 14–15.

Michener, C. (1975, September 8). Bruce is loose. *Newsweek*, p. 43.

Miller, D. (1984, June 7). Bruce Springsteen give the little guy something to cheer about. *Rolling Stone*, pp. 99–100.

Miller, J. (1980, December 8). The River. *Newsweek*, p. 96.

————. (1984, June 18). Return of rock heroes. *Newsweek*, p. 100.

————. (1987, April 13). Making a loud noise. *Newsweek*, pp. 74–75.

Mitchell, G. (1974, March). Bruce Springsteen: The Wild, the Innocent, and the E Street Shuffle. *Crawdaddy*, p. 71.

Moon, T. (1992, August 28). Bruce: A new message. *Philadelphia Inquirer* (NEWSBANK).

————. (1995, November 19). Solemn soliloquy. *Philadelphia Inquirer* (NEWSBANK).

Morse, S. (1992, December 11). Bruce's band: The Boss' leap of faith pays off. *Boston Globe* (NEWSBANK).

————. (1995, November 19). Springsteen picks the grapes of wrath. *Boston Globe* (NEWSBANK).

Nash, A. (1996, March). Bruce Springsteen hits the road. *Stereo Review*, p. 83.

Nelson, P. (1980, December 11). Records: Let us now praise famous men. *Rolling Stone*, pp. 51–53.

————. (1982, November). Bruce Springsteen's Nebraska. *Musician*, p. 114.

Nesin, J. (1984, September). Records: Long as he can see the light. *Creem*, p. 54.

Orth, M. (1975, October 27). Making of a rock star. *Newsweek*, pp. 57–63.

Palmer, R. (1985, August 6). Springsteen's music hits chord of America. *New York Times*, p. C13.

Pareles, J. (1985, August 18). Bruce Springsteen—rock's popular populist. *New York Times*, pp. C1, 7.

———. (1987, October 4). Springsteen looks at love. *New York Times*, pp. C1, 29.

———. (1995, December 14). Hard times and no silver lining. *New York Times*, p. C11.

Pond, S. (1981, October 1). Springsteen, other rock stars rally to help vets. *Rolling Stone*, pp. 80–81.

———. (1982, October 28). Springsteen delivers his bravest record yet. *Rolling Stone*, pp. 65–67.

———. (1984, August). Record reviews: Bruce Springsteen: Born in the U.S.A. *Musician*, pp. 86–87.

———. (1987, December 3). Bruce's hard look at love. *Rolling Stone*, pp. 77–79.

———. (1988, May 5). Bruce Springsteen's "Tunnel" vision. *Rolling Stone*, pp. 39–42.

Puterbaugh, P. (1995, April 6). *Bruce Springsteen: Greatest Hits. Rolling Stone*, pp. 60–61.

Racine, M. (1987, October 6). "Tunnel" Springsteen's worst. *Houston Chronicle* (NEWS-BANK).

Radel, C. (1984, June 10). Springsteen soars through low lyrics. *Cincinnati Enquirer* (NEWSBANK).

Rockwell, J. (1975, August 15). The rocky road to stardom. *New York Times*, pp. 37, 70.

———. (1975, August 29). Springsteen's rock poetry at its best. *New York Times*, p. 11.

———. (1975, October 9). New Dylan from New Jersey? It might as well be Springsteen. *Rolling Stone*, p. 9.

———. (1975, October 24). "Hype" and the Springsteen case. *New York Times*, p. 34.

———. (1984, May 27). Rock: Bruce Springsteen in concert. *New York Times*, p. 24.

Rogovoy, S. (1992, April 30). Springsteen: "New music" not so new. (Pittsfield, MA) *Berkshire Eagle* (NEWSBANK).

Samuels, L. (1986, November 14). The spirit of Springsteen. *Dallas Morning News* (NEWSBANK).

Schoemer, K. (1995, November 27). Back to the badlands. *Newsweek*, p. 90.

———. (1996, April 1). Heart of darkness. *Newsweek*, pp. 66–68.

Schruers, F. (1980, November 27). The Boss is back. *Rolling Stone*, pp. 11–12.

———. (1981, February 5). Bruce Springsteen and the secret of the world. *Rolling Stone*, pp. 20–23.

———. (1997, February 6). Bruce Springsteen finds "a sense of place." *Rolling Stone*, p. 18.

Shefchik, R. (1995, December 10). "The Ghost of Tom Joad." *St. Paul Pioneer Press-Dispatch* (NEWSBANK).

Simels, S. (1981, January). *The River. Stereo Review*, p. 102.

———. (1982, December). *Nebraska. Stereo Review*, p. 100.

———. (1984, September). *Born in the U.S.A. Stereo Review*, p. 86.

Slaughter, M. (1984). *Bruce Springsteen: An American classic.* London: Proteus.

Smith, P., and G. Martin. (1996, March 9). Hey Joad, don't make it sad . . . (oh, go on then). *New Music Express.*

Smith, R. (1985, September 8). These are the glory days for the guy who used to be the best-kept secret in rock. *Dallas Morning News* (NEWSBANK).

Smith, S. (1988, March 13). From rage to roses. *Chicago Tribune*, pp. 13:6, 8.

Springsteen, B. (1990). Speech at the Rock-and-Roll Hall of Fame. In E. Thomson and D. Gutman (eds.), *The Dylan companion* (pp. 286–88). New York: Da Capo.

———. (1998). *Songs.* New York: Avon.

Sterling, G. (1985, August 18). The "Boss" creating a legend in his own image. (Newark, NJ) *Star-Ledger* (NEWSBANK).

Strauss, N. (1995, May 7). Springsteen looks back but keeps walking on. *New York Times*, pp. B1, 30.

———. (1995, October). Human touch. *Guitar World*, pp. 57–60, 65–72.

Tannenbaum, R. (1990, January 11). Springsteen goes it alone. *Rolling Stone*, pp. 15, 66.

Tomlinson, S. (1987, September 24). Springsteen emerges from "Tunnel of Love." *The Oregonian* (NEWSBANK).

Tucker, K. (1984, June 10). In "U.S.A.," Springsteen's vision has never been clearer. *Philadelphia Inquirer* (NEWSBANK).

Van Matre, L. (1982, November 14). Nebraska. *Chicago Tribune* (NEWSBANK).

Varga, G. (1984, June 6). Springsteen strikes deep chord. *San Diego Union* (NEWSBANK).

Walls, R. (1983, January). Records: Darkness in the heart of town. *Creem*, p. 54.

Ward, E. (1974, April). Records: Bruce Springsteen: *The Wild, the Innocent, and the E Street Shuffle. Creem*, p. 69.

Weisbard, E. (1999, February). Retro Active: Bruce Springsteen's long-awaited box set reveals there's more to the Boss than meets the ear. *Spin*, p. 113.

White, T. (1990). *Rock lives: Profiles and interviews*. New York: Henry Holt.

Willwerth, J. (1975, October 27). The backstreet phantom of rock. *Time*, pp. 48–58.

Young, C. (1987, December). Records: Bruce faces all that stuff we're so scared of. *Musician*, pp. 104–6.

Young, J. (1983, January). Reviews: Bruce Springsteen: Nebraska. *Trouser Press*, p. 44.

index

About the Author

LARRY DAVID SMITH is an independent writer and lecturer who specializes in narrative critiques of popular media. His previous works include *Pete Townshend: The Minstrel's Dilemma* (Praeger, 1999), *Cordial Concurrence: Orchestrating National Party Conventions in the Telepolitical Age* (with Dan Nimmo; Praeger, 1991), and a variety of articles and chapters. He lives in Memphis, Tennessee.